THE WEST RIDING TERRITORIALS
IN THE GREAT WAR

MAJOR-GENERAL T. S. BALDOCK, C.B.

[Frontispiece.

The West Riding Territorials in the Great War

With a Foreword by Field-Marshal Earl Haig,
O.M., K.T., G.C.B., G.C.V.O.

BY

LAURIE MAGNUS

Fully Illustrated

LONDON
KEGAN PAUL, TRENCH, TRUBNER & Co., Ltd.,
BROADWAY HOUSE, 68-74, CARTER LANE, E.C.
1920

Printed and bound by Antony Rowe Ltd, Eastbourne

CONTENTS

CONTENTS

LIST OF ILLUSTRATIONS

LIST OF ILLUSTRATIONS

FOREWORD

When all Divisions, Regular, Territorial and New Army, from whatever part of Great Britain or quarter of the Empire they were drawn, have rendered such splendid service, it is difficult to refer particularly to individual units or formations.

The pages of this book, however, furnish in detail an account of the exploits of two gallant Territorial Divisions, to one of which, the 62nd, it fell to carry out an operation of outstanding brilliance on the occasion of the Cambrai attack on the 20th November, 1917.

Moreover, the history of both Divisions helps to emphasize the greatness of the debt due to the Territorial Force as a whole. The value to the State of the Territorial Force organisation at the outbreak of the war was immense. By volunteering freely for overseas service, the pre-war Territorials enabled the necessary reinforcements for the Army in the field to be maintained while the New Army was in the making. The gallantry of their subsequent performances should not be allowed to obscure the service they then rendered.

HAIG,
Field-Marshal.

PREFACE

While this book has been at press, the Territorial Force has passed into the Territorial Army, thus closing another chapter in the history of the British citizen-soldier. That closed chapter has still to be written, as a complete history of the Territorial Force, called into being by Mr. (Lord) Haldane, when Secretary of State for War, in 1907, struggling against adverse circumstances for existence and recognition from 1908 to 1914, and approving itself from 1914 to 1919, by the testimony of Mr. Secretary Churchill and Field-Marshals Earl Haig and Viscount French, as a saviour of the Empire in the Great War.

The present volume may supply material for one chapter of that history. In Book I, I try to trace the early annals of the Force within the confines of the West Riding of Yorkshire, and in Books II and III, I follow the Troops which were raised in that Riding to their war-stations overseas. As far as possible, I have observed the limits set by the scope of my narrative. General history before the war has been subordinated to the experience of the West Riding Territorial Force Association, and the history of the war has been told in relation to the part of the 49th and 62nd (West Riding) Infantry Divisions, which went to France in 1915 and 1917.

Principally, then, this book is concerned with the work of the Infantry. A brief account of the experience of the Yeomanry is given in Chapter XIV, and one or two other units (notably, a Company of the R.E., which served with the 29th in the Dardanelles, and a Casualty Clearing Station in France) are included in the main narrative. Another volume might well be filled with the doings of West Riding Territorials attached to other units during the war, but these records seem to belong to the units concerned more appropriately than to the present narrative. The story of the 2nd and 3rd Northern General Hospitals is likely to be fully told in the Medical History of the war, and will be found to reflect the utmost credit on the responsible authorities. These Hospitals were freely used by wounded men of all units from the front, and became the radiant centres of a large number of War Hospitals in the county. From the parent institutions in Leeds and Sheffield, Auxiliary Hospitals sprang up throughout the West Riding of Yorkshire, as many as 6,500 beds being affiliated to the 2nd Northern General Hospital alone. From August, 1914, till late in 1919, this splendid work, of which the foundations were laid in peace-time, was in full swing, and should form an important chapter in a complete history of the Territorial Force.

Special mention is also due to the uniformly brilliant record of the West Riding Divisional Artillery, which was employed throughout the war in all parts of the field. It has not proved possible in this volume to select its Brigades and Batteries for special treatment: the effect would have been too much disjointed; but, wherever they covered the Infantry, their work always won the highest praise, and their skill under arduous conditions is one of the marvels of the war. Something, too, should be said about Mechanical Transport, re-organized, like so much else, at the hour of trial in March, 1918, and of other Arms of the Service, subordinate to the Infantry Divisions. I must be content, however, with this passing reference to their exploits, and with such tributes to them as occur in the course of the main narrative.

My own connection with my subject is very slender. It happened that, in 1917, I was lent to the War Office by the Royal Defence Corps in order to do some special work in a branch then known as T.V.I. (in the Territorial and Volunteer Forces Directorate). The Director-General, Major-General the Earl of Scarbrough, had been Chairman from the start of the Territorial Force Association of the West Riding; and it happened again, in 1919, when the History Committee of his Association had been disappointed of the services of Professor G. S. Gordon, of Leeds University, a Captain in the 6th West Yorkshire Regiment, 62nd Division, and now Official Military Historian of the war, that Lord Scarbrough recommended me to write this local history in his stead. In the earlier chapters of the book, I had the advantage of Professor Gordon's assistance, and I gladly take this opportunity of thanking him for his valuable help. My work is also much indebted to the care of several of the General Officers Commanding the two Divisions; particularly, of Major-General Sir James Trotter in connection with Chapter VI, and of Lieut.-General Sir Walter Braithwaite, in connection with the important period of his Command of the 62nd in France. Lord Scarbrough's personal interest in all that concerns his Association has been extended, with great benefit, to this book in all its stages, and I have also to thank Brig.-General Mends, Secretary of the Association, and Captain Mildren, his assistant, for their unremitting trouble. The list of Officers from the Riding, who have placed at my disposal diaries, photographs, letters, notes, and valuable advice, is too long to enumerate. I should like specially to thank Major E. P. Chambers, Captains Tom Goodall, R. M. Robinson and J. C. Scott; but I will ask all, comprehensively, to accept the expression of my gratitude, and of my hope that I have not altogether failed to do justice to the praises which they have united in bestowing on the men whom they led.

For this, when all is said and done, is the beginning and the end of any instalment of a history of the Territorial Force. 'This wonderful force,' as Lord French has called it in his book, *1914*, was

PREFACE

founded on the 'patriotic spirit which has always been the soul of the Volunteers. It was reserved for Lord Haldane,' adds the Field-Marshal, ' to devise the scheme which was to make the fullest use of the Volunteers and bring them to the zenith of their reputation.' How high in military ardour and achievement that zenith proved during the Great War, may be judged, I hope, from this record, however incomplete and at second-hand, of the Territorial Troops from the West Riding, which it has been my privilege to compile.

L.M.

LONDON,
   March 23rd, 1920.

BOOK I

BEFORE WAR

CHAPTER I

THE WEST RIDING ASSOCIATION

At half-past five in the afternoon, on Monday, April 12th, 1915, the first detachment of troops in the West Riding (1st Line) Territorial Division left England for France. Their going, like all English goings and most English home-comings, was quiet and unobserved: the War Diary of the Division merely states that thus 'the move to France commenced'; further, that Divisional Headquarters left Doncaster the next day, embarked at Folkestone on the *Invicta*, and reached Boulogne 9-50 p.m.; that the General Officer Commanding the Division, accompanied by five Staff Officers, travelled by motor-car on April 14th through St. Omer and Hazebroucke to Merville, where Divisional Headquarters were established in the Mayor's house, 40 rue des Capucines; and that a telegram was received by the General from H.M. the King, and a loyal reply was despatched. So, the time of preparation was over, the time of action had begun.

The new adventure, which was to prove so searching, was founded securely in the past, and this latent sense of tradition explains, or helps to explain, why over 30,000 recruits were taken by the West Riding Territorial Force Association between the date of the outbreak of war and April 14th, 1915; why the strength of the County units had reached three-quarters of the pre-war establishment[1] fully as early as that date, and why the expedition to France proceeded in the ordinary course of duty. For the spirit of adventure was not new, though overlaid by many years of ease. Deep in the consciousness of Yorkshiremen, as of men 'from every shire's end of England', were echoes of long-ago wars in defence of their country on foreign soil, under Wellington, under Marlborough, under the Houses of York and Lancaster, and away back to the Plantagenet kings, when the first 'verray parfit gentil knight,' with his squire, 'as fresh as in the month of May', led his troops to fight for the right,

'In Flaundres, in Artoyes and Picardye.'

Thus Lord Haldane wrote correctly, in December, 1908: 'The organization of the Territorial Force, . . . novel as in material respects it is, . . . is the outcome of a process of development, the beginnings of which lie far back in the past.'[2]

Some account of that 'organization' in the West Riding, remembering its roots in the past, is necessary in advance of a history of what the troops wrought in the field. They did not spring fully armed from the head of Mars. On the contrary, their martial equipment

---

[1] This includes the 2nd and 3rd Lines. The last had recently been authorized for formation at, approximately, two-thirds of War Establishment. The Peace Establishment of the West Riding T.F. had been fixed for one Line only.

[2] Introduction to *The Territorial Force*, by Harold Baker, M.A.: London, Murray, 1909.

was a long and complicated affair, mixed up with questions of finance and administration, which were left, in the worst years of military ardour, to the public spirit of a few local men. The menace of foreign aggression in the consulship of Sir H. Campbell-Bannerman and Mr. Asquith was not a popular subject, and the Haldane Act, 1907, ' to provide for the reorganization of His Majesty's military forces, and for that purpose to authorize the establishment of County Associations, and the raising and maintenance of a Territorial Force,' was let loose on the counties of the United Kingdom at a time when, twice in one year, a general election was to be held on domestic issues unconnected with peace and war. There was worse than public apathy to contend with. Public apathy might retard enlistment under Section IX. of the Act, but a part of the opposition to the new measure was founded on more positive grounds. Speakers who went up and down the Riding to explain and recommend the scheme had to lay the spectre of ' compulsion ' : in those days of tumbling privileges the one unanswerable argument before which even duty was dumb. Thus, there is a report of a speech at Malton by Mr. (the late Colonel Sir) Mark Sykes on May 4th, 1908, in which,

> ' Surveying the present conditions of England in case of an attack, he said they had nothing to fall back upon but members of Rifle Clubs and Cadets. Should this Army scheme fail, they would have to look to conscription.'

There was a meeting at York on the same day, at which the elders of the Council discussed a recommendation of the Finance Committee ' to encourage corporation employees to join the Territorial Army.' On that occasion one councillor was of opinion, that

> ' there appeared to be a movement on foot throughout the country to induce large companies to close down their works and simply compel men to enlist in the Territorial Force, or be idle and have no wages at all.'

Another councillor considered that ' this was an attempt to establish municipal conscription.' Another gravely pointed out that ' to encourage ' did not necessarily mean ' to force,' but might be stretched as much as to mean ' persuade.'

We shall not attach names to these dead controversies. They have buried their dead to-day, and the graves of Flanders and Gallipoli bear mute but eloquent witness to the sudden glory of patriotism which dissolved ' encouragement,' ' force,' ' persuasion,' ' compulsion,' and ' conscription ' in the single light of national defence. But this perception was not yet, and the passive and active resistance which sections of opinion in the country, not excluding the West Riding, presented to Lord Haldane's Act was recognized by its author himself. Speaking at Leicester in the same week as the elders of York met in council, the Secretary for War declared—

> ' We are not militarists . . . All we want is to feel

Merville Church

49TH DIVISION, APRIL, 1915.

[Face p. 4.

secure in our hearths and homes, and to have the feeling that labour and commerce are alike adequately protected . . . He was against conscription and compulsion . . . He wanted to make the Army a people's Army';

and when a man at the back of the hall shouted that the scheme would lead to compulsory service, ' he was caught hold of by half a dozen police, and flung out '—to join the suffragettes. We cannot neglect these facts, old echoes though they be to-day. Nor shall we pause to ask if a bolder policy might not have been more successful, and if the appeal should have been directed to the real menace of German aggression. The whole tendency of the times was against emphasizing that aspect, and the pacific instinct of the nation was fostered rather than rebuked by the voices of responsible authority. It was not a healthy atmosphere for the New Act, and the Roman author of the maxim, *si vis pacem, para bellum*, never explained how to do it if a Government cried peace, and the Government was the people.

Still, the Act was launched, and the counties had to make the preparations.

There were two difficulties inherent from the start, and it is probably correct to associate them with the public apathy towards the scheme. For one thing, the burden of preparation fell a little obviously on a class, which, in the years before the war, lay under a cloud of mis-. representation. That it was a simulated and a temporary cloud, at least in its chief manifestations, the war itself was to prove; but it was spread fast enough and thick enough at the time to darken initiative and counsel. Not the best Government imaginable could contrive to have things both ways. If they chose to load certain classes in the community with the reproach of obstructing the ' people's will,' it was unseemly to rely on individuals from those classes to popularize a branch of their legislation. Thus, the recommendation of a ' people's budget' by abusive ridicule of landowners, and the promotion of a reform of the Second Chamber as the cause of ' people *versus* peers,' however expedient as a means of affixing a stigma for abuses, would prove impolitic, to say the least of it, when members of those orders were invited to take a leading part in recruiting for a ' people's army.' The same ' people ' might not see the point of leading and following at the same time. Yet the Territorial and Reserve Forces Act consti- tuted ' the Lieutenant of the County . . . president of the Association,' and the Lieutenant, thus placed in power, was, almost without exception, either a peer or a landowner or both. Next, it assigned to the Association the duty of ' recruiting for the Territorial Force both in peace and in war,' and we have seen that this duty was liable to be misconstrued as legalized conscription. The risk of such misconstruction was certainly not diminished by the obloquy which was poured, for other purposes of the legislature, on the order to which the presidents and some other of the more leisured members of the recruiting Associations belonged.   Secondly, these political conditions reacted on the Government to some extent.   For good or ill, the success of their plans for social betterment and domestic reform was a little obscurely involved with the maintenance of the open door to foreign imports, the rejection of commercial preference within the Empire, and, as a necessary corollary, with the doctrine that ' free trade ' would keep the peace.   This avoidance, on the highest principles, of any action likely to seem provocative abroad, so firmly upheld at the Foreign Office till the sixtieth minute of the eleventh hour, made us rig Dreadnoughts with apologies and raise recruits with muffled drums.   It followed from all these causes—the preoccupation of Ministers, the social status of county leaders, the talking peace to ensure peace—that, once the Territorial Act was launched, no member of the Government except Lord Haldane appeared openly anxious to make it go.   The early annals of Territorial Force Associations, as they came into being under the Act, are plaintively and miserably punctuated by what Sir William Clegg, in the West Riding, used to call the ' pin-pricks of the Army Council,' and a large part of their work of initiation, which is always the most difficult part, was achieved by personal effort against alternate or simultaneous doses of public indifference and official neglect.

Still, the Territorial Force grew.   Its foundations were well and truly laid on that old inexpugnable spirit which, as we saw above, was already alive in Chaucer's England, and which, when the new summons came, flared up through disappointment to success.   The six and a half years' record of the West Riding Territorial Force Association, from its inaugural meeting on January 17th, 1908, till the outbreak of war in 1914 is typical of the experience of other counties, alike in the obstacles which were encountered and in the resolution which partially overcame them.   It derives special interest from the fact that the population of the West Riding is much more than twice as large as that of any county outside London, except only Lancashire ; but the chief interest of the record lies in the after-history of the Association. The achievement of its units in the field is a final, triumphant vindication of the confidence of those who helped to raise them, a complete reward for the courage they displayed, and a proof, if proof were wanted, that the nation's need is the measure of the nation's power. Hence, if we dwell more particularly on some of the difficulties which confronted that Association during the epoch of preparation, the true merits of the Territorial Army scheme, when tried by the supreme test of action, will be more abundantly manifest.

First, as to *personnel*, H.M. Lieutenant for the Riding since 1904 had been Colonel the Earl of Harewood, A.D.C., of the Yorkshire Hussars, and formerly of the Grenadier Guards, who, accordingly, became first president of the Association.   With him were united as chairman   and   vice-chairman,   respectively,   Colonel   the   Earl   of

Scarbrough, A.D.C., commanding the Yorkshire Mounted Brigade, and formerly of the 7th Hussars, and Sir William Clegg, J.P., sometime Lord Mayor of Sheffield. These formed a powerful triumvirate, and 'had done their best,' as Lord Harewood remarked on January 17th, 1908, 'to set matters on a preliminary footing.' The president and chairman were still in office in 1920, but in February, 1917, Lord Scarbrough had received the appointment of Director-General of the Territorial and Volunteer Forces at the War Office, with the temporary rank of Major-General, and was thereafter compelled to interrupt his closer supervision at the Association. 'Our loss,' the president said at the next quarterly meeting, 'is a great gain to the country,' and the compliment paid to Lord Scarbrough by this appointment was appreciated by the Association as a whole. Sir William Clegg continued in office till the end of 1915, when, to his colleagues' great regret, his election as chairman of the Appeal Committee under Lord Derby's scheme and the pressure of other duties caused his necessary resignation. He was succeeded as vice-chairman of the Association by Brig.-General (Sir) R. C. A. B. Bewicke-Copley, (K.B.E.), C.B., in April, 1916.

It will be no derogation from the importance of the military members of the Association appointed by the Army Council, of the representative members similarly appointed on the recommendation of the West Riding County Council, the County boroughs of Bradford, Halifax, Huddersfield, Leeds, Rotherham, Sheffield and York, and the Universities of Leeds and Sheffield, and of the members co-opted by the Association to complete its statutory establishment,[1] if we turn next to the person of the secretary. The right choice of a candidate for this post was properly regarded as an essential condition of success, and at the inaugural meeting of the Association (January 17th, 1908), no other name was proposed but that of Brig.-General Horatio Mends, C.B., formerly of the 60th Rifles, at that time Brigadier General-in-charge of Administration, Northern Command. To the immense benefit of the Association, General Mends' term of office as secretary, except for a short interruption due to ill-health in 1909, continued right through the twelve years under review, and, alike in peace and in war, he has amply and fully sustained the confident belief expressed at the time of his appointment, that 'he combined every requisite which Mr. Haldane had laid down as essential for the secretary of an Association.' His assistants came and went according to the claims of other duties. They have included Captain J. U. M. Ingilby, Captain M. L. Porter, Major A. B. Boyd-Carpenter (later, Deputy Assistant-Director under Lord Scarbrough at the War Office, and, since December, 1918, M.P. for East Bradford), Major H. C. E. Smithett and Captain W. Mildren, M.B.E., of the T.F. Reserve, formerly Staff Q.M.S. in the Army Pay Corps, York, who was appointed superintending clerk at the beginning, and who has rendered admirable service.

[1] See Appendix I.

Second only in importance to a secretary was a place of meeting for the Association. It would need the powers of an epic poet to invoke the muse to sing the rival claims of Leeds and Sheffield as headquarters of the West Riding, and the historian who is not a York-shireman must be content to set the fact on record that York was finally selected for reasons which seemed sufficient to the high con-tracting parties. Once in York, there was no hesitation in approving premises at 9, St. Leonard's as a permanent local habitation.

We need not set out in detail the obvious necessary business of the appointment of committees, the distribution of duties, the drafting of regulations, and so forth. It was new work, and not very easy work, but the Association commanded the services of men of experience and affairs, and some spade work had been done in advance. One point particularly occurs to a reader of the Association archives : the concentration on the magical word, *Mobilization*. This event governed the deliberations of all concerned : not as a shadowy abstraction, which superior authority set them to work at in the dark, still less as a haunting terror, created by a jingoistic press, but as a real, present and an urgent duty, and as the test of validity for all their acts. This idea so con-stantly before them lent actuality to their proceedings. They spent no time in discussing if and when a state of war might arise. Their practical function was to assume the war and to prepare for it.

Apart from the recruiting problem proper, the provision, that is to say, of the full number of officers and other ranks required to complete the establishment of the units to be raised in the West Riding, there was an immense amount of work to be done, military as well as adminis-trative, before the Association could say to the War Office : press the button, and the troops will march out. The Haldane Act had created the machinery, and the Association had been formed to make it work ; and, since, at any moment from that date, the crisis of 1914 might have been precipitated, the new local authorities were well advised in aiming at instant readiness. But if we project ourselves back into the chaos of 1908, out of which Lord Harewood and his colleagues were entrusted with the task of evoking order, if we sympathize with their sense of responsibility, and recognize how gravely it was increased by lack of knowing when the crisis would occur ; in other words, if we look at the problem through the spectacles of the West Riding Association, we must be equally just to other aspects. The Haldane Act set up ninety-four Associations : ninety-four engines wanting fuel, ninety-four skeleton organisms awaiting breath and articulation, ninety-four committees hard at work as if each was solely responsible for building the Territorial Force. Translate this conception into the terms familiar to official routine in the placid years before the war. Imagine the accumulation of papers, the multiplication of minutes, and the comparative unexpectedness of the call to decide a series of questions which lengthened with the life of the Associations. True, a Central

Council of Associations was formed at an early date,[1] which served as a kind of clearing-house between the counties and Whitehall, and which, while it did not preclude the independent access of Associations, submitted as many as thirty-two recommendations from November, 1908, to July, 1909. A few of these topics are worth recalling. On November 9th, 1908, the Central Council recommended ' that travelling grants be given to individuals coming to Section, Company and Battalion drills over a distance of two miles.' A deputation waited on the Secretary of State on the following February 27th. In May, an intimation was sent that a circular Memorandum might be issued on the subject. In July, the matter was raised again, and another deputation was received on the 23rd of that month. On August 7th, the War Office decided not to make any grant for the payment of men in towns coming to drill. ' In rural corps, in which the companies, etc., are recruited over a scattered area, the War Office will consider an extra grant based on the cost of bringing in men of outlying sections for Company drill two or three times a year, and will shortly issue a letter asking for the necessary information on which a grant should be based.' That letter was issued on September 9th. On the 13th of the next month, the Central Council expressed the opinion that, ' if the Territorial Force is to be made of real value, . . . this can only be done . . . by giving financial assistance to men to enable them to come into drill.' On March 16th, 1910, a War Office letter was issued, granting a small allowance towards the cost of bringing in outlying sections to enable them to carry out squadron, battery or company training, but refusing to authorize as a charge on Association public funds, any expenses incurred by individual officers or men in travelling from their homes to their local troop or section headquarters to carry out their ordinary drills. A wise decision, no doubt ; certainly, a carefully considered one ; but, perhaps, a little disheartening in its extreme regard for the public purse and in the consumption of sixteen months during which voluntary recruits were not told what their patriotism would cost them. Sometimes the decisions came more quickly, but then they were usually in the negative. A proposal in February, 1909, ' that boots other than lace-up be supplied for wear by mounted men with overalls when walking out ' was refused in the following May. A recommendation during that May ' that a special grant of 6d. a head be allowed to Associations for provision of refreshments to men who are detained on parade, or on actual military duty, for not less than four consecutive hours,' was turned down on August 7th.

The general tendency should be clear from these examples. At the one end, in Yorkshire and elsewhere, throughout the ninety-four headquarters, were brand-new Associations, eager to sweep clean and to sweep swiftly. At the other end, in Whitehall, were the War Office

[1] The first Meeting of its Executive Committee was held on October 12th, 1908.

and the Treasury, fast bound by the traditions of their code, and tied particularly by a Government committed to retrenchment on Army estimates. We hardly know which to pity more, the Minister responsible to the House of Commons or the Territorial Force Associations which his Act had called into being.

Meanwhile, for historical purposes, it is essential to remember that, during this period of preparation, the Territorial Force *was* the Associations. It depended on them for recruits, premises, ranges, arms, equipment, clothing (even to ' boots other than lace-up for wear by mounted men with overalls when walking out '), everything that makes an Army ; and they depended in turn, far more closely than they had anticipated, on the decisions of a harrassed Army Council and the resources of a depleted Treasury. Happily, this period was protracted by the repeated postponement of war. In 1908 and, again, in 1911, the threat of war was averted, as we are now aware. Time was given, accordingly, if not for the complete fulfilment, at least for the partial satisfaction of the means devised for the fulfilment of the chief object of the Haldane Act. This was, as we saw,

' To provide for the reorganization of His Majesty's military forces, and for that purpose to authorize the establishment of County Associations, and the raising and maintenance of a Territorial Force.'

No time limit was laid down for the period of incubation in the Associations, and it is difficult to estimate what would have been our degree of unpreparedness if the accidents of European politics had allowed less than the six and a half years from 1908 to 1914.

A rough estimate can be formed, and it is worth computing in the present context, and in the security of peace after war, by reference to an open letter, dated February 26th, 1913, which was addressed by the Committee of the National Defence Association to Mr. Asquith, as President of the Committee of Imperial Defence.[1] The signatories included the Duke of Bedford, Lord Fortescue, Lord Glenconner, Lord Scarbrough and Sir Richard Temple (who were all connected with County Associations), Lord Lovat, Mr. Walter Long, Lord Methuen, Lord Peel, Sir Samuel Scott and other men of weight. While drawing attention to their consistent support of the Territorial Force scheme, they felt bound to point out ' that neither the Territorial Associations, nor the Territorial Force have yet taken sufficiently deep root as national institutions.' They stated ' with the utmost emphasis ' that ' no remedy involving extra financial assistance to the Territorial Force at the expense of the Navy or Regular Army would receive their support,' but they did not conceal their conviction that, ' if such a situation as existed in the autumn of 1911 recurred', ' the present training, equipment and numbers of the Territorial Force are inadequate for the task that would only too probably be laid upon

[1] This letter was published in the Press on February 28th, 1913.

it.' ' It has come to the knowledge of this Association,' they remarked in another paragraph of the letter, ' that a large proportion of Officers responsible for the training and administration of the Force now hold the view that it is incapable under present conditions of carrying out the duties allotted to it in any sudden emergency. We desire most strongly to support and emphasize this opinion.'

The warning was too grave to be ignored. The Territorial Act had been on trial for five years, and the war, which actually arrived in the summer of the following year, might break out at any moment.

Urgent action was taken, accordingly, by the Council of Territorial Associations, and it is particularly interesting to the present record to note that the basis of their action was a scheme submitted by the Earl of Scarbrough on behalf of the West Riding Association. After passing a strong resolution in April, 1913, pointing out the ' continued inefficiency ' in the establishment of Territorial units, and even stating that the success of the Force on a voluntary basis could be achieved ' only by a considerable improvement in the terms and conditions of service,' they lost no time in circulating the West Riding scheme through other Associations. So, at the October meeting of the Central Council, when replies and comments had come in, they were ready to ask the Prime Minister to receive a deputation, with a view to considering the whole matter.

This important interview took place on November 26th, 1913. On the one side were Mr. Asquith and General Seely, then Secretary of State for War ; on the other were Lord Dartmouth (Chairman), Lord Fortescue and Sir Hugh Shaw-Stewart, Bt. (Vice-Chairmen), and the following Members of the Council of the County Territorial Associations : Lord Scarbrough, Sir Richard Temple, Bt., Sir Hugh Bell, Bt., Lord Cheylesmore, Sir Edward Elles, Sir Arthur Anstice, Mr. Tonman Mosley, Lord Glenconner, Mr. Dalgleish, Mr. Adeane, Colonel Colvin, Colonel Lambert White, General Tyler, Lord Denbigh, General Mends, and the Secretary of the Council, Major Godman. The deputation represented eighty-one out of the ninety-four Associations, and was recognized by the Prime Minister as ' authoritative.'

It is well to recall at this point the essential dates in the situation. The Territorial and Reserve Forces Act ' for the reorganization of His Majesty's military forces ' became law in 1907. Early in 1908 the West Riding Territorial Force Association was brought into being under the Act, and set to work in a practical way to raise, clothe, train and otherwise prepare its troops for the day of mobilization. They had worked hard for six years, with the shadow of coming war across their path. Yet at the end of 1913, when the substance behind the shadow was apparent to all who knew, the chairman of the West Riding Association, one of the most populous County areas, administered by men of public spirit, and possessing in General Mends an untiring and a highly efficient secretary, came to the Prime Minister to say : Our proper establishment of troops is little more than 18,000 ; we fall short by 52 officers and 2,724 other ranks ; and ' that is roughly typical of the general shortage, which, with a few exceptions, exists throughout the Counties.' The failure was deplorable : ' It is the fact that the strength to-day is less than it was in the last year under the old Volunteer system.' But even more deplorable was the danger : ' In spite of all the efforts which have been made in these six years, it would appear that the high-water mark of voluntary effort in normal years and under present conditions falls greatly below the minimum laid down by the General Staff as necessary for National Defence'.

November 26th, 1913 : This was the date of the interview, and it was too late then to remedy the scheme. The total shortage of 1,400 officers and 66,000 other ranks ; the 40,000 members of the Force under nineteen years of age and ' only fit to be in a Cadet corps ' ; the absence from the annual camp of 1,362 officers and 33,350 other ranks, including 37 officers and 6,019 men ' absent without leave ' : these facts and figures might be cured by personal allowances to officers, efficiency bounties to other ranks, income-tax relief to employers for each qualified Territorial officer or soldier in their employ, grants to Associations for social purposes and for the provision of boots, shirts and socks, and by the rest of the moderate, wise and carefully devised recommendations which the Council of County Associations felt bound to propose to the Government, as ' the minimum improvement in the terms and conditions of service that we think would be effective in attracting the right class of men in sufficient numbers.' Public apathy, official discouragement, and the burden of other calls on the Exchequer might be purged of their worst effects by thorough changes of this kind. Even the evils pointed out by Sir H. Shaw-Stewart, that, ' owing to the exigencies of political combat, these same classes that I speak of (*i.e.*, landowners and employers) are just now being held up to the public as parasites, oppressors and robbers of the poor,' and that, ' except for Lord Haldane and his successor at the War Office, not one Cabinet Minister has ever had a good word to say for the work we are doing or, indeed, for the system we are endeavouring to carry out,' might at last prove capable of adjustment. But time was essential for such experiments, and the sands of time were running out. Mr. Asquith, indeed, in his reply to the deputation, affected to believe it all remediable. There were the proper compliments to ' the value of the work that has been and is being done.' There were other aspects of the numbers and the training, and certain ' encouraging features ' to be dwelt upon. There was a general undertaking that the Council's recommendations ' will be not only considered, and not lightly dismissed, but considered in a thoroughly sympathetic spirit.' There was the final valediction, as suave as it was impenetrable : ' We shall endeavour to produce as great an impression as we can on the Chancellor of the Exchequer consistently with his other requirements to meet your legitimate demands.'[1] And the Archduke Francis Ferdinand was assassinated, June 28th, 1914.

These, briefly, are the facts on which an estimate may be formed of the degree of preparedness reached by the Territorial Force more than six years after it came into being. Very happily, as we said above, this period was thus protracted. The defects were serious enough, but, had the crisis come earlier, Associations would have missed what the evidence of results proved to be valuable, that varied experience of organization, that knowledge of their own weak points, that sense of contact with officers and men, as well in their civilian relations as in their military capacity, and, generally, that power, essential to the satisfactory working of 'a highly complex structure o' various an' conflictin' strains,' which Mr. Kipling has illustrated in his story of *The Ship that Found Herself.* The consolation administered by the Prime Minister to the deputation of November, 1913, though a commonplace, or because it was a commonplace, was justified in the succeeding years of war :

' While we do not say that the present organization is in all respects satisfactory, we do believe that it is based on sound lines, and, so long as the same spirit which has existed from the beginning continues to animate officers and men, that the Force will increase every year in efficiency and capacity for the special functions which are assigned to it in our scheme of defence.'

The vista of years was contracted to less than one, our ' scheme of defence ' was unrecognizably extended, but the animating spirit did not fail.

How fortunate for the country it was that time was given to Associations to find themselves may be judged from the growing tension between the West Riding Association and the War Office. Sir William Clegg, speaking from the Chair on February 7th, 1910, complained of ' a kind of attempt on the part of the Army Council to treat the Association as a mere adjunct of the Army Council, and not as a free and independent body. If their deliberations and resolutions were to be treated in such a high-handed manner, he for one was not prepared to devote his time to the duties of the Association.' A few months later, on the motion of Alderman F. M. Lupton, of Leeds, seconded by Mr. A. J. Hobson, of Sheffield, a resolution was passed urging His Majesty's Government ' to give further effect to their own policy of placing the Territorial army under the control of the County Associations, and to permit these Associations, without undue interference, to perform their duty of providing a properly

[1] It is worth noting that the cost of the recommendations (including extra allowances to officers, efficiency bounties to other ranks, separation allowances during annual camp, insurance concessions, employers' income-tax abatement, grant for boots, shirts and socks, but excluding the proposed grant for amenities) was estimated at £2,300,000 per annum.

equipped Force on the grants allotted to them.' Relations became a little less strained after a personal interview between Lord Harewood and the Secretary of State, when a conciliatory reply was sent to the Association by the War Office. But in 1912 the situation had grown acute again, and Lord Harewood did not hesitate to describe it as a ' tension which had existed for a long time between the Army Council and that Association, especially the Finance Committee of the Association.' Sir William Clegg repeated his former protest, which was supported by Colonel Hughes and other members, while Lord Scarbrough referred to the case of the Association against the Army Council as, in fact, ' unassailable.' We shall not further recall the features of this dispute, which turned on a question of accountancy. It was not the details but the principle which mattered, and the principle which governed the deliberations of members of the West Riding Association was amply vindicated in their resolution, carried on July 1st, 1912 :

> ' That the Association welcomes the reply of the Secretary of State, as indicating complete satisfaction with the financial position of the Association, and notes with pleasure that, as a result of the protest made, there is now every reason to hope that the relations between the Army Council and the Association will be cordial and harmonious in future.'

So, the Association ' found itself ' at last. But the reconciliation came too late to make a prosperous new beginning. If war had still been postponed, opportunity might have been given to build up the Territorial Force on more generous and sympathetic lines, as suggested in the scheme of the West Riding, and to repair the disappointment of Associations. But, though Sir William Clegg spoke of ' a clean slate,' and Lord Scarbrough wrote more hopefully to General Bethune,[1] there was no time to take advantage of the change. The long threatened war was upon them, and, meanwhile, they had to encounter what Mr. Asquith, in November, 1913, called ' the abstraction, whatever Government is in power, who has the public purse under his immediate control.' This ' abstraction ' proved a very real obstruction.

---

[1] Lieut.-Gen. Sir E. C. Bethune, K.C.B., of ' Bethune's Horse '; General Cowan's successor as Director-General of the Territorial Force at the War Office, 1912-17, when he was succeeded by Lord Scarbrough.

CHAPTER II

THE WEST RIDING TROOPS

THE civilian effort before the war to create a 'people's army' under the provisions of the Territorial Force Act, was a fine national exploit, whether in the West Riding or elsewhere. Equally fine, if not finer, though no basis of comparison can be fixed, was the response of the men, including officers and other ranks, to whom the appeal was made.

It is essential to see this clearly. Parliament might pass the best Act which ever adorned the legislature. The Secretary of State for War and His Majesty's other Ministers might use all the eloquence at their command to popularize the Act in the country. The Territorial Force Associations, which were called into being under the Act, might attract the best brains in every county to crown the scheme with success. Throughout the complex organization, avoidable mistakes might be avoided, unavoidable obstacles might be overcome, and a kind of conspiracy of good luck might have surrounded the enterprise from its initiation. And yet, in the ultimate resort, one first condition must be satisfied : the men must be willing to come forward. For the Act spoke, as we have seen, of a 'reorganization of His Majesty's military forces'; and no power on earth, certainly no political power in England, could organize a voluntary force which was unwilling. If the troops out of whom the Territorial army was to be made were not willing to enrol in that army, and to bring to it the loyalty and devotion which had characterized voluntary service in the past, legislation would prove a dead letter. With or without the conditions which we have enumerated above (and some were lacking, as we are aware) the primary factor was the personal one ; conversely, if the heart of the nation was sound, no weakness in the Army Council or at the Treasury could wreck the scheme beyond repair.

Accordingly, it is useful at this point to look at events before the war from a different angle of vision. Men in high places, ' dressed in a little, brief authority,' have always this consolation, when they contemplate their shortcomings, whether within or without their own control, that the near view is fuller than the distant. If every Territorial soldier in the West Riding had been privy to Lord Harewood's difficulties, if every unit awaiting a headquarters had been admitted to the heart-breaking negotiations which preceded each grant of an eighth of an acre of ground, if every recruit grumbling at his boots had known how many pairs of boots were included in General Mends' requisitions, no progress at all would have been made with the raising of the Force or its equipment. But the men who were raised and equipped were spared these disappointments and dubieties. They took their troubles in single spies, not battalions ; and the single troubles which they encountered—too much rain, too few blankets, insufficient transport, and so forth—were counted as part of a day's work, not as items in a quarterly return. They did not multiply their grievances by the calculus familiar to an Association ; and it is precisely this restricted point of view which is valuable as a contrast and a corrective to Associational experience. For the final triumph of the Territorial scheme, as proved in the searching test of war, was a triumph achieved by individuals within the limits of their personal capacity.

It is well to recapture the spirit in which this triumph was achieved; and, fortunately for that purpose, we can refer to a West Riding unit, whose records go back from its War Diary of 1914 to the date of its original inception in 1859. A happy feature of this possession, unique and valuable in itself, is that the unit in question became in the fulness of time the same 4th Battalion of the West Riding Regiment, whose transport left England for France first of the 49th Division[1] ; and, with the added interest of that coincidence, its faded pages may be searched for evidence to the men's point of view.   It was Lord Haldane who wrote (December, 1908), in a passage referred to above[2] :

'The abstract and dry language of Statutes and Army Orders may command our rational assent, but what Cardinal Newman was fond of speaking of as *real* assent it will never command unless it is interpreted in the light which the historical method throws on it.'

Such a light is thrown by this record on the history of the previous half-century.

It began on May 25th, 1859, when Major-General Jonathan Peel, a brother of the great Sir Robert, and a predecessor of Lord Haldane's at the War Office, issued a circular to authorize the formation of Volunteer corps.   Two days later, a requisition was addressed to the Worshipful the Mayor of Halifax by a hundred and twenty-five inhabitants of the borough and its neighbourhood, praying him to convene a public meeting in order to consider ' the propriety of forming a Volunteer Rifle Corps for this district.'   The propriety was duly considered on the following Friday, June 3rd, in the Town Hall at Halifax, when and where a hundred and twenty good citizens, with Mr. Edward Akroyd[3] at their head, professed themselves willing to enrol as members of a Volunteer Rifle Corps for this Town and District, ' provided the cost of uniform, arms and accoutrements does not exceed £9 per annum.'   The crest selected was the Borough Arms ; the head-dress, familiar in caricature, was ' shako and plume ' ; the uniform a dark-green tunic ; the arms, a short Enfield muzzle-loader, and bayonet ; and the title of the corps was the 4th West Yorks Rifle

---

[1] See page 3.
[2] *Ibid.*
[3] Later, Colonel, and first Hon. Colonel of the Battalion.

Volunteers. Seldom have small beginnings been more amply fulfilled by noble ends.

The Rifle Corps grew and prospered. Colours, with crest and title, were worked by the ladies of Halifax and presented in September, 1860,[1] and Captain Akroyd had the satisfaction in that month of parading 455 men at a Review in York, and of publishing in Orders the next day, that ' the 4th West Yorks Rifle Volunteers, by their soldier-like bearing, their excellent discipline, and the steadiness of their movements, have earned for the Corps a high reputation among the Riding and County Battalions.' On March 10th, 1863, they paraded at the marriage of the Prince of Wales. They furnished a Guard of Honour, and guards and sentinel for the night, when His Royal Highness, on the following August 3rd, visited Halifax to open the Town Hall. In the same year, a capitation grant of 20/- for each efficient man was authorized for issue by the Government, thus relieving all ranks of a part of their voluntary expenditure ; and it is observed in the same context, though its precise bearing escapes us to-day, that the Government ' also repeated the gracious permission accorded by George II. of wearing hair-powder untaxed.' A drill-hall, designed by an assistant to Sir Gilbert Scott, and intended to serve both as the head quarters of the corps and as a public hall and concert-room, was started in 1868 and available in 1870. In 1874, the busby head-dress was adopted ; the tunic was altered to scarlet with dark-blue facings, and the long Enfield was substituted for the short. At the same time, the maximum establishment was fixed at 600 all ranks. The next year saw the first Camp, in tents on Castle Hill, Scarborough. In 1880, the Battalion was armed with the Snider breech-loader and bayonet, and the common helmet replaced the busby. In July, 1881, the Battalion, 480 strong, represented the county of Yorkshire at a Royal Review of Volunteers in Windsor Great Park. In 1883, a step forward was taken in the direction completed by the Territorial Act of 1907 : the 4th, 6th and 9th West Riding of Yorkshire Volunteer Corps were renamed the 1st, 2nd and 3rd Volunteer Battalions of the West Riding Regiment (Duke of Wellington's) ; the old Arms of Halifax were replaced by the badges of the West Riding Regiments ; and in 1887 the Battalion was re-clothed in a manner similar to the Line Battalions with which it had been affiliated, but with silver lace, buttons and badges. Ten years later, in 1897, a detachment of the Battalion was bivouacked in the ditch of the Tower of London, and did duty on London Bridge, on the occasion of Queen Victoria's Diamond Jubilee. A more serious call was to follow. On December 19th, 1899, after the so-called ' black week ' in the Transvaal, it was announced that ' Her Majesty's Government have decided to accept offers of service in South Africa from the Volunteers. . . . The terms of enlistment for officers and men will be for

[1] These Colours were deposited in All Souls' Church, Halifax, on April 3rd, 1910.

one year, or for not less than the period of the War.' Three days later, on December 22nd, Major W. H. Land, commanding the 1st Volunteer Battalion, West Riding Regiment (our old friend, the 4th Rifle Volunteers), was prepared to place the Battalion at the disposal of the Government, and an Active Service Company of Volunteers, with Lieut. H. S. Atkinson at their head, was complete for embarkation early in 1900, when they were entertained at a farewell banquet in Halifax. The occasion, historically so inspiring, has several features of present interest. Colonel (later, Sir) E. Hildred Carlile, remarked on the sense of ' promotion,' and the ' feeling that more would be required,' in the call to Volunteers to take a place side by side with Regulars in Line Battalions. Colonel Le Mottee discussed the ' spirit of militarism,' drawing a clear distinction between its fair and evil aspects ; and other speakers who followed referred with gravity and emphasis to the future needs of national defence. The draft sailed on February 17th, reaching Table Bay on March 14th, and, exactly a year later (March 16th, 1901), the Relief Company of the Battalion left Halifax for the same destination. Needless to say, their fighting record in South Africa was worthy of their regiment and Riding. They contributed to the final victory of British arms ; and, when the first members of the first Service Company returned to Halifax in the following May, they received the welcome which they deserved. A presentation of medals took place later in 1901, and inspired a pro-phetic speech by Colonel Le Mottee, which is well worth recalling to-day :

'The Volunteer movement,' he said, ' never stood higher in the estimation of the military authorities than it did now. The behaviour of the Volunteers showed that the spirit of the nation was as high as it ever was, and the question was how to utilize this fine material to the best advantage. Conscription was out of the question at present, and the only alternative was the extension of the Volunteer movement for the securing of efficiency for all who joined.'

This perception carries us a long way from 1859 and the Halifax Rifle Corps. We reach in the new century and the new reign, and in the brief peace after the South African War, the problem, or series of problems, which were honestly attacked, if not, as we have seen, fully solved, by the Territorial and Reserve Forces Act of 1907. But note the continuity of the history, and the secure foundation of that Act on material already existing. The Territorial scheme, like the British Constitution, grew up and developed by its own strength ; it was never imposed from without. Herein lay the secret of such measure of success as it achieved. The war in South Africa had revealed grave defects in military resources and in the means of national defence. ' Conscription was out of the question at present,' but the war of 1914 found the counties of Great Britain at least organized for an emergency which surpassed in its demands and its extent the most serious anticipations of the most foresightful. And the organization (this is the important point) was based on a tradition which could not fail. Everywhere in England, not in Halifax alone, had been men of public spirit, like Edward Akroyd, to petition their worshipful mayor on behalf of the Volunteer movement. Everywhere in England, for fifty years, the Volunteers had drilled and camped, had exchanged their shakoes for busbies, and their muzzle-loaders for breech-loaders, and had converted public ridicule into tolerance, and tolerance into appreciation, and appreciation at last into heartfelt gratitude to the ' people's army ' which sprang from English soil. We turn the old pages of *Punch*, and smile at John Leech's pictures of ' The Brook-Green Volunteers ' and others ; but behind our laughter is the sense that these long-ago, long-whiskered men were the true makers and only begetters of the Territorial Army in the Great War, and that Edward Akroyd and the hundred and nineteen who signed the resolution of enrolment at the public meeting in Halifax Town Hall on June 3rd, 1859, showed the way to the fighting men of the West Riding who helped Marshal Foch and Earl Haig to turn the tide of German advance in the summer of 1918.

This historic sense deepens as we approach the period immediately before the war. In May, 1902, the honorary rank of Lieutenant in the Army was granted to Captain H. S. Atkinson, with an award of the Queen's Medal with three clasps, in recognition of his services in South Africa. So, the Volunteer and the Regular had coalesced. In the following December, Lord Savile accepted the honorary Colonelcy of the Battalion, in succession, after a long interval, to its virtual founder, Colonel Akroyd, and testimony was borne to the fact that the troops were ' working on lines which lead to real efficiency of mobilization for home defence.' In 1905, the writing on the wall was conspicuous for all to read. Colonel Land observed, at the annual prize-giving, that the choice for the future now lay between ' the more effective training of the Volunteer forces, or compulsion. It rested entirely with the authorities and employers of labour to decide which alternative to adopt. One or the other was inevitable.' In 1907, the inevitable occurred, and early in 1908, when the Territorial Act was on the Statute-book, the Secretary of State for War addressed a stirring appeal to the male youth of Great Britain :

' The foundation of a Territorial Force or Army for home defence,' he wrote, ' is no light matter. The appeal which I am making to the nation is that its manhood should recognize the duty of taking part, in an organized form, in providing for the defence of the United Kingdom. The science of war is, like other sciences, making rapid strides, and if we would not be left behind and placed in jeopardy, we must advance. That is why it was necessary that the old Volunteer and Yeomanry forces should pass, by a process of evolution, into the organization of the new Territorial or Home Defence Army.'

Our survey of the progress of a single unit from 1859 to 1908 should enable us better to understand the precise bearing of Lord Haldane's language. What is true of a unit is true of the whole ; and we shall see, in the further annals of this corps of old Rifle Volunteers, who now bore ' South Africa ' upon their Colours, and counted a Regular officer among their Captains, how gallantly the Yeomanry and Volunteers responded to the call of tradition, and how fully ' a process of evolution ' describes the action which they took.

For they ' passed into ' the Territorial Army. As Colonel Land said to his men on a day in 1908 : ' The word " conscription " appears to be repulsive to the vast majority of Englishmen.' He did not share that repulsion, but for those who shared it ' What was the alternative ? Mr. Haldane thought the alternative was to enlarge and make effective use of the present auxiliary forces by reorganization.' So be it. A ' voluntary Territorial force stood between the country and conscription.' But in certain districts of England the Volunteer law was current among men, as the Scout law is, or should be, among boys : ' The Army Council was only asking all Volunteers to do what they in Halifax had done for years ' ; and, when only two alternatives were presented for selection, either to attest under the new Act, or to retire from the auxiliary forces and unwrite a chapter of local history which had been opened in 1859, ' they in Halifax ' were never in doubt. The 4th West Yorks Rifle Volunteers had changed their name in 1883, when they became the 1st Volunteer Battalion of the West Riding (Duke of Wellington's) Regiment. On April 1st, 1908, they consented to change their name again. The 1st West Riding Volunteers became now the 4th Battalion of the West Riding Regiment, with their uniform similar to the Line Battalion's, and scarlet facings for white and gold lace, gilt ornaments for silver and white, and the letter ' T ' to indicate Territorial. *Plus ça change, plus c'est la même chose* the ' process of evolution ' was complete.

We come back from the part to the whole, from Halifax to the West Riding. Our choice of Halifax has not been due to any exceptional conditions in that borough. In some respects, indeed, it lagged behind. Its city fathers contained at least their full proportion of anti-' militarists ' and anti-' conscriptionists,' and its recruiting record was never the best in the Riding. It has been clearer and more convenient, however, to illustrate the movement from start to finish, or, at least, from 1859 to 1908, by means of a concrete example, than to deal vaguely with the mass.

When the mass-problem was approached by Lord Harewood, as Lieutenant of the Riding, and his colleagues in the County Association, they found that the old Volunteer and Yeomanry forces were required to ' pass into ' the new Territorial Army to the number of about

18,300 of all ranks. On March 31st, 1908, the actual strength of those old forces was 414 officers and 9,683 other ranks ; so that, roughly, 8,000 in all had to be found additionally in the West Riding : eight more for every ten on the strength. The quota allotted to the Riding were a whole Division, a Mounted Brigade, and Army Troops.

We have already viewed this problem through the eyes of the West Riding Association, when we saw that the full numbers were never reached, and that a big new scheme was devised, and brought to the notice of the Prime Minister, in order to render the terms of service more attractive. We propose to look at the problem here through the eyes of the men themselves: not of those who did not enrol, but of the personnel which actually joined up. It is important to emphasize this aspect. A sermon preached at absent congregants always hits the regular church-goers ; and the repinings of Associations at a deficiency in establishment are apt to distract attention from the merits of the men on the strength. Thus, the keen inheritors of the tradition of the 4th West Yorks Rifle Volunteers were not less but, rather, more praiseworthy because their strength as a Territorial unit, after April, 1908, was always below establishment. Take the three last returns before the war :—

4th BATTALION, WEST RIDING REGIMENT, HALIFAX.

Date.	Establishment.		Total Strength.		Deficiency.	
	Officers.	Other Ranks.	Officers.	Other Ranks.	Officers.	Other Ranks.
31–12–1912	29	985	20	747	9	238
31–12–1913	28	978	21	596	7	382
31–5–1914	28	978	20	613	8	365

This was the kind of disheartenment which General Wright,[1] Commanding the Division, had to face at the outset of his task ; and, since it was the function of the Association to rebuke the absent 37 per cent., let us praise the present sixty-three. When three or four men in ten abstain, the virtue of the assentients is more conspicuous.

Certainly, it was easier not to join. We are not referring now to what we may call the permanent handicap : the passive resistance of some employers, the active dislike of others : the wave of pacific sentiment, fanned by hot blasts from Labour circles, and the acute

[1] Brig.-General Archibald John Arnold Wright, C.B., appointed April, 1908. This officer had served in Bengal, 1883-88, as D.A.A.G. (Musketry), and in the Chitral Relief Force, 1895. He was awarded the C.B. after the South African Campaign (Queen's Medal, 3 clasps ; King's Medal, 2 clasps), and subsequent to his retirement in 1910, was recalled to service, November, 1914, as Brig.-General Commanding the 90th Infantry Brigade.

suspicion of the hidden hand of compulsion. Nor are we referring now to merely local conditions, such as points of precedence and procedure, and minor grievances and jealousies, almost inevitable at the start of a novel and complex organization in an area as wide as the West Riding. These things loom large in the beginning, but the incidents of the quarrels disappear when the decisions shine in their results, and the wisest course is to believe that every honest conflict of interests is inspired by generous emulation. This, at least, is how we shall recall the discussion in 1908 whether the West Riding Horse Artillery, which was to form part of the Yorkshire Mounted Brigade, should be raised by the borough of Sheffield or by Earl Fitzwilliam, with its headquarters at Wentworth Woodhouse, and the ultimate acceptance of the latter offer in the public spirit in which it was made. No : the task set to General Wright and his colleagues, the purely military task, that is to say, was formidable enough, without attempting to weigh the imponderable. His record of service shows that he was least of all likely to be satisfied with a hollow or an illusory success. On July 7th, 1908, for instance, on the occasion of a visit to Leeds by their Majesties King Edward and Queen Alexandra, Regular and Territorial Troops were paraded to line the streets and to furnish Guards of Honour ; and the General Officer Commanding-in-Chief, Northern Command, in publishing the King's gracious message, expressed his personal

> ' gratification, that, on this the first occasion on which a portion of the recently-formed Territorial Troops of the Northern Command has paraded before the Sovereign, they should have merited the Royal approbation.'

The fact was gratifying, no doubt, but the responsible military authorities were probably much more concerned with the further facts that, at the same date, no equipment had been received for the Horse Artillery, only part equipment for the Royal Field Artillery and the Royal Engineers, and that the Infantry equipment had to be reported as ' generally bad, of obsolete pattern, and useless for active service.' It was not to earn Royal compliments on parade, but to have the Troops ready for mobilization, that these authorities were primarily concerned.

We are constrained to dwell upon this feature, because of its obvious connection with future deficiencies in numbers. Take the first Annual Training in Camp of the West Riding Division in the summer of 1908. Over 97 per cent. of other Ranks attended, of whom 72 per cent. were in attendance for the fifteen days : a very commendable record. The results on the whole were good. The Redcar Urban District Council expressed ' high appreciation of the gentlemanly conduct ' of the Troops, and hoped to welcome them again. There was not a single case tried for drunkenness, and discipline and bearing were notably improved. But, when we turn to the Report of the Divisional Commander, what do we gather as to his views, and what can we read between the lines ?

'As regards the equipment necessary,' he wrote, 'this is very far from being complete, and I hope, before many months pass, steps will be taken to remedy this great and dangerous defect. The Artillery were deficient of guns and wagons, and the harness is unsuitable for issue to Territorial Troops. . . . The Engineers were deficient in necessary equipment, consequently all ranks suffered as regards instruction and training.'

Danger and suffering are strong words, which General Wright would not have used without good cause. In the previous chapter we attempted to translate these grievances into the language of War Office routine, and after multiplying them by the ninety-four Associations, we were able to find some excuse for official hesitation in removing them. Here it is appropriate to translate them into the language of the rank and file, and to imagine, by no great effort, how, when the Camp was broken up, drivers of teams 'unsuitably' harnessed and victims of even worse defects would deter, unconsciously, it might be, their brothers and friends from joining up.

It may be urged that 1908 was the first summer in the life of the Force. Let us turn to the following year. At the Divisional Camp in 1909, the attendance of all ranks below officers reached 94 per cent., of whom 71 per cent. attended for fifteen days. But the Chairman's October report stated, with reference to an Army Council Order as to the purchase of boots : ' Under present conditions, should the Force be mobilized, it would be found to be incapable of marching.' Moreover, there were sundry deficiencies of guns, limbers, wagons, etc., and it is significantly observed :

'The Officer Commanding 2nd West Riding Brigade, R.F.A., has had a set of harness (six horses) converted from neck-collar to breast, at a cost of £9 10s. 5d. The Army Council has been asked to sanction and provide funds for the conversion of the remainder.'

Here, perhaps, we may interpolate a note, that in January, 1910, instructions were issued from the War Office,[1] authorizing County Associations, ' in view of the great influence and local knowledge ' at their disposal, to add to their existing heavy duties by making arrangements for the provision of the vehicles and animals required on mobilization for the Regular Army as well as for the Territorial Force. The West Riding Association, acknowledging this letter, remarked drily, that, while it was not aware that the provision of horses for the Regular Army on mobilization formed any part of its statutory duties, 'it is quite willing to undertake the work, subject to a clear understanding that adequate funds will be provided, sufficient, in its judgment, to carry out the work effectively.' And, if any reader is inclined to cavil

[1] Circular Memorandum, No. 131 of 14-1-1910 ; 9/Gen. No. 1700 (C. 3).

at the tautology in the last phrase, he may be recommended to study the experience of the West Riding Association as to the Army Council's view of the meaning of ' adequate funds.'

General Bullock[1] succeeded General Wright as Officer Commanding the Division in January, 1910. His first Camp was held partly in the Isle of Man, where, unfortunately, the weather was very bad. The attendance was 93 per cent. of other ranks, of whom 69 per cent. trained for fifteen days. ' No change ' was reported in the condition of the supply of guns, wagons, and saddlery ; most of the units were still deficient of binoculars ; ' the supply of horses was, on the whole, satisfactory,' and the provision of machine-guns in all units was complete. His second Camp (1911) showed a further fall in the percentages : 89 per cent. of other Ranks attended, of whom 58 per cent. trained for fifteen days. The Troops were encamped in various places, including Salisbury Plain, Ripon, Scarborough, Marske, Skegness and Aldershot. A Review of the Ripon Camp was witnessed by Major-General (Sir) John Cowans, afterwards Quartermaster-General, and at that time Director-General of the Territorial Force.

Sir George Bullock's command of the Division coincided with the pressure of three problems : the provision of horses on mobilization, to which reference was made above ; the formation of the Territorial and Veteran Reserves, with which progress proved very slow ; and the formation of Voluntary Aid Detachments, which it was decided to raise in the West Riding in accordance with the scheme of the St. John's Ambulance Association under the provisional name of County Companies (men's and women's). The first work of getting these companies afoot devolved upon General Mends, who, with customary zeal, doubled the duties of Association Secretary with those of County Director. In the Autumn of 1912, the designation of County Company was changed to Voluntary Aid Detachment, and shortly afterwards, when General Mends resigned the direction to Major G. D. Symonds,[2] he was able to hand over to his successor as many as fifty Voluntary Aid Detachments (16 men's, 34 women's), and at the same time to state his confident belief that the initial stages were safely passed and the movement was firmly established.

But these, after all, were side-shows, and, whatever success they achieved, or whatever labour they involved, they must not deflect attention from the main military business, which was always present to the minds of the Commanding Officers, and of non-Commissioned officers as well. It was their business to train for mobilization the

[1] Lieut.-General Sir George Mackworth Bullock, K.C.B., of the Devonshire Regiment. After distinguished service in India, he commanded the 2nd Devons in the South African Campaign, and was Major-General Commanding in Egypt, 1905-8. He was created C.B. in 1900, and K.C.B. an 1911, in the September of which year he relinquished the West Riding Command.

[2] Major Symonds was only able to hold the appointment for a few months. Thereafter, General Mends resumed it again, and carried on with conspicuous success till August, 1914.

Territorial troops of the Riding. The more keen and conscientious they were, the more they were haunted in their dreams by the shadow which took substantial shape on August 4th, 1914, and which grew so rapidly to dimensions undreamed of even by Lord Roberts. Yet this urgent business was performed, like the tasks of the Israelites in Egypt, without the necessary materials. Mr. Churchill, Secretary of State for War, at a meeting of representatives of Associations held in London on April 1st, 1919, in announcing his preliminary plans for the reconstitution of the Territorial Force, was moved to speak as follows :—

'I hope we shall always look forward rather than look back, so far as difficulties are concerned. The grievances of the Territorial Force in the years immediately preceding the war . . . are well known to most of those who are gathered here to-day ; and we should bear them in mind for the purpose of making sure that, so far as possible, a repetition of these hardships is avoided in the future.'

And the Minister went on to point out that—

'We have two great advantages which we have never enjoyed before . . . The days are past when the Territorial Force will have to put up with second- and third-rate weapons, and when every item of equipment and supply which it needed had to be obtained on painfully limited Army Estimates. . . . But, still more important than this, we have at the present time enormous numbers of war-trained veteran soldiers fresh from victorious fields,'

on whom to draw for the reconstituted Force. A happy state of things indeed : 'immense supplies, even immense surplus supplies of the very finest equipment in the world,' and numberless recruits 'versed in every aspect of war, who have the records of their achievements and of their experience vividly in their minds.' How many members of Associations, remembering the days that were past, must have listened to Mr. Churchill's words with more sorrow than anger in their hearts. The anger had faded and died in the fiercer emotions of the war, in part-preparation for which an earlier Secretary of State, just eleven years before, had reconstituted the old Yeomanry and Volunteers into the new Territorial Force. Now the new Territorial Force (after all, it was only eleven years of age) was to be reconstituted in another peace-time out of its own 'war-trained veteran soldiers'. It had sent, as Mr. Churchill stated, 1,045,000 men to fight against the best troops of Germany and Turkey. Six thousand five hundred of its officers and a hundred and five thousand other ranks had laid down their lives in that fight, out of a total casualty list of nearly 600,000 throughout the Force. Twenty-nine of its officers and forty-two of its men in other ranks had won the supreme honour of the Victoria Cross ; and there might well be sorrow in the hearts of many

present at that meeting, not only for the dead, the missing, and the
maimed, but for the 'painfully limited Army Estimates' from 1908
to 1914 ; for the 'second- and third-rate weapons,' or no weapons
at all, with which Territorial troops had been armed ; for the standing
order to train for mobilization and the recurring refusal to provide
the means, for all the unrecognized sacrifices of officers, N.C.O.'s
and men, badly clothed, badly housed, badly equipped, and for the
contrast between the generous recognition of what the Territorial
Force had done and the ungenerous treatment meted out to it in its
years of preparation for the doing. If Mr. Churchill's audience that
day agreed with him not to look back upon past grievances, at least
they might welcome his praise of

    'The vital part which the Territorial Force played at the
beginning of the war. . . . Had its organization been used
to build up the War Army,' he remarked, 'as was originally
intended and conceived by Lord Haldane, to whom we owe a
great debt, we should have avoided many of the difficulties that
confronted us at the outset, and we should have put a larger
efficient force in the field at an earlier stage.'

Our account of the West Riding Troops in the period before the
war were best concluded on this note. Up to the measure of their
achievement, they are entitled to their share of the praise, and no
useful purpose would be served by recounting in terms of drill-hall
and barrack-room accommodation the same tale of official procras-
tination and delay, some features of which we have noted in relation
to equipment and arms.

In September, 1911, General Baldock[1] succeeded Sir George
Bullock as General Officer Commanding the Division, and his term
of service extended into the war epoch. His summer camp in 1912
trained partly on Salisbury Plain (where the Mounted Brigade encamped for the first time outside Yorkshire), partly at Ad Fines, Buddon,
Skegness, and other places, with the 2nd and 3rd General Hospitals
at Netley. The weather was uniformly bad, so much so that a letter
was addressed by the Army Council to Northern Command, expressing
'their appreciation, and that of the Secretary of State for War, for the
excellent spirit which was shown by the Territorial Troops in Camp
this year. The weather has been most inclement, and the soldierly
spirit in which the Troops bore their discomfort was most praiseworthy.' The attendance of ranks below officers reached 85 per cent.
of strength, of whom 60 per cent. trained for fifteen days. The corresponding percentages for 1913, when the weather was remarkably
fine, rose to 88 and 66 respectively. Full arrangements were made
for an Annual Camp in 1914, at dates between May 21st and August

[1] Major-General Thomas Stanford Baldock, C.B. The General had served in South
Africa, where he was awarded the King's Medal with two clasps, and when he was
created C.B. His honourable record in France, 1914-15, will appear in a later chapter
of this book.

16th, and many units, as we shall see, were in training when the summons came to mobilize.

We may note, for historical completeness, some of the activities of the Command which were interrupted by that sudden summons. The whole machine was working steadily and regularly, but with slightly diminished velocity, and a certain sense, which is developed in fine machinery, of insufficient encouragement from above. Probably, from the point of view of the rank and file, the call seemed likely never to arrive. Even the keener officers and more intelligent N.C.O.'s might not unreasonably have begun to believe that the leisurely methods of the War Office still corresponded, as politicians certified, to a clear sky in Europe and a firm friendship with all foreign Powers, so that they, too, might pick their way slowly. Such pressure as was exerted, at any rate, came from within, not from without. As late as April, 1914, the new Headquarters at Halifax for the 2nd West Riding Brigade, Royal Field Artillery, and at Ripon for the Detachment of the West Riding Regiment, still awaited inspection by the Army Council. These were the last of a long series of premises, the acquisition and building of which had given endless trouble to the Association, not without serious detriment to the efficiency of the Troops. At the end of May, 68 Voluntary Aid Detachments (19 men's, 49 women's) had been recognized by the War Office, covering the following districts : Settle (1), Skipton (1), Ripon (1), Harrogate (12), York (5), Otley (7), Leeds (4), Aberfordia (9), Halifax (1), Wakefield (9), Osgoldcross (9), Huddersfield (3), Doncaster (2), Sheffield (2), Rotherham (2). The number of National Reservists had reached a total of 10,853, including 2,404 not classified in respect to their service-value. But of all the statistics available, the most interesting, finally, are numbers. On May 31st, 1914, the Establishment of the West Riding Territorial Force was 574 officers and 17,680 other ranks, 18,254 in all. Its total strength on that date was 537 officers and 14,699 other ranks, showing a shortage of 37 officers and 2,981 other ranks. In real numbers, the shortage amounted to 58 and 3,082 respectively, the discrepancy in figures being due to occasional surpluses in certain units.

Finally, we reproduce below a tabulated statement of the designations and peace-stations of the Corps which formed the Territorial Force of the West Riding shortly after the outbreak of war, and in the third column of that table we add the names of their then Commanding Officers. This, in fine, was the outcome of the six and a half years' work of the Lord Lieutenant and his colleagues in the Association. These Corps of gallant officers and other ranks were the open and visible sign of the response of the West Riding to the appeal of 1908. The Association might not have succeeded in discharging fully the duties numbered from (a) to (l) in Section II., Sub-section (2) of the Territorial and Reserve Forces Act. They might not have provided all the necessary buildings, nor have arranged with all employers of labour as to holidays for training, nor have supplied all the requisites on mobilization, nor have done half a dozen more things which they tried to do in the face of obstruction, and would have liked to do if they had been allowed. Their shortcomings were their misfortune, not their fault, and they have served since as a warning to the Army Council to prevent their repetition in the future. But in the spirit of the officers and men who were on the strength of the units in 1914, the West Riding had given overrunning measure. 'Any part of the Territorial Force,' it is written in Section XIII. (1) of the Act, ' shall be liable to serve in any part of the United Kingdom, but no part of the Territorial Force shall be carried or ordered to go out of the United Kingdom.' The Act of Parliament limited the liability ; we shall see how the action of West Yorkshiremen broke those limits, when the day came.

WEST RIDING TERRITORIAL FORCE
AT THE OUTBREAK OF THE GREAT WAR.

Unit.	Peace Station.	Commanding Officer.
YORKSHIRE MOUNTED BRIGADE.		
Yorkshire Hussars ... ... (less 1 North Riding Squad.)	York	L.-Col. E. W. Stanyforth, D.L., T.D.
Yorkshire Dragoons	Doncaster	Lt.-Col. W. Mackenzie Smith, T.D.
W.R. Roy. Horse Artillery ...	Wentworth Woodhouse, Rotherham	Capt. H. Walker.
MOUNTED BRIGADE.		
T. and S. Column	York	Capt. J. Brown, I.S.O.
Field Ambulance	Wakefield	Lt.-Col. W. K. Clayton.
DIVISIONAL AND ARMY TROOPS.		
1st W.R. Brigade, R.F.A. ...	Leeds	Lt.-Col. E. A. Hirst.
2nd ,, ,, ...	Bradford	Lt.-Col. E. N. Whitley.
3rd ,, ,, ...	Sheffield	Lt.-Col. C. Clifford, V.D.
4th ,, ,, ...	Otley (Howitzer) ...	Lt.-Col. W. S. Dawson, T.D.
W.R. Div. R.G.A.	York (Heavy Battery)	Major W. Graham.
W.R. Div. R.E. and Telegraph Cos.	Sheffield	Lt.-Col. A. E. Bingham, V.D.
5th Bn. W. Yorks. Regt. ...	York	Lt.-Col. C. E. Wood, V.D.
6th ,, ,, ...	Bradford	Lt.-Col. H. O. Wade.
7th \ (Leeds Rifles) ... 8th /	Leeds	{ Lt.-Col. A. E. Kirk, V.D. Lt.-Col. E. Kitson Clark, T.D.
4th Bn. W.R. Regt. ...	Halifax	Lt.-Col. H. S. Atkinson, T.D.
5th ,, ,, ...	Huddersfield ...	Lt.-Col. W. Cooper, V.D.
6th ,, ,, ...	Skipton	Lt.-Col. J. Birkbeck.
7th ,, ,, ...	Milnsbridge ...	Col. G. W. Treble, C.M.G.
4th Bn. K.O. Yorks. L.I. ...	Wakefield	Lt.-Col. H. J. Haslegrave, T.D.
5th ,, ,, ...	Doncaster	Lt.-Col. C. C. Moxon, T.D.
4th Bn. York & Lancs. Regt.	Sheffield	Lt.-Col. B. Firth, V.D.
5th ,, ,, ...	Rotherham ...	Lt.-Col. C. Fox, T.D.
R.A.M.C., 1st F.A.	Leeds	Major A. D. Sharp.
,, 2nd	Leeds	Lt.-Col. W. Macgregor Young, M.D.
,, 3rd	Sheffield	Lt.-Col. J. W. Stokes.
Div. T. and S. Column ...	Leeds	Lt.-Col. J. C. Chambers, V.D.
Northern Signal Cos. ...	Leeds	Lt.-Col. J. W. H. Brown, T.D.
2nd Northern Gen. Hospital	Leeds	Major J. F. Dobson, M.B., F.R.C.S.
3rd ,, ,, ...	Sheffield	Lt.-Col. A. M. Connell, F.R.C.S.
W.R. Div. Clearing Hospital	Leeds	Lt.-Col. A. E. L. Wear.

CHAPTER III

MOBILIZATION

No one in the present generation is likely to forget Tuesday, August 4th, 1914, A greater complexity of emotions was crowded into the twenty-four hours which ended at 11 p.m. (midnight by mid-European time) that day than was known before or has been known since. We moved from war to peace in 1918-19 through a gradual series of experiences : relief from fear, even from anxiety, growing hope, moral certainty, real conviction, the armistice, the surrender of ships, the peace conference, civil unrest, the return of troops, and so forth. We moved from peace to war in the space of a single night's experience. Who slept in the night of August 4th awoke the next morning to war. The more sanguine might hug the dream of a quick walk-over for the Allied Armies ; of France, with England's assistance, fighting victoriously on the West, while Russia, the ' steam-roller ' as they called her, crushed the soil of the enemy on his Eastern frontier. But not even the most credulous was immune from that sense of something new and unexpected which all the circumstances of the hour conspired to create. The extended holiday, the swollen bank-rate, the moratorium, the sessions of the Cabinet, the balance of responsibility which made Sir Edward Grey's least utterance an oracle ; the contrast between the dead tissue of domestic politics—Ireland, the House of Lords, the Welsh Church—and the living body of Belgium, already shaking at the thunder of German guns ; the quickened interest in foreign history, foreign policy, foreign naval and military resources ; the strange names of Treitschke, Nietzsche, and the vision of Professor Cramb ; above all, the sudden, overwhelming rush on respectable, commonplace minds of new, strange facts and ideas, and the haunting fancies which they evoked, in the midst of that August procession of harvest, foliage and heat, combined to produce an effect of change which no effort of ' reconstruction ' can unmake.

It fell least heavily on the Royal Navy and the Regular Army, which proceeded to or were found at their appointed stations, in calm reliance on the traditions behind them and without fear of the ordeal in front ; and next only to the service-men, who turned from peace to war as from one day's work to another, and changed their habits of life as quickly as a man might change his clothes, were the citizen-soldiers of the Territorial Force : landowners and tillers of the soil, doctors, lawyers and business-men, clerks, warehousemen and factory-hands, all the components of a great country's complex mechanism, united by the Haldane scheme to serve side by side in a ' people's army.'

The evidence may be sought from many quarters, but it is the source not the stream which varies. Take, summarily, General Bethune's tribute to the Force which he directed from 1912 to 1917[1];

> 'A few days after mobilization, the Territorial Force were asked by telegraph the number that would volunteer for foreign service. Ninety-two per cent. responded within a few weeks, and the complete total, I think, rose to ninety-six per cent. . . . Before the end of September, we had doubled the Territorial Force, and were proceeding to form 3rd Lines. . . . Recruits from August 4th, 1914, to January 19th, 1916, amounted in round numbers to 732,000. . . . The Territorial Force Associations, composed, as they are, of representatives of every class in a County, were eminently adapted for the work which they undertook and carried out so well. . . They relieved the War Office of an enormous amount of work which would not have been done in any other way.'

We shall have occasion to return to this official document.

Take, summarily, again, Lord French's tribute to the Territorial Force, based on his experience in Command at the front, in his book, *1914* (pages 293-94) :—

> 'It is true that by the terms of their engagement, Territorial Soldiers were only available for Home Defence ; . . . The response to the call which was subsequently made upon them shows quite clearly that, had they been asked at first, they would have come forward almost to a man.
>
> 'However, as it turned out, they were ignored . . . Officers and men alike naturally made up their minds that they were not wanted and would never be used for any other purpose than that for which they had originally taken service, namely, the defence of the United Kingdom.
>
> 'But the time for the employment of troops other than the Regulars of the Old Army arrived with drastic and unexpected speed . . . It was then that the Country in her need turned to the despised Territorials.
>
> 'The call came upon them like a bolt from the blue. No warning had been given. Fathers and sons, husbands and brothers left their families, homes, the work and business of their lives, almost at an hour's notice to go on Active Service abroad.
>
> 'It seems to me we have never realized what it was these men were asked to do. They were quite different to professional soldiers, who are kept and paid through years of peace for this particular purpose of war; who spend their lives practising their profession and gaining promotion and distinction ; and who,

[1] See page 14, note 1. The official Memorandum quoted in the text is dated October 31st, 1916.

on being confronted with the enemy, fulfil the great ambition of their lives.

' Equally distinct were the Territorials also from what has been called the New Army, whose Officers and men had ample time to prepare themselves for what they were required to do. I wonder sometimes if the eyes of the country will ever be opened to what these Territorial soldiers of ours have done. I say without the slightest hesitation that, without the assistance which the Territorials afforded between October, 1914, and June, 1915, it would have been impossible to have held the line in France and Belgium, or to have prevented the enemy from reaching his goal, the Channel seaboard.'

Take, in detail, the War Diaries of Officers Commanding Territorial Force units in the West Riding ; and first, for the sake of completing the record followed in the last chapter, that of the 4th Battalion, Duke of Wellington's (West Riding) Regiment. On July 26th, we read, they left Halifax for their Annual Training at Marske-by-the-Sea :

' The times were very unsettled, there were rumours of war, and it was thought that at any moment the order for mobilization would come. The training proceeded amidst intense excitement, and finally word came that Germany and Austria had declared war on England, France and Russia. The Special Service Section of the Battalion, consisting of two officers, Captain R. E. Sugden and Lieut. H. N. Waller, and 100 men were at once despatched to Grimsby. On August 3rd, the Battalion was ordered to return to Halifax, and at 7 p.m. on August 4th the order to mobilize was received . . . At about 1-30 p.m. on August 5th, the Battalion marched down Horton Street to the station, and took train to Hull, their allotted station, where the men were billeted.'

Among the officers who left Halifax with the Battalion were Lieut.-Col. H. Atkinson (the Lieutenant Atkinson of South Africa days[1]) and Major E. P. Chambers.[2] A few days were spent in making ready, and

' On August 13th, the Battalion marched to Great Coates, where the men were billeted in the village. The training was now commenced, and the days were spent in route-marching, Company and Battalion training, special attention being paid to musketry. The weather during the whole stay at Great Coates was absolutely perfect, glorious sunshine day after day.'

So the news reached Headquarters at Halifax.

Take the evidence of the 6th Battalion of the West Yorkshire Regiment. On August 5th, at 6 p.m , there were present at Headquarters in Bradford 575 members out of a total strength of 589.

[1] See page 18.
[2] To whom I am immensely indebted for the continuous archives of the Unit from 1859 to 1914. They were kept till 1910 by the late Major J. B. Howard, from whom Major Chambers took over the labour of love.

Before the close of that day 215 men had re-engaged and re-enlisted. On August 8th the Commanding Officer was in a position to telegraph to York that his Battalion was up to War Establishment ; 29 officers, 979 other ranks, 57 horses and the necessary transport : not bad going in August, 1914, for a unit of the Force, which, through its administrative council, had waited on the Prime Minister as recently as November, 1913, to discuss grave deficiencies in its numbers.

It is worth while to piece together this Unit's record, which may fairly be taken to typify that of the Territorial Force as a whole, within the West Riding or beyond, in these early weeks of the Great War. There is the detail of the horses, for example, insignificant, of course, in the perspective of a history of the Great War, but significant as an item of preparation in the sum of the country's enormous effort. The 57 horses were all purchased locally, 10 for officers, 16 pack, and 31 draught ; ' the latter being a good, heavy stamp from carters' wagons.' There is evidence of foresight in that touch. On August 11th the Battalion went by rail to its war-station at Selby, where Captain Anderton, billeting officer, had been making arrangements since the 9th. Ten men were discharged as undesirable, and it is observed that the enlisting was done at such high speed during mobilization, ' that it was impossible to inquire into the characters of many of the men.' About a hundred National Reservists, Class II, had been enlisted into the Battalion on August 8th, who proved ' a boon to the Battalion,' and repaid the hard work of General Mends and his assistants in this department. As old soldiers they served, despite their age, to steady the recruits. Recruit-training had to be started at once, in view of the many enlistments, and a special staff was organized for this purpose in order that the main business of training might be interrupted as little as possible. A welcome move from billets to camp (near Selby) was made on August 19th, and on the 24th they moved by rail and road to the Knavesmire Common, York, where Brigade Orders were received that the Battalion had been selected as the Service Battalion of the 1st West Riding Infantry Brigade : on the whole, a cheerful account of twenty days' experience of war conditions.

The newly selected Service Battalion was formed into complete Companies, which consisted entirely of personnel volunteering for service overseas, and in which the men from each Company were kept as far as practicable together. The remaining Companies were made up from Units, kept together in the same way, provided by the 5th, 7th and 8th Battalions of the West Yorkshire Regiment. After some practice in night-entraining and other exercises, the Battalion moved on August 31st, and marched with 1st Line Transport to take its place in the Brigade : ' a great change for the better,' it is added. Next day, the Brigadier-General addressed the Territorial troops of the Brigade on the subject of voluntary active service abroad, and by

September 15th the Battalion mustered 800 strong for overseas. Some strenuous weeks of training followed. On November 3rd, when the men were back in York, sounds of heavy firing in the North Sea raised a temporary alarm of German Dreadnoughts and Cruisers working North. ' In two hours,' we are told, ' the Battalion was ready to move off with transport loaded ' ; so, down South, we might sleep o' nights. At this date, too, we read of an ' enormous improvement in the general behaviour of the N.C.O.'s and men. Conduct excellent in the town.'

We come to November 22nd, 1914. Half the Battalion moved to Redcar, complete with transport, ammunition and tools, on trench-digging duty. Their place was taken by five Home Service Companies, who arrived, it is observed, without greatcoats or equipment. On December 2nd, the Machine-Guns with their detachments were ordered to Redcar, and proceeded under Captain R. G. Fell. On the 10th, an exchange was effected between the four Reserve Companies and the half-battalion at Redcar, which returned accordingly to York. A new programme of training was arranged, which lasted through January, 1915, and on February 1st came a welcome leave for twenty per cent. of officers and other ranks. At the end of February, the Battalion moved to Gainsborough, in Lincolnshire, to relieve the 4th Battalion K.O.Y.L.I., and were billeted on the inhabitants, four men in each dwellinghouse, ' a change for the better ', remarks the diarist, ' after being a platoon in a hired empty house at York '. The Battalion remained at Gainsborough till April 15th, when they proceeded in two trains to Folkestone, reaching Boulogne at 10-45 that night. Their transport and machine-guns, which had left Gainsborough the day before, and which travelled *via* Southampton and Havre, joined them at Boulogne. There for the present we may leave them to spend the night of the 15th in a Rest Camp, eight months and ten days after the order to mobilize had been received at Bradford.

Take the evidence of a unit in a different arm. Colonel A. E. L. Wear,[1] C.M.G., of the Army Medical Service, was in camp at Scarborough on August 4th, 1914, with the cadre of the 1/1st West Riding Casualty Clearing Station, later the 7th C.C. Station. The unit returned at once to its Headquarters at Leeds, where mobilization to war strength was completed, with the exception of the full complement of officers. Great care was taken to select men for the sake of their skill in special trades : joiners, tailors, boot-repairers, First-Aid experts, and so forth ; and the wisdom of this foresight was fully justified by events. Intensive training was started forthwith, in the French language, the duties of cooks and orderlies, field work by means of week-end bivouacs, and other practical departments, with the result

[1] Invalided home in November, 1916. About 47,000 patients passed through the C.C. Station during Col. Wear's two years' command. The C.M.G. was awarded to this Officer in June, 1915, when the Military Cross was conferred on his Quartermaster.

D

that Colonel Wear was able to inform the War Office as early as October that his unit was ready for overseas. Orders were received to proceed to France, and the officers scheduled on a waiting-list were enrolled, clothed and equipped. On November 1st, the passage was made to Boulogne, and on the 6th a detachment was employed in dealing at Poperinghe with the wounded from the first Battle of Ypres.

As this Medical unit from the West Riding preceded the Divisions to France, it will be convenient in this place to follow its fortunes a little further. Towards the end of November, 1914, it took over the Monastery of St. Joseph, which is situated just North of Merville, and which had been used in turn by German, French, English and Indian troops. A Casualty Clearing Station needs quiet and cleanliness, among the major virtues, and a perfect economy of minor details in order to ensure them. Colonel Wear proved equal to these demands. He apportioned the building into wards, stores, operating-theatre, dispensary, offices, etc., cleaned it all up and made it ready, and, after a little discussion with the Church authorities, turned the roomy main chapel of the Monastery into a serious case ward. Members of the unit (observe here the C.O.'s foresight in his selection of personnel) installed the heating-stoves, and concreted the paths, and built a large destructor to hold a 400-gallon iron tank, which supplied hot water to a bath-hut. They also did the washing for some time, but, later, arrangements were made for French female labour, and a regular laundry was fitted up. This feature was novel and successful. The work, seldom light, came in rushes, when day and night shifts (at times, even four-hour shifts) were organized, so as to carry on with the minimum of fatigue by means of a limited personnel. The unit numbered at full strength eight Medical Officers, a Quartermaster, a Dentist, two Chaplains, seven Nurses, eighty-four rank and file, nine A.S.C. and seventeen P.B. men. Perhaps its own simple statement gives its record in the most effective language : ' No man ever left the station without having his wound examined and dressed, and receiving a meal and a smoke.' From frost-bite, La Bassée, Neuve Chapelle, Aubers and Festubert, came the first streams of clients to this station.

We return to the centre of war activity at the Territorial Headquarters in York.

In a little book, written chiefly for America and published early in 1918, Major Basil Williams, later employed under Colonel Lord Gorell on educational Staff Duties, described in adequate terms the *Raising and Training the New Armies*[1]. We are not immediately concerned with the decision which called those Armies into being. Lord Kitchener was Secretary of State for War, and on August 8th, 1914, he called for that ' first hundred thousand ' whose spirit was so brilliantly conveyed in Mr. Ian Hay's volume of that name. He got them over

---

[1] Constable and Co., 1918.

A CASUALTY CLEARING STATION.

[Face p. 34

and over again, and it is no part of our purpose to discuss the Parliamentary Recruiting Committee's output of speeches, posters and 'literature,' by which, partly, under the grace of England's effort, the result was obtained. Nor shall we examine the evidence on which Mr. Churchill, as Secretary of State for War, based his expression of opinion, already quoted above, that, had the Territorial Force organization ' been used to build up the War Army, as originally intended and conceived by Lord Haldane, we should have avoided many of the difficulties that confronted us at the outset, and we should have put a larger efficient force in the field at an earlier stage.' What Lord Haldane intended in 1908 and what Lord Kitchener demanded in 1914 might well be corrected in the light of what Mr. Churchill knew in 1919. But even without the wisdom which is garnered after the event, we are entitled to quote one sentence from Major Williams' account of the New Armies. Towards the close of his review of ' the great awakening of the nation by the recruiting campaign,' 1914-1915, he wrote :

' All this time the Territorial Force, the original home defence force, nearly the whole of which had originally volunteered for service overseas, had been quietly raising recruits for itself, supplementary to the recruits raised by these different methods '.

' All this time ' and ' quietly ' are the *mots justes*. The ' time ' as we have observed, dated back through the Volunteer movement of 1859 to the immemorial tradition of shire-loyalty ; the ' quiet ' was that of boroughs and countryside, of mayors' parlours and manorial halls, of town-marts and village-greens in England—

' Grave mother of majestic works,
    From her isle-altar gazing down,
Who, God-like, grasps the triple forks,
    And, King-like, wears the crown.'

Her possession of the trident was first definitely challenged[1] since Trafalgar on August 4th, 1914, and in the West Riding of Yorkshire, as elsewhere, the means of defence were swiftly organized.

Swift forethought in County areas, it should be noted, did not invariably lead to sound action at the executive centre. A trivial example will suffice. Three weeks after the outbreak of war, a letter was written to the Army Council suggesting that the West Riding Association should make provision for cardigan jackets, warm drawers, and other articles of clothing, which the troops would require in the winter months. The Army Council sent a dignified reply, thanking the Association for their offer, but stating that these articles would be provided by the Army Council itself. Later, on October 9th, the Army Council intimated its inability to supply cardigan jackets, warm drawers, and other articles of winter clothing for the Troops, and

[1] ' We must grasp the trident in our fist ' said Kaiser Wilhelm II. at Cologne in 1897. The British Army occupied Cologne in 1918.

requested the Association to make provision.   So far the experience
was merely funny, but the sequel had a Gilbertian touch.   When the
Association made inquiry at the contractors, they were informed that
all manufacturers of the articles in question had been fordidden by
the Army Council to supply anyone else than the War Office.   ' These
facts are brought before the Association', remarked the Chairman in
his quarterly report, ' in order that members may know that everything possible was done to anticipate the requirements of the Troops,
and that any failure in this respect is due to causes beyond its control.'
It was well and temperately said.

The heavy increase of work in the secretariat was fairly met by
the voluntary help of the Hon. G. N. de Yarburgh-Bateson, Mr.
Talbot Rice, Mr. Peter Green, some eighteen or twenty volunteers
from the close of their day's work till late at night, two clerks from the
North Eastern Railway Company, a clerk from the York Probate
Office, twenty-six additional full-time clerks, Boy Scouts and other
useful helpers.   The County Director was assisted by Col. Sir Thomas
Pilkington, Bt.,[1] and Lieut.-Col. Husband, whom the G.O.C. had
appointed as officers superintending the Lines of Communication and
the arrangements for the care of the sick and wounded.   Advisory
Boards were formed for the 2nd and 3rd Northern General Hospitals
at Leeds (Training College, Beckett's Park) and Sheffield (Collegiate
Hall) respectively, which as early as the end of August had already
many patients from France and Belgium.   These Boards, consisting,
at Leeds, of the Lord Mayor, Alderman F. Kinder, Lt.-Col. Shann and
the Matron of the Infirmary; and, at Sheffield, of the Lord Mayor,
Lord Wharncliffe, Col. Hughes, Lt.-Col. Sinclair White and the Matron
of the Infirmary, were intended to relieve the Commanding Officers
of the Hospitals of some portion of their administrative functions.
leaving them freer for professional work and discipline.

We omit the long figures and many Army Forms with which
General Mends and his Staff had to wrestle.   The 5,000 blankets
and 2,000 sets of saddlery, the 32,887 complete suits of service-dress,
the 16,803 water-bottles and 4,242 bandoliers ; these requisitions and
the rest of then are as tiresome and uninteresting in retrospect as they
were absorbing and urgent at the time.   There is one feature of their
work, however, familiar by the mystic letters S/A, which cannot be
passed over without notice, for it imposed a very severe strain on the
Association's capacity for expansion.   S/A stands for separation
allowance, and the regular issue of this grant to the wives and dependents
of serving soldiers had been assigned by the Act of Parliament as part
of an Association's duty.   It was by no means an easy task.   Allowance has to be made for an inconvenient distribution of functions.
A soldier, whether Regular or Territorial, drew his pay from his

---

[1] Col. Sir T. Pilkington was given Command of a Regular Battalion at the end of 1914,
since when Col. Husband took sole charge of this branch.

Commanding Officer out of the monies supplied on vouchers presented to the Regimental Paymaster. In the Regular Army the same Pay-master kept the soldier's domestic account with his wife and children or other dependents; and, though errors inevitably occurred even when the accounts were thus linked, they could be checked and more readily adjusted, inasmuch as all the information was available in the same office. For the domestic account, it should be observed, was extremely sensitive to variations in the soldier's rate of pay, and was affected by the soldier's ' casualties,' whether major ones of death or desertion, or minor ones of leave, punishment and so forth. In the Territorial Force, however, the soldier's domestic account was kept by his County Association, presumably owing to the fact that they were more likely to be in touch with the personnel of the units which they administered. In peace-time this worked very well. When a Territorial soldier went into camp for a week or fortnight in the summer, it was com-paratively a simple matter for the local Territorial Force Association to pay the corresponding days' allowances to those whom he left at home. But the immense expansion of the Force in 1914, and the extraordinarily complicated system of accountancy, added to the distribution of pay-duties between the Regimental Paymaster for the man and the County Association for his dependent, overtook these heavily burdened bodies at a time when they were least well qualified to discharge the work effectively. They did not understand it. It was difficult to engage clerks. The Army Pay Department of the War Office could not spare sufficient trained instructors ; and, gener-ally, the urgent problems of the mobilization, equipment and (as we shall see) the duplication of the Force, tended to postpone attention to what seemed less pressing domestic matters. The early war annals of the West Riding Association are full of evidence to these conditions :

' The duty devolving on the Association of paying Separation Allowances and Allotments of Pay to the wives and families of the Territorial Troops entails very heavy work and responsibility. . . . The first payment was due to be made on the 9th August, and consisted of Separation Allowance only up to the 31st of the month. The September payment was duly made on the 31st August. The number of Money Orders sent out up to and for that date was 13,328, and on 3rd September, orders were received to also pay a compulsory Allotment of Pay for each married soldier.'
Though they split an infinitive in doing so, this payment, too, was duly made on September 11th ; but it involved a further 5,430 Money Orders with the corresponding, inevitable Army Forms.

It is no part of our present purpose to enquire into the possibili-ties of simplifying Army Pay ; least of all, to suggest the simplest method of a flat rate like the wage of a civilian. But it is within our province to point out the almost infinite possibilities of mistakes (even of the fraud which is so elaborately excluded) in the family register for each soldier of the number, sex and age of his children, in the paraphernalia of coupons, Postal Draft-books and Money-Orders, in the calculation and readjustment of rates owing to information advised from the soldier's unit or to domestic changes reported or detected, in the grading of ' unofficial wives ' and other official relationships, and, summarily, in the invention of a system which seems expressly designed to squeeze out of the officers administering it the last drop of the milk of human kindness without any compensating gain in the civil virtues of economy and efficiency.

In January, 1915, nearly 15,000 books of Postal Drafts, representing approximately £210,000, were issued to Postmasters by a directing staff at York, which consisted entirely of voluntary workers. In the following April, steps were taken to regularize the position of these gentlemen, in anticipation of the approval of the Army Council, in which connection notice was drawn to the ' unjustifiable system of differential treatment as between the clerical staff in Regular and Territorial Pay Offices,' clerks in the former being engaged at 35s. a week and in the latter being offered only 23s. In June, the number of cases in pay and in action for payment amounted to 36,538, while the Pay Department was working with 41 per cent. below the equivalent establishment of the Regimental Paymaster's Office. At last, on August 18th, 1915, more than a year after the outbreak of war, the War Office appointed an expert Paymaster to take charge of this heroic band of amateurs, a Government audit was instituted, and the Association was thankful to report that the department ' is now working in as satisfactory a manner as the complicated and constantly changing regulations will permit.' We shall leave the present branch of our subject on this note of moderate transport. That the Association had carried on so well is a proof of the continuity of function which won through to quicker results in other branches of its manifold activity.

We followed one or two units from the sudden hour of mobilization to the sea-ports of France and beyond. We may now look at this achievement, ' quietly ' performed, as we are aware, in the midst of the recruiting for the New Army, through the spectacles of the County Association. Thus, the Chairman's Progress Report, dated August 14th, 1914, referred to the confusion which was caused by the Division being in Camp when the fateful hour struck, but added that the task of mobilization ' may be considered as satisfactorily carried out.' A month later, he reported, in view of ' the present grave emergency,' that every West Riding unit in the Mounted Brigade, the Division and the Army Troops had qualified as a ' General Service ' unit, which meant service overseas. Consequently, the Association became responsible—this gives us a glimpse through its spectacles— for raising Reserve units in each case, which meant a duplication of the Force, or, roughly, another 18,000 of all ranks. Note here the

' which meant ' in each context. The plain meaning of the situation within a few weeks of the outbreak of hostilities, was that the pre-war units would be sent to France at full Establishment, and that the West Riding would have to supply equivalent units in their home-stations. The rapid march of events soon caused names to be given to these facts. In January, 1915, the Chairman stated in his Report that ' the first Reserve units are about to be organized as a Division,' and that ' as soon as the Imperial Service Division leaves for abroad, the first Reserve Division will take its place and a second Reserve Division will be raised. Orders have now been received to commence recruiting for the latter up to 30 per cent. of its Establishment.' Meanwhile, more than 7,000 National Reservists had rejoined the Colours in the West Riding, of whom about 2,000 had been mobilized for duty on Lines of Communication and in Prisoners of War Camps. This force was organized by Colonel G. E. Wilkinson, D.S.O., and ' the clothing and equipment,' it is added, ' have been provided by the Association.' In other directions, too, the energies of the Association were fully engaged. The 2nd Northern General Hospital at Leeds and the 3rd at Sheffield had treated over 4,000 and 3,000 cases respectively ; twenty-eight Auxiliary Hospitals had been approved, of which seventeen had been mobilized up to date, the whole of the staffs, except professional Trained Nurses, being provided free by the Voluntary Aid Detachments, whose beginnings we read of in the last hapter. Further, the West Riding Branch of Queen Mary's Needlework Guild had sent 91,866 articles for the use of the Troops abroad and at home.

And still the war went on, We are to imagine this machine, invented in an epoch of peace to raise 18,000 men for mobilized service at home, stretched now to more than twice its capacity and creaking under unexpected burdens, operated by a shifting personnel of re-called officers, part-time clerks, and inexperienced, however enthusiastic, voluntary workers, overwhelmed with Army Forms and Returns and the necessary business of accountancy, storing trousers by tens of thousands in a space provided for a quarter of the supply, yet vexed that ' certain articles, such as greatcoats, still come in very slowly, and boots, puttees, and gloves are extremely difficult to get,' and always overtaken by the demands of the inexorable German advance, which did not wait upon decisions by the Army Council. The essential letter was issued by the War Office, from the Adjutant-General's branch, on February 24th, 1915. It was numbered 9/Gen. No./4747, and it directed that the Imperial Service, first Reserve and second Reserve Units of the Territorial Force should be designated respec-tively, 1st, 2nd and 3rd Line. The organization of the West Riding Territorial Troops was altered, accordingly, to the West Riding Division, 1st Line ; the West Riding Division, 2nd Line ; and a 3rd Line on a Depot basis, with a strength temporarily limited to two-thirds of

War Establishment. The Yorkshire Mounted Brigade was similarly re-organized. The 3rd Line was eventually to furnish drafts for the 1st and 2nd Lines, and until it should be in a position to do so the 2nd Line was to provide drafts for the 1st, which went overseas, April, 1915.

So, we reach along another route the same point to which we followed certain units through their months of training at home. Many details have necessarily been omitted : that the Association's extra expenditure ' due entirely to the war ' between August 4th, 1914, and April 17th, 1915, amounted to £349,902 ; that 551 men of the 2nd Line Units responded to an appeal for volunteers to transfer to the Reserve of the Regular Battalions of the West Yorkshire, West Riding, K.O. Yorkshire L.I., and York and Lancaster Regiments ; that a Sanitary Section was added as a new unit to each 1st and 2nd Line ; that Territorial Depots were henceforth to be known as Administrative Centres, and to be manned by Home Service members of the Territorial Force[1] ; that up to March 31st, 1915, nearly 2,000 patients had been admitted to the Auxiliary Hospitals in the West Riding ; and so on, and so forth. For the local machine had many wheels, and every wheel was kept moving all the time. It revolved as smoothly as it might, but the motive force was not in York, nor in London, but, in the German Headquarters on the Western Front, and in the hate, which, reversing Dante's cosmogony, seemed, through those fateful months, ' to move the sun and other stars.'

Only one more change need be recorded before we follow General Baldock abroad. In May, 1915, his Division was re-entitled the 49th (West Riding) Division. At the same time its Infantry Brigades (the 1/1st, 1/2nd and 1/3rd) were re-named the 146th, 147th and 148th Infantry Brigades respectively.[2] A few months later, the 2nd Line Division, which was still in training at home, and to some features in whose early history we shall come back, was re-entitled the 62nd (West Riding) Division.[3] Under these names they won renown in the Great War.

[1] The Administrative Centres were independent of the Establishments of the three Lines. They were commanded by an Officer not below Captain's rank, and were charged with the duty of recruiting and of clothing all recruits prior to passing them to their units, and had charge of the Headquarters and Stores.

[2] By authority of a War Office Letter from the Adjutant-General's branch (No. 40/W.O./ 2481) of May 7th, 1915, published in IV. Army Corps Routine Order, No. 609, on May 16th. No change was made in the designation of the Artillery, Engineers and Medical units, but the number of the Division instead of the Territorial designation was attached to the Divisional Cyclist Company, Ammunition Column and Park, Signal Company, Supply Column, Train, and Sanitary Section.

[3] The General Officer Commanding the 62nd Division from February, 1915, to May, 1916, was Major-General Sir James Trotter, K.C.B. He had served in Bechuanaland and South Africa (Queen's Medal with two clasps, and C.B.), and was appointed C.M.G. in 1897, and K.C.B. in 1912.

BOOK II

WAR

CHAPTER IV

' MALBROUCK S'EN VA-T'EN GUERRE '

Once more the point of view changes. We have seen the 49th Division nursed by its ministering Association into the semblance of a military force. We have noted its cheerful submission to the discipline of drill and camp, and its fine-strung spirit of renouncement when the vague thought of active service at a remote date broke on the urgent call of the country's immediate need. Either aspect has been encouraging. Whether viewed individually or in the mass, this Territorial Division, one of many, which took the Imperial Service obligation and joined the Expeditionary Force in the spring of 1915, fills the spectator of so much courage and the narrator of so much effort with high hope for the Force as a whole.

Henceforth, we are to see the Division under a new aspect. Certain units from the West Riding were already in the field. We have visited a Casualty Clearing Station near Merville, and presently we shall come to the fine record of the 1st Field Company, West Riding Royal Engineers, which served in Gallipoli with the ' incomparable ' 29th Division. But, except for these isolated units, the war so far had passed it by. In its organic, military capacity, it had merely guessed at the course of the war from signs and tokens vouchsafed by the Army Council, from the duplication and triplication of its units, from the extreme difficulties of equipment, and from a general sense of haste without method. From this time forward, for four years and more, it was to learn warfare at first hand. It was to forget its separate existence as the sheltered nursling of a County Association, and to become a part, however small a part, of the British Expeditionary Force.

The B.E.F., France, at this date (April, 1915), needed all the reinforcements it could muster, and Sir John French[1] had already borne witness in his Fifth Despatch (February 2nd, 1915), to his hopes from the Territorial Force :

' The Lords Lieutenant of the Counties and the Associations which worked under them bestowed a vast amount of labour and energy on the organization of the Territorial Force ; and I trust it may be some recompense to them to know that I, and the principal Commanders serving under me, consider that the Territorial Force has far more than justified the most sanguine hopes that any of us ventured to entertain of their value and use in the field. Army Corps Commanders are loud in their praise of the Territorial Battalions which form part of nearly all the brigades at the front in the first line.'

And he had written again, as recently as April 5th :

' Up till lately, the troops of the Territorial Forces in this

---

[1] Field-Marshal Viscount French of Ypres (created 1915), O.M., K.P., etc., Commander-in-Chief of the Expeditionary Forces in France, 1914-15.

country were only employed by Battalions, but for some weeks past I have seen formed Divisions working together, and I have every hope that their employment in the larger units will prove as successful as in the smaller.'

Territorial soldiers had made good, and Major-General Baldock, Commanding the Division, as a complete unit from the West Riding, found his confident welcome assured.

He arrived at a critical time. It was the spring of 1915. At home, public opinion was to be convinced of the thoroughness of German methods by the sinking of the 'Lusitania' on May 7th. A reconstruction of the Cabinet by Coalition was announced on May 19th, and a Ministry of Munitions, with Mr. Lloyd George at its head, took shape on June 16th. This innovation was due to several causes, the ultimate origin of which is to be sought at a date a long way back from the outbreak of war. Accordingly, we may be absolved from any attempt to adjudicate between a Prime Minister, a Field Marshal, and a Secretary of State for War, as to the responsibility for the shortage of munitions which was revealed after war broke out. They did fall short of requirements, and high explosive shells had been postponed to shrapnel ; and, as far as public opinion could judge, the decision to repair these deficiencies (the political decision, that is to say) was expedited to some extent by the immediate effect of one sentence in a speech by Mr. Asquith, at Newcastle-on-Tyne, on April 20th. He was speaking, as he has since stated, to British workmen, with the object of speeding-up their output, but not without a proper regard to the cocked ears of the German Military Command ; and, partly in reliance on the expert information which he had sought, he said in the course of his speech :

' I saw a statement the other day that the operations, not only of our own Army, but of our Allies, were being crippled, or at any rate hampered, by our failure to provide the necessary ammunition. There is no truth in that statement.'

The assurance seemed to contradict the experience of gunners at the front. In his Seventh Despatch of June 15th, 1915, Sir John French affirmed quite clearly that,

' Throughout the whole period since the first break of the line on the night of April 22nd, all the troops in this area had been constantly subjected to violent artillery bombardment from a large mass of guns with an unlimited supply of ammunition. It proved impossible, whilst under so vastly superior a fire of artillery, to dig efficient trenches, or properly to re-organize the line.'

Indeed, on the very night when Mr. Asquith was speaking at Newcastle, a Territorial Force Officer (2/Lieutenant Geoffrey Woolley, of the 9th London Regiment) was earning his Victoria Cross for defending a position on Hill 60 against overwhelming enemy cannonade.

Hill 60, which was not a hill at all, but merely a hummock of railway earthwork, was in any case not visible from the Tyne, but the general disquietude at home at the time of the formation of the Coalition Cabinet reflected accurately enough the conditions which marked the place and time of General Baldock's arrival in France, with which we are immediately concerned. One word more will complete this impression :

'I much regret,' wrote Sir John French in the same Despatch, ' that during the period under report the fighting has been characterized on the enemy's side by a cynical and barbarous disregard of the well-known usages of civilized war and a flagrant defiance of the Hague Convention. All the scientific resources of Germany have, apparently, been brought into play to produce a gas of so virulent and poisonous a nature that any human being brought into contact with it is first paralysed and then meets with a lingering and agonizing death.'

The first such gas attack was launched at Ypres, on Thursday, April 22nd. On the previous Thursday night (the 15th), we left a West Yorkshire Battalion spending its first night in France at a Rest Camp, near Boulogne.

So the 49th went to the war on the eve of the Second Battle of Ypres, at a time of an outrage of gas and a shortage of shells.

They went in eighty-four trains and on five days between April 12th and 16th, embarking at Southampton Docks, Avonmouth and Folkestone for Havre, Rouen and Boulogne respectively, and they joined the 4th Corps of the 1st Army, commanded by Lieut.-General Sir Henry Rawlinson. Corps Headquarters were posted at Merville, and there the Divisional Commander reported with five of his Staff Officers, and established, as we saw[1], Divisional Headquarters in the mayor's house, 40 rue des Capucines. On April 18th, the following message was received from His Majesty the King :

' I much regret not to have been able to inspect the Division under your Command before its departure to the Front. Please convey to all ranks my best wishes for success, and tell them that I shall follow with pride the progress of the West Riding Division.'

A loyal reply was dispatched by General Baldock, and on the same day parties of Officers and N.C.O.'s, followed on the 19th by complete platoons, from the Battalions of the 2nd and 3rd West Riding (147th and 148th) Infantry Brigades were attached to units of the 23rd and 25th Brigades, 8th Division, for instructional duty in the trenches. On the 22nd, the 1st (146th) Brigade moved from Merville to Estaires, and was attached to the 7th Division, and placed under their orders. Sir Douglas Haig visited units of the Division on the following day. Divisional Headquarters were moved on the 27th to two houses and a farm in Bac St. Maur, and at 6 a.m. on the 28th, the Division took

[1] See page 3.

over a front of its own at Fleurbaix, covering sections 3, 4, 5 and 6 of
the IV Corps sector.

We may fill in a few details in this outline. After all, it was a
wonderful fortnight in the experience of the men from the West
Riding. A war on the Western front had been waged for more than
eight months, but it was all strange to new arrivals. Take, for instance,
the 1/6th Battalion of the West Riding (Duke of Wellington's)
Regiment, which slept at S. Martin's Rest Camp, about three miles
out of Boulogne, on the night of April 14th. The next day, which
was fine and warm, they marched nine miles to Hesdigneul, and
waited two hours at the railway station before entraining for Merville.
The entraining of a thousand and fifteen men presented no difficulty
to troops which had long since become expert in such drill. It was
carried out in batches of eight-and-forty, with a frontage of six men,
eight deep. At a given signal three men entered the truck ; the centre
man took the rifles of the rest, whom the two flank men helped in.
Merville was reached at 10-45 p.m. and the Battalion, preceded by its
Billeting party in a motor car, marched four miles to their billets at
Neuf Berquin, turning in after 3 a.m. : a long and tiring day's work.
The 16th and 17th were spent quietly. On the 18th there was Church
Parade, and in the afternoon motor-'buses were provided for a party
of fifty officers and N.C.O.'s to proceed to Fleurbaix, where they were
attached to the 13th Kensingtons for twenty-four hours' instruction
in the trenches. Even instruction had its perils, and this trench-party
returned one casualty ; Sgt. T. Richardson, ' slightly wounded.'
On the 20th, the motor-'bus came again for a party of twenty-six in
all, and next day a platoon from each Company in the Battalion studied
trench-warfare as pupils of the 25th Brigade. This instruction, which
included bomb-throwing, was continued till April 26th, when the
Battalion paraded at 4-45 p.m. and marched to new billets at Fleurbaix,
reaching Rue de Quesne at 8 o'clock. The next night at 11 p.m.
Pte. J. Walsh was killed by rifle fire, and on Thursday, April 29th,
Fleurbaix was shelled by heavy guns, which found the billets occupied
by this Battalion. A single shell killed two privates and wounded a
third : ' the dead were buried where the shell fell, owing to Pte. Pickles
being so mutilated. No service : Chaplain not available.'

This unhouselled grave may be taken as the initiation of the
Division into war, rumours of which, set flying in the Second Battle
of Ypres, reached units of the Division in their billets.[1] Their turn
was to come a little later, but the fighting throughout April and May
was so much of one piece and with one object that we may start, as the
battle started, on April 17th.

A straight line, 260 miles long, drawn from a point on the Rhine
midway between Cologne and Bonn, and terminating at the French

[1] On one occasion a scouring of latrines with a solution of chloride of lime caused a
rumour of the arrival of poison-gas.

coast about six miles north of Boulogne, will pass through Brussels and Ypres. That heroic town, in other words, the 'great nerve-

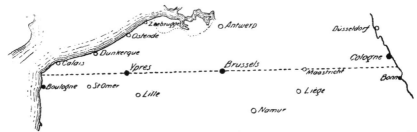

ganglion,' as it has been called,[2] was not merely the symbol and shrine of Belgium's resistance to the invader ; it was also a necessary stage in the German attempt at the Channel ports. They battered the line up and down, in the hope of breaking a way through, but their worst and heaviest blows were levelled at Ypres itself, which they wrecked but they did not capture. The second of these desperate assaults opened as we saw, at Hill 60, two and a half miles to the south-east of Ypres, where it flared into the horror of poison-gas

on April 22nd. A week of heroism and endurance brought this episode to a close by the withdrawal of the defence to a depth of about two

[2] By Sir Arthur Conan Doyle.

miles on a semi-circular front of nearly eight. An intensified fierceness of attack marked the renewal of the battle in May. The hottest days were the 13th and 24th, between which there was a kind of lull ; and thereafter the centre of fighting sagged away a few miles to the south, where the 49th Division was in waiting. The assault on Ypres had failed. Exhaustion-point had been reached on either side, but the defenders had paid an awful price. Their casualties numbered tens of thousands, and thousands had died in choking agony. The salient or semi-circle of troops, Belgian, French, Indian, Canadian and English, which had never stretched more than five miles out from its diameter on the Yser Canal, was flattened in even at the furthest to as little as two or three. Langemarck, the pivot of the first episode, which had lain on the rim of the salient, now lay more than two miles outside it ; Bellewaarde Lake, the pivot of the second, which had lain two miles inside the rim, was now on the edge of it or without. If the last stronghold of Belgium was to be saved, and the gate to the Channel ports kept locked, at least an equal power of resistance was required from the defenders in the next phase.

Moreover, we must look at a bigger map. Behind the actual fighting line lay Lille and Douai, railway-junctions of cardinal importance for the communication and supplies of the German armies. To strike at these towns through Lens, at the south-west corner of the triangle of which Lille formed the apex and Douai the heel, was an object desirable on its own account and full of promise for the succour of Ypres. If these plans, concerted with high hopes between General Foch and Sir John French, succeeded in threatening the railway-system behind, they were bound to react unfavourably on the German occupation of Belgium. And even if these larger plans failed, partly in consequence of the indentation of the semi-circle of troops guarding Ypres, there might still be a sufficient gain of ground and a sufficient slaughter of the enemy to affect his distribution of forces between the Western and the Eastern fronts. For the situation in Russia was already causing anxiety to her Allies.

Hostilities were opened on May 9th by an intense attack of French artillery to the south-west of Lens on the road from Arras to Béthune, between La Targette and Carency. 'That bombardment,' says a graphic writer,[1] 'was the most wonderful yet seen in Western Europe. It simply ate up the countryside for miles.' Unfortunately, the mileage was not wide enough to open the way to Lens, and day by ay the French advance was held up, pressed forward and held again, in a series of almost Homeric combats, which were measured by yards, even by feet, and in which the conspicuous names were White Works, Notre Dame de Lorette, Ablain, the Sugar Refinery, Souchez, the

---

[1] John Buchan, *Nelson's History of the War*, Vol. vii., p. 93.

cemetery at Neuville St. Vaast, and a terrible labyrinth of underground fortifications. The whole area, working up from the River Scarpe, was on a frontage of about seven miles, with Lens about six miles to the north-east. Each obstacle had to be surmounted not once only, but in many instances several times, and when, at the end of May, the German salient from the Lille-Douai road was flattened back at its southern extremity to the outskirts of Lens, which did not fall, the French success in the three weeks' fighting seemed hardly commensurate with the cost. We shall be in a position to estimate it more precisely when we have taken into account the results which were attained further north.

The French advance towards Lens from the south-west was supported by a British attack on a front facing east-south-east and

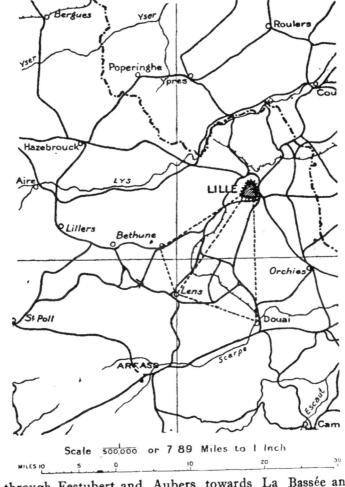

Scale $\frac{1}{500,000}$ or 7·89 Miles to 1 Inch

MILES 10   5   0   10   20   30

aimed through Festubert and Aubers towards La Bassée and Lille. We noted just now the triangle which is formed with Lille at

E

the apex, Douai at the eastern and Lens at the western foot.   On the
Lille-Lens line of that triangle, another and smaller triangle will be
found, of which La Bassée forms the westernmost angle.   The French,
we are aware, came up on a front converging on Lens from Arras and
the valley of the Scarpe.   The British advanced from the north-west
with a view to investing La Bassée, and if Lens and La Bassée had
both fallen, as the issue of these heroic endeavours, the double triangle,
or kite, would have been rolled up to its apex at Lille.

The British assault, like the French, opened on Sunday, May 9th.
The task of the IV Corps in the battle was assigned to the 7th and
8th Divisions, while the 49th Division took over the greater part of the
trench-line held by the Corps.   Their first object was to gain Fromelles,
but their main and ultimate objective was the Aubers Ridge.   The
general scope of the attack was disclosed confidentially to the troops
about to be engaged.   It was ' not a local effort for the capture merely
of Fromelles and Aubers villages,' but was 'part of a much larger
operation designed to break the enemy's line on a wide front.'   The
importance of the forces employed was also emphasized.   ' Not only
is the offensive being undertaken by the First Army', we read, but a
force of ' the best French troops, amounting to 300,000 or 400,000
men, is likewise advancing to the attack north of Arras.'   The disposition of the British troops made their objective quite clear.   They
faced the Lille-La Bassée road, curving round La Bassée at the
extreme right.   Their line was extended on the left to cover about
half the road to Lille.   The furthest point of that line from Le Bridoux
to Cordonnerie Farm was held by the 49th (West Riding[1]) Division,
and two of its Infantry Brigades, the 147th and 148th, were detailed
to occupy the German trenches which the 8th Division, followed by the
7th, and thus supported by the 49th, was to compel the enemy to vacate[2].
Unfortunately, the whole plan miscarried.   The first artillery attack
could not be sustained in sufficient strength to wipe out the barbed-
wire entanglements and free the way for the Infantry.   It followed
that the 8th Division could not press its heroic advance home, and the
West Riding Infantry Brigades were never called upon to discharge
their allotted task.   The first day's programme was thrown out from
the start.   Its features on the British front bore a tragic and curious
resemblance to those of the later days further south, when the advantage
won by the French bombardment had been neutralized by German
local fire.   The advance was broken, that is to say, into little pockets
and blood-spots of fighting, which sank into the soil where they occurred.
If the courage displayed in these encounters had been combined for

[1] Its numerical designation was not published in Corps Orders till the following week
(see page 40), but it is more convenient for use.

[2] The 146th Brigade was between the 7th and 8th Divisions, on the right of the rest of the
49th.   ' We were holding the line pretty thin.   My own Company,' writes an Officer
of the Brigade, ' had 650 yards of front line trench. . . . Thus, you will see we
did take part in the battle of May 9th, although we did not go over the top.'

the united effort which was intended, no troops born of woman could
have withstood it.   The record of every fighting unit tells the same
tale of desperate valour ; of a few exhausted and staggering survivors
hardly able to remember their own exploits, of endurance strained to
the limit of capacity, and of unwilling admiration extorted even from
a grudging foe.   But the net result on May 9th was failure ; it was
necessary to retire and to repair, and the part of the West Riding units,
to their own deep disappointment, was confined to occasional supporting fire, to relief-duty in the trenches, marked by little more than
its normal dangers, and, on the whole, to a comparatively quiet day.

   This battle of Fromelles, or of Aubers Ridge, which had the indirect
success of engaging sufficient German forces to assist the French
advance to Carency, was renewed a week later at Festubert, and was
not broken off till May 26th.   ' I had now reason,' wrote Sir John
French in his Seventh Dispatch, ' to consider that the battle, which
was commenced by the First Army on the 9th May and renewed on
the 16th, having attained for the moment the immediate object I had
in view, should not be further actively proceeded with ; and I gave
orders to Sir Douglas Haig to curtail his artillery attack and to strengthen
and consolidate the ground he had won . . . on a front of four
miles to an average depth of 600 yards.'   We may add that, if Lille
was not taken, Ypres, too, with its narrower front, still stood with its
back to the wall ; and behind that wall lay the Channel ports.   Moreover, the southern approach had been partially blocked by the reduction
of the German salient from Lens, and the fighting quality of our troops
was such as to deter the enemy from attempting a break-through on
one line without adequate resources on the rest.   In other words, a
see-saw movement was the chief obvious conclusion from the six weeks'
spurts of battle-fury to the east and south-east of Ypres.   A new
direct frontal attack would mean a new risk to Lens and on to Lille ;
a new attempt to throw out the Lens salient would mean a protusion
of the British salient from the Yser Canal.   The third or middle
course was to accept stalemate ; and to the limited but useful extent
of forcing this decision on the enemy, the heroes of the Second Battle
of Ypres, of the French pocket-battles in the Artois, and of the British
struggles round Aubers and Festubert are entitled to the full measure
of their renown.   Moreover, taking a wider survey, the stalemate
suited the combatants on other accounts besides exhaustion.   Germany
was waging war on two fronts.   Having pushed her western pieces
into positions, in which, save for minor attacks, they might be left
undisturbed for a time, she was anxious to concentrate on the east.
England, too, had another foe, whom it might be too late to overtake
unless she set about the work at once.   It became known as shortage
of shells, and Mr. Lloyd George, as we saw, was appointed in June to
devise rapid measures for its defeat.

   Turning back to the 49th Division, we note that on May 16th it occupied, again with the 8th Division, the extreme left of the British line. On the 22nd, orders were received for the 148th Brigade (the 4th and 5th King's Own Yorkshire Light Infantry and the 4th and 5th

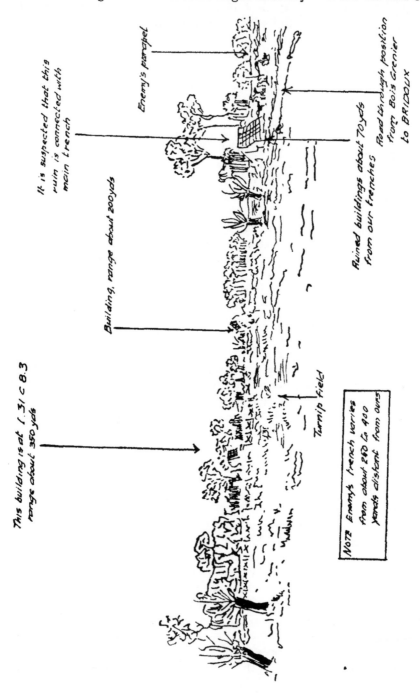

York and Lancasters) to throw forward the line to two ruined houses on the Bois Grenier-Le Bridoux road. (A panorama sketch of the site is given opposite). This meant the laying-out and preparation of a new front-line trench astride the road, and the necessary tools, sandbags, stakes, barbed-wire, and other paraphernalia were collected during the day of the 22nd and the early part of that night. Work was started about 11 p.m., when two Companies of the K.O.Y.L.I. under Major P. T. Chadwick and Captain Critchley, traced out and began digging the new trench. The two ruined houses, situated about half way between the British and the German lines, were found to be occupied by the enemy, who brought heavy rifle fire into play and considerably worried the working parties. In this encounter, Lieut. R. T. S. Gwynne was wounded, and died the next day. On the 23rd the same Companies went out again in order to strengthen the work commenced on the previous night. Heavy fire was drawn from the ruined buildings, but the enemy was forced to retire. Work was continued till daylight with satisfactory results, the cover being much improved and the communication-trench up to the new line being practically completed. By this means, certain operations which had been ordered by the Corps Commander on May 20th were enabled to be carried out. On the 24th these were opened by a bombardment from the ninety-six guns in the line at short intervals between 8 and 9 p.m. At 8-50 two Companies of the same 4th K.O.Y.L.I., under Captain A. C. Chadwick and Captain L. M. Taylor crossed the parapet of No. 6 trench and advanced up to the new trench prepared on the preceding nights : a journey of about seventy yards. The German machine-gun and rifle fire was exactly one second too late to find this party. The Companies quickly took position, and dug themselves in, and the ruined houses were put in a state of defence by a section working under Captain Creswick. Next morning, two Companies from the 5th K.O.Y.L.I. relieved their comrades of the 4th, and continued operations. From the 26th of May onwards for some days the Germans left them no peace, and a number of casualties ensued. But the operation had been carried out, and Sir Henry Rawlinson, Commanding the IVth Army Corps, desired that his high appreciation should be conveyed to the officers and other ranks of the 4th King's Own Yorkshire Light Infantry for the 'gallantry and precision' which had been displayed.

Further compliments followed. On June 12th, a message was received from the Adjutant-General at General Headquarters :

'The Commander-in-Chief notices with gratification the record of the 49th (West Riding) Division for the month of May, which shows that no single conviction by Court-Martial has occurred, a condition which does not obtain in any other Division of the Armies. He desires that his appreciation of this fact be duly conveyed to the 49th Division.'

And Major-General Baldock, commanding the Division, was informed by the General Officer Commanding the First Army, to which the Division had been transferred at the end of May :

'Sir Douglas Haig wishes to add an expression of his great satisfaction at the state of discipline in the 49th (W.R.) Division, and also desires to congratulate the Division on its soldier-like bearing and efficiency.'

A month later, the Division was re-transferred from the First Army, Indian Corps, to the Second Army, VIth Corps, commanded by Major-General Sir John Keir, when it moved to Proven, north-west of Poperinghe, and the surrounding villages in Belgium. The weather after May 23rd had become very hot, and there was one case of sunstroke in the trenches.

We shall return to the fortunes of the Division in the alternating periods of trench-life and billets which succeeded the intenser fighting of May. The whole Western front settled down to what seems like a phase of inactivity, but what was really a broken succession of diverse minor experiences, the monotony of which, like the sea's, was always movement, more apparent at close quarters than afar. Meanwhile, it will be appropriate to pick up the record of that isolated unit of West Riding Divisional Engineers, which, as we mentioned above, preceded the Division overseas. They, too, reached the scene of war in April, 1915. They fought in a different field, and were even more heavily engaged, but they earned by conspicuous gallantry not less honour than their comrades in France.

This unit, the 1/1st Field Company of West Riding Royal Engineers, under the command of Major Dodworth, formed one of three Companies which served under Lt.-Col. G. B. Hingston, C.R.E., in the 29th Division. Their original destination was France, but in February, 1915, it was decided to ship the Division with all possible speed to the Dardanelles, and, had this decision been carried out, the fate of British arms in the Peninsula might have been brought to a different conclusion. As a fact, owing to causes which have been made public, its departure was postponed till March, and, after a troublesome delay at Alexandria, the Field Company, with a strength of 6 officers, 201 other ranks, 62 horses and mules, and 12 vehicles, reached Tenedos on April 24th. At midnight on the same day they were selected, much to their delight, to sail with the covering force on the 'River Clyde' to the South Point of the Peninsula, and there, below Sedd-el-Bahr, the modern model of the Trojan wooden horse was beached at 7 a.m. on April 25th.

The events of that day of death and glory have been sung, and painted, and told, and require but brief reference here. 'No army in history,' says the poet who wrote a prose-epic called *Gallipoli*[1], 'has been set such a task. No other troops in the world would have made

---

[1] By John Masefield. Heinemann, 1916.

"MODERN MODEL OF TROJAN WOODEN HORSE."

[Face p. 54.

good those beaches,' and it is heartening to recall that troops from the West Riding of Yorkshire were included in this unique band.

For five months, from April till September, our Field Company of Royal Engineers remained on the Gallipoli Peninsula. The roads, the water-supply, the trenches, the night-wiring, the bridges, the jetties : every kind of engineering job came their way. They even manufactured hand-grenades, and gave practical lessons in the use of them, and they took their bellyful of fighting and of experience of Turkish shells. In June, for example, two of their sappers, A. Jennett and G. Packard, were awarded the Distinguished Conduct Medal for their gallant rescue of Captain Todd, of the Argyll Mountain Battery, who was lying with a leg blown off under heavy fire on the other side of a barbed-wire entanglement ; and the same decoration was bestowed on Lance-Corporal W. B. Owen, who snatched another wounded Officer out of a trench in actual enemy occupation, and carried him to a dressing-station two miles off, for the most part under fire. On September 22nd came a welcome fortnight's rest. They were back again early in October, and had a terrible spell of work after the great gale of November 26th, which helped to confirm the decision for evacuation. For the end of the adventure was approaching, and our Engineers remained till the end. After helping to clear Suvla and Anzac, they moved in January, 1916, to Helles, where they cut steps down the cliff to W. Beach. Thence they sailed at last in two parties reaching Suez, January 16th.

The rest of their story belongs to the Division in which they became absorbed. But the praise of their famous work in Gallipoli, to which they went straight from home, redounds to the credit of the West Riding, and may be added to the praises which we have quoted from Sir Henry Rawlinson, Sir Douglas Haig and Sir John French :

' The 1/1st West Riding Field Company Royal Engineers, which forms part of the " incomparable " 29th Division,' wrote Lieut.-General Sir Aylmer Hunter-Weston, Commanding that Division, ' did grand service on the Gallipoli Peninsula. . . . Engineers have always the post of honour in war, having to make entanglements, to mine, to sap and to carry out many dangerous jobs in the very forefront of the fray. Of all this work the 1/1st West Riding Field Company Royal Engineers had its full and more than its full share, and right well did all ranks rise to the occasion . . . The casualties among them have been heavy . . . but the results achieved by them have more than counter-balanced the loss incurred. They have covered themselves, their Unit, and the rest of the West Riding Divisional Royal Engineers with glory.'

This passage occurs in a letter written by Sir Aylmer Hunter-Weston on September 9th, 1915, and published with the next Quarterly Report of the West Riding County Association. In that Report,

Lord Scarbrough included an account of a visit paid to Flanders by himself, as Chairman of the Association, and by Brig.-General Mends, the Secretary. Their 'object was to ascertain in what ways the Association might best provide for the needs and comfort of the troops, and to study the conditions under which they have to work'; and it will not be out of place to examine Lord Scarbrough's conclusions in those respects in anticipation of what we shall find in the ensuing chapter.

He recalled to the memory of local patriots that the 49th Division was composed of Field and Heavy Artillery raised from Leeds, Bradford, Sheffield, Otley and York; of Engineers from Sheffield; of three Infantry Brigades from the West Yorkshire, West Riding, Yorkshire Light Infantry, and York and Lancaster Regimental Districts; of Army Service Corps from Leeds and York; and Field Ambulances from Leeds and Sheffield. They had left for France in April, and had been 'continuously in the fighting line ever since.' It would stimulate local patriotism to know that a Staff Officer wrote of the Division :

'I am very proud to have been connected with it. They are a real good lot, and I don't think there is a better Division in the country.'

To the 'amenities of war,' as likewise to the 'other side of the picture', we shall presently come back : such facts may be recovered from written evidence ; but what Lord Scarbrough and General Mends saw in the 'smiling faces', the 'spirit of cheerfulness' and the 'sense of mastery over the enemy,' is contained in no formal War Diary, and is the more valuable and vivid on that account. It brought comfort and encouragement to the West Riding in the dark days of the autumn of 1915 ; not merely to members of the Association, struggling, as we know, against the flood, but also to many wives and mothers, realizing that, 'in a campaign like this,' as the Report stated, 'casualties come fast,' and, lastly, to the various committees, Parliamentary Recruiting, Trades Union, and so on, which based their appeal for fresh efforts, in the last stages of voluntary enlistment, on the valorous record of the 'boys' who had already gone to the front. Alike in Flanders and in Gallipoli, that record was worthy of the West Riding.

CHAPTER V

THE DAY'S WORK

DURING January, 1916, the 49th Division was 'in rest': the first period of complete rest which the Division as a whole had enjoyed since the previous April, when it first entered the field.

Even before this complete rest the Division could look back on some months of comparative military inactivity. It had not been called upon to take part in the severe fighting at Loos in September, 1915 ; and no other big operations, on the scale of the warfare in May and June, had occurred since the Battle of Festubert. Yet there had been fighting every day. Every day of the intervening weeks and months between the close of the spring campaign and the order to rest in January had brought difficulties and dangers here and there, up and down the line of trenches in the neighbourhood of Ypres and the Canal, in which the 49th was engaged, and which it was essential to maintain as a barrier between the invader and the sea.

It is not easy to write the history of those days, when the Division was neither 'in rest' nor in action. We might review them in numerical sequence, long day after long day, when according to the Battalion chroniclers, 'nothing of importance happened,' or one unit relieved another, or there was an inspection by the Corps or Army Commander, or there was a 'bombardment of the whole line, varying in severity throughout the day and night.' These entries, and entries like these recur again and again in the Diary of every unit in the Division. Or, again, when autumn arrived, the weather compelled attention. 'Rained. Trenches very bad ; practically no work could be done. Heavy bombardment all day from 4 a.m.,' is a typical entry in October ; and we are left to read between the lines the accumulated miseries of that day's work, in which the worst hardship of all was that 'practically no work could be done,' in evil trenches sodden with rain and shaken by continuous fire. Minor miseries, perhaps, and less epical in retrospect than the Homeric combats of the spring, or the campaign on the Gallipoli peninsula ; yet real and serious enough in their hourly call on a man's endurance to warrant an attempt at narration.

We are told, for instance, that Sir Herbert Plumer was pleased if the Second Army casualties did not exceed two hundred a day in ordinary trench work, and a division of this figure into the Army total will yield a quotient from which we may deduce the average chance of danger in a quiet time. Or we may observe that the British first line trenches were distant from the line of German trenches by about 80 to 150 yards, but that where the line bent back on the north to the bank of the Yser Canal the distance from the German line was only 30 yards, with a very nasty corner at the bend.   We may note, too, the lack of rest at night : the constant flare of Very Lights across the trenches, and the incessant contest of wit (and luck) between the

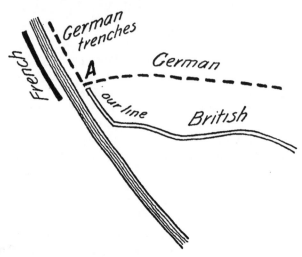

men repairing trenches or bringing up rations or ammunition and the snipers watching their opportunity.

Certain days at any rate may be selected for somewhat more detailed description, not because they differed essentially from the days that went before and that came after, but because, in the cycle of days, as in a cycle of numbers at a gaming-table, they are marked with adventitious interest.

Take, for instance, July 29th (we are writing of 1915 throughout) in the story of the 7th Battalion of the West Yorkshire Regiment. They were in dug-outs on the Canal, having completed a turn in the trenches just before midnight on the 25th.   On the 26th, 27th and 28th, nothing of importance happened.   On the 29th from half-past eight till noon, there was a heavy shelling of the dam at the rate of two shells every five minutes ; this rate was reduced by a half from noon till an hour after midnight, when the shelling ceased.   The dam was untouched, but the adjoining bridge was damaged in three places. One officer was killed and ten men were wounded.   Even so, the story is not exceptional, despite the 230 odd shells falling in sixteen hours.   But there is a sequel to the story, which is told in the following words : The Military Cross was awarded to 2nd Lieut. A. R. Glazebrook 'for conspicuous and gallant conduct, on the 29th July, in helping to dig out, at great personal risk, an officer and ten men whose dug-outs had been blown in, thus saving nine lives,' and Riflemen J. Bentley and H. Garrity received the Distinguished Conduct Medal 'for working with Lieut. Glazebrook.'

Take July 16th.   On the 15th the Germans had shelled the
Canal bank, and had fired three salvoes of shells into Divisional
Headquarters at the Château des Trois Tours.   Advanced Headquarters remained there, including the G.O.C. himself, the General
Staff Officers, 1st and 2nd Grade, the Brigade Major of the Royal
Artillery, and the Signal Company.   The rest moved back to St.
Sixte.   On the 16th, at 4-30 p.m., the grounds of the Château were
shelled again, and the grave difference between this day and that,
otherwise so alike in experience, was the inclusion of the General's
name in the casualty list.   He was just crossing a bridge which connected the Château with the mainland when he heard the shell coming,
and, though he doubled back to cover, he did not reach it in time,
and suffered a severe wound in the head.   It was the only casualty
at the time, though the house was riddled with shrapnel, and as soon
as the shelling had ceased, the gallant Officer was taken to Poperinghe,
where Sir Thomas Bowlby attended him.   Advanced Headquarters
were withdrawn to Hospital Farm.   The retirement was completed on July 18th, on which day the grounds of the Château were
once more heavily shelled soon after the General Staff had left.

The loss of Major-General Baldock's services was deeply regretted
by the Division, which he had commanded since September, 1911.
He had accompanied it from peace to war and commanded with
conspicuous success during the heavy fighting of May and June, and
' the whole Division loved him ', it has been written.   Happily,
he recovered from his wound, though he was not able to resume command, and on July 17th, 1915, Major-General E. M. Perceval[1], C.B.,
was appointed in his place.

Take the events of July 15th, in the new line of trenches occupied
by the 146th Infantry Brigade.   The 8th Battalion, West Yorkshire
Regiment, had relieved the 7th at midnight on the 13th, and came
in for some desultory shelling the next day.   On the 15th, the usual
patrol went on tour in front of the trenches.   It was composed of
Lieut. E. F. Wilkinson, and two Riflemen, Mudd and Clough.
By bad luck, Mudd was shot through the chest, and his cries
of pain attracted the German fire.   It was a very ordinary little
scene, but it is appropriate to imagine the sudden call on two lonely
men's courage and resourcefulness.   They carried the wounded
man back from in front of the German parapet under the heavy fire,
and were pulled up by their own barbed-wire mesh.   Clough went
in to find cutters, and Lieut. Wilkinson stayed out with Mudd.   The
tool was brought, the wire was cut, and the patrol came back with two

[1] General Edward Maxwell Perceval, of the R.F.A., served in India, Burmah, and South
    Africa, where he was awarded the Queen's and King's Medals (with 5 clasps) and won
    his D.S.O. He went to France, 1914, Commanding R.A., 2nd Division, and was
    promoted Major-General and appointed C.B. in the following year. He was acting
    as Sub-Chief of the Staff at General Headquarters when the accident to Maj.-Gen.
    Baldock gave him his appointment to the 49th Division, which he commanded till
    October, 1917.

candidates for decoration. Lieutenant Wilkinson was awarded the Military Cross and Rifleman Clough the Distinguished Conduct Medal for their cool and gallant action in this exploit. Next day, as war's tricky fortune had it, Lieut. C. Hartnell, of the same Battalion was killed by a shell in the front-line trench : the first officer casualty in that unit.

Take a few incidents in the trench life of the 4th and 5th Battalions of the York and Lancaster Regiment. On July 11th, the 4th relieved the 5th in an advanced trench on the East side of the Yser Canal, where the German and English lines met at an angle, with the French on the other side of the Canal, and were separated, as we saw, by a distance of only 30 yards. It was a recent capture from the enemy, and the trenches, we read, were ' in an awful state with both English and German dead. No work could be done on them because of shell fire.' Again, quite an ordinary experience, as trench life went in those days, but full of horror to its participants, and exacting to endure. On July 13th, the day was ' much quieter '—plainly a comparative term—till in the evening about half-past seven a heavy bombardment was opened all along the line, punctuated by explosions of gas shells, and followed by rapid rifle-fire. There was just a breath of wind blowing, but not enough to disperse the poisonous fumes, and for some hours the corner was unhealthy. The total casualties for the two days were 13 officers wounded, 17 other ranks killed and 55 wounded, and at 10 o'clock next night the 5th Battalion again relieved the 4th. Meanwhile, Sergt. W. Hutchinson and Ptes. J. W. Biggin and J. Cowlishaw were awarded the Distinguished Conduct Medal,

' for holding the flank of an advanced trench, which was partially demolished for 24 hours on the 13th July, in an isolated position, extricating themselves and the gun after they had been buried, and keeping the gun in action.'

Eighty-five casualties and three D.C.M.'s for two days' turn in the trenches : the period of standstill had its chances.

Take the worse experience of the 5th Battalion on July 10th, when they first took over these newly captured trenches. All day long the incessant German batteries poured their hail and thunder on the line, and not a single quiet hour was given for cleaning, clearing or repairing. The casualties mounted fast. Twenty-seven men were killed, and the list of wounded and missing included one Officer and 129 other ranks. Next day the following telegram was received : ' Army Commander desires to commend prompt action of troops 49th Division when attacked last night ' ; and the severity of the ordeal may be judged from the records of Lance-Corporals J. Yates and A. Calvert and of Pte. A. Gwynette, who were all awarded the D.C.M. : Yates,

' for attending with great gallantry, on the 10th July, under heavy fire and in full view of the German lines, to two wounded men who were cut off from the rest of the Platoon ' ;

Calvert,
> ' for assisting the Platoon Commander in steadying the men and keeping up their spirits, on the 10th July, when many other N.C.O.'s had been killed or wounded ';

and Gwynette,
> ' for attending to about twenty wounded men on the 10th July, during the heaviest part of the bombardment, and for keeping up the spirits of the men by his general bearing and conduct under heavy fire.'

These, surely, are the tests that tell. In these typical examples, selected almost at random from the day's work, we see in the making, as it were, that ' sense of mastery over the enemy,' which the Chairman and Secretary of the Association had observed on their visit to the front, and which was ultimately to dictate the terms of the Peace of Paris. On the East bank of the Yser Canal in the Summer of 1915, in stinking trenches filled with human wreckage, and exposed to a pitiless bombardment, the prospect of ' ease after war ' might well seem too remote for realization. It might seem, too, an idle thing, and below the fever-point of warfare, to respond in such dismal surroundings and with so dull a hope of martial glory to the constant, recurrent calls on a courage screwed to the sticking-place or a sense of duty as its own reward. Yet, somehow, in justice to the heroic dead, and to those who earned as well as to those who received decorations, the perception must be aroused that the war was won in the last resort by the private soldier, whether Regular, Territorial or New Army. In our Military Headquarters calculus he is not *Kanonenfutter*, food for guns : he is always, potentially, the wearer of a medal for the distinguished conduct, which he always seizes an opportunity to display ; and a period of comparative inactivity may provide more memorable opportunities of this kind than the stress and press of a big battle, precisely because the velocity of effort is measured by the daily round of marching from billets to trenches or of carrying out a normal patrol.

The word ' always,' though a big word, is appropriate, because this display of distinguished conduct is found to become a man's second nature and not to depend on a sudden impulse. Take the records, for example, of Drummer F. Thickett, of the 4th York and Lancasters, and Lance-Cpl. T. Best, of the 4th King's Own Yorkshire Light Infantry. On that night of the 13th-14th July, when the new trench was so heavily attacked, Thickett succeeded in wading through the Canal in order to carry a message from the firing-line to Headquarters, although the bridges had been broken and the telephone wires had been cut[1]. *He did it again* on the night of 8th-9th August. Unde heavy shell and rifle fire, and when all mechancial communica-

---

[1] One word about the field telephone will be in place. The whole countryside behind the British line was a network of telephone wires at this time ; ' one keeps tripping over them everywhere,' it was said, and there were probably 30 to 50 miles of wire to a single Artillery Brigade.

tion had broken down, he crossed the Canal on a single plank, and took the necessary message to its destination.   Best's record is in the same kind.   On July 20th and *again* on August 5th, a part of the trench where he was posted was blown in by enemy fire.   On each occasion he kept his men in hand, and started digging-out and rebuilding at once, with the utmost pluck and coolness, and without regard to German rifles and trench-mortars.   Best and Thickett were both awarded the D.C.M., which it will be ageed that they thoroughly deserved ; and we see in this habit of duty, acquired in daily experience and when no big forward movement set the pace, the ultimate secret of the success of British arms.

One more sample from these records may be selected.

On November 15th, the 6th Battalion, West Yorkshire Regiment, relieved the 8th Battalion in a line of trenches about two miles north-north-east of Ypres.   The weather was frosty, and the evil condition of the trenches was not improved by the fall of about a hundred ' whiz-bangs '[1] and thirty ' heavies ' between 9-0 a.m. and 3-30 p.m. on the 16th.   On the 17th, the shelling continued, with a regular reply by our Howitzers, and there was the ' usual sniping '.   On the 18th, as on the 17th.   On the 19th, the chronicler says : ' One of our Companies heavily shelled by enemy, six being killed and seven wounded. . . . . Battalion relieved by 1/5th West Yorks. Regt., and went into Divisional Reserve near Poperinghe.'   So far, the day's work was not exceptional, but there was to be a notable sequel to the day's story.   ' For most conspicuous bravery near the Yser Canal, on November 19th, 1915,' the supreme decoration of the Victoria Cross was awarded to Corporal Samuel Meekosha, of the 6th Battalion, in the following circumstances :

' He was with a Platoon of about twenty Non-commissioned Officers and men who were holding an isolated trench.   During a very heavy bombardment by the enemy six of the Platoon were killed and seven wounded, while all the remainder were more or less buried.   When the senior N.C.O.'s had been either killed or wounded, Cpl. Meekosha at once took command, sent a runner for assistance, and, in spite of no less than ten more big shells falling within twenty yards of him, continued to dig out the wounded and buried men in full view of the enemy and at close range from the German trenches.   By his promptness and magnificent courage and determination he saved at least four lives '.

It was the first V.C. in the 49th Division, and Captain Meekosha, who rose to Commissioned rank, reflected credit on the Riding which had raised it.

---

[1] So called, because they were on you and exploded before you heard the report.   As to ' heavies,' a visitor to the lines in September, 1915, wrote : ' Guns, particularly big Guns and Howitzers, are going to win this war, not rifles. . . I was shown a most interesting map giving all the German gun positions discovered by our aeroplanes . . Ours were shown, too, and they outnumber us by about three to one.'

Three hundred and seventy-six Honours in all, including 178 Mentions in Despatches, fell to the share of the Division during its first year's service in the field. Of these, the Victoria Cross, 16 Military Crosses and 71 Distinguished Conduct Medals were Immediate Awards for specific acts of gallantry. A few of those gallant acts have been brought back to memory here, not because they differed in kind from others for which awards were made (or, indeed, from many others for which, from lack of evidence or other causes, no recommendation was forthcoming), but rather to illustrate a catalogue which might prove wearisome *in extenso*. Thus on one day, December 19th, as many as ten M.C.'s and twenty-nine D.C.M.'s were won by Officers and Other Ranks, as the reward of valorous deeds on the occasion of a sudden gas-attack, which opened at 5-15 a.m. and continued for forty or fifty minutes. The fumes, reaching the support trenches, found many men still asleep, and these were gassed before they could be roused. The gas-attack preceded intense shelling, which went on, with a slacker daylight interval, until three o'clock the following morning. ' It was the most awful yet magnificent sight that I have ever seen,' writes a R.F.A. Officer : ' The whole country shaking with the explosion of shells, mostly big ; and a church near my Headquarters was hit with a 17-in. shell and blown to bits. The sky was one great glow like a vast electric light, and the atmosphere was laden with a choking and sickly heaviness. Our men are splendid,' he added. The total casualties of the day mounted up to :

			OFFICERS.		OTHER RANKS.
Killed ..	..	..	4[1]	....	46
Wounded	..	..	2	....	106
Gassed ..	..	..	8	....	191
			14	....	343

The decorations were presented by General Sir Herbert Plumer, Commanding the Second Army, on the following January 23rd ; and a week later the same Army Commander once more paraded the Division, in order to present awards for good service brought to notice in Dispatches. On the latter occasion he told the Division :

' This is a very pleasant ceremony to me, and I hope to you, with which to finish, for the time being, my connection, and that of the Second Army, with this Division. I have had the pleasure on two occasions lately ; one some weeks ago when you came out of the Line, and one the other day, when I gave ribbons representing decorations to Officers, N.C.O.'s and men of the Division after the recent gas-attack ; and on those two occasions I expressed briefly, but I hope quite distinctly, my apprecia-

---

[1] Including Colonel E. O. Wright, A.D.M.S., killed while organizing Ambulance traffic under heavy fire with his habitual gallantry.

tion of the way in which the 49th Division has carried out the duties entrusted to it during the last few months.   But now that it is settled for the time being that the 49th Division is to leave the Second Army, and go into another area, while I have nothing to add as regards appreciation of the work you have done, I should like to say to you how sorry I am that you are leaving the Second Army. . . . I cannot expect you to share my regret.   No one so far as I know, has felt any deep regret at quitting the Ypres salient ; but, while you will not regret your change of scene, when you look back at the time you have spent up here, notwithstanding the arduous time you have gone through, notwithstanding the losses of your comrades, whom we all deplore, you will, . . . I know, have some pleasant memories to carry away with you of your comrades of the Second Army. We, I can assure you, will follow your doings with the deepest interest, . . . and shall always feel a kind of reflected glory when we hear of the gallant deeds which I am quite sure you are going to accomplish both individually and as a Unit.'—

Stirring words, and a fine farewell, after what Major-General Perceval has described as ' nearly six months' continuous duty in the worst trenches of the Allied lines.   During the whole of this period,' runs the statement of the Divisional Commander, the men ' had unflinchingly sustained an unrelaxing bombardment,' and had borne ' with unfailing cheerfulness the most trying conditions of weather in permanently flooded trenches.'

So much for this aspect of siege warfare.

Before following the 49th Division from its well-earned period in Rest Billets to its next area of activity, we shall pick up some threads in the history of the 62nd Division (the West Riding 2nd Line, it will be remembered) from February, 1915, when Major-General Sir James Trotter assumed Command.   But, first, in order to complete the present picture, brief reference is due to what Lord Scarbrough, after his visit to the front, described as ' the amenities of warfare.' For these, too, were a part of the day's work, just as the hours of recreation are a part of a schoolboy's day.

The following are the relevant dates and facts :

July 28th. Divisional Baths opened at Steenje.
Aug. 5th. Divisional Armourer's Shop opened at Steenje.
Aug. 22nd. ' The Tykes ' Entertainment Troupe gave their opening performance at Peselhœk, near Poperinghe.
Aug. 23rd. Divisional Technical School of Instruction opened near Hospital Farm.
Sept. 10th. Divisional Farrier's Shop opened.
Sept. 15th. Divisional Band's first performance.
Oct. 11th. Divisional Horse Show held.
Oct. 15th. Divisional Grocery, Canteen and Coffee Bar opened.

LT.-GEN. SIR W. P. BRAITHWAITE, K.C.B.   MAJ.-GEN. E. M. PERCEVAL. C.B.

MAJ.-GEN. SIR R. D. WHIGHAM, K.C.B.   MAJ.-GEN. N. J. G. CAMERON, C.B., C.M.G.

MAJ.-GEN. SIR J. K. TROTTER, K.C.B., C.M.G.

[Face p. 64.

Nov. 9th.   Divisional Shop for repair of Gum Boots opened.

Dec. 6th.   Divisional Tailor's Shop opened.

There was also the Divisional Dump, where 6,000 rifles, for example, were salvaged in four months ; and, more definitely among amenities, there was the *Buzzer*, published as the organ of the Divisional Signal Company, which enjoyed a wide circulation and scattered enjoyment as it circulated.

The gracious visit of His Majesty the King on October 27th, when all Arms of the 49th Division were represented at an inspection of contingents from the Second Army, belongs to a different category, but it is gratifying to recall His Majesty's comment to General Perceval on the appearance and bearing of his men.

Plainly, the items in the above list owe their invention and inclusion to a common aim at recreation.   This aim might be simple and direct, as in the construction of a Dump for restoring derelict war material ; it might be a little less direct, as in the foundation of the Baths[1], which served partly for refreshment, and partly, taken in connection with their laundry, drying-sheds, etc., for the prevention of 'trench feet' and kindred ills ; it might be purely recreative, again, as in the programmes of the *Buzzer* and 'The Tykes' ; or it might be recreative-utilitarian, in the Gladstonian sense of a change of occupation, as in the establishment of workshops and schools ; and, in referring to any of these aspects, we should always keep clearly in mind the sharp contrast which they presented to the constant experience in the trenches, to and from which the men went and came.

Consider, first, this question of 'trench-feet.'   It was the fate of the 49th Division to occupy during this winter the most waterlogged trenches of the line.   They were 'permanently flooded,' as General Perceval said.   Yet he had the satisfaction of reporting that the number of cases of 'trench-feet' was among the lowest in any Division.   The total number was 760 ; the average number was six a day.   We have to add this feature to the day's work, but, with it, we add the measures that were taken to counteract the evil.   Not merely the three or four pairs of socks which each man took with him into the trenches, the arrangements for washing and drying them, and the provision of anti-frostbite grease and oil ; but also the care of the inner man ; soup-kitchens, hot cocoa and chocolate, supplies of Oxo and pea-soup, and the stress laid by the Divisional Commander on the importance of keeping the men's vitality high.   Nor should the gifts of the Association at home be forgotten in this context ; they sent the portable bath-house with oil-pumping engine and piping complete ; they sent 5,000 tins of 'Tinned Heat' (which sounds like an import straight from Hades) ; 10,000 small tins for anti-frostbite grease, 15,000 small cans for whale-oil, 4,885 short gum-boots, 722

[1] Sixteen men at a time were stripped, and given three minutes each under a hot shower-bath, their underclothing changed, and their uniform cleaned and fumigated.

F

thigh gum-boots, 7,000 mittens, 9,300 socks, oilskin-jackets, oilskins and sou'-westers, besides other contributions in kind.   There were still six cases every day, but the day's work was mollified by these means.

Another gift which reached the Division from the West Riding Association was the furniture and accessories for the theatre of ' The Tykes.'   This capable troupe of entertainers had begun in a very modest way on improvised platforms in the open air.   Perhaps they did not know, or were indifferent to the fact, that European drama, consummated in Shakespeare, had precisely similar beginnings. Though ' The Tykes ' did not produce a Shakespeare, they hardly fell short of his success in the pleasure which they afforded to their own audiences.   Historically, they were fourth on the list of Divisional Concert Parties, and it was on Christmas Day, 1915, that they definitely started on their career as a theatrical company.   In January, 1916, and again in the December of that year, they went home to the West Riding, where they played at the Empire Palace, Leeds, the Opera House, Harrogate, and the Empire Palace, Sheffield, exhibiting to enthusiastic houses the simple joys of the men at the front.   They performed in all in about fifty places, in improvised barns or converted stables, or very rarely in genuine halls, and they had the honour to be the first company to appear on the boards at Arras and Cambrai after their capture in 1918.   Even more impressive and gratifying is the fact that over 80,000 francs was handed by ' The Tykes ' to the Institutes' of the Division between 1916 and 1919, for the provision of additional comforts, sports, etc., to its units.   The original ' Tyke ' was Lieut. J. P. Barker, A.S.C., who was evacuated sick to England in September, 1918.   He really started and made them, and, if other names may be mentioned, we would refer to Lance-Cpl. A. Coates, of the Army Service Corps, and Pte. H. Marsden, formerly R.E., of the 243rd Employment Company, who were members of the troupe right through from August 22nd, 1915, to February 2nd, 1919.   A Divisional cinema, we may add, was established in March, 1917, and, after narrowly escaping destruction in the German advance at Berthen, April 9th, 1918, it survived to hand over a profit of 27,900 francs for the worthy objects of the Institutes' Fund.

Turning next to the facilities for education which were gradually developed in this period, we note the technical character of the instruction provided.   Thus, a Drainage Section was organized in the Ypres Salient, which laid down nearly 9,000 yards of main and subsidiary drains, with valuable results in the trenches.   Mining Sections were also formed to help Tunnelling Companies, and did excellent work while they lasted.   A Divisional Gas School gave lessons in the use and care of anti-gas appliances, and doubtless contributed to keep down the list of casualties on December 19th.   There were always Ambulance courses, and local opportunities for instruction in Sniping,

Scouting, Signalling, Bombing and other special branches.   The Divisional Technical School taught the use of Trench Warfare appliances, keeping parties of newly-arrived troops for twenty-four hours in mimic trenches, with the enemy trenches opposite also faithfully reproduced ; and a Divisional Training School was established to give both practical and theoretical instruction to junior Officers and N.C.O.'s of Infantry.

The workshops of the Royal Engineers turned out a quantity of stuff which was really remarkable in the circumstances.   All the made-up material for use in the trenches was prepared there, as well as the work in connection with the accommodation of men in the Rest Area.   When we read of one and three-quarter million sandbags, or of fifteen miles of road maintained and drained by civilian labour under the supervision of the R.E., or of seventeen bridges kept up and seven constructed by this Arm, or of four thousand tons of bricks drawn from ruined houses for horse-standings, or of thirty miles of trench-gridding[1] laid and fifteen miles of trenches maintained, we are able to form some idea of the unremitting toil and admirable skill displayed by the Divisional Engineers.

Reference, too, should be made to the fact that the grave defects in Field Artillery, which that Arm of the Division was so well aware of, and which it so particularly and gallantly endured, were to some extent corrected by the issue on October 29th of 18-pounder Quick-Firer Field Guns, instead of the existing 15-pounders, and on January 30th in the next year of 4.5-inch Howitzers instead of the 5-inch Howitzers in possession.

One more item of statistics may be mentioned.   In a year's constant journeys on bad roads for long distances, amounting in all to a total mileage of 900,000 miles, no lorry had to be replaced : an extremely creditable record for the Divisional Supply Column.

But these details are carrying us too far.   Our purpose in the present chapter has been to preserve an impression of the daily experience of the 49th Division from the end of June to the end of December, 1915.   The same things happened every day, though they might happen with a difference.   The day was fine, or the day was wet ; the patrol got back, or the patrol was wounded ; a shell exploded, or a shell fell ' dud ' ; distinguished conduct found a grave, or distinguished conduct won a medal : but always it was relieving or being relieved, throughout this long tour of duty under the exhausting conditions of the Ypres Salient.   We have sought to illustrate the life by selecting certain days for description, and we have sought, too, to set off that description by an account, however inadequate, of the other side of the picture : of the means provided from home or improvised on the spot, and alike approved by the Divisional Commander, to bring touches of warmth and colour into the chilling monotony of

[1] Wooden grids laid down like duck-boards to obviate the wet and slipperiness of the trenches.

trench-warfare.   How far such aim has been accomplished, even how far it is capable of accomplishment at this distance from 1915 and the bank of the Yser Canal, where the general gloom of the outlook was almost as difficult to banish as the mud on the physical horizon, cannot be predicated with any certainty.   What is clear to the present writer, however, and what he should have made clear to his readers, is that no opportunity was let go of doing a full day's work every day. They all pulled together all the time.   The result was that, though the long strain told on the physique of the Division, it did not tell on their spirits or their resolution, and, inasmuch as their appointed day's work was essential to the conduct of the war, and to the maintenance of equilibrium on the Western front, the 49th (West Riding) Division deserved well of their King and country in the last six months of the year 1915.

Tower of
the Cloth Hall
Ypres

[Face p. 68.

CHAPTER VI

SERVING IN RESERVE

THE intensive training of a 2nd Line Division, which was to take a conspicuous part in the battles of 1917 and 1918, is the subject of the present chapter.

The military confusion at home during the period prior to the passing of the first National Service Act, and prolonged to some extent through 1916, though it never affected the keenness and enthusiasm of the 2nd Line troops themselves, has yet to be taken into account in any impression which may be given of the conditions under which training was carried out. Reference to this factor will be found in the Memorandum on the Territorial Force written by General Bethune at the War Office, of which mention has been made before.[1] The then Director-General remarked : ' Great difficulty was experienced in training, as, with so many new Armies to be formed, the majority of capable instructors went to them, and our 2nd Line Territorial Force had to train themselves as best they could. The result,' he added, ' was extraordinarily good and surprised anyone who had anything to do with it.' We shall reach the element of surprise in due course. Here, for the moment, we are concerned with the ' great difficulty ' which was encountered, and more particularly with those aspects of the difficulty which lay outside the cognizance of the Territorial Force personnel, or, at any rate, outside their control.

Let us go back to first principles. The idea of a voluntary Army, despite the wastage of war and the unequal distribution of patriotic sentiment, or of the capacity to respond to it, was still, late in 1914, a sacred article of British faith. Another accepted article, if not of faith, at least of British practice, was the enlistment of that voluntary Army on a County basis. This procedure, which was laid down in Section IX. (I.) (a) of the Territorial and Reserve Forces Act, followed a similar provision in the Militia Act of 1882, and, tracing it back to that source, we discover that its primary cause was ' to estimate the extent of the County's liability in the event of the ballot being enforced.'[2] The tradition survived the ballot, and the rule of County enlistment was incorporated, as we have seen, in the organization of the Territorial Force. This rule worked well enough in peace-time, and might conceivably have continued to work well if it had been the only rule to be applied when war broke out on a scale not dreamed of by the authors of the Act of 1907.[3] But,

---

[1] See page 14, above.

[2] *The Territorial Force*, by Harold Baker (John Murray), page 246.

[3] Professor Spenser Wilkinson wrote in *The Sunday Times*, June 1st, 1919 : ' Lord Kitchener does not seem to have been aware of the existence of an organization—the County Associations—for the purpose of raising new troops upon a Territorial basis.'

historically speaking, and without attempting to judge the issue, it was decided very early in the war to vary that rule, and to raise recruits for the new Armies on a system which crossed the method handed down to the Territorial Force by the old Militia and Volunteers. The Counties were reaped of their best men by a Secretary of State who knew not Lord Haldane. The first hundred thousand disappeared into the vast abyss of war from every town and village in the country. Members of Parliament came down to recruit for Kitchener's Army, and forgot, or were not reminded by the Mayor, of the claims of Haldane's Force. Bonds of brotherhood in arms, by trades, professions, even by height or religion (*e.g.*, ' Bantams,' ' Jewish ' Regiment, etc.) drove their wedges through the County bond ; and under these new and distracting conditions, the old rule of enlistment by Counties became to a large extent a pious memory of peace, and enlistment by hook and crook, by picture-posters, white feathers, and worse devices, became the feverish rule of war.

This was the 2nd Line problem viewed through the spectacles of Territorial Force County Associations. The men themselves did not see it from the same angle. Their great desire, with insignificant exceptions, was to prepare themselves for service overseas with the utmost possible expedition. In their camps or billets or drill-halls, they were probably as unconscious of as they were indifferent to the serious administrative difficulties created for their County chiefs by the constant changes of policy on the part of the Army Council. Nor is the Army Council unduly to be blamed. The pace of the war itself was quicker than anyone had anticipated, and social and industrial conditions at home did not readily adapt themselves to its imperious needs. If we refer to these forgotten problems, out of which the successive National Service Acts were forged, as a partial solution, we shall be understood to refer to them solely in explanation of the ' great difficulty ' which was experienced, and not in the least in derogation of the great zeal with which that difficulty was surmounted to the ' surprise ' of everyone concerned.

We have further authority as to the difficulties. In a Memorandum kindly prepared by Major-General Sir James K. Trotter, K.C.B., who was appointed to command the West Riding 2nd Line Division[1] in February, 1915, he writes as follows of the early days of his Command :

> ' The difficulties affecting training were at this stage very serious. The troops were not all provided with uniform. They were without equipment ; the Infantry had no arms, except a few d.p. rifles ; the Artillery no guns ; the Mounted Troops, Artillery and Engineers no horses, and the Transport nothing but a few hired carts. But the want most sorely felt was that of the young, active, trained N.C.O. to instruct and to give life to

---

[1] The numerical designation, 62nd Division, was affixed, as we have seen, in August, 1915 ; for convenience we shall henceforward employ it by anticipation.

the movements of the young soldiers. Competent instructors were not to be had. Every available N.C.O. was taken up by the 1st Line Territorials and the New Service Army units, and this Division was at this time left to its own very limited resources. The Regimental Officers were in the main new and untrained, and though the Command Schools of Instruction gave short courses to as many as possible, it was very remarkable to observe the time necessary to convert the raw recruit into a trained soldier under these conditions. . . What was lacking was the atmosphere. Nevertheless, some real progress in elementary training was made in the early Spring (1915), and some young officers displayed considerable energy and initiative.'

Lack of atmosphere is the burden of this complaint, and a brief map of the conflicting winds which were blown across the path of Territorial Force organization may account, in part, at least, for these disturbed atmospheric conditions. Summarily, the war policy of the Army Council in regard to the Territorial Force may be marked by the following five steps : (1) They decided to raise Reserve or 2nd Line units behind the Imperial Service Units of the original or 1st Line. The practical distinction between the two was based on their state of preparedness to fulfil the overseas obligation. Thus, the distinction was always fluid. It varied, that is to say, according to the degree of training reached by the individual personnel, and there were always frequent exchanges between the 2nd and 1st Lines. The only constant element in the Reserve units were the men, who, owing to age or health or other conditions, would never be fit for Imperial Service. Divisional and other military organization was the same in both Lines, but the 1st was composed of Officers and other Ranks ready for service abroad, the 2nd was composed partly of surplus Imperial Service personnel, partly of troops prepared, so far, only up to Home Service, which still formed the statutory function of the Territorial Force. (2) The next stage occurred when the 1st Line units went overseas. Then a 3rd Line, or 2nd Reserve, was authorized for formation, behind the Home Service units composed partly, as we have seen, of men ready, in a military sense, to go overseas, and this 3rd Line was presently constituted into a series of (3) Draft-producing Depots, with establishments varying from time to time according as their corresponding 1st Line units were stationed at home, or on garrison duty abroad, or with an Expeditionary Force. A little later (4) steps were taken to weed out the Home Service personnel still remaining with the 2nd Line units and to distribute them into newly-constituted Home Service units, and finally (5) the National Reservists were formed into Supernumerary Territorial Force Companies, with a fixed establishment of about 120 all Ranks, for the protection of Lines of Communication and Vulnerable Points at home. To complete a brief account of a long process which was not worked out with a very clever perception of its intention from the start, we may add that these Super-numerary Companies were transformed by Royal Warrant, in 1916, into the Royal Defence Corps, when they passed out of the County administration. But all through 1915 the position was extraordinarily complex from an administrative point of view. Territorial Force Associations were responsible for maintaining their 1st Line units overseas, their 2nd Line units at home, their 3rd Line Draft-producing Depots, their Provisional Home Service units and their Supernumerary Territorial Force Companies.

In justice to the West Riding Association, which was hard put to it to keep an even keel in this welter of conflicting currents, we may examine the policy which they pursued, in somewhat more detail. From the first they declined to be hustled. As early as October, 1914, the Chairman, Lord Scarbrough, remarked in his Quarterly Report to members of the Association, that ' In consequence of the great difficulty of obtaining supplies of clothing, boots, necessaries, etc., and the lack of Officers and qualified Instructors, it was considered best not to push recruiting for the Reserve units, but to endeavour to raise them very gradually as Instructors and clothing and equipment could be provided. By so doing,' he pointed out, ' the efficiency of these units is not likely to be retarded, and the waste of time and dis-couragement entailed by collecting large numbers of men without Officers, Instructors, arms, uniform, boots, or any provision for their well-being, has been to a large extent avoided.' But his policy, however sound at the outset, could not be indefinitely maintained. The time came, and it came more quickly than some even of the shrewd-est of observers had foreseen, when the Reserve, or 2nd Line, units had to be allowed to recruit up to full establishment, despite those deficiencies in equipment which so seriously embarrassed their Commanding Officers, in the urgent work of training them for service overseas. So the ' large numbers ' continued to come forward, and might not be refused. As early as November, 1914, for example, the 2/6th Battalion of the West Yorkshire Regiment had a strength of over 1,400, and this splendid record was not unique in the 2nd Line Division. The real problem faced by General Trotter in the Spring of 1915 was not shortness of numbers, though this, too, became a source of some anxiety at County Headquarters, when the new Armies were competing with the Territorial Force ; it was still less lack of keenness for foreign service, but it was always the old problem of Israel in Egypt—how to make bricks without straw. We quoted just now the General's own account of the problems which he had to face in this regard. We may quote here his further account, by no means too rosy in certain aspects, of the progress in elementary training which was made in the early Spring of 1915. It will be remembered that the 1/1st West Riding (49th) Division went abroad in the middle of April. The 62nd Division was then appointed to take over its duties. The Infantry, it is reassuring to find, were now in possession of rifles, which had been obtained from Japan, and the Artillery, about the same time, received an armament of French guns, made in 1878, and 'evidently discarded,' writes General Trotter, 'for many years. The tangent scales were graduated in metres, and the shells were provided with a graduated time-fuze. But no one could be found to connect the graduation with the range scales, and no book of instructions existed. . . . No ammunition was available for practice, and the whole time this weapon was in the hands of the Artillery, *i.e.*, till December, 1915, it was only used for training purposes, and then only to a limited extent, the breech action and sights being of obsolete pattern. If,' adds the General, 'the Artillery had, according to the plans in force, been called upon to take part in the defence of the coast, the casualties it would have caused would have been at the breech-end of the guns'. There were other interruptions to training, as seen from a Commanding Officer's point of view. The competition in recruiting, to which so frequent reference is necessarily made at this period, produced, in places, almost humorous results. Thus, a Divisional Commander of the Territorial Force units would be pressed in some places by the local authorities to supply bands for recruiting-meetings held for the purpose of enlisting men in units of the New Armies. Again, industrial conditions created unforeseen anomalies. It often happened that the first men to enlist were the key-men in their respective factories, and these men, after having been put through a course of military training, and having become efficient soldiers in the comparatively shorter time corresponding to their superior capacity, had eventually to be returned to the works from which they came, or to other works engaged in producing war-materials. Another increasing source of embarrassment to the Divisional Commander and his subordinate Officers lay in the calls which were made on the 62nd Division, during 1915, to supply drafts for service overseas. Even the extraction from 2nd Line units of the men fit only for Home Service upset the composition of those units, and interrupted the continuity of training and the growth of an *esprit de corps*. Take, merely as an example, the experience of the 2/8th Battalion of the West Yorkshire Regiment. On March 8th, 1915, ten of their men were drafted to the 1/8th. Sundry other exchanges of personnel between the 2/8th and 1/8th, before the latter went to France, in April, resulted in a numerical loss to the unit remaining at home. On May 17th, 4 Officers and 188 other Ranks were transferred to the 26th Provisional Battalion for coast defence; and were followed at subsequent dates by a further 17 men. On August 15th, 54 men went out to the 1/8th Battalion. On the 27th came the gratifying news that Lieut. E. F. Wilkinson, formerly of the 2/8th Battalion, had been awarded the Military Cross in France : *sic vos, non vobis*. In October, orders arrived that the Battalion was to be reduced to 600 all ranks, that unfit men were to be posted to the 26th Provisional Battalion, and the remaining surplus over the new establishment, to the 3/8th Battalion West Yorkshires. It is obvious that changes of this kind, which may be paralleled in any other unit, were no light drawback. The success of the training of the Division during the period, May to October, 1915, when it was in camp in Sherwood Forest, might have been even more seriously affected except for the loyal co-operation of Officers, N.C.O.s and men in carrying out the programmes arranged for them. They were moved by an increasing resolve to prepare themselves for the call for embarkation, the hope of which, though renewed from time to time, seemed always so slow to materialize.[1] Meanwhile, work was carried on with this object always in view. Particular attention was devoted to the duties of the Platoon Officers and Company Commanders, and General Trotter bears witness that 'during the summer and autumn months, the Division made remarkable progress in training, administrative work and discipline.' In October, they left their encampments, and were stationed, at the end of November, in the Northern Command, with Headquarters at Newcastle-on-Tyne, where the Brigades were allotted to the Tyne defences, and the units were occupied in making and improving the trenches. About this time the Artillery at last had received a serviceable weapon ; 18-pounder, breech-loader guns were issued to three Brigades, and 5" Howitzers to the fourth. In December, news arrived that the Division had been selected as the first of the 2nd Line Territorials Divisions for service in France, and orders were issued to move to Salisbury Plain. Sir James Trotter, whose organizing ability had so well and truly laid the foundations of the military efficiency of the Division, was succeeded in its Command, on December 24th, by Major-General Walter Braithwaite, C.B.,[2] who took over the Division at Newcastle.

It is interesting to dovetail the accounts of the retiring and succeeding Divisional Commanders. General Braithwaite notes that ' the Battalions were commanded mostly by Territorial Force Officers of a certain age and standing, with personal knowledge of the men in their units, and with experience, in many cases, of Territorial Force conditions as they existed before the war, but, naturally, with no experience of war as it was being waged. The material was excellent, and all that was lacking was to adapt it to the conditions obtaining at the Front.' Accordingly, at Lark Hill Camp on Salisbury Plain, where the Division arrived in January, 1916, application was at once made to the War Office for men with fighting experience to fill posts on the Divisional Staff, and for the appointment of Brigade Majors

[1] The official figures of the draft sent out from the 62nd to the 49th Division from March to August, 1915, are : Officers, 116 ; Other Ranks, 2,778.

[2] Walter Pipon Braithwaite, served in Burmah (1886–87) and South Africa (1899–1902 ; Brevet-Major, Queen's Medal, 6 clasps ; King's Medal, 2 clasps) ; C.B., 1911 ; Major-General, 1915 ; K.C.B. and Lt.-General (Commanding IXth Army Corps), 1918.

of the Infantry Brigades in order to set to work to make the Division completely war-worthy. The response was prompt and satisfactory, and perhaps the most satisfactory feature from the Divisional Commander's point of view was the loyal readiness of individual Officers who felt themselves and were too old for the strain of active service to make way for younger men, who had either been wounded or invalided from France. An ideal General Staff Officer, 1st Grade, was found in Lieut.-Colonel the Hon A. G. A. Hore-Ruthven, V.C. Lieut.-Colonel R. M. Foot, to the great benefit of the Division, was appointed Q.M.G. ; Brig.-General A. T. Anderson arrived from France to take command of the Divisional Artillery, with Capt. W. J. Lindsell as his Brigade Major, and these Officers, with Lieut.-Colonel Gillam in command of the Royal Engineers, made, we are assured, ' an excellent beginning.' Mention is also due to the arrival at this date of the Rev. C. M. Chavasse as S.C.F., and we may add here that he served with the 62nd Division for the whole period of its active service, with the exception of a very short time when he was promoted to be Senior Chaplain of the Corps. The Brigadiers of the 185th, 186th and 187th Infantry Brigades, respectively, who were also appointed about this time, were Generals V. W. de Falbe, who had commanded a Battalion in France ; F. F. Hill, who had been invalided from Gallipoli, and R. O'B. Taylor, who happened to be home from leave in Egypt, and who had also been in Gallipoli. These arrivals, as might be expected, added immensely to the strength of the Division. Its efficiency, from February onwards, increased by leaps and bounds, and the Division was fortunate, too, in receiving from time to time the latest ' tips ' from Officers serving in or invalided home from France, and anxious to place their experience at the disposal of those about to proceed there.

Still, it was not all smooth sailing. In May, 1916, after service rifles had been issued, and when training was in full swing, orders were suddenly received for the Division to find a draft of over 4,000 men for France, and it looked as if the Division was to be turned into a mere draft-producing unit, and its fighting efficiency to be impaired accordingly. Happily, this order, like so many others, was cancelled. A further and more actual disappointment ensued a month or so later, when the Division was sent to the East Coast to be employed in reserve for the defences, with the intimation that it was likely to stay there. We are left to imagine the consternation of the troops, already straining at the leash, and the difficulty of the Divisional Commander and his subordinate Officers in accommodating their programmes and policy to these shifting counsels from above. Certainly, the East Coast was not as convenient for training, and did not provide the same facilities as were available on Salisbury Plain. The Brigades were separated by some distance : the Headquarters of one Brigade and the bulk of the Artillery being round about Bungay, another group being at

Henham Hall (Lord Stradbroke), and a third at Somerleyton (Lord Somerleyton, formerly Sir Savile Crossley), near Lowestoft. But once more the prospects changed. Fresh orders presently arrived, stating that the Division was selected for service in France. On July 26th, the King came down to inspect the Division prior to embarkation, and His Majesty expressed himself extremely satisfied with all that he saw.

Time went on, however, and no embarkation orders came. Drafts for Service units abroad and for Service units definitely allotted to home duties continued to be called for throughout this Summer and Autumn, and still the Division was in doubt as to its ultimate use and destination. Still the Divisional Pelican waited to put his foot down on German soil. The men now enjoyed opportunities, of which they gladly availed themselves, of working on training instructions which had been received direct from the front. Trench-digging, air-raid duty, rifle-practice with Charger-Loading Lee Enfields, gas-drill, concentration-marches, musketry and Lewis-gun courses, assaults-at-arms, aquatic sports, and other martial exercises and recreations, were all included in the preparation for battle. The whole life of the soldier in France was, so far as was possible, copied as faithfully as it could be during this strenuous period. Officers on light duty in England, who had been wounded, were sent down in batches and

distributed among the Battalions, which were eager, as we saw above, to take advantage of the benefit of their experience. Young Officers, with a war record behind them, were appointed to command Battalions, Batteries and Companies. Sketches of the latest types of trenches were received and re-produced in practice ; and, briefly, except for the actual atmosphere of active service, the Division became during these months a living organism capable of assimilating all the lessons which experience could teach it, and likely, with its splendid material, to give a good account of itself at the Front.

And, at last, the summons arrived. In October, 1916, orders were received to proceed to Bedford and Wellingborough in order to complete the Division with all necessary stores, and to hold itself in readiness to go overseas. The actual order for the move was still postponed till the last days of December, and the final scenes may be quoted fron the War Diary of one of the West Riding Battalions :—

   ' January 4th, 1917.—Order of the Day issued by Major-General Braithwaite, containing farewell message from His Majesty the King to 62nd Division, on the eve of their departure overseas.

   ' January 4th, 1917, 9 a.m.—Farewell service of Holy Communion at St. Paul's Church, Bedford, before proceeding on Active Service. ' January 11th, 1917.—Left Bedford for France. Right half Battalion left the Ballast Pit Sidings, Bedford, at 3-25 a.m. Left half Battalion left at 5 a.m.'

' I do not think,' writes General Sir Walter Braithwaite, at the conclusion of the Notes with which he has been kind enough to supply the present writer, ' a more happy and contented Division, or one better found and equipped, ever left the shores of England, and I think it was as well trained as a Division could be, thanks to all the help I received from the Staff and Commanding Officers, and to all the kind friends in France, who kept us supplied with the latest training instructions.[1] I cannot close this short sketch of our training period without alluding to the great help we received throughout the period from Lord Scarbrough and Brig.-General Mends. They were "father and mother" to the Division; made several visits to us; took endless trouble to help us, and, in fact, made all the rough places smooth. Also, I cannot but acknowledge the patriotism of those Commanding Officers who, feeling themselves too old for active service, made way for young up-to-date Commanders.'

It will be interesting to conclude this account with a conspectus of the Order of Battle of the 62nd Division from February, 1917, when it first entered the field, during the 22 months of its brilliant fighting record, till February, 1919, when demobilization was in active course. The purpose of this information, which is arranged for convenience in tabular form, is to show, in the first column, the units which composed the Division when it first landed in France ; in the second column, the units which joined the Division between that date and February, 1919 ; in the third column, remarks explanatory of the information in columns one and two ; and in column four the names of the respective Commanding Officers at the time of the embarkation of the Division. It will be observed that certain Battalions of the 1st and 2nd Lines were amalgamated during 1918, and these tables should be referred to, accordingly, in cases where any consequent changes in nomenclature may puzzle the reader of later chapters.

1 It may be worth while to note that the 62nd was the first Division to proceed to France with an equipment of steel helmets complete.

ORDER OF BATTLE OF 62nd (WEST RIDING) DIVISION between February, 1917, and February, 1919.

Landed with Division, Jan.-Feb., 1917.	Joined Division between Feb., 1917, and Feb., 1919.	Remarks.	Commanding Officer (Jan., 1917).
DIVISIONAL F.A.			
310th Brigade, R.F.A.	—	Remained throughout.	Lt.-Col. G. R. V. Kinsman, D.S.O., R.A.
311th Brigade, R.F.A.	—	Became Army Brigade early 1917.	Lt.-Col. A. Gadie.
312th Brigade. R.F.A.	—	Remained throughout.	Lt.-Col. E. P. Bedwell, R.A.
62nd Div. Ammunition Col.	—	Remained throughout.	Lt.-Col. F. Mitchell.
62nd T.M. Batteries	—	Remained throughout.	
—	14th Bde. R.H.A. & B.A.C.	Joined November, 1918.	
DIVISIONAL ENGINEERS.			
457th Field Company. R.E.	—	Remained throughout.	Major W. A. Seaman.
460th Field Company, R.E.	—	Remained throughout.	Major L. St. J. Colley.
461st Field Company, R.E.	—	Remained throughout.	Major E. J. Walthew.
Signal Company.	—	Remained throughout.	Capt. R. V. Montgomery (Som. L.I.).
185TH INFANTRY BRIGADE.			
2/5th West Yorks. Regt.	—	Amalgamated with 8th W. Yorks., August, 1918.	Lt.-Col. J. Josselyn.
2/6th West Yorks. Regt.	—	Amalgamated with 6th W. Yorks. to 49th Div., Feb., 1918.	Lt.-Col. J. H. Hastings.
2/7th West Yorks. Regt.	—	Disbanded June, 1918.	Lt.-Col. Hon. F. S. Jackson.

ORDER OF BATTLE OF 62nd (WEST RIDING) DIVISION between February, 1917, and February, 1919 (Continued).

Landed with Division, Jan.-Feb., 1917.	Joined Division between Feb., 1917, and Feb., 1919.	Remarks.	Commanding Officer. (Jan. 1917).
185TH INFANTRY BRIGADE (Contd.)			
2/8th West Yorks. Regt.	—	Amalgamated with 1/8th W. Yorks., Feb., 1918.	Lt.-Col. W. Hepworth, V.D.
185th T.M. Battery.	—	Remained throughout.	
	1/8th Bn. W. Yorks. from 49th Div.	Amalgamated with 2/8th W. Yorks., Feb., 1918.	
	1/5th Bn. Devon Regt.	Joined June, 1918, from Egypt.	
	2/20th Bn. London Regt.	Joined August, 1918, from Egypt.	
186TH INFANTRY BRIGADE.			
2/4th Bn. West Riding Regt.	—	Remained throughout.	Lt.-Col. H. E. P. Nash (R. Scots)
2/5th Bn. West Riding Regt.	—	Amalgamated with 1/5th Bn, Feb., 1918.	Lt.-Col. T. A. D. Best, D.S.O., (R. Innis. Fus.).
2/6th Bn. West Riding Regt.	—	To 49th Div. for amalgamation with 1/6th, Feb., 1918.	Lt.-Col. J. Mackillop.
2/7th Bn. West Riding Regt.	—	Disbanded June, 1918.	Lt.-Col. Clifford, D.S.O. (North. Fus.).
186th T.M. Battery	—	Remained throughout.	
	1/5th Bn. West Riding Regt.	From 49th Div. Amalgamated with 2/5th, Feb., 1918.	
	2/4th Hants. Regt.	From Egypt, June, 1918.	
187TH INFANTRY BRIGADE.			
2/4th Bn. K.O.Y.L.I.	—	Remained throughout.	Lt.-Col. E. Hind, V.D.

ORDER OF BATTLE OF 62nd (WEST RIDING) DIVISION between February, 1917, and February, 1919 (*Continued*).

Landed with Division, Jan-Feb., 1917.	Joined Division between Feb., 1917, and Feb., 1919.	Remarks.	Commanding Officer (Jan., 1917).
187TH INFANTRY BRIGADE (*Contd.*)			
2/5th Bn. K.O.Y.L.I.	—	Amalgamated with 1/5th Bn., Feb., 1918.	Lt.-Col. W. Watson (Som. L.I.).
2/4th Bn. Yorks. & Lancs. Regt.	—	Remained throughout.	Lt.-Col. F. St. J. Blacker.
2/5th Bn. Yorks. & Lancs. Regt.	—	Disbanded Feb., 1918.	Lt.-Col. P. Prince (Shrops. L.I.)
187th T.M. Battery	—	Remained throughout.	
PIONEER BATTALION	1/5th Bn. K.O.Y.L.I.	From 49th Div. Amalgamated with 2/5th, Feb., 1918.	
	9th Bn. Durham Light Inf.	From 50th Division, Feb., 1918.	
DIVISIONAL TRAIN.			
62nd Divisional Train	—	Remained throughout.	Lt.-Col. H. H. Wilberforce.
525 Company, R.A.S.C.	—	Remained throughout.	Major A. P. Wright.
526 Company, R.A.S.C.	—	Remained throughout.	Lt. S. G. Shaw.
527 Company, R.A.S.C.	—	Remained throughout.	Lt. W. N. Roberts.
528 Company, R.A.S.C.	—	Remained throughout.	Capt. H. P. Peacock.
DIVISIONAL R.A.M.C.			
2/1st (W.R.) Field Ambulance	—	Remained throughout.	Lt.-Col. W. Lister.
2/2nd (W.R.) Field Ambulance	—	Remained throughout.	Lt.-Col. C. W. Eames.

ORDER OF BATTLE OF 62nd (WEST RIDING) DIVISION between February, 1917, and February, 1919 (*Continued*).

Landed with Division Jan.-Feb., 1917.	Joined Division between Feb., 1917, and Feb. 1919.	Remarks.	Commanding Officer (Jan., 1917).
DIVISIONAL R.A.M.C. (*Contd.*)			
2/3rd (W.R.) Field Ambulance	—	Remained throughout.	Lt.-Col. W. S. Keer.
62nd Divl. Sanitary Section	—	Remained throughout.	Capt. Moss-Blundell, C.B.
2/1st Northn. Cas. Clearing Stn.	—	Remained throughout.	Lt.-Col. W. A. Wetwan.
—	33rd Sanitary Section.	Joined after Armistice.	
DIVISIONAL MACHINE GUN BN.			
—	201st M.G. Company.	Joined 1917 ⎫ Formed into 62nd Bn. Machine-Gun Corps, Feb., 1918	
—	208th M.G. Company	Joined 1917 ⎬	
—	212th M.G. Company	Joined 1917	
—	213th M.G. Company.	Joined 1917 ⎭	
DIVISIONAL M.T. COMPANY.			
62nd Div. M.T. Company	—	Remained throughout.	Major H. J. C. Hawkins.
MOBILE VETERINARY SECTION.			
2/1st (W.R.) Mob. Vet. Sect.	—	Remained throughout.	Capt. P. Abson, A.V.C.
DIVISIONAL EMPLOYMENT CO.			
—	252nd Employment Co.	Joined June, 1917, and remained throughout.	

G

The Staff Officers in January, 1917, were as follows :—

G.O.C.	Major-(Lieut.-) General (Sir) W. P. Braithwaite, (K.) C.B.
A.D.C.	Lieut. G. H. Roberts.
A.D.C.	Sec.-Lieut. J. C. Newman.
G.S.O. (I)	Lieut.-Col. Hon. A. G. A. Hore-Ruthven, V.C., D.S.O., Welsh Guards.
G.S.O. (II.)	Major W. G. Charles, Essex.
G.S.O. (III.)	Capt. J. A. Batten Pooll, 5th Lancers.
A.A. and Q.M.G.	Lieut.-Col. T. M. Foot, C.M.G., R.L., late R. Innis. Fus.
D.A.A. and Q.M.G.	Major H. F. Lea, R.L., late Yorks. Regt.
D.A.Q.M.G.	Capt. F. J. Langdon, R.L., late The King's.
A.D.M.S.	Col. de B. Birch, C.B., R.A.M.C. (T).
D.A.D.M.S.	Major T. C. Lucas, R.A.M.C.
D.A.D.O.S.	Lieut. R. M. Holland.
A.D.V.S.	Major F. J. Taylor.
A.P.M.	Major G. D'Urban Rodwell.
C.R.A.	Brig.-Gen. A. T. Anderson, R.A.
A.D.C.	Lieut. Anderson, R.A.
Bde. Major	Capt. W. G. Lindsell, R.A.
S/Capt.	Capt. A. J. Elston.
C.R.E.	Lieut.-Col. F. Gillam, R.E.
Adjt.	Capt. G. D. Aspland.

185TH INF. BDE.

G.O.C.	Brig.-Gen. V. W. de Falbe, C.M.G., D.S.O.
Bde. Major	Major R. E. Power, The Buffs.
S./Capt.	Capt. W. A. C. Lloyd.

186TH INF. BDE.

G.O.C.	Brig.-Gen. F. F. Hill, C.B., C.M.G., D.S.O.
Bde. Major	Major C. A. H. Palairet, The Fusileers.
S./Capt.	Capt. W. O. Wright.

187TH INF. BDE.

G.O.C.	Brig.-Gen. R. O'B. Taylor, C.I.E.
Bde. Major	Major R. B. Bergne, Leinster Regt.
S./Capt.	Capt. F. M. Lassetter.

CHAPTER VII

I.—PREPARATIONS ON THE SOMME

We return from the 62nd Division in England to the 49th in France, in the same year, 1916. The battles of the Somme were fought mid the pleasant, folded hills of Picardy, where the Sussex Weald almost seems to have crossed the Channel into France, and Spring renews every year the glad tokens of that poets' May, when the sons of Champagne and Picardy, between the valleys of the Marne and the Somme, made France splendid in history as the mother of fable and romance : classic soil, a French writer tells us, ' entre Orléans, Rouen, Arras et Troyes, en pleine terre française, champenoise et picarde, dans toutes ces bonnes villes et villages.'[1]

Classic, too, in another aspect, as the scene of repeated assaults, in the Hundred Years' War, and before and after, by invaders envious of Paris. The last and heaviest of those assaults, since Paris fell in 1871, now occurred in 1916, between February and June, at the eastern gate guarded by Verdun. In 1914 and again in 1918 the invader pushed nearer to Paris ; but neither in the first year nor in the last year of the War were his hammer-blows quite so destructive or his heart of hate quite so hot as in the middle year, 1916, when the Crown Prince Wilhelm of Prussia staked his army and his dynasty on the attempt. We are not directly concerned with all that Verdun means to France. Vaguely we read from the map that it is distant about a hundred and fifty miles from Paris, and dimly we perceive that its fall, like the surrender of Strasbourg and Metz, might well, if swiftly accomplished, have brought disaster on the capital. But what even an Englishman cannot realize, despite the *entente cordiale* and the fellowship binding the *entente*, is the intense passion of the cry of General Petain's troops on the Meuse : *Passeront-pas*, they shall not pass. The Crown Prince threw his brave soldiery (for their valour is the measure of French endurance), first, against the series of forts of which Verdun was the citadel, next against Verdun itself, which was no longer an objective but a symbol, and lastly, and vainly at the last, against a resolve not to yield the pass, even when the force of the resistance had robbed the passage of all profit.

This, briefly, is the story of Verdun in the early months of 1916. It is French history from start to finish. The wider vision of fuller knowledge is aware that there was unity of purpose even before there was unity of command. Sir Douglas Haig's great Second Despatch contains several references to this feature : ' The various possible alternatives on the Western front had been studied and discussed by General Joffre and myself, and we were in complete agreement as to

[1] Gustave Lanson.

the front to be attacked.'   ' It was eventually agreed between General
Joffre and myself that the combined French and British offensive
should not be postponed beyond the end of June.'   ' To cope with
such a situation unity of command is usually essential, but in this case
the cordial good feeling between the Allied Armies, and the earnest
desire of each to assist the other, proved equally effective.'   The
French time-table at Verdun was partly regulated in conformity with
these counsels.   Partly, too, the situation at Verdun was affected by
movements outside France : by Russia's successes against Austria,
and by the Battle of Jutland on May 31st, from which the Germans
brought back so little except damaged ships and a broken moral to
support their loud claims to victory.   But the German tidal wave at
Verdun, whatever considerations intervene, was repelled finally by
French bayonets and by the spirit of France behind her steel :

> ' They lie like circle-strewn soaked Autumn-leaves
> Which stain the forest scarlet, her fair sons !
> And of their death her life is.'

The place and the time, as we see—The Somme valley and the
end of June—had been agreed between General Joffre and Sir Douglas
Haig ; and, in accordance with their decisions, the three-fold object
of which was :

'   (i.) To relieve the pressure on Verdun,
    (ii.) To assist our Allies in the other theatres of war by
           stopping any further transfer of German troops from
           the Western front,
   (iii.) To wear down the strength of the forces opposed to
           us '[1],

steps were taken betimes to make the necessary, elaborate preparations.
It will be appropriate to follow those preparations in connection with
one or more units of the 49th (West Riding) Division, which we left,
it will be remembered, enjoying a welcome term of rest after their tour
of duty on the east bank of the Yser Canal.

Take, for instance, the 7th Battalion of the West Yorkshire Regiment.   We select it partly for the chance that Lt.-Col. Tetley, D.S.O.,
then Major, 2nd in Command,[2] kept a separate diary of the Battalion,
which we have had the advantage of perusing, partly because, as will
appear, the second Victoria Cross in the Division was awarded to a
non-commissioned officer of this unit for conspicuous gallantry on the
first day of the Somme campaign.

The first fortnight of 1916 was spent by the Brigade[3] at Wormhoudt, where, after Company training every forenoon, ' the men had

---

[1] *Despatches*, page 20.

[2] He succeeded Lt.-Col. A. E. Kirk, V.D., in Command of the Battalion, August, 1916.

[3] Brig.-General M. D. Goring-Jones, C.M.G., D.S.O., of the Durham L.I., had succeeded
Brig.-General F. A. Macfarlane, C.B., in Command of the 146th Infantry Brigade,
after a brief interregnum by Lt.-Col. Legge (December 20th, 1915, to January 12th
1916).

plenty of time to themselves . . . The Tykes gave their entertainment every night.' On January 15th, this easeful life ended, and a march of eight miles to Merckeghem was followed on the 16th by a sixteen-mile march to Zutkerque, which the men ' stood very well.' On the 17th, another sixteen miles brought the Brigade as far as Calais, where they went into camp on a ' sandy common, which was very like Strensall Common ' in Yorkshire : there is a family likeness in gorse-bushes. The New Year Honours of that date brought Major H. D. Bousfield's D.S.O. and Captain J. D. Redmayne's Military Cross. From 8-30 p.m. on February 1st till 3 a.m. on the 2nd the Brigade travelled by rail from Calais to Longeau, just east of Amiens, with all transport and baggage on board : the relief of Verdun had begun. About a week was spent near Amiens, where the Yorkshiremen found the landscape a pleasant ' contrast to that round Poperinghe,' and ' not unlike the Yorkshire wolds.' From February 10th to 12th the march was resumed to Authuille, where the 5th and 7th Battalions were in support and the 6th and 8th in the trenches. The 7th remained in support for eight days. On February 20th they went into the trenches on the north-east edge of Thiepval Wood. On the whole, the trenches were good and dry, but they ran down on the left to a marsh made by the River Ancre, and on the right they had been damaged by trench-mortar fire ; still, it was a change for the better from the Yser. Snow was falling heavily at this time, and the trench-tours were kept down to four or five days. After three weeks of this experience, the Battalion was relieved on March 5th by the 9th Inniskilling Fusiliers, of the 36th (Ulster) Division, and went into billets at Harponville. It is observed that ' during the three weeks the Brigade had been in the trenches, a great deal of work was done by the newly appointed Intelligence Officers, and practically everything possible was known about No Man's Land.' The Intelligence Officer in the 7th West Yorkshires was 2/Lieut. Beale, but for old acquaintance' sake, we select an example of such service, which provided valuable knowledge for future use, from the record of Lieut. E. F. Wilkinson, M.C., of the 8th Battalion of the same Regiment. At mid-day on February 28th he went out to certain cross-roads. Again, on the afternoon of March 2nd, he waded up the stream which flowed under a stone bridge just west of these cross-roads, and found a plank bridge twenty-five yards up-stream, which, judging by the marks on it, was regularly used by the Germans. The information which this officer obtained in his daylight prowlings helped to compose the map of No Man's Land ; and it is worth observing that a German War Diary (2nd Guard Reserve Division), to which we refer later on, acknowledges that British Officers ' were provided with excellent maps, which showed every German trench systematically named, and gave every detail of our positions.'

We are writing of the preparations for the Somme battles. ' These preparations ', said Sir Douglas Haig,[1] ' were necessarily very elaborate and took considerable time. Vast stocks of ammunition and stores of all kinds had to be accumulated beforehand within a convenient distance of our front. To deal with these, many miles of new railways, both standard and narrow gauge, and trench tramways were laid.' In the Harponville period, we now read, all the Companies of the 7th West Yorkshires ' were employed in working on a new railway, which was in course of construction from Daours to Contay. ' This work, assisted by good weather, ' nearly every day being warm and sunny,' was finished on March 26th. On the 30th, there was an inspection by Lord Kitchener, who expressed his approval of the appearance and turn-out of the men. The 5th Battalion of the West Yorkshires, which was billeted in Harponville at the same time, shared in the work and the inspection. Day by day they were called upon for working-parties to construct new roads, new railways, or both ; and ' all this labour,' Sir Douglas Haig reminds us, writing of the Army as a whole, ' had to be carried out in addition to fighting, and to the everyday work of maintaining existing defences. It threw a very heavy strain on the troops, which was borne by them with a cheerfulness beyond all praise[2].' Certainly no sign of lack of cheerfulness is revealed in the diary of any unit. ' The men liked the change of work,' we are told.

Throughout April and May Battalions were busily engaged in various forms of training and fatigues. On May 29th, while in the billets at Vignacourt, orders were received by the 7th West Yorkshires to march to Aveluy Wood, just east of Martincourt, in order to provide working-parties to dig a buried-cable trench for the 36th (Ulster) Division. The move was accomplished in two days' marches, and the 8th Battalion of the same Regiment joined them in Aveluy Wood on June 1st. The weather here was bad, the accommodation poor, and German shells were rained on the camp from an early hour in the morning on June 2nd. But the work of preparation went on apace, and the Battalion remained in Aveluy Wood till June 19th. Meanwhile, the King's Birthday on June 3rd had brought further honours to the 49th Division. The Distinguished Conduct Medal awarded to a Company Sgt.-Major ' for general good work and devotion to duty since the Battalion came to France in April, 1915,' and the Military Medals awarded to a Sergeant, a Lance-Corporal and a Rifleman for devotion to duty on December 8th, 1915, when their Battalion, in front-line trenches on the Yser, was exposed to heavy shell fire, are typical of the record of the whole Division.

The time of preparation was nearly over. The appointed hour of action was close at hand. ' It was agreed ', we remember, between General Joffre and Sir Douglas Haig, ' that the combined French and

[1] *Despatches*, page 21.
[2] *Ibid*.

British offensive should not be postponed beyond the end of June.' Before the curtain rises on that drama, opened punctually on July 1st, and on the part taken at the opening by the gallant Battalion which we have accompanied from Wormhoudt, we may glance more rapidly at the experience of other units in the Division which Major-General Perceval led to the Somme.

Take the 5th Battalion, York and Lancasters. On February 3rd, they entrained for Longeau, marched four hours to Ailly, and reached Oissy by motor-'bus on the 4th. ' Hilly country,' they note again with satisfaction. Their machine-gunners were struck off strength to form a Machine-Gun Company under Captain Rideal. March was spent in railway work and training : ' Regular hours and a fortnight's rest have worked wonders with the Battalion, ' we read after a month's manual labour. ' The slackness due to nearly a year's trench-life is no longer apparent, and an entirely new stock of N.C.O.'s are beginning to give promise for the future.' And the future began to show more clearly. A whole week's work at the end of April was ' devoted to training,' especially to an ' attack on trenches south of Naours, which undoubtedly represent the German lines opposite the Authuille Section. The 49th Division in reserve attacks the German 3rd Line, the 1st and 2nd Lines already having been taken by other Divisions, probably of the Corps ' (we are quoting from an account of training-practice) ; and the Officer Commanding the Battalion, Lt.-Col. Shuttleworth Rendall, D.S.O., added with keen anticipation : ' All training and the similarity of the ground seem to point to the fact that, at a date not far distant, the 49th Division will attack the actual 3rd Line of the German trenches in front of Authuille.' It happened very much as Colonel Rendall foresaw ; and, when we come presently to the actual fighting, we shall see that this gallant Officer was, unfortunately, severely wounded shortly after the ' date not far distant ' from the rehearsal which he here reports. Meanwhile, on June 26th, Brigade Operation Orders were received at Battalion Headquarters : ' the utmost secrecy still preserved. Day of attack, alluded to as Z day, not yet notified. On Z day at Zero hour, artillery bombardment will lift from German front line and attack will commence.'

There were four X and Y days still to run. Bad weather accounted for a postponement from the 28th to the 30th June ; and, while awaiting the summons to the Assembly-trenches in Aveluy Wood, we may follow the story of preparation in the log-book of yet another unit, the 4th West Riding (Duke of Wellington's) Regiment, with which we first made acquaintance in Chapter II.

On January 15th they marched from Houtkerke, where they had lived for a fortnight in farm-billets, to similar accommodation at Wormhoudt. The Battalion remained in rest : ' Company-drill, bayonet-fighting, route-marching, bomb-throwing, etc., have been carried out, and the men appear to have greatly benefited by the change '.

On February 2nd came the move to Longeau, and the march through Amiens to Ailly, which preceded, as with other units of the Division, the tours in the trenches north of Authuille and the working-parties of March to May. Lt.-Col. (later, Brig.-General) E. G. St. Aubyn, D.S.O., at that time in Command of the Battalion, was allotted special duties at Corps Headquarters at the end of June, when Major J. Walker took Command. (Major E. P. Chambers had been attached since early in April as Claims Officer to the Division). The Birthday Honours included a D.S.O. for Major R. E. Sugden, two Distinguished Conduct Medals and a Military Medal. At 2 p.m. on the last day of June, the Battalion moved to Senlis, ' to take part in operations.'

Every unit repeated the same experience : rest and recuperation in January from the severe strain of the trenches on the Yser ; a move south-south-west early in February to the hilly country about Amiens ; trench-work and trench-warfare in the valleys of the Somme and the Ancre ; intensive training in offensive ; elaborate, tireless fatigue-duty in all kinds of labour behind the line : railways, tramways, causeways, dressing stations, magazines, water-mains, communication-, assembly- and assault-trenches, mining operations, and so forth ; often under enemy fire, with the weather ' bad, on the whole,' and ' the local accommodation totally insufficient,[1] ' and, at last, at the end of June, on the agreed date, ' to relieve the pressure on Verdun.'

II.—OPERATIONS ON THE SOMME

We are to remember in the first instance that the French and British objective was limited. In order to relieve the German pressure on Verdun, it was not necessary, however desirable it might be, to drive the enemy out of France and Belgium. Strictly speaking, he was never driven out ; he begged an armistice for retirement ; and, though his retreat became a rout, it falls into its place in the war-history, as Sir Douglas Haig indicated in his last Despatch, as the final stage of a gradual process, in which, compared with older battles, months and miles were consumed like hours and yards. A fairly clear perception of what was happening, albeit two years before the end, was present to the mind of the British Commander when he wrote his Second Despatch in December, 1916. There he represented the Battles of the Somme as a phase, or stage, in a longer battle, and the objects of the fighting on the Somme as subsidiary to the objects of the war. Accordingly, we are not to expect, as at home, and racked with acute anxiety, we were eager to expect at the time, that the German defeat on the Somme would be equivalent to an Allied victory in the war. Still less are we to repeat the practice, too common in 1916, of dividing the yards of Allied gains into the miles of territory in German occu- pation, in order to calculate a time-ratio from the quotient. Space

[1] *Ibid.*

and time were never measurable by one calculus. Even a surrender
of space, as General Petain proved on the Meuse, and as Marshal Foch
was to prove in 1918, might diminish instead of increasing the force
of the enemy's offensive. Always the war was greater than its battles,
and always a chief object at every stage was to wear down the enemy's
resistance. Sir Douglas Haig, as we saw in the last chapter, was well
aware that the Battles of the Somme had not broken the enemy's
strength, ' nor is it yet possible to form an estimate of the time the war
may last before the objects for which the Allies are fighting have been
attained. But the Somme battle,' he declared with conviction, ' has
placed beyond doubt the ability of the Allies to gain those objects.'
This, after all, was all that mattered, and we do well to see the view
from Olympus before descending into the valley of the Somme.

It is the evening of June 30th, 1916. The diaries of units agree
in their accounts of these crowded, fateful hours. The 1/7th West
Yorkshires' record says :

' June 30th. Battalion marched to Aveluy Wood, *via* Hedauville,
Englebelmer and Martinsart, after dark. All transport moved to
position south-east of Hedauville, between that village and
Bouzincourt.

' Not more than 25 Officers per Battalion were allowed to go
into action ; the remainder, with a certain number of Signallers,
Lewis Gunners and Bombers went to Bouzincourt, ready to be
called upon when wanted.

' July 1st. Battalion received orders about 8 a.m. to move to
assembly-trenches in Thiepval Wood, and all had arrived there by
noon. There was a good deal of shelling of the assembly-trenches
while we were getting into them, and a good many casualties were
caused, especially among the Lewis gun teams.'

The 1/5th York and Lancasters state :

' June 30th. 11 p.m. Battalion clear of Warloy on road to
assembly-trenches.

' July 1st. 3-45 a.m. Whole Battalion in assembly-trenches,
Aveluy Wood.

——— 6-20 a.m. Intense bombardment commenced, and lasted
for one hour.'

The 1/6th West Yorkshires, write :

' June 30th. Battalion marched to assembly-trenches in Aveluy
Wood.

' July 1st. 6-30 a.m. Heavy bombardment by our artillery of
enemy trenches. Battalion moved across the River Ancre and took
up a position in Thiepval Wood.'

The 1/4th West Ridings' record runs :

' Battalion moved from Senlis at 11-7 p.m. (30-6-16), marching to
assembly-trenches in Aveluy Wood, arriving about 2 a.m. (1-7-16)
under heavy shell-fire.'

We need not multiply this evidence. We should already be able to imagine the quick, dark scheme of concentration, so far as the 49th Division was concerned, in the first stage of the Allied programme for the relief of the pressure on Verdun.

At this point we may look at the map (page 92).

We spoke on a previous page[1] of the line drawn from Douai to Lens, working from east to west, on which a break-through by the French would have shaken the defences of Lille at the apex of a triangle formed with Lens and Douai at its bases. We are now to strike south of this line, and taking Douai as our apex to draw a second triangle with Arras and Bapaume at the lower angles (the further extension of this sketch is explained at page 124 below):

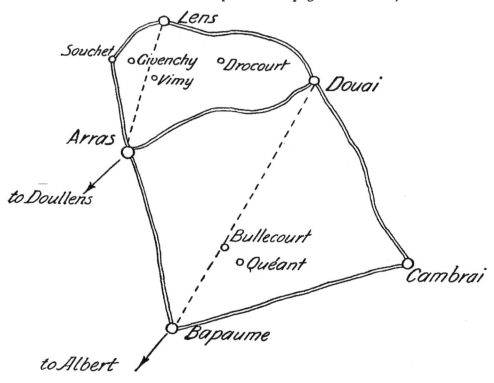

For the great battle for Paris or the coast, the great German invasion of France, which was also an attack on British sea-power, has shifted its centre from Ypres; and, while the Crown Prince of Prussia is hammering at Verdun, as the eastern gate to Paris, the French and British Army Commanders in the north-west of France have resolved to try to advance (to push the Germans further back, that is to say), on, roughly, a north-easterly front, looking from Amiens through Albert to Bapaume. This, broadly, is the key to a situation,

[1] See page 49.

which we have been following in diminishing degrees from the big, strategic plans in high places to the disposition of units and individuals. We have watched the preparations for that advance : the movements of troops by rail and road ; the eyes of the army in the air ; the ears of the army underground ; the elaborate collection of war-material ; the construction of permanent ways, and so forth. We see now the relation in space of the campaign of 1916 to the campaign of 1915. The tidal wave has ebbed away from Ypres, and has surged more furiously against Verdun; we are to change our focus, accordingly, from the Yser Canal to the River Somme, and from the Channel ports to Paris ; and in this sector, narrowing our survey, as the vast movement unfolds into details, we are most particularly concerned with the straight line, laid on a Roman road, which runs south-west from Bapaume to Albert. It is rather more westerly in direction, and about half the length of the road down to Bapaume from Douai. Travelling along its well-laid surface from north-east to south-west, we pass through Le Sars, Pozières and La Boisselle, the last a little to the left of the line. The nodal point, or meeting-place, or starting-place, is the town of Albert on the Ancre, ' a small, straggling town built of red brick along a knot of cross-roads at a point where the swift chalk-river Ancre, hardly more than a brook, is bridged and so channelled that it can be used for power.'[1] Westward from Albert is Amiens ; eastward we saw, Bapaume. Next, follow the chalk-stream of the Ancre, northward under Albert's bridges, through its native banks and braes. For our range of vision is being contracted, and we are coming through Army Commanders' plans to the men appointed to carry them out in their destined stations along the line. About two miles north of Albert on the west bank of the Ancre are the first trees of Aveluy Wood, where our assembly-trenches lay. Martinsart lies behind this Wood, Mesnil and Hamel are beyond it, Bouzincourt just below it to the rear. Opposite, on the east bank of the Ancre, about three miles to the north of Albert, lies the village of Authuille, north of which again is Thiepval Wood, looking backwards at Hamel and Mesnil on the safe, west side of the little river, and facing ' the German line opposite the Authuille section,' just as Colonel Rendall (and, doubt-less, many others) had imagined the situation in that dress-rehearsal by Naours which we attended at the end of April. Thiepval village is on the German side of our front line.

So we reach by gradual delimitation, by a *diminuendo* process, as it were, the task allotted to Major-General Perceval, Commanding the 49th Division, on July 1st, 1916.[2] ' Z ' day has arrived at last. The vast plans for the relief of Verdun are now about to be set in motion. Home Governments have expressed their approval, and have sent the

[1] John Masefield. *The Old Front Line*, Heineman, 1917.

[2] It will be remembered that the Division, being in reserve, was directly under the orders of the Corps Commander.

THE SOMME FRONT.
BRITISH.

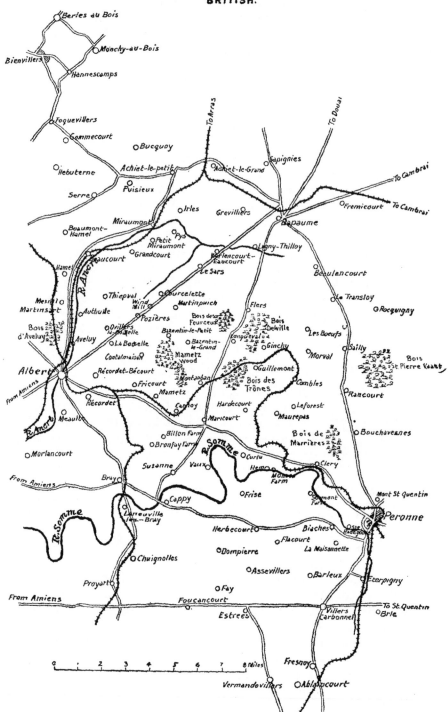

munitions and the men.   Due weight has been given to outside considerations in this war on many fronts : to the needs of Italy and Russia, the disappointment of Germany at sea, the inclination of the United States of America.   From the dunes of Calais to the Picardy hills, north-west France has become an armed camp, with the ceaseless movement of the immense accumulation of animate and inanimate material which nearly two years' experience has proved to be essential for modern warfare.   All the while, as Sir Douglas Haig reminds us in his great Second Despatch, 'the rôle of the other armies holding our defensive line . . . was neither light nor unimportant. While required to give precedence in all respects to the Somme battle, they were responsible for the security of the line held by them and for keeping the enemy on their front constantly on the alert.'   Verily, a huge organization to be stated in terms of unit action and of the prowess of individual men.   It was a long way from Sir Douglas Haig to Aveluy Wood : the 49th was only one of five Divisions (the 12th, 25th, 32nd, 36th and 49th), which composed the Xth Corps of the Fifth Army.

Our business lies between Authuille and Thiepval.   We have fined down the vaster issues to the operations east of Authuille, where the British line bulged towards the Ancre in an ugly angle known as the Leipsic Salient.   The fighting to which we now come is all round and about that Salient, between the point where the British front line crossed the River Ancre at Hamel to the point where it met the Albert-Bapaume road.   If we realize that the object of this fighting was to straighten and push back that bulge, and so to contribute to the advance of the long Allied line on the Somme battlefield, we may return to the men who fought there in the early days of July, 1916.   It is one thing to show on a map, on however large a scale, the increasing depth of the British front line at various dates after July 1st ; it is another thing to visualize that line in the actual mud, trees, slopes, which composed it, and to recount the conditions day by day, under which it swayed forward and back, in front and beyond and across the magnificently fortified German trenches.

Take the 7th West Yorkshires, for example.

We left them at noon on July 1st in their assembly-trenches in Thiepval Wood.   While the sun was still high in the heaven, about half-past five in the afternoon, Brigade orders (146th Infantry) arrived for the attack.   The 5th and 6th Battalions of the Regiment were to go over the top in an attempt to capture Thiepval village, the 8th was detailed for support, and the 7th for reserve.   Some hot hours of confused fighting ensued.   The 7th Battalion was told off to man the original British front line trench, from the point where it touched the east bank of the Ancre to a point known as Hammerhead Gap, at the top of Thiepval Wood.   This move was being completed with great difficulty, owing, mainly, to the congestion of the trenches by the wounded and stragglers of the 36th (Ulster) Division, when an Officer of that Division, Commanding the 9th Royal Irish Rifles, made an earnest request for help to reinforce his men in the German lines. Two Companies (C and D) of the 7th West Yorkshires made their way to these captured trenches, leaving A and B Companies to hold the British front and support lines. The fall of night brought no rest to this unit. The 36th Division became able to hold its own, and the half-Battalion from the 49th was ordered to withdraw. This order was not easy to carry out in the darkness, weariness and general *mêlée*, and about forty men of C Company found themselves stranded for the night (July 1st-2nd) in the disagreeable hospitality of the German line. They were well led by a non-commissioned Officer, Corporal (later, Sergeant) George Sanders, who was recommended for his valuable work and great personal bravery by the Officers of the Royal Irish Rifles. Later, Sanders received the supreme decoration of the Victoria Cross[1] for his gallant conduct in this action, and six of the brave men with him were awarded Military Medals. The whole Battalion was withdrawn to Aveluy Wood, and reached the assembly-trenches about 11 o'clock on the night of July 2nd ; thirty-six hours, or a little less, after they had assembled on the 1st. They had lost 16 killed, 144 wounded and about 20 missing ; they had gained a Victoria Cross, some experience, and—four days' rest.

Take another unit of the 49th Division : the 5th Battalion of the York and Lancaster Regiment, in the 148th Infantry Brigade. We left them proceeding to Aveluy Wood just before midnight on June 30th. The first instalment of their story in the present action is to last almost exactly a week : from 1-30 p.m. on July 1st, when the Battalion moved out of the assembly-trenches, till 8-30 p.m. on July 8th, when they were relieved by the 7th West Ridings, and went into huts in Martinsart Wood. The story makes sad but gallant reading. They sustained in those seven days and nights a total of 307 casualties. Their Commanding Officer was wounded and missing, their Officer 2nd in Command was killed, another Officer had died of wounds, thirteen more were wounded or missing. In other Ranks, 56 were killed and three had died of wounds ; 204 were wounded and 44 missing : a heavy toll to be extracted from one Battalion towards the relief of the pressure on Verdun.

---

[1] The award to Sgt. Sanders, V.C., was notified in the *London Gazette* of September 9th, 1916, in the following well-merited terms :—

' For most conspicuous bravery. After an advance into the enemy's trenches, he found himself isolated with a party of thirty men. He organized his defences, detailed a bombing party, and impressed on his men that his and their duty was to hold the position at all costs.

' Next morning he drove off an attack by the enemy and rescued some prisoners who had fallen into their hands. Later two strong bombing attacks were beaten off. On the following day he was relieved after showing the greatest courage, determination and good leadership during 36 hours under very trying conditions.

' All this time his party was almost without food and water, having given all their water to the wounded during the first night. After the relieving force was firmly established he brought his party, 19 strong, back to our trenches.'

The price was paid without reckoning the cost, and we shall not follow in detail the experiences of this unit during that week. They moved first to where the British front line touched the left bank of the Ancre. Major Shaw took A and B Companies to the north side of that line ; Lt.-Col. Rendall, with C and D Companies was posted on the south side. Captain G. A. G. Hewitt at this juncture retired to hospital suffering from shock. The fighting went on from hour to hour with very varying fortune : at one time, there seemed a possibility of a successful assault on St. Pierre Divion, the next village north of the line ; at other times, the utmost efforts were required to extricate the wounded. On July 5th, Aveluy Wood was shelled practically for the first time. High explosive, shrapnel and lachrymatory shells were employed, and found all the assembly-trenches ; captured maps and prisoners' information were no doubt responsible for this disaster. Early in the morning of the 6th, seven officers and eighty other ranks went out in two bombing parties to capture a front-line trench ; no Officer and twenty-two other Ranks returned. It was in this action that Lt.-Col. Rendall, D.S.O., Commanding the Battalion, had to be left wounded in a German dug-out, and that Major Shaw, 2nd in Command, was killed. The failure was due to the good German sniping, too heavy bombs for effective throwing, and a communication-trench not deep enough to pass them through. It was stubborn fighting, we see, and very difficult progress was made. But one Division in one Corps of one Army was not the whole fighting force which the Allies brought to the Somme, and some relief may be found by looking through German eyes at the results on July 1st in another sector. We have already referred to the War Diary for this period of the 55th Reserve Infantry Regiment (the 2nd Guard Reserve Division), which was holding the German line in front of Gommecourt six or seven miles north of Hamel. Their experience is no doubt typical of the enemy's sufferings all along the line. Thus we read of an intense bombardment, 'overwhelming all the trenches, and sweeping away the wire' ; of the 'thick charging waves of English infantry' ; of every round from the English guns pitching into the trench, 'thus rendering its occupation even by detached posts impossible' ; of telephonic communication destroyed by the bombardment, so that 'Regimental Headquarters were without news of the progress of events' ; of the English 'excellent maps,' and the 'most disturbing effect' of English aeroplanes : and, so reading, we begin to perceive another side to the picture. Such records of failure and disappointment, of forlorn hopes and forfeited successes, as occur in the journals of our own units are seen in a truer perspective when the long line of battle is displayed. Even the rain in which some wet Yorkshiremen spent a miserable night (July 7th) by the roadside fell impartially on the other side of the road, and was duly chronicled by dripping Germans ; and, when we are told that C and D Companies of the 6th Battalion of the West

Yorkshires, who ' went over the parapet to the attack ' at 4 p.m. on July 1st, had to retire to their own trenches with their Signalling Officer (Lieut. Dodd) killed, their Commanding Officer (Lt.-Col. Wade) and two other Officers wounded, we take consolation from the entry which follows next in the same journal : ' Enemy reported to be massing opposite our front for a counter-attack, which, however, did not develop.' ' Enemy ' did not have it his own way all the time.

Let us follow this unit a little further. During the first fortnight of July, step by step, and with many a step backward before two steps forward could be taken, German trenches in the Leipsic Salient had been occupied, and improved footholds had been won. Every effort was being made to consolidate and extend the new positions, and it happened on July 14th, at 4 o'clock in the afternoon, that this Battalion (the 6th West Yorkshires) took over that portion from the 7th. The 7th had had a rough experience. In the early morning of July 13th they had been attacked by German bombers, who, according to Colonel Tetley's testimony, evinced ' great bravery and disregard of danger.' At one time they rushed a British trench, ' but were bombed out by 2/Lieut. F. J. Baldwin and men of A Company . . . . Practically all our bombers were casualties.' The Battalion lost 15 killed and 92 wounded in this exploit, but Major-General Perceval assured them that their ' stubborn fighting had materially assisted in the success of the larger operation on the British front,' and Lieut. Baldwin was awarded the Military Cross and two N.C.O.'s the Distinguished Conduct Medal.

The night of the 14th-15th was fairly quiet. Both sides were attending to their wounded. But early in the morning of July 15th, when the 6th Battalion had relieved the 7th, the Germans returned to the attack, and this attempt, very pluckily repulsed, is memorable for the use of a weapon, new in the experience of the defenders, and hardly less horrible in its first effect than the surprise of poison-gas at Ypres. We have the advantage of a graphic description of the three hours' fighting on that morning from the pen of Lieut. Meekosha, V.C., who took part in it as a non-commissioned Officer.[1] He writes :

' About 3-30 a.m. the Germans launched their dastardly attack with liquid fire, the only warning we received being the terrifying shrieks of those unfortunate sentries who came into contact with the flame. Then came a hail of hand grenades, a few of the Boches coming as far as our own parapet, hoping to find our men demoralized. For their pains they were each presented with at least one well-aimed bullet. Our men then lined the parapet with as much speed and ammunition as possible, and let the Hun have it for all they were worth. Another party of Boches, well stacked with bombs, had already stormed one of our saps, which had been blocked about half way. Our Battalion bombers

[1] See page 62.

were at once called out to deal with this party, and, fighting their
way foot by foot, cleared every living Boche from the sap, a fact
which reflected no little credit on our men, being, as they were,
at a disadvantage from the very beginning. Our Stokes Mortar
Battery was then set to work on the German front line, and to see
old Fritz jump on to his own parapet, run a few yards as hard as
he could go, and then into his own trench again (provided that he
did not get a bullet in the attempt, our machine-guns and rifles
being on the look out for opportunities) was the best amusement
I had had for weeks.   This went on for about three hours, during
which time the work of our Officers and N.C.O.'s was cut out in
stopping our men from rushing headlong into the Hun trenches
in their eagerness to kill as many Boches as possible in as little
time as possible.   Unfortunately, a few of the good men lost their
lives during this fighting, but we had the satisfaction of knowing
that, for every one lost, the Hun lost at least four.

' Thus ended our first experience under liquid fire.

' After this, our boys set to and cooked for themselves the
breakfast they so richly deserved.'

It was after this fashion that the pressure on Verdun was relieved.
Sir Douglas Haig is quite clear on this point. He admitted that,
' north of the valley of the Ancre, on the left flank of our
attack, our initial successes were not sustained ';   that ' the
enemy's continued resistance at Thiepval and Beaumont Hamel
(29th Division) made it impossible to forward reinforcements
and ammunition, and, in spite of their gallant efforts, our troops
were forced to withdraw ';   and that ' the subsidiary attack at
Gommecourt also forced its way into the enemy's positions; but there
met with such vigorous opposition that . . .   our troops were
withdrawn'[1].   These were the first day's experiences.   The succeeding
days, as we have seen, brought certain adjustments for the better, even
in the difficult region where General Perceval's gallant troops had to
fight their troublesome way up slopes of mud from the valley of the
Ancre to the deeply fortified positions which the Germans held with
machine-guns, rifles and liquid flame.   But they did not bring conspicuous success.   They were not expected to bring it, as a fact.
As we have looked at the fighting at close quarters, so we are to look
at the results through Command spectacles.   The Battle of the Somme
was not won, nor was it intended to be won, between Thiepval village
and Authuille, where the Leipsic Salient bulged inwards. ' The
British main front of attack,' we are told in the same Despatch, ' extended from Maricourt on our right, round the Salient at Fricourt,
to the Ancre in front of St. Pierre Divion ';   that is, from the bank of

---

[1] *Despatches*, page 26. In a footnote to this passage, Sir Douglas Haig writes : ' In the
course of this fighting, a Brigade of the 49th Division, Major-General E. M. Perceval,
made a gallant attempt to force Thiepval from the north.'

the River Somme to the Albert-Bapaume road and north of it.   But
' to assist this main attack by holding the enemy's reserves and occupying his Artillery ' (not, note, by capturing his defences), ' the enemy's
trenches north of the Ancre, as far as Serre inclusive,were to be assaulted
simultaneously ' ; and, further north, ' a subsidiary attack ' was to be
made at Gommecourt.   So clear did this distinction become in the
early stages of the battle, and so plain was the dividing line between
the holding and the pushing forces, that Sir Douglas Haig decided to
separate the Commands : ' In order that General Sir Henry Rawlinson
might be left free to concentrate his attention on the portion of the front
where the attack was to be pushed home, I also decided to place the
operations against the front, La Boiselle to Serre, under the command of General Sir Hubert de la P. Gough. . . . My
instructions to Sir Hubert Gough were that his Army was to maintain
a steady pressure on the front from La Boisselle to the Serre Road, and
to act as a pivot, on which our line could swing as our attacks on his
right made progress towards the north.'   Moreover, ' our attacks on
his right ' (Sir Henry Rawlinson's on Sir Hubert Gough's) must be
associated, in a larger survey, with the simultaneous French attacks
under their own Command.   Accordingly, it is wholly just to say that
the containing action of the 49th Division, when the first impetus of
the units had been checked, developed exactly according to plan, in a
military phrase rendered famous by another Army.   Up to July 7th,
the enemy's forces north of La Boisselle ' were kept constantly engaged,
and our holding in the Leipsic Salient was gradually increased ' ;
and, after July 7th, as the Commander-in-Chief wrote, ' the enemy
in and about Ovillers had been pressed relentlessly, and gradually
driven back by incessant bombing attacks and local assaults,[1]' among
which, one among many, may be mentioned a very gallant night attack
by the 8th West Yorks.   Thus, Sir Douglas Haig's view from Olympus
informs the Battalion records, and we shall see in the further course
of the Somme battle how fully his instructions were observed till the
time came to swing round on Sir Hubert Gough's pivot.

[1] *Despatches*, pages 25, 27, 30.

CHAPTER VIII

I.—OPERATIONS ON THE SOMME—(*Continued*).

It is not seemly to be too modest about the Somme, nor to insist over-much upon the limitation of the Allied objective. We know that it was not intended to drive the Germans out of France ; at least, not in 1916. As a fact, in the Spring of 1917 there was a big German retirement, which was only voluntary in the sense that the enemy bowed to necessity before necessity broke him, and again, in the Autumn of 1918, there was another big German retreat, which brought the war to an end. They take a short view who fail to see the direct and intimate connection between the campaign of 1916 and the decisive results in the following two years. The British Commander, while the future was still veiled, had no illusions on this point. Wielding, like the Castilian knight of old, ' now the pen and now the sword,' Sir Douglas Haig, when he indited his great Despatch on December 29th, 1916, stated without reserve, that :

> ' Verdun had been relieved ; the main German forces had been held on the Western front ; and the enemy's strength had been very considerably worn down. Anyone of these results is in itself sufficient,' he avowed, ' to justify the Somme battle. The attainment of all three of them affords ample compensation for the splendid efforts of our troops and for the sacrifices made by ourselves and our Allies. They have brought us a long step forward towards the final victory of the Allied cause.'[1]

' A long step forward,' not necessarily in the eyes of the old men and children who stuck pins in their wall-maps at home ; and yet not a short step either, even when measured by this exacting standard. Let us look at the map once more and stick in some imaginary pins on our own account. First, take the straight, white road from Albert to Bapaume, and divide it into eleven equal parts, representing its length of, approximately, eleven miles. Just before the second milestone (or mile-pin) from Albert, mark the point where the Allied line crossed the road on July 1st, 1916, and just beyond the eight milestone mark the point where the Allied line crossed the road on December 31st. They had devoured (or ' nibbled ' was the word) six miles in six months, including the villages of Pozières and Le Sars, and were less than three miles distant from Bapaume. Next, observe the effect of this protrusion on the reach, or embrace, of the Allied arms. Take the Ancre and the Somme as frontiers, and prick out from the point by the second milestone a line running

[1] *Despatches*, page 51.

northwards to the left of Thiepval and across the Ancre to Beaumont-Hamel, and southwards to the left of Fricourt and Mametz, then to the right of Maricourt, then left of Curlu to the Somme. This was the Allied line on July 1st. Take the same boundaries again, and prick out from the point by the eighth milestone a line running northwards to the left of Warlencourt and Grandcourt, then to the right of Thiepval, Beaucourt and Beaumont-Hamel, and southwards to the right of Flers, Lesbœufs, Sailly, Rancourt, Bouchavesnes and Cléry to the Somme. This, roughly, was the Allied line on December 31st. The pricked-in area, rhombic in shape, which means neither round nor square, encloses a large number of square miles re-captured from reluctant Germans. It did not include Bapaume itself, nor Peronne, nor St. Quentin, nor Brussels ; the time for these had not arrived. But it took in many towns and hamlets which had known the foot of the invader, it broke huge masses of fortified works which had been designed to shoe the invader's foot, and, consequently, it seriously shook the moral power of German resistance. We shall not measure the acres of French territory released, for we have no standard by which to calculate the effect of Verdun relieved on the German armies driven homewards between the Ancre and the Somme. Nor is a yard by yard advance properly expressed in terms of mileage. Take any one of the positions re-captured : Mametz, Trônes, Combles, Thiepval itself, and review it for a moment in the series of defences, artificial and natural and natural-artificial, which the tenacious attackers had to overcome. Thus, between Fricourt and Mametz Wood were Lonely Copse, the Crucifix, Shelter Wood, Railway Copse, Bottom Wood, the Quadrangle, etc. : every name a miniature Waterloo to the gallant men who fought and fell there. Nowhere in all that area could a sixteenth of a mile be gained without an elaborate battle-plan and a battle, or several battles, taxing to the utmost the endurance of troops dedicated to victory and resolute to death. So, 'they brought us a long step forward towards the final victory of the Allied cause.'

We are to contract our range once more to the scope of the 49th Division, and to consider that 'step' more particularly in the region north of Albert by the Ancre, where Sir Hubert Gough commanded the Fifth Army. It was not a sensational record. If we follow the Diary of that Army, say, from July 21st to the end of September, we receive, mainly, an impression of containing work excellently done, while the shock of battle broke afar. A few of these entries may be cited :

'July 21st. 49th Division in Leipsic Salient. . . .

'July 23rd. Attack by 48th Division and 1st Australian Division. Good progress. 49th Division front South of River Ancre. . . .

'July 29th. 49th Division left of 12th Division to River Ancre. . . .

' Aug. 27th.   49th Division relieved 25th Division. . . .
' Sept. 3rd.   South of Ancre 49th Division attacked. . . .
' Sept. 24th.   18th Division relieved 49th Division. . . .
' Sept. 27th.   11th Division captured Stuff Redoubt.
' Sept. 28th.   18th Division attacked Schwaben Redoubt.'

Except on September 3rd, to which we shall come back, the work of the 49th Division, seen from this angle of vision, appears more passive than active.

Let us enlarge the angle considerably.   Instead of Sir Hubert Gough's, consult Major-General Perceval's Diary, the Divisional instead of the Army Commander's.   We come nearer to action in that aspect.

Between July 21st and the 27th there were ' three encounters with the enemy in the Leipsic Salient.'   On the 21st, he made a bombing attack ; on the 22nd, the 4th York and Lancasters ' attempted to extend our position in the Salient to the east by surprise,' but were foiled ; on the 23rd, the 4th King's Own Yorkshire Light Infantry made a similar attempt, ' but consolidation was prevented by a heavy counter-attack from all sides, and our troops retired to their original line.'   From the Army Commander's point of view, a single entry sufficed for these exploits ; the Divisional Commander had to account for nearly five hundred casualties in the period.

Take the 28th of July to the 4th of August.   There were 279 casualties in the Division, due, partly, to ' a considerable amount of trench-mortar fire on the Leipsic Salient and Authuille Wood' ;   and who shall say but that every wounded man made a definite contribution to the Somme advance ?   Yet Sir Hubert Gough was content to observe : ' 49th Division left of 12th.'   Or, August 26th to September 1st.   General Perceval's entry on the 27th merely repeats (or we should say, anticipates) Sir Hubert Gough's at greater length : ' Divisional Headquarters returned from Acheux to Hedauville, and at mid-day the Command of the line from Thiepval Avenue (exclusive) to River Ancre passed from 25th to 49th Division.'   There is a further entry in this Diary, which, being a record of work done in the ordinary course of duty, the Army Commander did not reproduce : ' With a view to an attack on German trenches north of Thiepval Wood, the new saps and parallels to the north of the Wood have been completed, ammunition-trenches improved, and dumps formed and filled with ammunition, bombs, R.E. stores, etc.'

So far the Divisional Commander, in expansion of Sir Hubert Gough.   There are next the Battalion Commanders to be consulted ; and, still omitting at present the Divisional record of the week including September 3rd, when ' 49th Division attacked,' we may once more enlarge the angle, and examine this preparation for attack from a Battalion Commander's point of view.   Thus, we read that :

' On August 26th, the Battalion[1] was sent up to the trenches on the right of Thiepval Wood. . . . Captain R. Salter was killed instantaneously by a shell as soon as he got to Battalion Head-quarters.   We were in this line for only two days, but had 52 casualties as there was a good deal of shelling. . . . The Battalion was relieved on August 28th by the 5th K.O.Y.L.I., and went into huts in Martinsart Wood ; from here we had to find large working parties in the front line for two or three days, and then had a rest until the attack on September 3rd.'

We are brought back, like Master Pathelin, *à nos moutons*.   The ' long step forward ' was achieved, the Battle of the Somme was won, by the Allied Armies working to the plans of Sir Douglas Haig and Marshal Joffre.   Those plans included the provision of a separate Army on the Ancre, to hold the German forces in that area, and to make what progress they could.   The Commander of that Fifth Army was Sir Hubert Gough, and Major-General Perceval's West Riding (49th) Division was included as a unit of its Xth Corps.   What happened, then, on September 3rd, when the new saps and parallels had been constructed, the communication-trenches improved, and the dumps filled with bombs and ammunition ?   How did the 49th attack, and what have the Officers Commanding its Battalions to add to the bare record of Sir Hubert Gough or the more expansive Diary of the Divisional Commander ?

The units immediately concerned were the 4th and 5th Battalions, West Riding Regiment, and the 6th and 8th Battalions, West Yorks. The 7th Battalion of each Regiment was stationed in reserve.   The week's casualties in the Division were high :

	OFFICERS.	OTHER RANKS.
Killed	14	196
Wounded	47	994
Missing	17	611
	78	1801
Total		1879

and the bulk of them occurred on September 3rd.   The large per-centage of missing in all ranks (more than a third of the whole) seems to indicate a hasty retreat from untenable positions.

The presumption is borne out by Battalion records.   These agree that co-operation was interrupted by a bad block in communica-tion, and that Battalions were not able to render one another all the support that was expected.   Each unit tended to believe that its own advance was held up, or, rather, that its withdrawal was necessitated, by what had happened on its right or left ; and, consequently, the

[1] The 1/7th West Yorkshires.

exploits of individuals were more conspicuous than the conduct of the attack. Zero hour was 5-10 a.m., and the Companies left the trenches punctually and went over in good order. But the half-light caused some confusion, and communication proved very difficult. In the instance of several Battalions no definite news was received for three hours or more. Runners failed to get through, and rumours were not satisfactory. At last, about 9 o'clock, tidings began to arrive of heavy losses incurred in trying to consolidate captured positions under a cross enfilade of machine-gun and rifle fire. Remnants of Companies, driven back after a long morning's heavy fighting told of the exhaustion of their bombs, and of their messages lost in No Man's Land. Stray parties cut off in the attack, found cover in shell-holes until nightfall. One Commanding Officer frankly wrote, ' the whole attack failed.' ' The objectives were gained,' he summed up, ' but the first casualties in Officers and N.C.O.'s were heavy, and therefore the men with power of "leadership" were lost when most needed to hold on. The presence of the enemy in the Pope's Nose (a machine-gun nest at an early point) upset all chances of reinforcements and supply except across the open '—an almost impossible condition. The runners, as we saw, did not get across, and the light was too bad for the observation posts to give effective help. On the other hand, the daylight was too strong to consolidate under fire the battered German trenches which had been captured. There was, unfortunately, a ' but ' or an ' if ' which qualified every record of success; and we may quote the following statement from a Battalion Diary, which gives a very fair impression of the whole episode :

' From the reports of the two Officers who returned to Battalion Headquarters from the battle, it was ascertained that for the most part a really good fight was put up. If Battalion Headquarters had been able to get any information back, it is practically certain that the position would not have been lost. The men fought splendidly, and in many cases without N.C.O.'s or Officers, and the losing of the captured position was a piece of bad luck.'

' What remained of our assaulting troops,' says General Perceval, ' were back in our trenches,' about 10 a.m., having ' sustained heavy casualties and lost most of their Officers.' A re-attack was planned for 6 p.m., but was countermanded during the afternoon, and the 146th Infantry Brigade was withdrawn to Forceville and the 147th to Hedauville. So, the 49th Division had attacked, and the whole attack had failed ; but between these two bald statements lie detailed records of a courageous attempt, which we shall not pursue further, but which contributed in this hard-held sector to the ' long step forward ' which was being taken on the Allied front at large. German records, so far as we have seen them, confirm the seriousness of the attack. We read there how ' matters had meanwhile become still worse,' and how

Company was added to Company in order to meet the impending danger. ' Lieut. Engel's Company signalled " Please send support, " ' and his experience was repeated in other sectors ; ' our *Minenwerfer* intervened at the most opportune moment '.   On the whole, the enemy's accounts increase admiration for the 49th Division.

It is particularly interesting to record that, in the course of this summer and autumn, a Regiment of Yorkshire Yeomanry met their friends of the 49th Division in and about the defences of Thiepval. We shall come, in Chapter XIV below, to the experiences of the Mounted Troops who left the West Riding for France during 1915. There we shall see how they served as Divisional Cavalry for several months, and how, in May, 1916, they were re-organized as Corps Cavalry, and were set to do various duties, not always appropriate to their Arm, which they discharged with a thoroughness and an efficiency worthy of the best traditions of the Service.   The Yorkshire Dragoons were posted to the IInd Corps, which, on July 25th, 1916, took over that sector of the Fifth Army front which lay between Ovillers-la-Boisselle and Thiepval.   The hopes of a Cavalry situation, unfortunately, never materialized, but the Dragoons did excellent work during the Battle of the Somme by maintaining Observation Posts in forward areas, thus short-circuiting the means of communication between Corps Headquarters and Battalion Commanders.   ' During operations,' we are told, ' information received in this way and from other sources was embodied each day in maps and reports, which were sent up by despatch rider during the night, and reached front line units in time for the usual attack at dawn. . .   The observers were sometimes asked to undertake special work of great importance.   Before several attacks they were required to reconnoitre and map the enemy's wire.   The slightest mistake might have lost hundreds of lives, but it was never made.'   Among the names which we may mention *honoris causa* in connection with this service are those of Captain, later Major, R. Brooke ; Major, later Lieut.-Col., R. Thompson ; Sergts. Storer and Tinker (Military Medals), and Corpl., later Sergt., Cranswick (Bar to M.M.).

Let us consult the map once more.

In the extreme right-hand corner will be seen the village of Pozières on the straight road (Albert-Bapaume), which ran diagonally across the battlefield.   In the extreme left-hand bottom corner are Martinsart and Martinsart Wood, on the safe side of the River Ancre, where spent Battalions of the 49th Division used to withdraw to lick their wounds.   The course of the Ancre is clearly shown from just above Albert to Miraumont, winding its stream under Authuille and Hamel Bridges ;   and between Authuille and St. Pierre Divion lie Thiepval and Thiepval Wood, the possession of which was so hotly contested since the battle was first joined on July 1st.   The more we look at this timbered countryside, with its chalk-pits, its farms and mills,

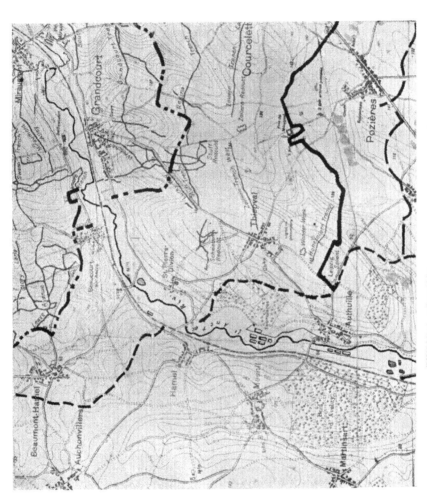

THIEPVAL DEFENCES.

[Face p. 114.

the more unsuitable it seems to the red carnage of 1916.   Yet the troops behaved magnificiently, and Sir Douglas Haig sent several messages during these trying weeks to express his thanks and appreciation.   To one Battalion he sent on August 30th by the hands of the Divisional Commander a sprig of white heather as an emblem of good luck.   Hard though the going was, and bad though the luck seemed to be, making acclimatization tedious and difficult, it rarely happened, even among raw troops, that the conditions proved too exacting. Very typical of the spirit of the Division, in the midst of its harassing experiences, where the room designed by nature for smiles was too narrow almost to contain its special circles of man's inferno, was the part borne in the third week of September by the 7th Battalion of the West Riding Regiment.   They had been at Hedauville since September 4th, at two hours' march from Martinsart Wood, whither, in order to go into the line, they moved on Friday, September 15th.   There they had tea, and took rations for the next day, and were loaded with two bombs per man, and so proceeded from 7 p.m. to new trenches, south of Thiepval, which had been captured only the night before. The relief was delayed in execution partly by artillery barrage, partly by an attack of German bombers, partly by heavy rain, and partly by too few guides ; there was only one guide to each Company, ' and these were strange to the trenches and had difficulty in finding the way. ' It was completed by 4-20 in the morning (September 16th), and during ' intermittent shelling ' all that Saturday arrangements were concerted for an attack on the German trenches in the evening of the 17th.   This operation was most successful ; on the left an objective was gained, and held, 350 feet in advance of schedule.   The details are not uninteresting, and will repay closer study, not because the area of the attack was large in proportion to the whole battle-field, but because it was difficult *terrain* and the obstacles were well overcome.

Just north of the famous Leipsic Salient on the map, lay, first, the Hohenzollern Trench and, secondly, the Wonder Work : two strongly fortified positions.   Eastward out of Thiepval, from the point where the road from the Cemetery meets the main road in a right angle, ran the Zollern Trench, terminating (for present purposes) at the Zollern Redoubt north of Mouquet Farm.   Further along the road from the Cemetery, at a point about as far north of the Crucifix as the Cemetery is south of it, the Stuff Trench started to run eastwards, parallel to the Zollern Trench below.   It was very elaborately fortified, and terminated in the Stuff Redoubt still further above Mouquet Farm. The Regina Trench ran further eastward, from about the point where the Stuff Trench terminated.   Parallel with the road from the Cemetery and Crucifix, the Lucky Way ran up towards Grandcourt, and the Grandcourt Trench branched off eastward a little below the village, again in a parallel line with the Regina and Zollern Trenches.   West of that Cemetery road and crossing the Divion Road about half-way between the Cemetery and St. Pierre Divion was the horrible Schwaben Redoubt ; and, though these names do not exhaust the German defences of Thiepval, they recall sufficiently the opposition to the 7th West Ridings and their support on this third Sunday in September.   The assault was made in four waves at intervals of fifteen, twenty and fifteen feet, the unit being a Platoon.   A Bomb Squad, consisting of one N.C.O. and eleven other Ranks, accompanied each half-Company, and every man of the last two waves carried either a pick or a shovel.   Report Centres, main and subsidiary, Battalion Scouts, and other special parties were detailed for duty, and all Troops were reported in position at 6 p.m. Nearly everything went right, except that a portion of D Company, including both Lewis Guns and their detachments, were believed to have advanced towards the Row of Apple Trees, and were either taken prisoners or wiped out by machine-gun fire.   About 7 o'clock reports were received that the objective had been captured, though it was doubtful how the left flank had fared.   The total casualties in this little action were five Officers and 215 other Ranks.   Certain valuable lessons were learned : the action proved that the jumping-off trench should be parallel to the objective (this precaution enabled direction to be kept accurately) ; that every man, and not merely the last comers, should carry a pick or shovel, fastened to his body by rope or tape ; and that the consolidating parties should either be kept back till the barrage stops or require dug-outs : trivial details, perhaps, but they saved life and added to efficiency.   We may add that the Army Commander, Sir Hubert Gough, visited the Battalion on September 19th, and expressed his satisfaction with the operation, which gained an important part of the enemy defences after five previous attempts had failed, and served to straighten the line held by the 147th Infantry Brigade north of the Leipsic Salient.

A still more important lesson had been learned, and the means were now at hand to apply it.   If these formidable blockhouses were to be crushed, a new military weapon was essential, and early on September 15th the first Tank waddled into warfare.   From this date to the end of September, by a brilliant series of advances from the south, across and along the Albert-Bapaume Road, a victorious crown was put to the tenacious vigil and hard fighting of the Fifth Army, and the attack swung round at last on the pivot held by Sir Hubert Gough.   This attack (September 26th) was described by Sir Douglas Haig as not less than

'a brilliant success.   On the right,' he narrated, 'our troops (2nd and 1st Canadians Divisions of the Canadian Corps, Lieut.-General Sir J. H. G. Byng) reached the system of enemy trenches which formed their objectives without great difficulty.   In Thiepval and the strong works to the north of it the enemy's resistance was more desperate.   Three waves of our attacking troops (11th and 18th Divisions, II. Corps, Lieut.-General

C. W. Jacob) carried the outer defences of Mouquet Farm, and, pushing on, entered Zollern Redoubt, which they stormed and consolidated. . . . On the left of the attack fierce fighting, in which Tanks again gave valuable assistance to our troops (18th Division), continued in Thiepval during that day and the following night, but by 8-30 a.m. on the 27th September the whole of the village of Thiepval was in our hands. . . . On the same date the south and west sides of Stuff Redoubt were carried by our troops (11th Division), together with the length of trench connecting that strong point with Schwaben Redoubt to the west, and also the greater part of the enemy's defensive line eastwards along the northern slopes of the ridge. Schwaben Redoubt was assaulted during the afternoon of the 28th September (18th Division), and . . . we captured the whole of the southern face of the Redoubt and pushed out patrols to the northern face and towards St. Pierre Divion "[1]:
grand exploits these, and infinitely welcome to the gallant Territorials of the West Riding, who had shared since July 1st in the long and formidable task of holding that north-west corner till the appointed hour struck for its fall, and their work could be resumed and fitted in with the larger plans of the Allied Commands.

We might close the present chapter here. The full story of September 15th and the days which followed at Thiepval is involved with other volumes of war history than that of the 49th Division. The romance of the coming of the Tanks belongs to the Machine-Gun Corps, Heavy Section ; the death of Raymond Asquith in the attack belongs to the Grenadier Guards, and to the eminent family of which he was a member. What belongs to us, as the inalienable heritage of the Troops commanded by General Perceval, is the fact that for three months, less three days, from their first assembly in Aveluy Wood, they held on firmly and grimly to that narrow foothold in the Ancre Valley which was dominated always by German guns. They went and came to the muddy, bloody trenches, from Authuille Wood, Aveluy Wood, Martinsart Wood, day by day, under a pitiless harvest sun or a yet more pitiless autumnal rain ; and by their steadfastness and tenacity, even more than by their toll of German life or their fragmentary captures of German trenches, they enabled Sir Douglas Haig to perfect, without haste and without undue anxiety, the long, slow sweep of his advance which swung back on Thiepval at the last. And, though the details at this stage must be kept subordinate to the main features, lest we should seem to claim more than a just share, yet it is satisfactory to observe that certain Battalions of our Division participated in these final operations. Thus the 5th West Yorkshires were detailed as support to the 7th Bedfordshire Regiment for the attack on Schwaben Redoubt on September 27th. They

[1] *Despatches*, page 44.

were formed up on that afternoon, and again before daybreak the
next morning.   Zero hour was fixed finally at 1 p.m.   On that day
the three supporting Companies became a part of the main advance,
and the final Brigade objective was reached by a mixture of both
units, the men from Yorkshire and Beds.   It was a fine conclusion
to the waiting orders imposed after July 1st, and it elicited the following
fine testimony from Major-General T. H. Shoubridge, C.B., C.M.G.,
Commanding the 54th Infantry Brigade, in a latter dated October
1st, 1916, and addressed to Major-General Perceval :

> ' I feel I must write and tell you how splendidly the 5th West
> Yorkshire supported the attack of the 7th Bedfordshire Regiment
> on the Schwaben Redoubt. . . . The Battalion had, I fear,
> a trying time, as the attack was postponed, and I had to bring
> them up in support at night, though they had practically been
> told they would not be wanted that night.   In spite of all diffi-
> culties, when the final attack took place, they formed up in perfect
> order and advanced during the attack with marked determination.
> I was very struck with the soldierly qualities of the men and the
> keenness they displayed, and I am very proud to have had them
> under my Command. . . . All my Battalions are full of praise
> for the Artillery support afforded them both during the attack on
> Thiepval and the subsequent attack on Schwaben Redoubt. . . .
> We all feel very grateful to the troops of your Division associated
> with us. . . . Forgive type,' added the gallant General,
> ' Have just come out of the battle, and have no ink ! '

Recognition, too, eminently merited, reached the 49th Divisional
Commander from Lieut.-General C. W. Jacob, Commanding, as
we saw, the II. Corps.   He wrote, on October 3rd :

> 'As the Division under your Command has now been
> transferred to another Corps, I take this opportunity of thanking
> you, your Staff, the Commanders of Brigades, and all Ranks
> of the Division, for all the good work you put in while you were
> in the II. Corps.

> ' The conditions were trying, and your casualties heavy.
> The calls made on units necessitated great exertions, which were
> always cheerfully carried out.   The gallantry of the Officers and
> men is shown by the large number of decorations won by
> them, and the spirit of all Ranks is good.   The clearing of the
> Leipsic Salient, the prompt way all calls for raids on the enemy's
> trenches were met, and the heavy work done by the Division
> in the preparations for the final attack on Thiepval are gratifying
> records . . . It was unfortunate that the Division as a
> whole could not take part in the final capture of Thiepval, but
> you will all be glad to know that your representatives in that
> battle, the 49th Divisional Artillery and the 146th Infantry

Brigade, did excellent work, and added still further to the good reputation of the Division.'

Schwaben Redoubt, we may add, was not retained without a struggle. There was still one corner to be seized where the Regina Trench branched out in the direction of Courcelette, and, running north of that village, came down towards the Albert-Bapaume Road, almost immediately above Le Sars ; and these gains, too, were made and held despite desperate counter-attacks before the middle of November. So, when winter came down on the Somme battlefield, and the warring armies went to earth, the Allied line which had bulged in towards Albert now bulged out towards Bapaume. 'That these troops should have accomplished so much under such conditions . . . constitutes a feat of which the history of our nation records no equal.'[1] We have tried to describe this feat, in so far as concerns the part, modest in area, indeed, but very exacting in performance, which was played by the 49th Division and we have tried to exhibit that part in its true relation to the drama as a whole.

We may now touch upon one or two details.

Before the close of 1916 a third Victoria Cross fell to the share of the 49th Division. The recipient was Major (then Captain) W. B. Allen, of the 1/3rd West Riding Field Ambulance, attached to the 246th Brigade, Royal Field Artillery. The gallant Officer had already received the decoration of the Military Cross, and we cite here the official record of the circumstances in which the supreme reward was won :

> ' For most conspicuous bravery and devotion to duty. When gun detachments were unloading H.B. Ammunition from wagons which had just come up, the enemy suddenly began to shell the battery and the ammunition, and caused several casualties. Captain Allen saw the occurrences and at once, with utter disregard of danger, ran straight across the open, under heavy shell fire, commenced dressing the wounded, and undoubtedly by his promptness saved many of them from bleeding to death. He was himself hit four times during the first hour by pieces of shell, one of which fractured two of his ribs, but he never mentioned this at the time, and coolly went on with his work till the last man was dressed and safely removed. He then went over to another battery and tended a wounded Officer. It was only when this was done that he returned to his dug-out and reported his own injury '.

Every Arm of the Service had its heroes. Major Allen in the R.A.M.C. earned the Victoria Cross ; Major Alan F. Hobson, D.S.O., in the West Riding Divisional Royal Engineers, who was killed on August 26th, earned the following tribute from a brother-officer of his unit :

[1] *Despatches*, page 53.

" Poor Hobson, our Major, was killed about three days ago by a shell in the neighbourhood of our work.   One has read of lovable, brave leaders in personal histories of previous wars. Hobson was one of those men whom writers love to describe as the best and truest type of an Englishman.   He never asked one of us to go where he would not go himself.   He was always happy, even-tempered and just."

A hero's grave or the Victoria Cross : it was a common choice, settled by fate during the war, and at no time commoner or more inevitable than during these Battles of the Somme.   A few extracts from the letters of a fallen Officer may be given in conclusion to this period, not because they differ essentially (for a happy style is an accident of fortune) from other letters sent home from the Western front, but because they express in word-pictures, compiled on the spot and at first hand, the spirit of the very gallant men whose cheerful devotion in 1916 made possible the victory of 1918.

First, an account of an ordinary sight by the roadside :

' While we were waiting for orders there was a constant procession of troops going up and troops going back from the front line.   It was an intensely interesting procession to me, but there were some terribly sad sights of mangled men being brought back on stretchers.   The " walking cases " were very pathetic ; one in particular I remember.   A young Officer leaning heavily upon the arm of one of his men, the right side of his face bandaged up.   His left eye closed in agony, along he stumbled, while on each side of him our guns went off with a roar that must have been trying to a man evidently so shattered in nerve, and all the time he was exposed to Boche shelling.'

Another extract from the same letter :

' It is a pitiable sight to see horses badly wounded, poor dumb things, so brave and patient under shell fire.   When one is riding near one of one's own batteries, and guns suddenly belch forth flame and smoke over one's head, these dear creatures hardly wince.   From the time the first shell fell among the horses until we left the town—about two hours later, we were dodging shells. When we were outside, the warning hiss of a Fritz caused a funny sight.   Those near buildings jumped to a sheltering wall, some of us who were near trees embraced their trunks and dodged round them when we thought the burst would be on one side. We screamed with laughter at each other, but when one burst rather too close, our heads ached and our hearts thumped (anyway, mine did, and it is no use disguising the fact).'

And from the last of this series of dead letters :

' Presently our trench crossed No Man's Land—at least, it once was No Man's Land ; now it belongs to us until we can turn it over to its proper owners.   We examined Fritz's handiwork where he had spent months of watching and fighting.   We could see what British fighting was like by the evidence there. . . . At one place we were within forty yards of him, but we heard no sound.   The only sound that broke the stillness of that beautiful day was the bang of our own guns and the swish of our crumps overhead.   At one point, close to the tangled wire of Fritz's front line, we saw a sad sight, perhaps the saddest sight of war, groups of our own lads, sleeping, sleeping, sleeping.   Heroes, they had done their bit and there they lie.   They have died so that others can live to be free from the yoke of a monster in human form, whose greed for power must be stifled.'

' Sleeping, sleeping, sleeping ' : this iterated note conveys, now that the war is over and the maps are folded and put away, a tender thought properly keyed, at which to close our account of the Somme battlefield.   It is a field of great achievement and of pious memories, hallowed for all time in English history, and the ' more ' that remained to be done, as foreseen in the vision of this writer, could not be more worthily accomplished than in the spirit of the heroes of the Somme.

II. WINTER, 1916-17.

It was the peculiarity of the war in France and Flanders that there was no clear ending to any battle.   At Ypres, at Verdun, and on the Somme, the tide of war flowed with full flood, and ebbed away without definite decision.   There was a little more erosion of the trenches on one side or the other, a few more miles of territory submerged, or disengaged from the invader, revealing, when the tide rolled back, the waste and ravage and destruction, and then a temporary lull, till

' The tide comes again,
And brims the little sea-shore lakes, and sets
Seaweed afloat, and fills
The silent pools, rivers, and rivulets,
Among the inland hills.'

We reach such a coign of observation, such a lull, less real than apparent, for brave men were being killed every day, in the period from November to January, 1916-17.   It lay between the exhaustion of the Somme offensive and the refluent wave of battle-fury up and down the line in early spring ; and this brief interval may be utilized to pick up a few stray threads.

Let us look at home in the first instance.

The West Riding Territorial Force Association had by now settled down to its stride.   We left its members in 1915[1] struggling, perhaps a little breathlessly, with difficulties of accountancy in their Separation Allowance Department, with the organization of Auxiliary Hospitals, the equipment of 2nd and 3rd Line units, the formation of a National Reserve, and the constant perplexities of the recruiting problem.

[1] See page 40, above.

We find them at the close of the next year with one Division crowned with honour in the field, with another Division straining at the leash, and with a certain reduction in their commitments, owing partly to National Service legislation, partly to firmer methods at Whitehall, and partly to other causes.   Necessity had nationalized the war ; and, though more than 52,000 accounts of soldiers' wives and dependants were now on the Paymaster's books, though more than 3,000 beds in 53 Auxiliary Hospitals were now available in the Riding, and more than 21,000 pairs of socks and 45,000 other comforts had been despatched to the troops during the winter, the Association had thoroughly mastered the technique of war administration when the original triumvirate of Lord Harewood, Lord Scarbrough and General Mends, as President, Chairman and Secretary respectively, was broken up in February, 1917, by Lord Scarbrough's transfer to the War Office as Director-General of the Territorial and Volunteer Forces.[1]

The appearance of the words ' and Volunteer ' requires a brief note of explanation.   The Chairman informed his Association in January, 1917, that the local administration of the Volunteer Force had, at the request of the Army Council, been undertaken by County Associations.   ' Generally speaking,' ran the writ,[2] ' the division of functions between the local military authorities and T.F. Associations in regard to the Volunteer Force will correspond to that obtaining in the case of the Territorial Force in times of peace.'   It was not, perhaps, the best precedent to select, but it was the best available in the circumstances, and an historian will surely arise to tell the story of the part-time soldier in the Great War, what he did and what he might have been used to do.   Such historian will be endowed with imagination to sympathise with the buffeted patriot in the early days of the war, and he will possess sufficient knowledge of the facts to follow his tangled skein of fortune through the maze of legislative enactments and contracting-out tribunals, which cast him up on the lap of his tired country, in November, 1918, half a volunteer and half a conscript and the most melancholy mongrel of the Army Council.   This, happily, is not our present business.   We are simply concerned to show how the Volunteer Act of 1916, which had become law late in December, brought the Volunteer Force into the orbit of the County Associations on the one part and of the Director-General of the Territorial Force on the other.   That Act made provision for Volunteers to enter into an agreement with His Majesty for the performance of certain duties of home defence ' for a period not exceeding the duration of the present war.'   The time-clause was the essence of the contract. Till then, under the Act of 1863, a Volunteer, prior to mobilization, which could only ensue in case of imminent invasion, and which never ensued during the late war, had the right to quit his Corps at his own

[1] See page 7, above.
[2] Army Council Instruction, No. 1830, of September 21st, 1916 ; 9/V.F./128 (T.F. 2).

option on giving a fortnight's notice to his Commanding Officer. Under these conditions he was plainly no soldier, however elastic the terms of his employment. He could neither be clothed nor trained at the public expense, for the public would have no value for their money if the Force, or any part of it, walked out at fourteen days' notice. Permanence of service was then first obtained when the Volunteer Force was reconstituted out of personnel bound by agreements entered into under the new Act of 1916; and thus it happened at the beginning of the next year that the work of Associations was increased by responsibility for the local administration of the Volunteer units raised in their respective counties, and that these duties were tacked on to the machinery of the Territorial Force organization. How heavy the duties became may be measured by a single item of statistics: as many as 217 Army Council Instructions referring *exclusively* to the Volunteer Force were promulgated before the date of the Armistice.

Lastly, reference is due to German action during this lull, or to what we know or may infer about it. Plainly, their moral had been badly shaken. Sir Douglas Haig was resolute on this point, and the extraordinary ' all but ' luck which dogged their campaign on the Western front from the beginning to the end of the war, and of which the full military explanation must await the evidence from their side, was as characteristic at Verdun as anywhere. They all but got home to their objective : so nearly that the German Emperor's telegrams, which he used to compose after the model of his grandfather's in the 1870-71 campaign, just missed being accurate by a few yards ; and this ' little less, and what worlds apart,' which separated the Crown Prince from victory, however cleverly wrapped up in the language of public despatches, must have caused more than common chagrin. For actually it was Verdun which was wanted, the right breast of the mother of men, and not the outposts of its defences, nor even the serried rows of French dead. These might serve in less vital regions to dazzle the eyes of the world ; at Verdun, they drew attention to the defeat. Nor was consolation to be derived from the results of that attempt to relieve Verdun which we have followed in the battles of the Somme. The higher ground, or ridges, still remained in German possession, but it was a precarious hold, as we shall see, and, while the mere configuration of the ground was soon to tell in favour of the Allies, other factors, which cannot be mapped except in an atlas of psychology, were beginning already to count. The repeated losses of fortified positions, culminating in the Wonder Work and Redoubts which had resisted the assaults of July 1st, were disastrous not only on their own account but also as indicating a weakness which might conceivably spread to the Rhine. If the theory of defence proved unsound, no degree of valour in practice would ever avail to put it right. We must not prejudge this question. We are not writing the German history of the war. But it is legitimate to say that, apart from

I

the general retirement which the Germans ordered in March, 1917, and which reached a rate of ten miles a day, our troops gradually discovered a change in the enemy's system of defences. He began, first on the British and afterwards on the French front, to abandon the formal lines of trenches, and to employ the natural features of the soil, when and where these might occur, as the basis of his defences. The crater, or shell-hole cavity, was brought into use in this way, and no outward mark was allowed to distinguish a fortified group of craters, subterraneously connected with one another and otherwise rendered formidable, from harmless groups in its immediate neighbourhood. Thus, the cession by the Germans of ' only our foremost crater-positions,' or of a ' craterfield ' *tout court*, began to figure in their reports for the edification or delusion of German readers. An integral part of the crater-system, as worked out more elaborately at a later date, was the ' pill-box,' or sunk blockhouse, which was strengthened towards the foe and left more thinly built on the home side, so as to render it useless as a weapon should its fire be directed by its captors. We may conclude that the blows which had been dealt at the continuous lines of trenches in the battles of the Ancre and the Somme had alarmed the German High Command ; and that a part of the motive for the retirement (and a very effective part it proved) was to prepare those fortified groups and concrete nests of deadly machine-gun fire at all kinds of irregular distances. The intention was partly to deceive the airman's eye, and to stop that preparation of exact trench-maps to which the Germans had borne testimony on the Somme. But partly, too, the modification of the defence-system implied that our offensive had not been vain. Its immediate effect, accordingly, however serious and impeding it was to prove, was not without good hope. The vaunted theory of ' impregnability ' had been shaken, and, though the end of the war was still out of sight, yet Thiepval, like Jutland, bore a message which the rest of the war was to expound.

Full information on these problems is still lacking from the German side, and without it, as indicated above, our conclusions must be indicated hypothetically. But all the evidence now available makes it clear that they are reasonably correct. Thus, Ludendorff, writing after a tour of the Western Front in December, 1916, laid stress on the urgent need of re-organizing the fighting power of the German Infantry. The machine-gun had become the chief fire-arm, and 'our existing machine-guns', he declared, 'were too heavy for the purpose. . . . In order to strengthen our fire, at least in the most important parts of the chief theatre of war, it was necessary to create special Machine-gun Companies—so to speak, Machine-gun Sharp-shooters.' Attention is also called in the German Commander's authoritative *Memoirs* to the need of hand-mines, grenades, and all quick-loading weapons, and to the formation of storm troops. ' The course of the Somme Battle,' continues the General, ' had also supplied important lessons with respect to the construction and plan of our lines. The very deep undergound forts in the front trenches had to be replaced by shallower constructions. Concrete " pill-boxes," which, however, unfortunately took long to build, had acquired an increasing value. The conspicuous lines of trenches, which appeared as sharp lines on every aerial photograph, supplied far too good a target for the enemy Artillery. The system of defence had to be made broader and looser and better adapted to the ground. The large, thick barriers of wire, pleasant as they were when there was little doing, were no longer a protection. They withered under the enemy barrage ' ; and an angry tribute is paid in his chapter to the equipment of the *Entente* Armies with war material, which ' had been developed to an extent hitherto undreamed of,' and to 'the resolution of the *Entente*, their strangling starvation blockade, and their propaganda of lies and hate which was so dangerous to us.'

It is good to see ourselves as our enemy saw us after the Battle of the Somme. And, perhaps, though we are anticipating a month or two, we may conclude this chapter by a quotation from a German Army Order, hitherto unpublished, of April 4th, 1917. It illustrates from another angle the effects of those '*Entente* Armies' and 'their propaganda ' to which Ludendorff alludes in such embittered terms. The Order ran :

'A National Day has been decreed at home for April 12th, in the sense that members of the large Trade Unions and Associations give up that day's income, salary or wage for the benefit of the Fatherland.

'The wish has been expressed that this programme may be supported as follows : *viz.*, that Officers and other Ranks may volunteer to give up their pay for one day.

'All Officers and other Ranks who are willing to abandon for one day the amount of pay due to them will apply to,' etc.

The captured papers do not disclose the extent of the response to this appeal, but, plainly, at the beginning of 1917, all was not well with the Fatherland.

CHAPTER IX

WITH THE 62ND IN FRANCE

THE eleven miles from Albert to Bapaume, eight of which we travelled in the last chapter, should be familiar by now. In order to gain a clear view of the activities of the 62nd Division after its arrival in France, we may now draw a rectilineal figure enclosed by four main roads, with the Albert-Bapaume road as a portion of the base. Call the Albert-Bapaume road A, B. Extend it to C, Cambrai, on the east°; draw a line C, AA, from Cambrai to Arras, north, north-west ; draw a line, AA, D, from Arras to Doullens, west, south-west, and join D, A, Doullens to Albert, to complete the figure. On C, AA. Cambrai-Arras, a triangle maybe erected with Douai at its apex, thus connecting this new rectangle with the country, Douai, Lens, La Bassée, Lille, which we visited in Chapter IV. On D, A, Doullens-Albert, another

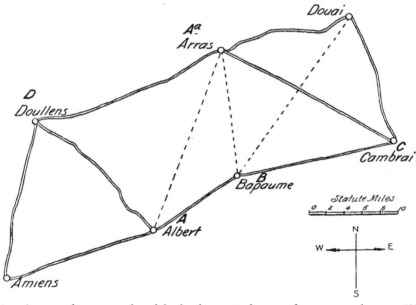

triangle may be erected, with Amiens at the south-western base. We have thus a fairly accurate outline of the lie of the land to which General Braithwaite took his troops in January, 1917, and we know, approximately, at least, how much of that land had been set free by the Battles of the Somme and the Ancre.

The gains in those battles are to be exploited. We shall be occupied for some time to come within the four sides of that shell-ridden quadrangle. The upper road from Doullens to Arras was free, though it was not wise to try to enter Arras except under cover of darkness, as the approach to it from the west was exposed to observation and shell fire, and the town itself had been badly damaged by bombardment.   The lower road was free, as we know, till within three miles of Bapaume, whence our front wound round to below Arras. The object now is, to drive the Germans back on the whole long line from Ypres to Reims, and, especially, within this area, to drive them back between Arras and Bapaume, nearer to Douai and Cambrai. That object was achieved, we shall see, in three great battles during 1917 :—

Arras in April and May,
Ypres (3rd) in June till September, and
Cambrai at the end of November.

Keeping this large view in mind, and recalling, generally, its relations, as remarked briefly in the last chapter, to the configuration of the soil and the effect of this and of other conditions on the plans of the German High Command,[1] we may follow for a few days the story of one unit's experiences, in order to set these in relation to the Division, the Corps, and the Army.   For from the night of January 11th-12th, when the 62nd Division first slept, or tried to sleep—for it was so cold—on French soil, till the Battle of Arras in April, every Battalion in that Division was engaged in the same driving work : in the same work of driving the Germans back, of anticipating their retreat to prepared positions, of consolidating small but important gains, of proving their own worth as a fighting unit, of breaking out, between Thiepval and Hebuterne, to Serre, Puisieux, Miraumont, Achiet, Irles. Pys, always nearer to the Bapaume-Arras road.   We may select for this purpose the 2/5th Battalion of the Duke of Wellington's West Riding Regiment.   It was another Battalion of the same Regiment whose fortunes we followed in Chapter II. from its earliest volunteer beginnings, and now, as then, we possess the advantage of consulting a personal diary kept by an Officer of the selected unit.[2]

The first thing, where everything seemed strange, was to get to know the way about.   A ride to Auxi le Château gave opportunity for a ' very interesting talk ' with an Officer in the 1/5th Battalion of the same Regiment (49th Division).   A day or two later came a tour of the trenches in an old London General omnibus.   The party visited Acheux and Warlencourt, and then drove along the Doullens-Arras road, which was closed to traffic at one point owing to shelling. They went through Arras, noticing its damage by fire and incendiary shells, and reached the line held by the 7th East Surreys.   Here they had an opportunity of watching the system of relief : the East Surreys

[1] " The configuration of the ground in the neighbourhood of the Ancre Valley was such that every fresh advance would enfilade the enemy's positions, and automatically open up to the observation of our troops some new part of his defences.   Arrangements could therefore be made for systematic and deliberate attacks to be delivered on selected positions."—*Despatches*, page 63.

[2] Captain Tom Goodall, D.S.O., M.C., to whom I am much indebted for the loan of this diary, and of some documents, etc., which he was at pains to collect and has kindly put at my disposal.

by the 6th West Kents. ' It was a daylight relief and worked out very well indeed.' The reserve and front-line trenches were examined : the latter were highly complicated ; all the Platoon dug-outs were in cellars, owing to the ruined state of the houses and factories ; at one point, only twenty-five yards from the German front-line. Patrols went out clothed in white to match the snow. A Company cook-house was blown in by trench-mortar fire, wounding two servants and ruining the breakfast. And so back to Doullens and Bus-les-Artois, rejoining their Battalions. This was in January. On February 3rd, ' the weather was so cold that the ink in my fountain-pen was frozen.' On the 7th, ' the cold was so intense that the oil on the Lewis guns froze.' On the 13th, a tour in the trenches before Serre, in relief of the 1st Dorsets : ' the sights one saw in and about the trenches rather opened one's

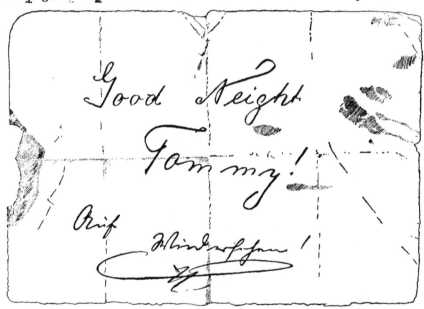

eyes. The dead, both our own and the enemy, were lying about partially buried ; rifles, grenades, unexploded shells, bombs and equipment. The trenches themselves did not exist as such, as in most cases they had been blown in.' On the 15th, the thaw commenced, and in some respects was more intolerable than the frost. The mud in places was two feet deep, and reliefs and so on were considerably hampered.

The shadow, or, rather, the light, of the coming German retreat lay over all. Every trench which was captured brought a wider view and a larger prospect into sight, and there is no doubt that the 62nd Division, to that extent more fortunate than the 49th, arrived at a time and in a locality which afforded, in business parlance, small turn-overs and quick returns. The long waiting experience which ate the heart out of constantly harassed troops was now, temporarily, if not definitely, passed ; they were pushing outwards hopefully to open country and signs of the retreat occurred every day. Thus, on February 25th, at 2 o'clock in the morning, the enemy was reported to have vacated Serre, which, if a straight line be drawn from Albert to Arras, may be pricked in just to the left of that line at a point about two-fifths along it. Puisieux lies on the line just above Serre. Achiet-le-Petit, Achiet-le-Grand and Sapignies lie behind Puisieux eastwards, at distances roughly, of two miles. Miraumont is south of Puisieux, Irles south of Achiet-le-Petit, and Pys south of Irles. They are all in the Albert-Arras-Bapaume triangle within the shell-ridden quadrangle above.

Let us start at Serre on that dark February morning. A push was made out and up towards Puisieux. There were strong positions to be negotiated : Gudgeon Trench, Sunken Road, Orchard Alley and Railway. Two patrols were sent out early on the 26th under subaltern Officers of the 2/4th King's Own Yorkshire Light Infantry, and reported Gudgeon and Orchard trenches clear. Later, it was discovered that the patrol's Gudgeon was a trench not shown on the map, and that the patrol's Orchard was the true Gudgeon ; mist and mud and an unmapped trench are ugly extras in patrol-work. Three Companies (A, B, D) of the Battalion were pushed up to the real Gudgeon trench with orders to put out posts on the Sunken Road in front and an observation-line on the Railway in front of that. They succeeded in placing two outposts, but machine-gun fire stopped the observation-line. There remained the heavily fortified Wundt Werk, which we have not yet mentioned, and which was held by C Company under the Officer Commanding the Battalion. Many fine deeds were performed on this day of continuous exposure to shell and rifle fire. A non-commissioned officer, for example, was sent forward to take charge of a small party, who had been badly knocked about. He kept them under cover in a shell-hole all the rest of the day, and by his coolness and trustworthiness undoubtedly saved their lives.

The 2/4th K.O.Y.L.I. were relieved during the night by the 2/5th West Ridings, to whom we accordingly return. Their new orders were to take Orchard Alley and push outposts in the Sunken Road running from Puisieux to Achiet-le-Petit. At 8 p.m. on Februa y 27th, the Commanding Officer advised the Brigadier that Orchard Alley had been captured ; at an early hour the next morning, the outposts in Sunken Road had been established, and later in the day these positions had been consolidated, and touch had been obtained with the 2nd Royal Warwicks on the left and the 2/6th West Ridings on the right. The Brigadier wired his appreciation, and, later, the Military Cross was awarded to Lieut. P. R. Ridley in the following circumstances :—

  ' On the evening of 27th-28th February, 1917, the Officer

was in charge of a party of three Officers' patrols, each of one Officer and fifteen other Ranks, detailed to rush Orchard Alley from Gudgeon Trench.   Lieut. Ridley was responsible for maintaining the direction, marching on a compass-bearing for 500 yards across unknown and difficult country.   This Officer led his party with great dash, shooting one German and capturing another on entering the trench.   He showed considerable coolness and ability in the attack, and in organizing the defence of the trench.'

The Military Medal was awarded on the same occasion to Lance-Cpl. Herbert Priestley, who had been in command of a Bombing Section in that party, and who, despite a wound in the head, led his men in a most gallant manner.   These were the first honours (first of a long list) in the 62nd Division.

There was to be an attack on Achiet-le-Petit.   The course of the offensive indicated it, and it was indicated too, by attack-practices early in March, when 500 men of the 2/5th West Ridings were employed at Forceville in digging trenches similar to the German system at Achiet-le-Petit.   On March 15th, after completing sundry exercises, the Battalion proceeded to Miraumont, where they took over a line from the 2/5th King's Own Yorkshire Light Infantry, half a mile south-east of Achiet-le-Petit.   They found the 2/4th of the same Regiment on their right and the 2/7th on their left during this tour. On the 17th, the 2/4th reported that they had occupied an enemy trench 300 yards in advance of their line without meeting opposition ; at the same time patrols of the 2/5th found 300 yards in front of them free from the enemy.   Hopes rose, as the country began to open out. B Company was promptly ordered to push on through Achiet-le-Petit, and to occupy Sunken Road, north of that village.   The remaining Companies also moved forward, and occupied the support-trenches. Later on the same day, a further push was made to Achiet-le-Grand ; gaps were to be cut in the wire to let the Cavalry through, and D Company was to push on to Gomiecourt.   The wire proved a formidable obstacle ; but just before midnight on the 17th the Brigadier was informed that the orders had been carried out.   By 4-30 a.m. on March 18th, D Company was in occupation of Gomiecourt.   They had encountered only slight machine-gun fire, and five hours later the Cavalry went through.   Thenceforward to the end of March, the Battalion stood fast on the ground occupied.   There was plenty to do in consolidating it, and plenty of German material left behind which served that purpose.   But all existing accommodation had been destroyed, the majority of trees had been killed, several dug-out entrances had been mined, and important road-junctions had been blown up.

We may read a part of this story in more detail.   Little exploits fully related illuminate the history which they helped to make.   What part was borne by B Company (above) in this adventure ? They were commanded by Captain Joseph Walker, whose orders were to hold Resurrection Trench south of Achiet-le-Petit and to capture that village.   For three days and nights they came in for a very heavy bombardment, in which the trench was obliterated in parts and severe casualties were suffered.   On March 17th, an hour before dawn, two battle-patrols were sent out to the flanks of the village.   The rest of the Company followed under Captain Walker, and, despite some machine-gun fire, they took the village and passed through it.   They dug-in on the north side and threw out a defensive flank, which drove off the enemy rearguard.   Achiet-le-Petit was promptly blown to bits by ' a terrific barrage of heavy stuff,' but B Company had not waited for it.   At mid-day the Corps Pigeoner arrived with a basket of birds, and reports were sent back to Headquarters.   In the evening, instructions came for the whole of the line to move forward and'attack Achiet-le-Grand and Gomiecourt.   Before this could be done, the German wire had to be cut to allow the Cavalry to pass through. ' The wire was nearly a hundred yards in depth in three broad belts, and so thick that it had to be dug up in parts.'   The task was completed before daylight by B and C Companies.   B Company then advanced to their objective and occupied the western side of Achiet-le-Grand, and A Company cleared Logeast Wood : a good day's work, it will be admitted.

This narrative may still be expanded : the day's work is typical of what was happening throughout the district.   From Achiet-le-Grand to Gomiecourt, two villages otherwise insignificant, the distance is under two miles.   At 1 a.m., March 18th, 1917, there was a heavy mist, and it was difficult to find the road ; so ' we struck across open country on compass-bearing,' say the records, ' and arrived in the trenches west of Gomiecourt at 3-30 a.m., occupied these, and then sent out two patrols through the village, but they did not find a soul ' : a deserted village, but from other causes than Oliver Goldsmith's. ' The junction of every road in the village had been mined and blown up, and everything of value had been destroyed.   All fruit-trees had either been cut down, or an incision made round the bark so that the sap would not rise.[1]   All wells had been blown in, and one had been poisoned with arsenic,' so the R.E. Officer reported to our diarist.   The R.E.'s took 700 lbs. of unexploded charge out of the cellar of the only village *château*, where the front stairway had fallen in and there was a big hole in the floor of the entrance hall. We read an interesting note, too, on March 26th : ' Walked with Lieut. Ridley ' (we watched him win his M.C.) ' across country to Bapaume ' (the eleven miles had been cleared at last). ' Noticed the Hôtel de Ville still standing ; most other buildings had been blown

[1] Later in the year, the surgical skill of French gardeners succeeded in some instances in joining the severed arteries of these trees.

up. Then went south of the town towards the trenches, but, as these reminded one too much of Beaumont Hamel, had lunch and then came back. Walked along the Bapaume-Arras ' (B, Aa) ' main road as far as Ervillers ' (a third of the way from Bapaume) ' and then struck across country to Gomiecourt. Bapaume Town Hall and Sapignies Church had both been mined and left by the enemy and blew up during the night.' So, the deserted villages bore traces of their late inhabitants.

If a straight line be drawn from Bapaume to Douai, bisecting the Cambrai-Arras road (C, Aa, of our quadrangle), and if that straight line be divided into three equal parts, the village of Bullecourt will be found at one-third of the way from Bapaume and two-thirds from Douai. It is thus well within our quadrangle, yet well on the further side of the road from Bapaume to Arras, along which we just now walked to Ervillers. We shall be occupied with Bullecourt for some time : on April 11th in a snowstorm, when ' an attack was made against the Hindenburg Line, in the neighbourhood of Bullecourt,' and again on May 3rd and following days, when ' it was advisable that Bullecourt should be captured without loss of time.' [1] For the German retreat was at an end.

Bapaume had fallen on March 17th, Peronne on the following day. South and east of Peronne, on the 21st, the Fourth Army had captured forty villages. French troops reached the outskirts of St. Quentin, and counted their villages by the score. The Cavalry, mounted and dismounted, had come in for a bit of their own, and a fine exhilaration of open fighting had been blown like a freshening breeze along the east wall of the shell-torn quadrangle. But after the third week of March the pace of the retreat began to slacken ; and, as soon as the first days of April dispelled the cover of the mist, and the wind and the sun dried up the mud from which the Germans had been retiring, their slower pace stiffened into resistance, and their resistance hardened into battle. All along the Hindenburg Line, so much advertised, yet in places so elastic, which was to guard the ridges of observation, the Battle of Arras was engaged in April, May and a part of June, and during the course of that Battle, Bullecourt was won and lost and won again.

No more need be said about the retreat. The precise ratio between initiative and compulsion, precisely how far, that is to say, it was carried through according to plan and directed by forces under German control, will not be settled till the official war-histories of both belligerents have been published, and may even be disputed thereafter. Certainly, it was admirably executed ; less certainly, it was voluntary in all its parts ; most certainly, it was accompanied by

[1] *Despatches*, page 102.

incidents which indelibly stained the reputation of the German Military Command. That 'the systematic destruction of roads, railways and bridges in the evacuated area made unprecedented demands upon the Royal Engineers,' or that in four and a half days, for example, from the morning of March 18th the Somme at Brie was rebridged for our troops,[1] were facts of warfare as legitimate for the enemy as they were creditable to his pursuers. What was illegitimate and irreparable was the not less systematic destruction, forbidden in the Pentateuch, as Mr. Buchan[2] notes, of 'trees for meat' and water for drinking. We have remarked these features in petto : the single trees felled or slashed, the single wells poisoned or blown in, the single monuments gutted or mined ; and France knows the full tale of her own wrongs.

So we come to the Battle of Arras, which opened definitely on April 9th and rolled in thunder along the northern ridges to its renewed flood in the Third Battle of Ypres.

We may look at the map again. The Battle of Arras was fought on a front of sixteen or seventeen miles, stretching, roughly, nine miles to the north and seven or eight to the south of Arras. Arras, as we know, was within the British line ; its cellars and sewers, as a fact, had been prepared for the accommodation of our troops, though they were not long in request. The British line to the south of Arras (we are writing of the opening of the battle) crossed the Arras-Cambrai main road almost immediately below the town, facing Tilloy-les-Mofflaines on the right, and running down to Croisilles and Ecoust, which looked across the line to Bullecourt. Below Bullecourt, two miles or so to the right, and about three miles above the Bapaume-Cambrai road, the village of Quéant should be observed for the sake of its trench-connection with Drocourt in the north (east-south-east of Lens), which formed a switch to the Hindenburg Line, in case of German accidents behind Arras. It was the Quéant-Drocourt trench-system which made Bullecourt so important to its defenders. The British line to the north of Arras (still at the opening of the battle, but outside of our original quadrangle) crossed the River Scarpe in the eastern suburbs of the town, and ran up with a bearing to the left between Souchez and Givenchy, turning to the right again between Loos and Lens. Vimy, with all its fortifications, both natural and artificial, was the key to an advance in this area. The situation should be studied on a larger map, but it is useful to see it, too, in miniature ; and for this purpose we repeat once more our sketch on page 90 above. On the rough square, Arras-Bapaume-Cambrai-Douai, we erect now on the northern side the road-junctions from Arras to Douai through Souchez and Lens. The British line ran up, as we have said, between Souchez and Givenchy, with Vimy and its ridges on the right, and ran down to the west of

[1] Despatches, page 76.
[2] Nelson's History of the War, Vol. XIX., page 23.

Bullecourt, which helped to guard the Quéant-Drocourt switch.   It
only remains to observe that from Lens to Ypres was a journey of less
than thirty miles, and that an attack at Messines and Wytschaete formed
an obvious corollary to successes at Bullecourt and Vimy.

We are not directly concerned with the bigger strategy of
this Spring campaign.   Sir Douglas Haig made it clear that
he regarded the capture of the Vimy Ridge as necessary in
itself and important for the view which it would afford over the plains
to Douai and beyond.   When this object should be achieved he proposed to transfer his main offensive into Flanders.   ' The positions
held by us in the Ypres salient since May, 1915, were far from satis-

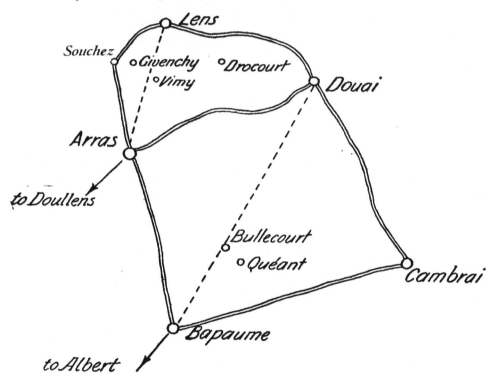

factory,' he wrote.   ' They were completely overlooked by the enemy.
Their defence involved a considerable strain on the troops occupying
them, and   .   .   .   our positions would be much improved by the
capture of the Messines-Wytschaete Ridge, and of the high ground
which extends thence north-eastwards for some seven miles.'   These
plans were re-adjusted to some extent by arrangement with the French
Command : ' The British attack, under the revised scheme, was, in
the first instance, to be preparatory to a more decisive operation to
be undertaken a little later by the French Armies,' and though, as
the British Commander wrote, ' my original plan for the preliminary

operations on the Arras front fortunately fitted in well with what was required of me under the revised scheme,' yet, in order to give full effect 'to the new rôle allotted to me in this revised scheme, preparations for the attack in Flanders had to be restricted for the time being to what could be done by such troops and other labour as could not in any case be made available on the Arras front.[1]'

So much in this place for the plans. What were the troops entrusted with their execution? Looking at a larger map again, and assuming for a moment that a week's fighting (April 9th to 16th) has already taken place, and that the British front has been advanced, as indicated, from the outskirts of Lens in the north to Croisilles in the south, we may now enumerate Sir Douglas Haig's forces as they were distributed from north to south in order of battle on April 17th. Note that the First Army was commanded by General Sir H. S. Horne, the Third by General Sir E. H. H Allenby, the Fourth by General Sir Henry Rawlinson and the Fifth by General Sir Hubert Gough : great Generals all, and tried Commanders. We give, first, the positions, so far as they can be located for certainty in the third line which resulted from a week's fighting, and, next, in descending scale of military organization, the Army, the Corps, the Division, and the Regiments :—

ORDER OF BATTLE, 17th April, 1917.

Position.	Army.	Corps.	Division.	Regiments.
VIMY	I.	Canadian	1st, 2nd, 3rd, 4th Canadian, 5th British.	
North of RIVER SCARPE	III.	XVII.	51st (Highland)	Gordon Highlanders A. & S. Highlanders. Seaforth Highlanders. Roy. Scots. Black Watch.
			34th	Roy. Scots (2 Bns.). Lincolnshire, Suffolk, Northd. Fus. (9 Bns.).
FAMPOUX			9th (Scottish)	Black Watch. Seaforth Highlanders (2 Bns.). Scottish Rifles. Roy. Scots (2 Bns.). A. & S. Highlanders. Cameron Highlanders. S. African Bde. (4 Bns.). K.O.S.B.

[1] *Despatches*, pages 82–83.

ORDER OF BATTLE, 17th April, 1917—(*Ccntinued*).

Position.	Army.	Corps.	Division.	Regiments.
FAMPOUX	III.	XVII.	4th	Household Bn. Roy. Warwickshire. Seaforth Highlanders. R. Irish Fus. Somersetshire L.I. E. Lancs. Hampshire. Rifle Brigade. K.O. (R. Lancs.) Lancs. Fus. Duke of Wellington's (W.R.). Essex.
South of RIVER SCARPE near MONCHY		XVIII.	12th (Eastern)	Norfolk. Suffolk. Essex. R. Berkshire. R. Fusiliers (2 Bns.). R. Sussex. Middlesex. Queen's (R.W. Surrey). Buffs (E. Kent.) E. Surrey. R.W. Kent. Northants.
			14th (Light)	K.R.R.C. (3 Bns.). Rifle Bde. (3 Bns.). Oxford & Bucks L.I. K.S.L.I. Somerset L.I. D.L.I. K.O.Y.L.I. Durham L.I. King's (Liverpool).
			30th	Liverpool (4 Bns.). Manchester (4 Bns). Beds. Yorks. R. Scots. Fus. Wilts. S. Lancs.
			37th	R. Fus. (2 Bns.). K.R.R.C. Rifle Bde. R. Warwickshire. E. Lancs.

ORDER OF BATTLE, 17th April, 1917—(*Continued*).

Position.	Army.	Corps.	Division.	Regiments.
South of RIVER SCARPE near MONCHY	III.	XVIII.	37th	N. Lancs. Beds. N. Staffs. Lincolnshire. Somerset. Middlesex. York. & Lancs.
		VI.	29th	R. Fus. R. Dublin Fus. Lancs. Fus. Middlesex. K.O.S.B. Inniskilling Fus. S. Wales B. Border. Essex. Hampshire. Worcestershire. Newfoundland.
Advanced, via ARRAS			15th (Scottish)	Black Watch. Seaforth Highlanders. Gordon Highlanders (2 Bns.). Cameron Highlanders (2 Bns.). R. Scots. R. Scots. Fus. A. & S. Highlanders K.O.S.B. Scottish Rifles. Highland L.I. (2 Bns.).
?			3rd	K.R.R.C. 10th R. Welsh Fus. West Yorks. R. Scots. Gordon Highlanders. R. Scots. Fus. R. Fusiliers. Northd. Fus. Suffolk. K.O. (Roy. Lancs.) E. Yorkshire. 7th K.S.L.I. 12th King's (Liverpool)
?	III.	VI.	17th (Northern)	W. Yorkshire. E. Yorkshire. Yorkshire.

ORDER OF BATTLE, 17th April, 1917—(*Continued*).

Position.	Army.	Corps.	Division.	Regiments.
?	III.	VI.	17th (Northern)	Dorsetshire. Lincolnshire. Border. S. Staffs. Sherwood Foresters. Northd. Fus. Lancs. Fus. Duke of Wellington's (W.R.). Manchester. Yorks. & Lancs.
South of VIth. Corps		VII.	21st	Northd. Fus. (3 Bns.). E. Yorkshire. Yorkshire. Durham L.I. K.O.Y.L.I. (2 Bns.). Leicestershire (4 Bns.). Lincolnshire.
Between R. Cojeul and R. Sensée			33rd	R. Fusiliers. K.R.R.C. King's Queen's. Suffolk. Worcestershire. Scottish Rifles (2 Bns.). Middlesex. A. & S. Highlanders. R. Welsh Fus. Highland L.I.
?			50th (Northumbrian)	Northd. Fus. Durham L.I. Yorkshire.
?			56th (London)	London. Middlesex.
BULLECOURT	V.	V.	7th	Border. Devonshire (2 Bns.). Queen's. Gordon Highlanders. H.A.C. R. Welsh Fus. S. Staffs. Manchester (4 Bns.). Warwickshire.

ORDER OF BATTLE, 17th April, 1917—(*Continued*).

Position.	Army.	Corps.	Division.	Regiments.
?	V.	V.	11th (Northern)	D. of Wellington's. W. Yorkshire. Yorkshire. York. and Lancs. Lincolnshire. Border. S. Staffs. Sherwood Foresters. Dorsetshire. Northd. Fus. Lancs. Fus. Manchester. E. Yorkshire.
BULLECOURT			58th (London)	London, 2nd Line, T.F.
			62nd (W. Riding)	W. Yorks. (4 Bns.). D. of Wellington's (4 Bns.). K.O.Y.L.I. (2 Bns.). York. & Lancs. (2 Bns.).
LAGNICOURT		Australian		

It was a strong force, as is apparent, and except in the extreme southern sector, from Ecoust (opposite Bullecourt) to Lagnicourt, no 2nd Line Territorial troops were engaged. There, with Londoners on their left and Australians on their right, twelve battalions from the West Riding took their part.

The operation was not successful. 'The attacking troops of the Fifth Army,' wrote Sir Douglas Haig, 'were obliged to withdraw to their original line.'[1] Thus they missed the more sensational advances which were secured at Vimy and Monchy-le-Preux. But they contributed by their action to those results, and their gallantry earned a high encomium from the British Commander-in-Chief, and established for the 62nd Division, in its first engagement on a big scale, a record worthy of more veteran troops.

Let us start in this sector on April 9th, the day of the opening of the Battle of Arras.

It was explained to the Front-line Battalions that, in the event of the attack of the Third Army on Neuville Vitasse being successful, and of the advance being pushed forward to Fontaine-les-Croisilles and Cherisy, the enemy might evacuate his positions. Patrols were sent out, accordingly, in order to ascertain the facts; and the 2/6th West Yorkshires, for example, if we may select one Battalion out of

[1] *Despatches,* page 93.

K

the twelve, were ordered to hold themselves in readiness to advance after 12 o'clock noon at one hour's notice. A provisional scheme of operations was laid down, in anticipation of the sequence of events, should the Hindenburg Line be evacuated on that part. These plans missed fire, however, and on the next day (10th) the unit which we have selected was still stationed at St. Leger. In the early morning information arrived of an impending German counter attack, and, after orders had been issued for a move at ten minutes' notice, Brigade Orders arrived during the afternoon for a night march to Ecoust. This move was duly accomplished. The object was to capture Bullecourt and Hendecourt, and then to move forward in the general direction of Cagnicourt, on the further side of the Quéant switch. Shortly after midnight on April 11th, the troops were informed to this effect; Zero hour was 4-30 a.m.

We have to record that the operation, as planned, could not be fully carried out. Briefly, it had been devised as follows : unless, as seemed improbable, the Hindenburg Line should be found to have been evacuated, the Australian Division, supported by Tanks, was to push forward to Riencourt and Bullecourt. As soon as their work rendered it possible, the 185th Infantry Brigade (Brigadier-General V. W. de Falbe, C.M.G., D.S.O.) was to push one Battalion into Bullecourt from the south-west, with another Battalion in support. The Tanks (two, followed by four), after clearing Bullecourt, were to move out of the village, and clear the Hindenburg Line up to a stated position, where they would come under the orders of General de Falbe, in command of an Advanced Guard, detailed to capture Hendecourt and to move forward as indicated above. This formed the operation, as planned. The operation, as executed, starts with Battalion reports to the Brigade, at 5-15 a.m., 6 a.m. and 7-10 a.m., to the effect that not a Tank was in sight. We may imagine the anxiety at Headquarters. Reconstruct the surroundings on that April morning : the immense line of British Troops stretching right away beyond Vimy, the noise of guns, the open country on the other side ; remember the significance of Bullecourt, not merely as the objective of the 62nd Division, but as the last stronghold of the enemy in that sector before he retired to the Quéant switch behind the real Hindenburg Line ; multiply every missed appointment and its consequent inconveniences in civil life to the nth power of calculation ; add a responsible sense of the great issues depending on prompt action ; and then conceive what it meant to Lt.-Col. John H. Hastings, D.S.O., the Officer Commanding the 2/6th West Yorkshires (to return for a moment to this unit), to have to report three times in two hours that, so far as he was aware, the conditions precedent to his pushing on to Bullecourt still remained unfulfilled. Item one : the Tanks had not arrived. Item two : there was still no news of the Australians having entered Bullecourt. Colonel Hastings went forward to make enquiries, and to discuss matters with the Australian Division. On his return, he advised the Brigadier that the situation was ' very obscure.' His patrols, he said, had not reported, but there was no sign of the Australians clearing Bullecourt, and several enemy machine-guns had been located on the south-east fringe of the village. This report crossed a message from the Brigade (through the 2/8th Battalion, West Yorks.), stating that Tanks had been seen at a factory between Bullecourt and Hendecourt, and adding : ' Please take immediate action, without waiting for Tanks to arrive, to clear up situation in Bullecourt and seize Hindenburg Line to the west of the village.' (This message in original was received an hour later.) A reply was sent through the 2/8th Battalion to the effect that the instructions seemed to be ' based on faulty and erroneous information ' : the main point was that the Australians had not entered Bullecourt, and that reports from the patrols were still awaited. While this reply was on its way, the Brigadier visited the Battalion Head-quarters, and ' was evidently dissatisfied with the want of progress.' He admitted to Colonel Hastings that the conditions laid down as pre-liminary to the advance still appeared incomplete (which means that the Tanks had not operated), but he was anxious that the push should be attempted, and Colonel Hastings went up again to investigate.

Meanwhile, what about the Tanks ? Major W. H. L. Watson, D.S.O., of the Machine-Gun Corps, Heavy Section, writing in *Blackwood's Magazine*, June, 1919, stated that, ' of my eleven Tanks, nine had received direct hits and two were missing.' He pointed out that the sudden change of plans between April 10th and 11th had proved somewhat upsetting, that the crews were composed of tired men, that a blizzard was blowing, and that the snow proved bad cover. He added that the Australian troops were turned distrustful of Tanks for some months, and that a British Brigadier, to whom he was paying a farewell visit, told him, ' with natural emphasis, that Tanks were "no dammed use." ' Further than this, we need not pursue the question. A day was to come very soon when the new weapon would outpace the Infantry, and help effectively to win its battles. At Bulle-court, on April 11th, the co-operation was not adequate.

At 11 o'clock that morning, Colonel Hastings, ruling out the Tanks, expressed his deliberate conviction that the village could not be captured by daylight, except by very great sacrifices. The wire was uncut, the snipers were active, and there was very little cover. Three hours later, Brigade orders arrived to withdraw the patrols, and at dusk the Battalion relieved the 2/7th Battalion of their own Regiment in the right sector of the front facing Bullecourt. The relief was completed at 1 a.m. on April 12th, and another long and trying day was spent in tapping the Bullecourt defences, which were found to be still formidable. By 5 a.m. on the morning of the 13th, the relief of the Battalion in its turn by the 2/7th West Ridings was completed, and they returned to Ervillers on the Bapaume-Arras road.

They had suffered badly during this experience. On the 11th, Lieut. C. F. R. Pells, 2/Lieut. A. G. Harris and 31 other Ranks were killed, and the wounded amounted to 30.   Fine work was done by the 174th Tunnelling Company, R.E. (Major Hutchinson, M.C., Commanding), in digging out the victims of a collapsed house in which two Officers were killed : they worked thirty hours continuously and rescued nine men alive.

Meanwhile, Bullecourt had not been captured. If a detailed map be consulted again, it will be seen that the British lines of April 16th and 24th both met at their southern extremity on the wrong (north) side of the River Sensée, and formed a dangerous salient, or inward bulge, with the British line running south from Croisilles. The Hindenburg Line at Bullecourt still guarded the switch-line at Quéant ; and this failure was the more disappointing in view of the easterly advances along the River Scarpe behind Arras, and, further north, behind Vimy and its woods and hills. Tanks had shown fine capacity during that fortnight. The gallant Infantry had accomplished by their aid what it took them nearly as many months to accomplish with much worse casualties on the Somme in 1916. For the missing weapon had been found, though its full use was still to be discovered, and obstacles even more formidable than had held up the 49th Division at Thiepval were levelled or reduced.

We pass at once to the renewed assault on Bullecourt between May 3rd and 17th.

The 62nd Division was once more engaged. The new weapon was brought again to the attack, and, though further experience was still wanted before its masterly employment at Cambrai in November, the last phase of the Battle of Arras clearly demonstrated to all those who chose to see the immense value of co-operation between Infantry and Tanks. That the brunt of the Infantry fighting in these experimental days fell on the troops from the West Riding, will find a place in military history as well as in Yorkshire records.

Brigade Orders with reference to the fresh assault were received immediately after the old. Already on April 15th, the plan of operations was to hand, and the intervening seventeen days was spent mainly in rehearsals. The order of advance from the right was the 185th Infantry Brigade (de Falbe), the 186th (Hill) in the centre, and the 187th (Taylor) on the left. Each Brigade had its definite objective, and they advanced to the attack side by side. The Third Army operated eastwards in the direction of Fontaine-les-Croisilles, with the 2nd Australian Division on the right. Tanks were to crawl up in sufficient numbers. The day was fixed for May 3rd. Zero hour was 3-45 a.m. Once more we may quote Major Watson[1] as to the part borne by the Tanks in this attack. ' A costly failure,' is his

[1] *Blackwood's Magazine*, July, 1919. See page 131, above. The articles have been collected in book-form since this chapter was in type.

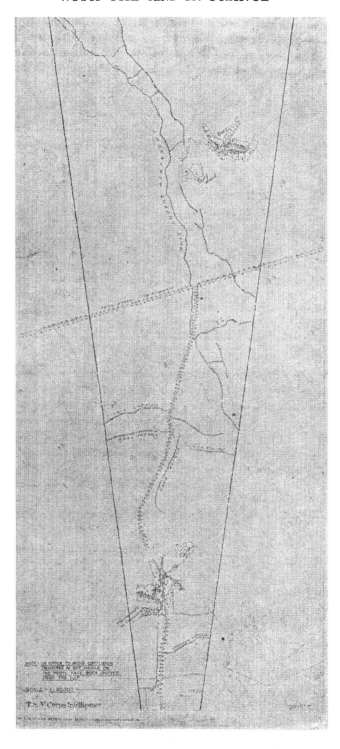

description of the day's work.   Major R. O. C. Ward, D.S.O., who
was killed in the following November, was out with his Tanks in
front, ' but the Infantry could not follow,' he complained.   ' Attack
unsuccessful.   Casualties heavy,' is the bare statement in one of the
Battalion diaries.   Before consulting a more expansive authority, it
will be interesting to examine the accompanying photograph of Hendecourt from the air.   Above the village, we see the main road from
Arras to Cambrai, which runs from north-east to south-west.   Crossing
that road, we see the switch trench-line from Drocourt to Quéant,
which ran roughly, from north to south.   The trenches guarding the
village, Orix, Opal, Hop, Morden, are indicated on the face of the
photograph, and are still more clearly displayed in the ground-plan sketch
which we also reproduce (p. 133).   Turning back now to May 3rd, we
have the advantage of some notes by an Officer of the 62nd, who
watched the opening barrage from the top of the railway embankment.
It was an unforgettable sight.   ' Shells of all sizes screamed through the
air, and bullets from our machine-guns sped towards the enemy lines.
The noise was deafening and appalling.   Then the Tanks went forward to do their part in the attack.   Hundreds of Very lights and
coloured signals were sent up by the enemy all along his line ' ;   and
to the careful watcher and time-keeper, these lights and signals brought
evil tidings.   For after two Companies of one Battalion of the 62nd
should have been in the enemy second-line trench, ' enemy lights
were still sent up from that direction.'

We turn to a Company record.   Take, for instance, B Company
of the 2/5th West Ridings.   They advanced steadily to the attack,
and fought their way up the slope to the ridge on the left of Bullecourt.
But they met very formidable opposition.   Some think that the sound
of the Tanks deploying in their assembly positions may have reached
acute enemy ears ;   but, whether or not this was the case, and,
on the whole, the evidence is against it, a devastating machine-gun
fire and a terrific barrage of high explosive and shrapnel were
suddenly opened on the advancing Company, while hidden concrete
emplacements protected the enemy guns.   The survivors gallantly
rallied, and pressed on into the Hindenburg Line through a ' tornado
of bullets.'   Lieut. O. Walker was killed at this point, as he was
charging at the head of his platoon, rifle in hand, through the German
wire.   Two enemy machine-guns were captured, and their crews
killed by our bombers.   Captain J. Walker, M.B.E., Commanding the
Company, with a mere handful of men, still pushed on and forced a
broken way to the next strong point of hidden emplacements.   Here
the little party held out for three awful days and nights.   They had
no water and only their iron rations, and they were bombed and shelled
all the time.   On the second day, the enemy tried to take them prisoners,
but the attempt was repulsed.   On the third day, when the position
was blown in through our own Batteries having shortened range, this

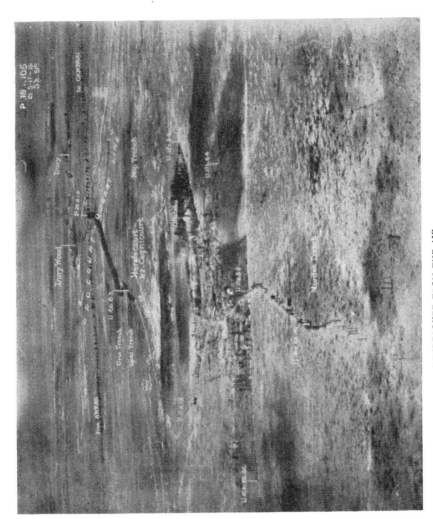

HENDECOURT FROM THE AIR.

[Face p. 134.

very brave Officer and his few surviving wounded men contrived to fight their way back through the German outpost line, in broad daylight and fired at from every side. A nine hours' struggle brought them home ' by a miracle.'[1] Bullecourt was still uncaptured, but its blood-soaked ridges and trenches had taught the Prussians the meaning of Yorkshire grit.

The story may be repeated, if it is not clear enough, from the diaries of other Battalions. Take the 2/4th York and Lancasters, for example. It is a vivid narrative, which may be quoted almost verbatim :

By Zero hour on May 3rd, the men had marched on to the tape line, extended, and formed waves, as ordered, each man fixing his bayonet and lying down directly he got into his place. Just as the head of the 6th line came into its alignment, a shell burst close by, wounding Lt.-Col. Blacker, Commanding, and about six other Ranks. ' Don't mind me, get the lines out,' was the gallant Officer's order, which was instantly obeyed : though the shelling was heavy all the time, the operation was completed as if in a practice-attack. The Adjutant found the lines absolutely correct, and men lying close to shell-holes had in many instances refrained from taking cover for fear of spoiling their interval. It was this kind of spirit which beat the Germans, though they kept us out of Bullecourt on May 3rd. Colonel Blacker, with the assistance of his servant, returned to Battalion Headquarters, and Major Richardson arrived from Brigade to take over the Command of the Battalion. A rum-ration was served out at 3 a.m., and the first line advanced at Zero (3-45 a.m.) less eight minutes. In order to understand what followed, it must be borne in mind that there were 900 yards to be traversed before the first German trench was reached : 900 yards through the heavy smoke and dust of the barrage depicted above. To keep intervals, distance and direction was not an easy task even for the best-trained troops. Still, all was going well, till some confusion was caused by another unit crossing their front between the 4th and 5th lines. These troops were ordered to withdraw and re-form, but the order was mistaken by about 70 men of the right rear Company of the invaded Battalion. They thought it was addressed to them, and withdrew, accordingly, to the railway embankment. The rest, steadily led, despite the mixture of units, pushed on to the first German trench, but the waves had lost their formation before the second line was reached. Major Richardson was killed in a courageous attempt to find out exactly what was happening, and, later, Brigade orders arrived to parade all available personnel for a second attack in two lines. It ended miserably in shell-holes, which afforded insufficient protection from casualties out of proportion to the result, and about 4 o'clock in the afternoon of the long day the

[1] The present writer is indebted to Captain Joseph Walker for the particulars of this gallant and desperate exploit.

order came to retire to the railway cutting. The 7th Division relieved the 62nd.

We need not multiply the records. ' The attacking troops eventually withdrew to the railway cutting ' ; ' finally forced to retire about 11-30 a.m. on the railway embankment ' ; these entries and entries like these recur with maddening iteration in the narratives of the units on this date, and the loss of life was terribly high. But Bullecourt fell in the end. Ten men had been left in the coveted village by troops which had reached it on May 3rd, but had fallen back from all but its fringes, and these ten men were rescued on May 8th. Day by day, the stubborn fight was waged, with attack and counter-attack of intense ferocity and varying fortune, till at last, on May 17th and following days, Territorial Troops of the County of London and the West Riding drove out the last remnants of the German garrison from their last stronghold in front of Quéant. Let Sir Douglas Haig tell the tale of these successes, which brought to a victorious close the series of fighting known as the Battle of Arras :

'At 3-45 a.m. on the 3rd May, another attack was undertaken by us . . . While the Third and First Armies attacked from Fontaine-les-Croisilles to Fresnoy, the Fifth Army launched a second attack upon the Hindenburg Line in the neighbourhood of Bullecourt. This gave a total front of over sixteen miles. Along practically the whole of this front our troops broke into the enemy's positions . . . . To secure the footing gained by the Australians in the Hindenburg Line on the 3rd May, it was advisable that Bullecourt should be captured without loss of time. During the fortnight following our attack, fighting for the possession of this village went on unceasingly. . . . On the morning of the 7th May, English troops (7th Division, Major-General T. H. Shoubridge) gained a footing in the south-east corner of Bullecourt. Thereafter gradual progress was made, in the face of the most obstinate resistance, and on the 17th May, London and West Riding Territorials[1] completed the capture of the village. . . . . . . On the 20th May fighting was commenced by the 33rd Division (Major-General R. J. Pinney) for the sector of the Hindenburg Line lying between Bullecourt and our front-line west of Fontaine-les-Croisilles. Steady progress was made until by the 16th June touch had been established by us between these two points.'[2]

We had intended to close here the present chapter. But our impression of life at the front with the 62nd Division is incomplete without reference to the mimic warfare and the relaxation from war which likewise formed part of its experience. On that very day, June 16th, when the Bullecourt sector was finally consolidated, Divi-

[1] 58th and 62nd Divisions, Major-General H. D. Fanshawe, Commanding the 58th Division.
[2] *Despatches*, pages 99 and 102.

COLISEUM MADE OUT OF A GERMAN CRATER.

[Face p. 136.

sional Sports were being held at Achiet-le-Petit. In a Coliseum made
out of a German crater, which we illustrate from a pencil-sketch on
the spot, the Divisional Band was playing on June 14th, and boxing
contests were being fought. Two days later, a Gymkhana was held,
in which some of the chief events were dribbling a football on horse-
back,[1] driving a pair of mules tandem,[2] and collecting stones to drop
into a bucket.[3] On June 20th, three Officers of the 2/5th West Ridings
rode from Achiet-le-Petit to Thiepval, and went over the ground which
had been fought by the 1st Line Battalion of their Regiment nearly a
year before. ' Forsan et haec olim meminisse juvabit,' they may have
thought, as they contrasted their leisurely ride with the heat of battle
which the site recalled ; and the same thought, applied to their own
experience, may have revealed the hope of a future day when Bullecourt, like Thiepval, would be remembered as a past stage in a victorious
advance.

[1] Competitors mounted and armed with a pick-handle dribbled the ball 100 yards, then
round a post and back to shoot through a goal.

[2] Ride a mule and drive another (tandem) round a course through various obstacles, finish
with 100 yards down the straight.

[3] Run in heats of 16 or less. In front of each competitor, standing dismounted in line,
is a row of stones at 10 yards distance from each other. At the word ' go,' mount, and
bring each stone severally and drop it into bucket.

CHAPTER X

I.—THE NORTHERN RIDGES

BETWEEN the Battle of Arras in the Spring and the Battle of Cambrai in the Autumn came the Third Battle of Ypres in the Summer. This middle battle in time (with which, in the history of the West Riding, we shall not be much concerned) was the northernmost battle in space, and its success, if it had been fully successful, would have been amphibious in kind. It would have rendered untenable by Germany the sea-bases of her submarine campaign, thus relieving the food-problem for the Allies, and it would have removed the military peril, fought out to a standstill in 1915, which threatened Paris and the Channel ports. On this account, as we saw in the last Chapter, the northernmost battle of the three was originally the chief in significance according to Sir Douglas Haig's plans. If we may regard the long Allied line, say, from Reims to the sea, throughout, and even beyond, the fighting season of 1917, as the scene of a single battle, we must add that the course of that battle did not follow Sir Douglas Haig's wishes. We read above of a 'revised' scheme, of 'restricted' preparations for the attack in Flanders, and we infer (indeed, we are informed) that, if Haig had been in sole Command of the Allied Forces on the Western front, he would have disposed the programme a little differently. Happily, it is not our business to judge the strategy of the war. Our task is to narrate the part which was played by a few thousand Yorkshiremen in bringing the war to a victorious close. Strategy was not in their contract : the Colonel obeyed his Brigadier, the General his Corps Commander ; and even in a larger sphere, Sir Douglas Haig was less than supreme. In the triple battle of 1917 many factors entered into account. To burn out the submarine nests, to countervail Italy's fate of arms, to anticipate Russia's defection, to release French industry and railways : these were a few of the considerations which affected the movements of the Allied Armies between Verdun and Ypres, the two flagstaffs of French and British ardour. That they were, primarily, political considerations does not mean that they were wrongly brought into account. Always the strategical initiative, as distinct from the tactical, lies partly outside the control of the fighting men. But there was worse than this in the series of conditions which determined the fighting of 1917. The sequence of battle-areas (Arras, Ypres, Cambrai) might be dictated by causes which prevailed over the best-laid plans ; the course of the battles themselves, especially of the Summer-battle about Ypres, was dictated by less calculable chances. Among these were the 'pill-boxes' and the mud, the solid and the fluid conditions. When to break off that last battle was almost more difficult a problem than when to engage it ; and if its commencement was postponed by causes outside Haig's control, we can read between the lines of his Fourth Dispatch the hesitation with which he carried it on :

> 'After weighing these considerations, as well as the general situation and various other factors affecting the problem, among them the desirability of assisting our Allies in the operations to be carried out by them on the 23rd October in the neighbourhood of Malmaison, I decided to continue the offensive further
>
> . . .
>
> 'Though the condition of the ground continued to deteriorate, the weather after this was unsettled rather than persistently wet, and progress had not become impossible.   I accordingly decided to press on while circumstances still permitted . . .
>
> 'By this time the persistent continuation of wet weather had left no further room for hope . . .'[1]

it would be unnecessary to complete this final sentence, except that it closes with the definite statement, that, 'in view of other projects which I had in view, it was desirable to maintain pressure on the Flanders front for a few weeks longer.'   Once more, we are not required to judge, but, at least, we may note the implication that, even when there was 'no further room for hope' (surely, a grave obstacle to progress) it was still necessary to 'maintain pressure for a few weeks longer.'

The West Yorkshire troops did not come in till close to the end of this middle battle, and we shall presently be more fully concerned with the 'other projects' elsewhere.   But we can imagine what it meant to those spent and battle-weary soldiers to 'maintain pressure' beyond the hope of progress.   'Physical exhaustion,' we read, 'placed narrow limits on the depth to which each advance could be pushed' ; and how far those limits should be forced was a matter of very difficult discretion.   'Time after time,' runs the Despatch, 'the practically beaten enemy was enabled to re-organize and relieve his men, and to bring up reinforcements behind the sea of mud which constituted his main protection' ; and at what point a 'practically beaten' enemy should be left behind his barrier of mud was, again, very hard to decide. Hard and difficult decisions for the High Command ; but the hardship and the difficulty of the fighting fell heavily on the fighting men, and the Summer-battle of 1917, which was prolonged far beyond the Summer, entailed, as Sir Douglas Haig tells us, ' almost superhuman exertions on the part of the troops of all arms and services.'[2]   The great Commander chose his word well.   If the triple battle of 1917 were to be fought out again, with all the conditions constant except

---

[1] *Despatches*, pages 127, 129, 130.   In a footnote to the first passage (page 127) F.M. Earl Haig has amplified the causes which led to the continuing of the Ypres offensive by a summary of a speech delivered in the House of Commons (August 6th, 1919) by Major-General Sir John Davidson, M.P.

[2] *Ibid.*, page 133.

those which strategists could vary, there would be, conceivably, a new time-table and a new distribution of effort at Arras, Passchendaele and Cambrai : there would still be the 'superhuman' effort to overcome the German advantage of irregular, murderous blockhouses, like Martello-towers sunk in a sea of mud, and of not less irregular rain.

We come to closer quarters with this middle battle.   It opened on June 7th with an explosion of nineteen mines, which caused enormous rents in the enemy front-line trenches, and which effectively assisted the Artillery and the Air Force in their preparations for the Infantry advance.   Impressive from a spectacular point of view, it was no sudden thing, this explosion.   It represented many months of patient labour by highly-skilled miners and engineers, the memory of whose devotion to duty, under conditions of constant horror, should help, in industrial times, to soften acerbities at home.   It was, further, the great surprise of the attack.   British enterprise had to burrow underground in order to escape the observation of an enemy, who, since 1915, when the Ypres salient was inevitably contracted,[1] had occupied all the commanding ground in a stretch of country where 60 feet was the measure of a mountain.   Messines, Wytschaete and Oostaverne were all captured on that first day (June 7th), together with more than 7,000 prisoners and 450 pieces of Artillery.   General Sir Herbert Plumer and the Second Army, who had acted as wardens of these marches through so many weary and exacting months, reaped a swift reward in the second week of June.

Unfortunately, it did not end as it began.   The obliteration of two Battalions on the Yser between Nieuport and the sea on July 10th belongs to the history of the Northamptons and the King's Royal Rifles, whose heroic defence of a position cut off from succour or support is Homeric in its quality.[2]   Canadian historians will tell the tale of the capture of Hill 70 from the Prussian Guard, and of the long struggles in the outskirts of Lens.   The season was still young, however ; the initial operations had been successful, and the results achieved in June encouraged Sir Douglas Haig to extend the area of his attack right along the ridges and their spurs from Messines to Houlthulst Forest.   These movements started on the last day of July, with the Fifth Army under General Sir Hubert Gough and the Second under General Sir Herbert Plumer.

Slowly, resolutely, painfully, a way was forced up the difficult slopes.   After twenty days a big advance could be recorded, but the going had been hard and expensive, and already the pace began to tell. The halt called in mid-August by exhaustion was employed for further preparation, and a month later, when the full attack was re-commenced, the highest points were still in enemy hands.   It was now the middle of September : battle had been joined in the first week of June, but

[1] See page 48, above.

[2] ' Any port except Nieuport ' became a catchword.

Glencorse Wood and Inverness Copse and a series of minor positions had still to be won, in order to render Passchendaele untenable and so to complete the capture of the ridges.   The programme, we see, was out of gear ; the price paid was out of proportion to the gains.   The battle-fury surged up and down in gusts and lulls, and ebb and flow, shaped less to a regular advance than to a series of shocks and with-drawals, with the battle-mark always a little higher, but, behind it, in an ascending scale, loss of life, and devastated country, rain and ruin, and desperate endeavour.   Was it worth while ? was one urgent question.   How long could it be kept up ? was another.

Every Battalion of the 49th Division was engaged : the West Ridings, the King's Own Yorkshire Light Infantry, the York and Lancasters, and the West Yorkshires, and at last they reached the top of the main ridge.   The date was October 9th-10th, and the 49th was moved to the attack with the 66th Division on their right and the 48th on their left.   The St. Julien road lay behind them, Passchendaele was a mile or two ahead.   Three stout Infantry Brigades, eager to crown the Summer's struggle, took part in the front of the operation : the 146th in the centre, the 148th on the right, and the 144th (48th Division) on the left.   The 147th was the Reserve Brigade.   The centre Battalion of the centre Brigade was the 1/7th West Yorkshires ; they found the 1/5th of the same Regiment on their right, and the 1/8th on their left : the 1/6th was their Reserve Battalion.   The heavy casualties in these two days' fighting made exact information hard to collect: in three Companies of the middle Battalion all the Officers and senior N.C.O.s had been permanently or temporarily disabled, and as early as 7-30 on the first morning (October 9th) the Reserve (147th) Brigade was ordered to be ready at an hour's notice.   In these circumstances, an hour to hour narrative could not be accurately com-piled.   The details were too much confused.   Touch was lost between Companies and between Battalions, and one Officer's summary of a part must stand for the record of the whole : 'The Brigade (the 146th) reached its first objective, but was unable to proceed further.'   Still, an advance was made on these two days, which count among the worst experiences on the Western front, and the Troops very thoroughly merited the congratulations of the Corps Commander, Sir Alexander Godley, on their achievement 'under the extremely adverse con-ditions.'

The congratulations were renewed a few days later (October 18th) when Major-General Perceval, C.B., took leave of the 49th Division, which, despite the 'adverse conditions' and the 'almost superhuman exertions,' which we have read of, he had commanded so gallantly and with so much hope.   We are told that, at the Brigade Parade, he appeared to feel the parting very keenly, and we know how warmly his regret was reciprocated by the whole Division.   He had succeeded to the Command in 1915, when General Baldock was injured by a shell,[1] and he had led the 49th Division in the Battles of the Ancre and the Somme, culminating in the capture of Thiepval, during 1916.[2]   He was succeeded now by Major-General Neville J. G. Cameron, C.B., C.M.G. (1916), of the Cameron Highlanders, who had served on the Nile and in South Africa, and whose proud privilege it became, as an Infantryman, to command a Territorial Infantry Division till the end of the war.

We return from this personal note, arising out of the change of Command, to the intense struggle outside Houthulst Forest.   It was renewed three times in October, a bloody October for the 49th Division, as for the British Army as a whole, and, at last, on the last day of that month, the British line had been carried, foot by foot, till within about 300 yards of the contested village of Passchendaele. One more week of effort was demanded of the Troops exhausted by four months' bloodshed, and the final assault was delivered on November 6th, when the village fell to the Canadians.   In the course of four days' further fighting the last crests of the ridges were secured, and the long Third Battle of Ypres was definitely terminated.

Who had won it ?   Counting July 31st as the first day of that phase of the Third Battle, it had cost the Germans over 24,000 prisoners. They had lost positions from Messines to Passchendaele, roughly, on a front of twelve miles, the value of which, small in area, had been recognized as cardinal in three great battles in three years.   Because they had lost the positions, we may conclude that they had lost the Third Battle, as they had lost the First (1914) and had been stalemated in the Second (1915).   But this conclusion does not contradict another, that Sir Douglas Haig had not won.   He had not won the victory which he sought.   If we compare the close with the opening of this long and brilliant Despatch ('the Campaigns of 1917'), we see clearly by how much he had contracted his original bold design, and how grievously his large hopes had been disappointed by extraneous events.   'The general conditions of the struggle this year,' he recorded, 'have been very different from those contemplated at the conference of Allied Commanders held in November, 1916.   The great general and simultaneous offensive then agreed on did not materialize.'   We turn back to the plans at that Conference, so far as the British Com-

---

[1] See page 59, above.

[2] A Special Order of October 19th contained the following message from the retiring General Officer Commanding :

'On giving up the Command of the Division which I have held since July, 1915, I wish to thank all ranks for their invariable loyal support, and to express my great admiration for their gallant conduct and for the cheerful manner in which they have borne the many hardships which they have had to endure.

'It will always be a special source of pleasure and pride to me that I was in Command of the Division in the recent action.   Nothing could be finer that what the Division accomplished on that occasion.   The performance of the Division will remain my chief interest in life, and I feel sure that, whenever opportunity offers, more fine records will be added to those already possessed.'

mander reveals them.[1]   They 'comprised a series of offensives on all fronts, so timed as to assist each other by depriving the enemy of power of weakening any one of his fronts in order to reinforce another.' The Arras battle was not to be pursued beyond its first objective : 'it was my intention to transfer my main offensive to another part of my front . . . I hoped, after completing my spring offensive further south, to be able to develop this Flanders attack without great delay, and to strike hard in the north before the enemy realized that the attack in the south would not be pressed further.'   But it 'did not materialize,' as has been said.   The task of the British and French Armies had proved far heavier than was originally anticipated, and, on the other hand, the enemy's means of resistance had proved 'far greater than either he or we could have expected.'   We shall see in a later chapter how these disappointments imposed a change from the offensive to the defensive in the renewed campaign of 1918.   Here we observe that, to this extent, the Summer battle of 1917, protracted almost too long for the endurance even of British soldiery, could not be counted victorious.   Nor was the final outlook better, when the results on a wider front were added to those of the Third Battle of Ypres. On no front had we suffered defeat ; on none, as German reports prove, was the enemy free from anxiety or confident of military success. But our great efforts were frustrated by outside causes : military opinion is hardening to the conviction that the Western battles of 1917 worked out, on a balance, to our disadvantage, and the dark shadow of the Russian Empire in solution fell across the concluding pages of the British Field Marshal's Fourth Despatch.

II.—BETWEEN THE BATTLES.

WHILE the 49th Division was struggling up the northern ridges, the 62nd was spending a brief and busy interval between the Battle of Arras in the Spring and the Battle of Cambrai in the Autumn.

Not an hour of that interval was wasted.   The noise of the guns was never ceasing ; and it is especially interesting to observe how admirably the Divisional Training, set on foot at once between the battles, fitted the daily calls which were to be made on all units of the Division.

But first, for the sake of its pleasant reading, and as a proof that merit found reward, take Lord Harewood's statement to the West Riding Association in October, 1917, of the Honours awarded to their Troops.   The 62nd had figured in an Honours List as early as the previous April, and there had been a good sprinkling from its units in June.   Now, every unit had been fighting, and every unit had won distinction.   Thus, we met Lieut.-Colonel Hastings at Bullecourt,

---

[1] Some revelations have been made from French documents, but in a limited history of Territorial troops it has not appeared necessary to discuss matters not bearing immediately on these operations.

and we read here of his well-merited D.S.O., and of as many as sixteen Military Medals awarded to gallant men in his Battalion. In point of fact, the Honours which were awarded were far fewer than the Honours which were deserved ; and, confining ourselves to figures only, since it is not seemly to select names[1], we observe that, out of fourteen Military Crosses which fell to the 62nd Division, four went to subaltern Officers in a single Battalion of the West Ridings. In the 49th Division, there were twenty-four awards of the Military Cross ; four men received Bars to their Military Medals ; and there were over a hundred fresh Military Medals and other decorations. Many mothers and maids in the West Riding had cause to be proud of their sons and lovers.

So much in this place for the past fighting.   Meanwhile, let us follow one unit of the 62nd to its interval of rest between the fights. Here, too, we need not particularize.   We noted at the end of the last chapter how quickly sport succeeded war, and in all units alike, at Achiet-le-Petit and elsewhere, the typical Battalion Sports Officer would 'get a move on' very quickly.   We may imagine the kind of man he was ; say, a subaltern Officer with a wound-stripe, perhaps recently rejoined, and wearing, no doubt, the ribbons of a Military Cross and a Croix-de-Guerre.   We may imagine, too, the shell-pocked field, which, in order to exercise his men, he would set himself to convert into a football ground, with its holes neatly patched and darned, and its goal posts and other appurtenances requisitioned as urgently as ammunition.   Or take the signal example of the great crater-coliseum,[2] on which a whole Battalion had been set at work, and which was ingeniously constructed to accommodate about two thousand spectators.   It was chiefly used for boxing contests, and the R.E. took a hand in erecting its 18-foot ring.   The next step was to find and train the teams, and special mention is due to the middle-weight champion of the 62nd Division, Company Sgt.-Major Schofield, D.C.M., of the 2/5th West Ridings, whose fight with Pte. Hayhurst, of the 2/6th Duke of Wellington's, filled the Coliseum one fine day. They were not too particular about the seasons.   When the weather was hot, they played cricket ; when it was not, they played football, and an inter-Brigade Summer football match resulted in the victory of a team composed of the R.E. and R.A.M.C. ; the 2/4th West Ridings being second, and the 2/5th West Ridings third.   Later, a Divisional Cup was competed for at Beaulencourt, and was won by the 2/5th West Ridings, who beat the R.E. and R.A.M.C. by the handsome score of six goals to one.

The old saying about the playing-fields at Eton and the Battle of Waterloo recurs to memory as we write.   The preparation for war in sport was illustrated again and again.   Three times in the course

---

[1] Complete lists will be found in Appendix II.
[2] See p. 136, above.

of this Summer, a certain Company out of a Battalion of the 62nd was stationed in a position known as the Apex, which had formed part of the Hindenburg Line, south-south-west of Riencourt. The first occasion was towards the end of June, and the Company Officers found cause to bless the foresight of the authorities who had organized so many forms of sport. Take their excellent shooting, for example. A party of the enemy, about six in number, had been observed on the sky-line walking in single file on the top of a communication-trench. The range was, approximately, 1,200 yards. Six men were sent out in a good lying position, and the sights were harmonized between 1,000 and 1,400 yards. After the third round, we are told, the enemy rapidly dispersed, and contracted their sphere of activity. Or, take the raid on the Apex on September 13th, which was shown by prisoners' testimony to have been carefully rehearsed by a considerable enemy force of Storm-Troops, Infantry, and others, under orders to destroy all dug-outs near the Apex and to inflict as much damage as possible on our garrison. The attack fell on the 2/6th West Yorkshires, and was very gallantly repulsed ; chiefly by the courage and determination of Captain G. C. Turner, who was killed, and of L.-Sergt. W. Pearson (No. 241038), who lived just long enough for General Braithwaite to recommend him for the award of the D.C.M. It was a typical ' No surrender' exploit, and merits special recognition. Or, another incident at the Apex back in August. On this occasion a private soldier distinguished himself, and was awarded the M.M., in a voluntary patrol to clear up an obscure position. In full day-light he went, unaccompanied, up a gulley some 35 to 40 yards, and located an enemy party. He reported the position to his Officer, who dealt with it successfully the same night by the aid of some rifle-grenadiers. It was the same private, by the way, the crack shot in his own crack company, who brought down some partridges in September, within a few yards of the enemy posts. Either for the game or for other causes, the men of this Company became so keen on patrol work at the Apex, that they petitioned for a double tour duty and stayed out eight consecutive nights. Insignificant details, perhaps, but good shooting and keen soldiership won the war ; and the Division thoroughly earned the compliments of the Commander-in-Chief and Army Commander on their exploits during this period, which showed ' skill and enterprise.'

They were as good at salving as at sniping. The tale is told of a Platoon near Bullecourt, which had become liable to a complaint that Salvage orders were being neglected. The complaint was quickly set to rights, and within a very short time a remarkable collection was accumulated outside Company Headquarters. A derelict Tank had been found hidden fast in high undergrowth, and as many as seven Lewis guns and some forty magazines in more or less bad condition were brought to join the Battalion dump. By the side of

L

another Tank the bodies were identified of four men of the Royal Warwicks, and, as the Yorkshiremen themselves had once been engaged in the same sector, they began an organized search, which resulted in at least forty casualties being transferred from 'missing' to 'killed.'

So, the pause between the battles were filled up. With raids and counter-raids, and martial exercises, and military sports, and play imitating work, the exhaustion after Bullecourt was repaired, and the spirit of Bullecourt was renewed. Field-work on the open fighting system completed the training at Beaulencourt where a move was made into hutments in October, and it is noted that the shooting was so much improved that one Platoon, at the end of its intensive practice, scored a total of 405 out of 450 points in a 'mad minute' competition. Early in November, a new Brigadier was appointed to the 186th Brigade in succession to Brig.-General Hill, whose gallantry and leadership had won him the affection of all ranks, when the limits of age compelled his retirement. The veteran's place was taken by a very junior Officer, R. B. Bradford, V.C., who fell in action at the end of the same month, and whose name may stand, on the eve of the Autumn fighting, to typify the *personnel* of the Division, certain units of which we have visited here and there in the training period between Arras and Cambrai. Roland Boys Bradford was born in 1892; he joined the Durham Light Infantry in 1912, and went out to the war two years afterwards. Thus, his chance came early in life, and he made the fullest use of every phase of it. His promotion was as rapid as his valour was remarkable. He won the M.C. and the V.C. (1916), and was several times mentioned in Despatches, and accounts agree that this youthful Brigadier, when he reached that military rank at the early age of twenty-five, was a soldier of very brilliant promise. He died young, according to civil standards, but he achieved a fine professional record under exacting conditions of active service; and General Braithwaite's 62nd Division was fortunate, in November, 1917, in possessing, on the Cambrai front, Brigadiers so thoroughly conversant with their duties and so fully qualified to lead their men as General Viscount Hampden, commanding the 185th, General Taylor, commanding the 187th, and General Bradford, commanding the 186th, whose swift death is the just pretext for this brief excursus.

III.—THE BATTLE OF CAMBRAI (FIRST PHASE)

We reach now the final stage of the campaign, which had been planned with such hopeful anticipations at the November conference just a year before.

There are several ways of regarding the Battle of Cambrai. We may look at it through big, strategic spectacles, as a means, opportune, but timely, of engaging and distracting German Forces which might otherwise have been sent to Italy. This view is not without authority, and it is stated with his usual lucidity by Mr. Buchan in his popular narrative :

> ' Italy, fighting desparately on the Piave, deserved by all the laws of war some relief in the shape of an Allied diversion.   Weary as his troops might be, Sir Douglas Haig was not able to grant them the rest which they had earned and most urgently required.'[1]

It is not within our province to strike a balance between this assumption of 'all the laws of war' and the degree of weariness of Sir Douglas Haig's troops.

Again, we may look at this battle through the narrower spectacles of a tactician.   It was designed in the nature of a surprise.   It was unexpected in time and place, and it brought into operation a new weapon in the form of a mass attack of Tanks in lieu of Artillery preparation,   In this aspect the Battle was victorious : it evoked von der Marwitz's Order to the German Second Army (November 29th) :

> 'The English, by throwing into the fight countless Tanks on November 20th, *gained a victory* near Cambrai.   Their intention was to break through ; but they did not succeed, thanks to the brilliant resistance of our troops.   We are now going to turn their embryonic victory into a defeat by an encircling counter-attack.   The Fatherland is watching you, and expects every man to do his duty.'

Once more, we shall not attempt to strike a balance.   We gained a victory, according to this Order, but it was embryonic and not a success. At the same time, we know that things were serious when the Fatherland was said to be watching.

A third way of looking at this battle, and the way best suited to our present purpose, is to regard it as a very gallant enterprise, worthy of the finest traditions of the British Army, and not less worthy because a large part of its hardest demands fell on Territorial Troops.   They might muffle the joy-bells in England when the full story of the battle was revealed, but at least they had rung them spontaneously in recognition of a brilliant feat of arms, and the bells still peal in celebration of the dash and heroism of British soldiers.

We turn back for a moment to the sketch on page 116, especially to A B C, the road from Albert through Bapaume to Cambrai.   The British line has swallowed up the eleven miles (A B), where the fighting was so intense in 1916, and it struck now (November 20th) across that road at a point just east of Boursies, about half-way between Bapaume and Cambrai.   Thence it forged right into the triangle, of which Arras is the apex, leaving Quéant in German occupation on the east, and Bullecourt in British on the west, to the northerly country where we have been adjourning.   Turning next to the position before us, we see what advantage would accrue from a deeper bite

[1] *History of the War*, Nelson, Vol. XXI., page 94.

on the same road. Not primarily to capture Cambrai, though this, too, might enter calculation, but to roll up the British forces from below the road in such a way as to threaten Cambrai and to disturb the German Winter dispositions, was a hazard worth the stake in late November. Roughly, the scheme of the attack was to push out between Boursies and Gonnelieu in a north north-easterly direction, lapping up the strong positions like a flame, and to spread in a converging semi-circle up to the main road (Bapaume-Cambrai) and beyond.

The troops at Sir Julian Byng's disposal [1] were, first, a fleet of four hundred Tanks, commanded by General Hugh Elles ; next, the following six Infantry Divisions : the 36th (Ulster), 62nd (West Riding), 51st (Highland), the 6th, 20th and 12th ; next, four Cavalry Divisions ; and, finally, three more Infantry Divisions (3rd, 16th and 29th), of which the 29th, of Gallipoli fame, was actively engaged. It will be seen that the 62nd had a place of honour in the attack, and it was allotted the task of capturing Havrincourt, the strong point of the enemy's line. This task required all the powers the Troops could bring : unfaltering leadership, indomitable mettle, and untiring endurance. The methods and needs of the attack had been the subject of constant discussion since the original scheme of operations had been laid before Divisional Commanders at a conference on October 31st. The 51st and 62nd Divisions had been trained close to one another in order to facilitate co-operation, and the preparation of Artillery positions, begun on November 4th, was carried out night and day till the 19th. No detail was too small to engage the personal attention of the Officers in charge of the operation, various features of which were modified from day to day in accordance with practical experience.

On the night of November 17th-18th, the two leading Brigades of the 62nd Division took up their battle front ; the 185th on the right, and the 187th on the left. Detachments of the 36th Division were kept in the out-post line, so as to avoid any chance of the enemy spotting the relief ; and, though he rushed one of these posts, and captured two men of the 36th, he was not made aware of the date or time of the attack, or of the fact that Tanks were to be used. These lumbered off from the advanced Tankodrome at the south-west corner of Havrincourt Wood, and reached their lying-up places by midnight on Y Z night, November 19th-20th. The pace of the Tanks was calculated, after practical experience, at a hundred yards in five minutes, and the Artillery barrage and Infantry advance were regulated accordingly. The two leading Infantry Brigades were to attack on a two-Battalion front, preceded by twenty-two Tanks. The remaining two Battalions

[1] Lt.-General the Hon. Sir Julian Byng, G.C.B. (1919), K.C.M.G., Commanding the Third Army since June, 1917, when he succeeded General (Lord) Allenby, transferred to Palestine ; created Baron Byng of Vimy, 1919.

of each Brigade, preceded by eight Tanks, were to leap-frog through the leading Battalions, picking up all surviving Tanks on their way.

Second only, if second, to the Tanks in novelty and effectiveness was the new, great weapon of surprise, perfected by the lessons of a hundred mistakes. We may quote the evidence of a contemporary Battalion diarist, who ascribed the initial success, first, to the Tanks ('these dealt extremely effectively with the enemy wire, which was very formidable in places'), and, secondly, to secrecy ('even in the marches up to the line the destination of the Battalion for that night was not made known to anybody below the rank of an Officer. That this policy paid well may be judged from the fact that the enemy was obviously taken completely by surprise'). This record, taken from the account of the 2/4th York and Lancasters, is repeated in almost every diary. In order to keep the secret, very elaborate precautions had been taken. Aerial photographers were deceived by marches on the off-side of roads. Lorries going northward carried lights, lorries going southward carried none. No fires were allowed. There was no preliminary bombardment, and, as indicated above, no one in the Division knew the destination of the Division. Zero hour on November 20th was 6-20 a.m., and at 6-20, on that foggy morning, the first intimation to the Germans of the 62nd Division's attack was the sight of a sheet of flame from every gun, and of heavy Tanks looming through the mist. No wonder, that the first bound of the eager Infantry started with conspicuous success, and was attended by comparatively few casualties.

That first bound of the Infantry was to carry them to Havrincourt and Flesquières, and Havrincourt, as we saw, was to be the prize of General Braithwaite's Troops. We shall come to the fighting in a moment. Here let us straightway say that the Division acquitted itself brilliantly. Sir Douglas Haig, in his Despatch, expressly used this rare epithet. 'The 62nd (West Riding) Division (T.), (Major-General W. P. Braithwaite),' he wrote, 'stormed Havrincourt, where . . . . parties of the enemy held out for a time,' and 'operating northwards from Havrincourt, made important progress. Having carried the Hindenburg Reserve Line north of that village, it rapidly continued its attack, and captured Graincourt, where two anti-Tank guns were destroyed by the Tanks accompanying our Infantry. Before nightfall, Infantry and Cavalry had entered Anneux, though the enemy's resistance in this village does not appear to have been entirely overcome till the following morning' (November 21st). 'This attack of the 62nd Division,' added the great Field Marshal, 'constitutes a *brilliant achievement* in which the troops concerned completed an advance of four and a half miles from their original front, over-running two German systems of defence, and gaining possession of three villages.'[1]

[1] *Despatches*, pages 155, 156.

As a fact, their advance on that day, the third Tuesday in November, covered a distance further in actual mileage than any other of Sir Julian Byng's Divisions ; further, indeed, than any Division of the British Army had advanced in one day under like conditions since war was engaged in the Western Front.   Starting from a point just below the big bend of the Canal du Nord, they took Havrincourt by assault (which meant, among other factors, (1) secrecy, (2) Tanks and, as we show below, (3) Infantry-rush) pushed straight forward to Graincourt, and reached and occupied Anneux, at the edge of our B C road, and opposite the south side of Bourlon Wood : over 7,000 yards, as a crow flies, and a wholly exceptional day's march for soldiers fighting every foothold.

We have drawn attention to the secrecy and the Tanks.   'The measure of further success,' so ran an order of the day, 'is entirely dependent on the speed with which the operation is carried out.   Every minute is of importance. . .   Once the enemy is on the run, every man must put forth his utmost efforts to press on and to prevent his rallying.'   Here, again, the 7,000 yards of the 62nd Division bear witness to exemplary team-work in training for this Infantry-rush both in the period of Divisional rest and of intensive preparation. One more detail may be set down in this place.   At the Dinner of the 62nd Division, held at Leeds on September 9th, 1919, when Major-General Sir James K. Trotter took the Chair, General Braithwaite, on leave from his Command in Cologne, announced that a site for a Divisional Battle Memorial had been sought and courteously granted in Havrincourt Park—an announcement which, as we shall see, derived additional force and appropriateness from the further record of the Division at Havrincourt in the victorious advance of 1918.

Meanwhile, still on that first day, when the Tanks went crashing through the fog, the Highlanders (51st Division) were repeating against Flesquières on the right, the 'bound' of the 62nd against Havrincourt.   Its capture was reported about 11 a.m., but two hours later authentic news arrived, that, though the troops were holding the front trench of the Hindenburg Support Line in front of the village, machine-gun and rifle fire had broken the assault ; a large number of Tanks had been put out of action ; the Support Line and Flesquières itself were still in enemy hands.   This retardation of the programme affected immediately the advance of the 186th Infantry Brigade (Graincourt).   Its right wing was dangerously exposed ; and the two Field Artillery Brigades to the east of Havrincourt, deprived of the hope of Cavalry assistance, were also left hanging.   Still, the Infantry pressed on.   The results achieved were too good and too promising to be sacrificed to a risk which might eventuate either way, and it would at least be practicable to call a halt on the Graincourt-Cambrai road till the position at Flesquières was clearer.   This plan was exactly carried out, and shortly after 5-30 that afternoon the

HAVRINCOURT: CANAL DU NORD BRIDGE.

HAVRINCOURT: IN THE PARK.

[Face p. 150.

186th Brigade had captured Graincourt, and was resting (or at any rate not advancing from) a line north of the Cambrai road.

We shall come back to the epic battle of November 20th. Passing now to November 21st, the objective of the Division on the second day was the high ground west of Bourlon and Bourlon Wood. The gallant 186th Brigade was entrusted with this attack, and all available surviving Tanks were put at their disposal. One Regiment of Cavalry was attached to the Division, and Zero hour was fixed at 10-0 a.m. It had been hoped to push forward the Artillery during the night of 20th-21st, but the rain which had been falling since the afternoon interfered with this programme. However, despite the opposing mud, all four Artillery Brigades were in action between Havrincourt and Graincourt early in the afternoon of the 21st. The night of the 20th had passed quietly. About 8 o'clock the next morning, the 51st (Highland) Division had completed their capture of Flesquières, and were advancing on to the Marcoing-Graincourt Road. Prisoners' tales reported that Bourlon Wood (the 62nd's objective) was held by the 32nd and 224th Brandenburghers, indicating that a Reserve Division had been brought up by the enemy. It was time to get on, and punctually at Zero-hour the 186th Infantry Brigade, with the 185th in close support and the 187th in reserve, were started on their way, while the Artillery bombarded Bourlon village and put a smoke barrage on Tadpole Copse. Eighteen Tanks in all was the number of available survivors, but, owing to trouble with petrol-supply, etc., not all of these were ready to time, and some delay ensued in the execution of the operation.

Before estimating the results of the severe fighting in which the Brigade was involved, one or two facts may be stated as to the participation of some of its units.

The 2/4th West Ridings were detailed to capture Anneux and Anneux Chapel. The village, though strongly held by Infantry and Machine-Guns, duly fell to their splendid efforts, but further advance was stopped at the edge of Bourlon Wood. The Company detailed to take the Chapel performed skilful work with heavy casualties, and, after making good their advance to the edge of the wood, and capturing at least 300 prisoners, were withdrawn shortly before dark to the sunken road.

The 2/5th and the 2/7th West Ridings were badly handicapped for lack of Tanks. Instead of the frontal attack which had been intended, the uncut wire compelled them to have recourse to an attack by bombs, with consequent loss of impetus. A single Tank, which arrived in the afternoon, was utilized to the utmost of its capacity. The 2/6th Battalion, which was to have been kept in Brigade reserve, and to have been used for the capture of Bourlon Village as soon as the leading Battalions had reached their objectives, had to be employed to reinforce the assault and to fill up gaps in the line. Similarly, the Cavalry were dismounted in the later hours of the afternoon, and helped to complete the line held in front of Anneux by the 2/4th West Ridings.

Though Moeuvres and Anneux (inclusive) had been captured, and were held, it was evident that Bourlon Village would not be taken that day. Orders were issued, accordingly, to relieve the 186th Infantry Brigade in their present positions, and their relief by the 185th was duly carried out that evening.

The general situation on the night of November 21st was somewhat vague, and next day, though the Division was to have been relieved during the night of the 21st/22nd by the 40th Division, it was decided to make one more effort to capture the ridge west of Bourlon Wood, which overlooked all the ground west and south of Graincourt. They tried, and struggled, and tried again, but, despite much desperate fighting, no capture ensued, and, owing to the enemy's counter-attack and the consequent disorganization, the attempt had to be abandoned. On the same day, the 51st Division took and lost Fontaine. In the night, the relief of the 62nd was duly effected by the 40th.

We break off here for a moment to set down one or two of the gallant deeds which were done in the three days' battle. And, first, we should quote in full the special Order of the Day, which General Braithwaite, Commanding the Division, published on November 24th, the first full day of the relief. The Divisional Commander, it stands written,

'has the honour to announce that the Commander-in-Chief and the Army Commander have expressed their high appreciation of the achievement of the 62nd Division in the battle.

'The Divisional Commander had the most implicit confidence that the Division would acquit itself with honour.

'To have advanced 7,000 yards on the first day, taken all objectives, held them against counter-attacks and handed over all gains intact to the relieving Division is a feat of arms of which any Division may be justly proud.

'The number of prisoners taken is not far short of 2,000. Thirty-seven guns have been captured, which include two 8-inch Howitzers, one complete Battery of 4·2, one complete Battery of 5·9, and the remainder, guns of various calibres, many of which were brought into action against the enemy.

'The number of Machine-Guns, Granatenwefer, etc., etc., which have fallen into our possession is so considerable that it has not been possible yet to make an accurate tally of them.

'The advance of the Artillery to Graincourt, and the accuracy of the barrage, is worthy of the best traditions of the Royal Regiment. To C Battalion, the Tanks, all ranks of the Division express their admiration of the skill, bravery and the splendid self-sacrifice which made success possible.

'The discipline, valour and steadiness of all ranks has been beyond praise.

'It is with great and legitimate pride that I have the honour to sign my name as Commander of the 62nd (West Riding) Division.'

November 24th, 1917—the years that have elapsed and that will elapse since General Braithwaite signed this Order cannot diminish its praise. The glowing words breathe and live ; they survive the *neiges d'antan* which cover his gallant men's graves between the Bapaume road and the Canal de l'Escaut.

Here, too, is the place to mention the visit on November 22nd of Sir Douglas Haig himself to the Headquarters of the 62nd Division (a visit preceded the day before by the dispatch of an A.D.C. by the Commander-in-Chief), in order personally to congratulate General Braithwaite, and to tell him to let the Division know how splendidly, in his opinion, they had acquitted themselves.

Or take the record here and there (it can be but a casual selection) of the acts which won these praises in the three days' battle which we are reviewing. It was at the very beginning of the battle, early in the morning of November 20th, that the 2/5th Battalion of the West Riding Regiment, going forward in column of route to try to get through the gaps in the wire in front of Havrincourt, lost Lt.-Col. T. A. D. Best, D.S.O., their Commanding Officer, described by the General at his graveside as 'one of the finest soldiers and the most perfect gentlemen he had had under his command.'

The same Battalion, if we may follow it a little further, continued its advance on the first day to a point on the further (north) side of the Bapaume-Cambrai road, where it succeeded in establishing touch with the 36th Division on the Canal bank. This attack was a 'record at the time for depth in one day's advance, the Battalion going about 7,000 yards from the old British Front Line to the final objective for the day.' Its captures for the day included more than 350 prisoners, fifteen Machine-Guns and a Trench Mortar, and the total casualties in the Battalion were three Officers and ten other Ranks killed, one Officer and fifty-five other Ranks wounded, and four men missing. Its honours included two appointments to the Distinguished Service Order, in the persons of Captains Goodall and C. S. Moxon ; and next day, November 21st, when Major F. Brook was appointed by the G.O.C. to the Command of the Battalion, in consideration of his gallant conduct and brilliant leading after the death of Colonel Best, Captain (Temporary Major) Goodall, Senior Company Commander, became second in command.

Records similar to the above might be lifted out of the Diary of each and every Battalion engaged on those days. Our selection of a single example will have sufficed to typify the spirit which animated all units in all ranks ; and when we turn from the exploits of a Battalion to the exploits of individuals, the same tale of courage is repeated.

Take, for instance, the following record of an exploit by two young Officers : it is regarded by the Divisional Commander as one of the most remarkable during the battle.   In the 187th Brigade, the G.O.C., Brigadier-General Taylor, in his determination to be prepared for all eventualities, had impressed upon his Officers the necessity of pushing forward at Zero hour, whether or not the Tanks had arrived.   This meant that the Infantry must know their way, and, consequently, during Y Z night, two Officers of the 2/5th King's Own Yorkshire Light Infantry crept out between midnight and dawn to reconnoitre the route.   They actually succeeded in creeping up to the enemy's wire, and marked out the route which they would have to follow, if the Tanks were late the next morning, by placing tapes to guide them.   It was well that they did so, for the unexpected happened.   The Tanks, which were to lead the Battalion, were delayed ; and it was due to the initiative and enterprise of these two gallant Officers,[1] that the Battalion was able to start without the advance-guard of Tanks, and to march straight to their first objective, which they captured at the point of the bayonet.

Take, again, seven exploits in the ranks, each of which won a Military Medal.   We select them as typical acts, in the various arms of the Service ; and, though the extracts from the records are accurate, we shall not identify them by names, since many pages of this narrative could be filled with similar accounts.   In each instance, the date of the exploit is November 20th or 21st, and they all redound to the credit of the 62nd Division.

(1) A Private displayed great courage and devotion to duty during the attack on the Hindenburg Support system near Graincourt.   He acted as runner, and was on duty two days and one night with his Company, often taking messages under machine-gun fire to Platoons on the Front Line, thereby keeping his Company Commander in constant touch with what was happening.

(2) A Private displayed great bravery and resolution whilst acting as Company runner during the operations near the Hindenburg Support Line.   Throughout the day, under heavy fire, he continued to carry messages to and from Battalion Head Quarters and Companies on the flanks.   He set a fine example of devotion to duty and showed a complete disregard for his own safety.

(3) A Private displayed his bravery and coolness during the attack on the Hindenburg Support Line, north of the Cambrai road.   When his Company was temporarily held up by machine-gun fire from the Front, and its flank was threatened by a strong

---

[1] Captain Lynn and 2nd Lieut. James.   We mention their names *honoris causa*.   They were the first men in the enemy's trenches that morning.

enemy bombing party, this man took up a position in the open, in front of the German wire, and continued, under heavy fire, firing off rifle-grenades until incapacitated by wounds. His gallant action frustrated the attempt to turn the flank of his Company.

(4) A total disregard to danger and devotion to duty was shown by a Private, while acting as Stretcher-Bearer during the attack on the Hindenburg Support system near Graincourt. He dressed wounds and got back casualties during the whole day under machine-gun fire, and went out alone next day and brought in a badly wounded man from the front of the forward line, thereby undoubtedly saving a life.

(5) A Non-Commissioned Officer showed great bravery and initiative during the attack on the Hindenburg Support Line. When the Company was temporarily held up by enemy machine-gun fire both flanks, he took out a Lewis-gun to the left flank of the Company, and, though under continuous and heavy fire, engaged the enemy machine-gun with direct fire, and thus enabled the Company to advance.

(6) A Non-Commissioned Officer displayed courage and initiative during the attacks between Anneux and Bourlon Wood. He was in charge of a Lewis-gun team on the right flank of his Company. Heavy casualties were being caused by a party of the enemy firing from the direction of Anneux. Without waiting for orders, the N.C.O. crept forward under rifle and machine-gun fire to a commanding position, and opened fire with his Lewis gun on the enemy, killing several and dispersing the rest of the party.

(7) A Non-Commissioned Officer displayed conspicuous bravery during the attack on the Hindenburg Support Line and Hughes Switch. A hostile Trench Mortar was in action from a point slightly in advance of Hughes Switch. This N.C.O. rushed forward and bayoneted the men in charge of the Trench Mortar, and took prisoners an officer and eight men who emerged from a dug-out close at hand.

These seven examples, casually selected from the records of fighting in the opening phase of the Battle of Cambrai, illustrate what General Braithwaite meant when he wrote (November 24th) of his 'implicit confidence' in the Division. They illustrate, too, what Sir Douglas Haig meant when he wrote that it was 'reasonable to hope' that his operations at Cambrai would be successful. For success and confidence in war depend in the ultimate resort on how the soldier obeys orders. The runner who takes messages under fire is an essential link between his Company Commander and Divisional and Army Headquarters. The man who frustrates a turning movement, or who enables his Company to advance, helps directly to bring the issue into accordance with the plan of operation, and, in this regard, these few typical examples are worth more than a chapter of battle stories, as the spirit is worth more than the letter.

IV.—BATTLE OF CAMBRAI (SECOND PHASE).

WE turn back at this point to the main narrative.

The 62nd Division, as we saw, was withdrawn during the night of 22nd/23rd November, and was relieved by the 40th. This relief proved of short duration. November 24th, the day of the Special Order, was spent in necessary re-organization, but shortly before midnight on that day, after barely thirty-six hours' pause, Corps orders were received, that the 62nd were to relieve the 40th during the following evening.

We have the advantage of an impression of that day (November 24th, 1917)—an impression from without, as it were—from the private diary of Major-General the Earl of Scarbrough, at that time, it will be remembered, Director-General of the Territorial and Volunteer Forces, and still Chairman of the West Riding Territorial Force Association. In the company of General Mends and Captain Atkinson-Clark, the Director-General was paying a visit to his County Divisions at the Front. He had lunched on the 23rd at Ypres, with Major-General Cameron, Commanding the 49th Division, in a dug-out just inside the walls. The Division were then in the line, with one Brigade (the West Yorkshires) in reserve, and Lord Scarbrough had visited their camp, and seen their Commanding Officers, who were 'living in a sea of mud.' At 8 a.m. on Saturday, the 24th, the visitors left the Second Army, travelled by motor-car through Bapaume, and, passing over a part of the Somme battlefield, where 'every village had been shelled out of existence,' reached the operation area of the Third Army. Thus, the Chairman and other Officers of the Association enjoyed the unique experience of taking lunch with Major-General Braithwaite, Commanding the 62nd Division, on the day following their visit to the Headquarters of the 49th. Lord Scarbrough notes that the G.O.C. was 'immensely pleased' with the work of his Division, and that Sir Douglas Haig had visited the General and thanked him for their 'remarkable success.' Though the Division only came out the day before, after three heavy days' fighting, and were naturally 'dog-tired,' they had just been called upon to be ready to send a Brigade back into the line at half-an-hour's notice. The enemy had begun a heavy counter-attack on Bourlon Wood, 'which was the key of his position, and which dominated the Bapaume-Cambrai Road, the main road of supply for his troops in the line further north.' The 40th Division, the visitors heard, were reported to be having a bad time, as the German Artillery had been reinforced, and a Division brought from the Russian front had been thrown into the line. These notes, written at the time, are exactly confirmed by the records prepared more carefully later on when all the available facts had been ascertained.

If we look at a map once more, we observe that the wider swing-round on the eastern portion of the Bapaume-Cambrai Road had been held up at Crèvecoeur and Rumilly. The consequence was (the causes were uncontrollable, and concern the historian of other Divisions) to increase the German pressure on Bourlon Wood and on the village beyond. The 40th Division had attacked and captured the greater part of these positions during November 23rd, but by reinforcements and counter-attacks the enemy had succeeded in reversing these successes. Orders were issued, accordingly, for the 62nd Division, less the Artillery and R.E., to relieve the 40th Division, less the Artillery, R.E., and Pioneer Battalion, in the Bourlon Section of the line, with the 186th Infantry Brigade on the right, the 187th on the left and the 185th in Divisional Reserve ; the Headquarters of the two leading Brigades being located at Graincourt. The relief was carried out without incident, except for a considerable amount of shelling, which caused some casualties in the 186th Brigade. Next day (November 26th) there was a Corps Conference at Divisional Headquarters, where, after long discussion, it was decided that the Guards and the 62nd should attack the following morning with the assistance of Tanks, in order to capture Fontaine and the remainder of Bourlon Wood and Village. The night of the 26th was very cold, with a blizzard blowing of snow and sleet. Zero-hour next morning was fixed for 6-20 a.m. The Tanks, of which 20 were available (16 being allotted to the 187th Infantry Brigade for the capture of Bourlon Village), reached their rendezvous punctually at 2 a.m., and the Infantry were all in position fifty minutes before Zero-hour. A projected bombardment of the village during the day of the 26th was not proceeded with, since three Companies of the Highland Light Infantry (40th Division) were missing, and it was thought that they might still be holding out in Bourlon. Coming now to Zero-hour on the 27th, and observing that, about 10 a.m., Brigadier-General Taylor, Commanding the 187th Brigade, reported that his attack had been unsuccessful and that his troops, which had entered Bourlon, had been compelled under heavy fire to retire, we may enumerate at least four causes which contributed to this comparative failure. The first was darkness and mud : the men, and their rifles and Lewis guns, were covered with mud from the start, and every man in the Brigade was chilled by his long exposure to the driving snow. Secondly, there were strong points south of Bourlon, which, owing to heavy machine-gun fire, had not been dealt with by the Tanks. Thirdly, the village barricades likewise opposed the Tank advance ; and, fourthly, in and beyond Bourlon, the enemy were able to bring to bear very effective machine-gun fire. Or we may quote, in illustration of these obstacles, the experience of a Company Officer, from Zero-hour 6-20 a.m., to the time, a few hours later, when he, like so many others, became a casualty :

'Immediately on leaving the forming-up line,' he wrote, ' we came under very heavy machine-gun and rifle fire. We pressed on. The machine-gun fire became more intense, and the enemy shelling more severe. The casualties here amongst the Company were very heavy indeed. Despite this, the Company, with dauntless courage, still pressed on, but my casualties were appalling, and further progress became impossible.'

It was about this time (say 10 a.m.) that the 185th Infantry Brigade were ordered to place another Battalion at the disposal of the 187th. Meanwhile, frequent reports of hard fighting on the front of the 186th Infantry Brigade had been received, and now they sent a message to say, that, though their troops had all reached Bourlon Wood, the left Battalion of the Guards had been driven back to its original line. At noon it became evident that the advance of this Brigade had left both flanks dangerously exposed. Partly in order to meet this danger, the 185th Brigade (less one Battalion already sent forward), reinforced by a Battalion of the 2nd Cavalry Dismounted Brigade, were ordered to relieve the 187th, and to extend their line round the south edge of Bourlon Village, so as to keep in touch with the 186th ; and the 2nd Cavalry Dismounted Brigade (less its one Battalion) was ordered to keep itself in readiness to relieve the front Battalions of the 186th. The advance of this last-named Brigade was continued during the day, and they reached practically all their objectives and were consolidating in depth. By this time, however, they were very tired and were subject to heavy counter-attacks, and the full effect of the new dispositions were not felt in time to achieve their aim.

We need not follow this fighting further. During the night of November 28th/29th, the 62nd Division was relieved by the 47th. It moved back to Havrincourt for the night, and marched next day into the reserve area at Bertincourt and Lebucquière. Thenceforward, until the battle was broken off, except for intermittent shelling, the 62nd Division took no further active part in the operations. They had done extraordinarily well, and the fine fighting of the 187th Infantry Brigade in Bourlon Wood on November 27th stands out in the record of brilliance achieved by the 62nd Division during this week at Cambrai. We know what happened immediately afterwards : how the fighting odds proved too tremendous, and the great offensive ended with a retirement on December 4th to the 7th, back from Bourlon, back from Fontaine, back from Mesnières and the Bonavis Ridge, to points corresponding approximately to the line held on November 20th, with certain gains in the regions of Flesquières and Havrincourt, though a little closer to Gouzeaucourt in the South. It would be idle to mini- mize the disappointment at this result, especially when it was realized at home. In the larger issues of the war, the Battle of Cambrai takes a smaller place than it occupies in the records of the troops which took part in the fighing.   A victory had been gained by those troops which could not be turned to defeat, though the advance was turned to a retirement.   As a battle, it had been lost ; as an experiment, it had succeeded, though the measure of the success was laid up in the future. But the troops were competent to measure it.   Their military sense, developed by a year's continuous campaigning, seized the broad issues

of the experiment, and all ranks of the 62nd Division were filled with a just sense of elation.   Their allotted task had been performed with what Field-Marshal Lord Haig, in his foreword to this volume, describes as ' outstanding brilliance,' and a consciousness of this performance, however modestly concealed, was present to the minds of all who survived the battle.

The casualties had been severe. In the first phase (November 20th to 23rd), they amounted to 75 Officers and 1,613 other Ranks ; in the second phase (November 25th to 28th), to 79 Officers and 1,565 other Ranks.[1] The honours had been not few[2] ; but, apart from the measure of achievement which casualty and honours lists supply, we take count of the enhanced spirit of the Division, which, though it had 'found itself' before, may be said to have vindicated at Cambrai its title to a place in the front rank. The Divisional Pelican, as we see, was still waiting to put down his foot, but by fine team-work and fine individual work, the Division had proved its merit as a fighting force, and had won the rare praise of the Field-Marshal and the grateful thanks of the Divisional Commander. Viewed, too, in relation to earlier actions, the Cambrai battle, whatever its issue, is to be claimed as a conspicuous success. It first proved the efficacy of Tanks, and their power of timed co-operation with the Artillery and Infantry arms ; it first proved the value of secrecy as an essential factor of victory ; and the lessons learned at Cambrai incomparably modified the memory of past work at Bullecourt and Thiepval.

[1] We may note here that the ascertained casualties in the Territorial Troops of the West Riding up to December 31st, 1917, amounted to 44,049 all Ranks, included 406 Officers and 5,242 other Ranks killed.

[2] Details as complete as is practicable will be found in Appendix II. Here we select for mention a few particulars from the Divisional lists, completed to January, 1918. In the West Yorkshires, 62nd Division, for example, there were 19 awards to the 2/5th, 33 to the 2/6th, 30 to the 2/7th, and 28 to the 2/8th, headed in each instance by a D.S.O. (or a Bar to his D.S.O.) for the O.C. the Battalion. The four Battalions of the West Ridings in the 62nd carried off over 110 awards, including Col. Best's (killed) Bar to his D.S.O., three D.S.O.'s, and six M.C.'s. These items are typical of the Division.

BOOK III

WAR'S END

M

CHAPTER XI

FATEFUL DAYS IN 1918

ALL accounts agree that the close of 1917 found the Allies very unfavourably situated. The balance seemed to be shifted against them ; and the contrast, in retrospect, is striking between the natural elation of the troops who had taken part in the push at Cambrai, and had put to a practical test the three-in-one new factors of success—Tanks, secrecy and speed—and the equally natural depression of public opinion at home, and even at the front, wherever the chances of the campaign were accurately weighed. The mere strategic satisfaction at having relieved the pressure on Italy, or, at least, at having kept it short of full strength, by tactical operations in France, afforded inadequate compensation for the knowledge, growing to certainty, that the issue of 1917 would be a German offensive in 1918. All the credits on the side of the Allies were likely to mature in the remote future. All the debits, the heaviest of which was Russia, could be calculated at once.

Take, for instance, Sir Arthur Conan Doyle's fifth volume.[1] It opens on a very *piano* note. ' The late winter and the early spring of 1918 saw the balance tilted against the British and their comrades in the West, through causes over which they had no control. . . From November [1917] to March [1918] an endless succession of troop trains were bearing the divisions which had extended from the Baltic to the southern frontiers of Russia, in order to thicken the formidable array already marshalled across France.' Or take the expert evidence of Major-General Sir Frederick Maurice[2] : 'In Europe 1917 was a year of disappointment for the arms of the Allies. . . From the beginning of November onward they [the Germans] were moving troops from the Russian to the French front as fast as their trains could carry them. It was calculated that the Germans would be able to increase their strength on the Western front between the beginning of November and the end of April by not less than a million and a half of men' : a very nasty calculation for the Allied Command, and for the two Governments behind it at home.

Moreover, there was not much time. This was the key to the situation. Troops moving as fast as they could travel would reach their destination earlier than troops which were moving through a longer distance at a slower rate. ' While it would be possible,' wrote

[1] *The British Campaign in France and Flanders : January to July*, 1918. Hodder and Stoughton, 1919.
[2] *The Last Four Months : The End of the War in the West*. Cassell, 1919.

Sir Douglas Haig,[1] 'for Germany to complete her new dispositions early in the new year, the forces which America could send to France before the season would permit active operations to be recommenced would not be large': again, a very simple calculation, but it entailed serious consequences. The first was, that 'it became necessary to change the policy governing the operations of the British Armies in France'[2]; or, rather, this was less the first consequence than the sum-total of the consequences, which involved in their train all kinds of major and minor changes. The policy governing the operations of the British Armies in France had to be changed. 1918 had to be adjusted to 1917; and, while the process of adjustment unmade, or, at least, disturbed, the whole basis of British dispositions, and robbed the seed-time of the harvest, it was by no means clear that the new course would be either satisfactory or complete. For the change from an offensive to a defensive policy, under the urgent threat of a German advance, was accompanied by (1) a reduction in the British fighting strength, (2) a deficiency in defensive training, and (3) an extension of the British front by over twenty-eight miles. Such, briefly, was the problem at the opening of December, 1917, while General Braithwaite's gallant troops were still winning laurels in front of Cambrai, and public opinion in England was still uncertain whether the 'break-through' had come or not. As a fact, it was coming from the other side. It was coming with a weight of men and guns unequalled in the history of warfare. It was coming before the United States could pour their forces into Europe. It was coming against spent soldiers, unprepared with rear-line systems or with the latest developments in defensive fighting. It was coming, when our man-power was at its lowest, measured by the demand that it had met, and by the demands which it had to meet. It was coming, accordingly, when Army Commanders, from the Field Marshal downwards, were upset, if we may use an expressive term, by the necessity of defending an extended front with numerically reduced forces. The re-organization of Divisions from a 13-battalion to a 10-battalion basis affected, of course, even the smallest unit, and every Commanding Officer had to adapt himself to the new methods. That the fighting efficiency of units was impaired is a conclusion contradicted by events. That it could not be otherwise than impaired, under these novel and cumulative conditions, is an inference in accordance with expectation.

We may select a very simple entry from the Diary of the 1/6th Duke of Wellington's West Riding Regiment (49th Division). On January 29th, 1918, when the battalion was at Hondegem, a draft of eight Officers and one hundred and ninety-five other ranks from the 1/5th West Riding Regiment was posted to it, 'the 1/5th W.R.R.

[1] *Despatches*, page 177 (July 20th, 1918).
[2] *Ibid.*

having been transferred to the 62nd Division.' Next morning, this draft was posted to companies, 'after which all companies re-organized on a 4-platoon basis.' Take the 2/4th Battalion of the same Regiment, and its entry on January 31st, 1918 : ' The Brigade was reduced to three Battalions, the 2/6th being broken up, ten Officers and two hundred and twenty other ranks being transferred to the 2/4th Duke of Wellington's Regiment.' On the same day, seven Officers and one hundred and fifty other ranks were posted to the 2/5th West Yorkshires from the 2/6th West Yorkshires, ' who were disbanded'; and, briefly, if reference be made to the Order of Battle of the 62nd Division, given at the end of Chapter VI above, the range and complexity of the changes in *personnel*, consequent on the supreme need of defending a longer line with fewer men, and defending it against imminent assault, may be judged by these random examples. There was not a Company Commander in all the Divisions of the British Armies who did not *feel* the effects of the new policy in the early days of 1918.

Purposely, we have dwelt on the soldier's view. To him it mattered not at all that the Versailles (Supreme War) Council had been formed at Rapallo in the previous November, or that Mr. Lloyd George, on his way home through Paris, had delivered a rousing speech on the topic of the barrier in the West. Neither Council nor speeches would break that barrier, the dams of which were about to burst on *him*. To him, again, it mattered little more that, before the dams burst in fury on his long, thin, tired khaki line, the same doubts, or nearly the same doubts, weighed heavily on the minds of his Commanders as had oppressed them in 1915, when the 49th Division first came out to France. Now, as then, behind the narrow wall of Troops, which still guarded Ypres from the invader, lay Dunkirk, Calais, Boulogne. We may call this the horizontal line, leading from Brussels to the sea, and across the sea to hated England. That way lay the end of the war, and Prussia's satisfied ambition. Now, as then, too, a vertical line pointed southwards from Ostend to Paris, through Arras, Albert and Amiens, and the battlefields of 1916. That way lay a bisection of the Allied Forces, a spectacular occupation of the French capital, and, at best, a prolongation of the war into 1919 and even 1920. Either way lay disaster to British arms ; and the stars pointed both ways at once. To the soldier, as we say, it mattered little that a kind of choice had to be made, and a kind of balance had to be struck, between two alternative enemy aims, which were yet not mutually exclusive. His business was to fight, not to think, and, in the fighting days to which we are now coming, he fought tenaciously till he fell, leaving to those whom they concerned the fate of London and Paris. Yet, because their fate was involved in the disposition of the Allied Armies at the beginning of 1918, we are bound to consider the problem by which Sir Douglas

Haig was confronted. ' In the northern portion of the British area,' he wrote, in the Despatch which we have already quoted in this chapter, ' lie the northern channel ports, the security of which necessitated the maintenance of sufficient troops in the neighbourhood. Little or no ground could be given up on this front. . . In the central portion,' he continued, ' lie the northern collieries of France and certain important tactical features which cover our lateral communications. Here, also, little or no ground could be given up.' What could be given up ? A hateful consideration for the High Command, but it had to be faced and answered, in order to save what could not, or to concert, at least, the best measures for its safety. ' In the southern portion of the British area, south-east of Arras,' it was held, ' ground could be given up under great pressure without serious consequences.' The ' great pressure ' was certain to be applied, and it afforded some consolation to reflect that, in contrast to the central and northern portions, the forward area of this sector consisted chiefly 'of a wide expanse of territory devastated by the enemy last spring in his withdrawal.' He had held it in 1916. Early in 1917, as we saw, he had partly retired from it and had partly been driven back, destroying and ravaging as he went, to his prepared lines in the rear. Let him come again in 1918. We knew the ground as well as he. The ground ' to be given up under great pressure ' was sacred to the heroes of the Somme, and would not be given up for ever.

The time passed quickly to the appointed day.

We return to the 62nd Division, in rest on January 1st in the Reserve area of the XIIIth Corps in the Maroeuil district, above Arras. ' It was evident,' runs the great Despatch, dated July 20th, but going back to the previous November, ' that the enemy was about to make a great effort south of Arras. An attack on this front would undoubtedly have as its object the separation of the French and British Armies and the capture of the important centre of communications at Amiens. To meet this eventuality more than half our available troops were allocated to the defence of this sector, together with the whole of the cavalry.' On January 5th, the front from Gavrelle to Oppy, at right angles to the Arras-Douai road, was taken over from the 56th by the 62nd, with the 185th Brigade holding the left section all the time, and the 186th and 187th alternating on the right. On January 9th, Major-General Braithwaite, the 62nd Divisional Commander, assumed command of the sector. On the 18th, a German runner was captured, and valuable information was elicited from him as to the enemy dispositions. The 240th German Division was opposite the 62nd ; many troops, mostly from Russia, had been collected in the back areas ; the appointed day was plainly drawing nearer. There had been heavy snow and a sudden thaw : ' Conditions in the line very bad,' writes a Battalion diarist (January 19th), ' but men *very* cheerful and happy ' (the italics are his).

When they were not in the line, they were providing working parties ; when they were not at work, they were undergoing training. ' The construction of new communications and the extension of old, more especially in the area south-east of Arras, involved the building of a number of additional roads and the laying out of railways, both narrow and normal gauge. All available men of the fighting units, with the exception of a very small proportion undergoing training, and all labour units were employed on these tasks.' So far, the Field Marshal in his Despatch, and we may quote Sir A. Conan Doyle's comment : ' There were no enslaved populations who could be turned on to such work. For months before the attack the troops . . . were digging incessantly. Indeed, the remark has been made that their military efficiency was impaired by the constant navvy work upon which they were employed.'[1] It may be. But Sir Douglas Haig bore testimony, that ' the time and labour available were in no way adequate, if, as was suspected, the enemy intended to commence his offensive operations in the early spring . . .'

On January 31st, as we saw, the re-organization of the Division took place. Under the new scheme of nine battalions *plus* a Pioneer Battalion to a Division, the nucleus of Battalions to be amalgamated arrived from the 49th Division further north. In the 185th Brigade, the 2/6th West Yorkshires were disbanded, and the 2/8th were amalgamated with the 1/8th to form the 8th West Yorks. In the 186th Brigade, the 2/6th West Ridings were disbanded, and the 5th West Ridings were formed out of an amalgamation of the 1st and 2nd Line Battalions. In the 187th Brigade, when it left the line, the disbanded unit was the 2/5th York and Lancasters ; the 2/5th King's Own Yorkshire Light Infantry were amalgamated with the 1/5th as the 5th K.O.Y.L.I.

February sped, like January, in preparation varied by raids, and by rumours more or less authentic. ' Training and range-firing till noon. Route march from 2-5 p.m.' is a characteristic extract from a Battalion diary, dated February 19th. On February 28th, the 62nd Division relieved the 31st in the left sector of the XIIIth Corps. On March 10th, an increase of activity was observed in the enemy aircraft and artillery. On the 12th, information was to hand that an attack in the neighbourhood of Arras might be expected at an early date, and the Division was held in a state of readiness. On the 17th, under cover of darkness, two officers and eighty other ranks of the 2/7th West Ridings made a successful raid on the enemy trenches north of Fresnoy. On the 21st, news arrived that the enemy offensive had started opposite the Third Army, on a front of about twenty-seven miles from the north of Gouzeaucourt to the south of Gavrelle. The Army Commander was General the Hon. Sir Julian Byng, with the Vth, VIth, IVth and XVIIth Corps

[1] *Op. cit.*, page 82.

under the respective commands of Lieut.-Generals Sir E. A. Fanshawe, Sir G. M. Harper, Sir J. A. L. Haldane and Sir C. Fergusson, Bt.

    March 21st, 1918: the story has been told a hundred times, and will be re-told in every book of the British Army until the 'pussyfeet' of warfare prohibit the writing of military history. A

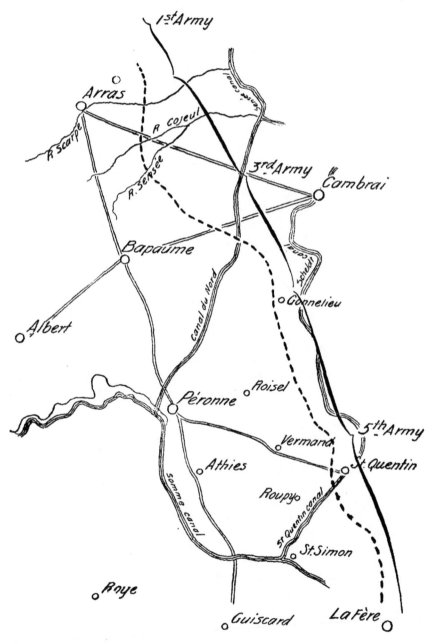

few words must be said about it here, though it happened that on the day itself no troops from the West Riding were engaged. The Fifth Army, commanded at that date by General Sir Hubert de la P. Gough, extended immediately south of the Third, and consisted of the VIIth, XIXth, XVIIIth and IIIrd Corps, under Lieut.-Generals Sir W. N. Congreve, Sir H. E. Watts, Sir F. I. Maxse and Sir R. H. K. Butler respectively. At its southern extremity, it touched the junction of the British and French lines; its total front was about two-and-forty miles, with an average of about 6,750 yards to each Division in the line compared with an average of about 4,700 yards per Division in the line in the Third Army. We should remember, too, that the southernmost portion of the front had only recently been taken over from the French, and the ' navvy ' work spoken of above was even more incomplete than in other parts. By so much more difficult, accordingly, was Sir Hubert Gough's task than Sir Julian Byng's. The German General opposing the Fifth Army was von Hutier, the conqueror of Riga, and the Crown Prince of Prussia was afforded this unique opportunity of winning his coveted laurels in the final battle to be known as the *Kaiser-schlacht*. Further, at least sixty-four Divisions of super-trained enemy troops took part in the operations on the first day, against eight in the line of the Third Army (with seven in reserve) and eleven in the line of the Fifth Army (with three Infantry and three Cavalry in reserve). Two-thirds of the German Divisions were allotted to the assault on General Gough; and ' never in the history of the world,' it has well and soberly been said, ' had a more formidable force been concentrated on a fixed and limited objective.'[1] We are not directly concerned with the story of the Fifth Army on that day, but since its ' apparent collapse ' has been (or was) contrasted with the ' glorious defence ' by General Byng, we may be permitted to cite here the opinion of Major-General Sir F. Maurice, that ' the burden which Gough's troops had to bear was incomparably the greater.' He summarizes with admirable brevity the facts which we have recounted above :

' In the first stage of the battle very nearly twice as many German Divisions attached Gough as fell upon Byng. Each of Gough's Divisions had on the average to hold nearly fifty per cent. more front than had Byng, while the Third Army reserves were nearly twice as strong as those of the Fifth, yet at the end of the first day's battle Gough's left, where the gallant 9th Division beat off all attacks, had given less ground than some of Byng's Divisions further north had been compelled to yield.'[2]

Pending the appearance of an official history of the war, no narrative of March 21st can be otherwise than inadequate, which

[1] Sir A. Conan Doyle, *op. cit.*, page 10.
[2] *The Last Four Months*, page 38.

holds the scales less evenly between the two Armies primarily engaged than this temperate statement by Sir Frederick Maurice.

Even so, we have omitted the fog, which, after five hours' incessant bombardment (from 5 to 10 o'clock in the morning), had been drawn up from the soil in a white, impenetrable blanket, and which, in Sir Douglas Haig's words, ' hid from our artillery and machine gunners the S.O.S. signals sent up by our outpost line,' and ' made it impossible to see more than fifty yards in any direction.' This efficient aid to the attackers, which had often been simulated in battle by artificial means with smaller success, affected the defence all along the line ; and the only answer to the fog, we are told, was to strengthen the Infantry in the trenches, involving, if it were to be done, a fresh weakening of our too weak reserves.

But we are not writing the history of the Second Battle of the Somme. On March 21st, as we have said, General Braithwaite's troops were not engaged in that long line from Oppy to La Fère, on which, as we read above, ' ground could be given up under great pressure without serious consequences.' The pressure proved greater than had been anticipated, and the measure of the ground given up increased the seriousness of the consequences.

On the 21st, those fifty-four miles were held from north to south by the following Divisions in order of line : 56th, 4th, 15th, 3rd, 34th, 59th, 6th, 51st, 17th, 63rd, 47th, 9th, 21st, 16th, 66th, 24th, 61st, 30th, 36th, 14th, 18th, 58th. The Guards Division was at Arras, and from various points in the Reserve-area, again working southwards from above the Scarpe, the 31st, 40th, 41st (west of Albert), 25th (at Bapaume), 19th, 2nd, 39th, 50th, 20th, and the 1st, 3rd and 2nd Cavalry Divisions (at Péronne, Athies and Guiscard respectively) were brought up and thrown into the line. The first battle-honours belong to these, and no sketch, however imperfect, of the conditions under which they were won, can miss the splendour of their winning, or the valour of the living and the dead.

We pass over the next few days. Their story is written on the map in four days' battle positions (March 23rd to 26th), all of which were swiftly obliterated in the further retreat and the last advance. What can never be obliterated, however, so long as gallant deeds are traced on the map of human character, is the memory of those British Divisions, outnumbered, befogged, giving ground, but retaining, with their backs to the wall, the heroic quality of victors. We merely note that, on March 26th, at a conference held at Doullens between the French and British Army Commanders, Lord Milner (representing the British Government), M. Poincaré (President of the French Republic), M. Clemenceau (Prime Minister) and the French Minister of Munitions, it was decided, in view of the imminent danger of the capture of Amiens, ' to place the supreme control of the operations of the French and British forces in France and Belgium in the hands of General Foch, who accordingly assumed control.'[1]

On March 23rd, the wave of withdrawal reached the 62nd Division. The 187th Brigade was moved to Arras, where it was placed at the disposal of the 15th Division, but this order was cancelled almost at once, under the stress of immediate circumstances, and the whole Division was allotted to the XVIIth Corps. On the night of March 24th/25th new orders were received to join the IVth Corps, and early in the morning of the 25th the three Infantry Brigades of the Division were moved to Ayette.

It proved a long day's work, and the beginning of an exacting time. We are back again now in the old, shell-ridden quadrilateral : Doullens-Arras (north), Doullens-Albert (west), Albert-Bapaume (south), Arras-Bapaume (east). Bucquoy, to which the Division was to move at once, lies just to the east of the centre of the diagonal Arras-Albert, and the south-west road from Bucquoy to Albert passes through Thiepval and Auchy, where the 49th Division from the West Riding suffered so severely in 1916. We remember how, a little more than a year ago, in January, 1917, when the 62nd had just arrived in France, some Officers of the 2/5th Duke of Wellington's made 'a tour of the trenches in an old London General omnibus. The party visited Acheux and Warlencourt, and then drove along the Doullens-Arras road, which was closed to traffic at one point owing to shelling.'[2] The problem then was to push the Germans back, back between Arras and Bapaume, always nearer to Douai and Cambrai. A year's hard battles had been fought, and now, in March, 1918, Bapaume had fallen, Albert was to fall (March 26th-27th), and the problem was to prevent the enemy's 'double hope of separating the French and British Armies and interfering with the detraining arrangements of our Allies by the capture of Montdidier.'[3] In this effort the now veteran 62nd was to bear a conspicuous part.

[1] *Despatches*, page 208. The appointment of the future Marshal of France as Generalissimo (C. in C. of the Allied Armies) was confirmed on April 14th.

[2] See page 117, above.

[3] *Despatches*, page 206.

CHAPTER XII

WITH THE 62ND AT BUCQUOY

GENERAL BRAITHWAITE, then Commanding the 62nd, has said to the present writer that he regards the action at Bucquoy as, perhaps, the finest achievement of his Division. They were hurried to Ayette early as March 25th, and there, as stated, the Staff Officer who had been sent on to IVth Corps Headquarters brought Orders for the Division to proceed at once to Bucquoy. Divisional Headquarters reached it at about 8-30 in the morning, and the General went forward to the Headquarters of the 40th and 42nd Divisions, just West of Bucquoy, in order to learn the tactical situation. (The 40th had been in reserve on March 21st till it was pushed into the line near Bullecourt; the 42nd had arrived since that date). The leading Troops of the 185th Brigade began to reach Bucquoy about 10 o'clock, but the roads were so much blocked with transport of all kinds that concentration was not completed till 11-30. Meanwhile, Corps Orders had been received for the men to have a meal and to get rested, and for the Division, which had been up all night and had already marched twelve miles, to hold itself in readiness for a move at short notice. The General also paid a visit to the Headquarters of the 41st Division (in reserve at Albert on March 21st, and also pushed into the line), now likewise stationed at Bucquoy, and shortly afterwards Lieut.-General Sir G. M. Harper, Commanding the IVth Corps, arrived.

The situation, as it revealed itself, was simple and serious. Briefly, with or without Albert, which fell on the night of March 26th, the urgent, essential task was to stabilize a line. The Germans had thrust, and thrust again, here, there, wherever they found an opening. They had driven us back in five days (March 21st to 25th), on the front of the Third Army, right up to the line of the old trenches at Achiet-le-Grand, Miraumont, Pozières. More ground might still be yielded 'under great pressure,' but the vital danger lay further south, where, still to the north of the River Somme, at the junction of the Third and Fifth Armies, withdrawals on the night of the 26th were to reach a line from Albert to Sailly-le-Sec. What this meant to the French forces nearer Paris, to the important centre at Mont-didier, and to the railway from Amiens to the capital, was coming very insistently into view; and the severe strain on the 62nd Division, among other gallant Divisions, on March 25th and following days, was due above all to the necessity of arresting the advance about the Ancre, and of preventing the German hope of breaking through the receding British line. Once broken, it could never have been mended, and our real triumph in defeat was our disappointment of Luden-dorff's design of cutting off one force from another. The line went back, irregularly, unsteadily.   Perilous salients were bulged out, to be straightened by retirements on the wings.   Troops were pushed from place to place, or assembled by spontaneous conglomeration. to stop a dangerous gap.   Different units became hopelessly mixed, and sorted themselves out into novel formations.   Platoons, Companies, even Battalions improvised barriers of their own dead.   But still Ludendorff was disappointed.   Still his weary men, flung in desperation, however magnificently led, spent their last ounce of strength in vain.   Still, in retreat after retreat, touch was maintained between Brigades, between Divisions.   Still fighting the enemy to a standstill, dog-tired, attenuated, unconquerable—still a line held.

It was to a patch of that line, covering, roughly, the centre region in the Doullens-Albert-Bapaume-Arras quadrangle, to which we have frequently referred, that the attention of Major-General Braithwaite was directed by the IVth Corps Commander at their anxious conference in Bucquoy about noon on March 25th.

The 186th Brigade was now arriving at Bucquoy, and the two Brigadier-Generals (185th and 186th) were ordered, as soon as they would be ready, to move to Achiet-le-Petit, and to cover that village, the 186th on the right and the 185th on the left.   The object of this move was to prolong the front of the 62nd Division (at Logeast Wood, due East of Bucquoy, and midway between Ablainzevelle and Achietle-Grand), so as to enable other Divisions which had been heavily engaged, to withdraw and re-organize.   The Brigades reached their positions between 4 and 5 o'clock in the afternoon, with two Battalions each in line and one in reserve, and with one Company of the Machine-Gun Battalion attached to each Brigade.   It is to be observed that these were the first operations, since the Machine-Gun re-organization, in which that Battalion had taken part, and, in ideal country for that weapon, and with the improved moral of the Companies under new conditions, the results fully justified the change.   During the early evening of March 25th, the various Divisions affected (19th, 25th, 41st, 51st) gradually withdrew behind the line held now by the 62nd with the 42nd, and at 7 o'clock Major-General Walter Braithwaite, Commanding the 62nd Division, took over Command of the front, with Headquarters at Bucquoy, and the Headquarters of the gallant 41st were removed to Souastre in the rear.   At 9-30, General Braithwaite's Headquarters withdrew to Gommecourt, to which a line had been run during the afternoon, but, owing to the heavy traffic on the roads, the move was not completed till 11 p.m.   About that hour, the Corps Commander sent a telephone message to say that it would be necessary to withdraw not later than next morning to the line Puisieux-Bucquoy-Ablainzevelle, and to ask the Divisional Commander if he preferred to make the move sooner, while still under cover of darkness.   We should note that a trench East of Bucquoy had been dug during the afternoon by the Pioneer Battalion of the 62nd (9th

Durham Light Infantry), in order to cover that place in the event of our Troops being driven in, and that about 8 p.m. the 187th Brigade was ordered to concentrate on Bucquoy in Divisional Reserve, and to move forward a Battalion into the new trench.   Meanwhile, the Divisional Artillery had arrived, and went into action, covering the withdrawal, during the night of the 25th.

General Braithwaite decided to take advantage of the darkness, but, though a Staff Officer was sent back at once to communicate his decision to the Brigadiers, the Order did not reach them till after 2 o'clock next morning (March 26th), so heavy was the congestion in the roads ; and the actual start was made in early daylight.   In the night, the 186th Brigade was subjected to enemy fire, and some changes in the dispositions had to be made, but the successful withdrawal of the Division was completed about 8 a.m., when the 185th Brigade took up a position on the high ground East of Bucquoy. The 186th were in touch with them, and extended to a point about five hundred yards North-east of Puisieux, with two Battalions in the front line, and the third and Pioneer Battalions in support.   The 187th were in Divisional Reserve in the neighbourhood of Biez Wood, with two Battalions East of the Wood, and the third in the trenches South and South-west.

This was on March 26th, and another heavy and difficult day ensued.   The Germans were advancing all the time in a westerly direction, which developed during the day into a determined north-westerly attack from the neighbourhood of Puisieux and Serre against the right flank of the 186th Brigade.   Two Battalions of that Brigade (5th Duke of Wellington's and Pioneers) were accordingly withdrawn a short distance, so as to face more directly to the South, with their right resting on Rossignol Wood (between Bucquoy and Hébuterne), so as to cover the exits from Puisieux.   Three Companies of the 2/4th Duke of Wellington's (in Reserve) were moved forward to prolong this line, and a Battalion of the 187th Brigade (Reserve) was further used to extend their flank on the high ground West of Rossignol Wood.   This occurred in the late afternoon, when five heavy attacks by the Prussian Guard on Bucquoy, and between Bucquoy and Puisieux, had been repulsed ; and the causes why the German advance in this area had shifted slightly to the North (roughly, in the direction Serre to Hébuterne) were, briefly, two : (1) To the South of Puisieux and Hébuterne, early on March 26th, there was a gap in the line of three or four miles between the 62nd and 12th Divisions.   About a thousand men from various units of the 19th Division were holding the defences round Hébuterne, and it was known that the New Zealand Division was well on its way to fill the gap.   Their leading Brigade, however, could not arrive till the late afternoon, and it was actually about 10 p.m. before it filled the southern half of the gap, with its left resting on Colincamps.

THE CHURCH, BUCQUOY.

[*Face p.* 174.

Meanwhile, about 7 p.m., the 4th Brigade of the Australian Division, which had been put at General Braithwaite's disposal, relieved the elements of the 19th in the defence of Hébuterne, and got in touch during the night of the 26th and early morning of the 27th with the second Brigade of the New Zealanders, to the South of the village. This gap, then, and the delay in filling it, were one main cause of the concentration on the West of Bucquoy.   The second (2) was subsidiary, and arose from the fact that, during the morning of March 26th, constant reports were received of mounted enemy troops seen in Hébuterne and even to the West of it.   Possibly, isolated patrols had reached the edge of the village, but, as the result of these rumours, ' unauthorized orders were issued by persons totally unknown, in a more or less excited state,' to clear all transport westwards, and some valuable hours were lost in collecting and bringing back those units.

This bare account of one day's fighting leaves much to the imagination.   But an hour by hour recital of the deeds of unit by unit in the Division would make too much of a day's work, which was only the beginning of a hard battle.   We must not lose the perspective in a contemplation of detail, and this perspective is admirably rendered in the few lines devoted by Sir A. Conan Doyle to the 62nd Division on March 6th. ' South of Puisieux,' he writes, ' there was a gap of four or five miles [the Divisional Commander says ' three or four '] before one came to British troops.   Into this gap in the very nick of time came first the 4th Brigade of the Second Australian Division, and later the New Zealand Division in driblets, which gradually spanned the vacant space.   It was a very close call for a break through without opposition.   Being disappointed in this, the Germans on March 26th spent the whole afternoon in fierce attacks on the 62nd Division, but got little but hard knocks from Braithwaite's Yorkshiremen,' who, we remember, had been on the move since early morning the day before. ' The 186th Brigade on the right,' it is added, ' threw back a flank to Rossignol Wood to cover the weak side.'[1]   We shall not further expand it.

Next day, March 27th, after a comparatively quiet night, the attacks on Bucquoy were resumed on the front held by the 185th and the left of the 186th Brigade.   Our Lewis guns took ample toll of the advancing enemy lines, and the assault failed with heavy loss.   Shortly after noon another attack was begun to the East of Rossignol Wood, where the 5th Duke of Wellington's, who had suffered so severely the day before, were primarily engaged on their right.   Their Lewis guns and rifles proved effective in the open, but the bombers swarming the old trenches which existed in that part of the line were less easy to repulse : the German was a skilful thrower, and it happened at that time and in that locality that rifle bombs and Stokes Mortars were very difficult to procure.   Despite extraordinary courage and

[1] *Op. cit.*, pages 63-64.

untiring effort and resourcefulness, bombing parties continued to work their way up the intricate systems of old trenches ; and, though two determined attacks between Rossignol Wood and Hébuterne (between 1 o'clock and 2-30) and two others on Bucquoy (at 4 o'clock and again at 5-30) were severally defeated, the 2/4th Battalion of the King's Own Yorkshire Light Infantry were driven to the high ground East of Hébuterne and a Company of the 2/4th York and Lancasters were driven out of the Wood.   The North-westerly move of the enemy, which we noted as his direction the day before, seemed, accordingly, more critical, since a gap had been made between the right of the 186th Brigade and the Australians in Hébuterne.   To meet this crisis, the trenches East of Gommecourt, lying further to the North-west, were manned by two Companies of Australians, and the 187th Brigade was ordered immediately to counter-attack.   There was some delay in getting this order through to the two left Battalions of the Brigade (the 2/4th York and Lancasters and the 5th King's Own Yorkshire Light Infantry), but about 7 in the evening, after the 4th Australian Brigade had been ordered urgently to co-operate, using, if necessary, the whole of their Reserve Battalion, the Brigadier-General Commanding the 186th got into personal touch with Lieut-Colonel O. C. S. Watson, D.S.O., Commanding the 5th K.O.Y.L.I. (187th Brigade), and ordered him to counter-attack Rossignol Wood, with the help of four Tanks, which the Brigadier was able to put at his disposal. This counter-attack succeeded, and at 11 p.m. the Officer Commanding the Battalion reported that he had regained part of the Wood and the high ground to the South-west of it.   He had gained great glory at the same time, as is shown by the following extract from the *London Gazette*, May 8th, 1918 :

'VICTORIA CROSS

' Major (A/Lt.-Col.) Oliver Cyril Spencer Watson, D.S.O. (R. of O.), late King's Own Yorkshire Light Infantry.

'For most conspicuous bravery, self-sacrificing devotion to duty, and exceptionally gallant leading during a critical period of operations.   His command was at a point where continual attacks were made by the enemy in order to pierce the line, and an intricate system of old trenches in front, coupled with the fact that his position was under constant rifle and machine-gun fire rendered the situation still more dangerous.   A counter-attack had been made against the enemy position, which at first achieved its object, but as they were holding out in two improvised strong points, Lieut.-Colonel Watson saw that immediate action was necessary, and he led his remaining small reserve to the attack, organizing bombing parties and leading attacks under intense rifle and machine-gun fire.   Outnumbered he finally ordered his men to retire, remaining himself in a communication trench to cover the retirement, though he faced almost certain death by so doing.   The assault he led was at a critical moment, and without doubt saved the line.   Both in the assault and in covering his men's retirement he held his life as nothing, and his splendid bravery inspired all troops in the vicinity to rise to the occasion and save a breach being made in a hardly tried and attenuated line.

'Lt.-Colonel Watson was killed while covering the withdrawal.'

We have only to add to this record of the 27th, that the 185th Brigade should have been relieved on that day, but the operations round Rossignol Wood and the loss of Ayette (by the 31st Division on the left of the 42nd) postponed the relief for twenty-four hours.

The night passed quickly and fairly quietly.   On March 28th, there was an early bombardment of the whole Divisional front and of the back area over the Woods (Biez and Rossignol), and an intercepted advance on Bucquoy, which was subjected to heavy shelling all that day.   Splendid work was done in that morning battle (10 a.m. till noon) by the 186th Brigade under Brig.-General J. L. G. Burnett, a very worthy successor to Bradford, whose services we commemorated above.   One Platoon of the 5th Duke of Wellington's, which occupied an advanced post, became isolated from the rest.   When last heard of at about 1 o'clock, it was known to be still holding out, but no particulars of its experiences are available.   The heroic record remains, to the imperishable honour of Yorkshiremen, that, when the position was finally reached, this Platoon had been overwhelmed, and not a man was left alive.

More serious than attacks in the open, which were sometimes stopped, and which, if they developed, were repulsed, were those bombing-parties working their way up the trenches, who had done so much damage the day before.   They were very active again on the 28th, and sometime between noon and 2 o'clock they contrived to drive back from the ridge East of Hébuterne and from Rossignol Wood the 5th Battalion of the King's Own Yorkshire Light Infantry, who had made so gallant a sacrifice to hold that position overnight.   Rossignol Wood was not recovered on that day.   Two Tanks were derelict in the Wood, and formed effective cover for the enemy, and there was a partial failure, too, in an attempt by the 124th Brigade (41st Division). At 7 o'clock, fresh orders for the re-capture were given to the 8th West Yorkshires (in reserve to the 185th Brigade), who were placed at the disposal of the 187th, and at the same time the 4th Australian Brigade was to drive the enemy out of the trenches South-east of Gommecourt. This bombing encounter proved successful in releasing five hundred yards of trenches, and by early morning of March 29th the West Yorkshires had reached the Northern end of the contested Wood.   There they were held up by heavy machine-gun fire, but the twofold countermeasures had eased the situation, and the gap between the 186th and

N

the Australian Brigades was satisfactorily filled. The postponed relief of the 185th by the 42nd Division was duly completed during that night.

Next morning (March 29th), progress was made with the urgent work of re-organizing the 187th Brigade. It had performed magnificent service in exceptionally difficult circumstances, which included the absence through illness of its Brigadier-General. Lt.-Col. Barton, D.S.O., who had been temporarily in Command, had also fallen ill, and was replaced on March 28th by Lt.-Col. C. K. James, D.S.O., the Officer Commanding the 2/7th West Yorkshires. The Brigade had been almost continuously in action since its hurried departure from Ayette in the early hours of March 25th, and the V.C. awarded posthumously to the Commanding Officer of the 5th K.O.Y.L.I. is an indication of the splendid resistance which it offered time after time to the enemy assaults on its front. The Brigade was now located in the trenches North and West of Rossignol Wood, in touch with the 186th on its right and with the 41st Division on its left. One Battalion of the 185th was moved up in close support during the afternoon. Bombing fights between the Australians and their assailants about Gommecourt and Hébuterne were the chief incidents of the day which proved the growing exhaustion of the enemy. March 30th and 31st were spent, too, in comparative quiet : an important document captured by the Australians showed how heavily the Germans had suffered. But the 62nd had suffered too. We referred above to Colonel Watson. Two other Commanding Officers, who fell at the head of their respective Regiments, may also be mentioned here, as splendid types of fighting Officers, first beloved and then mourned by their men. These were Lieut.-Colonels A. H. and C. K. James, of the 7th and 8th West Yorkshires, known, of course, as James the Seventh and James the Eighth, who, though not related to each other, were firm comrades in life and death. On the night of March 31st-April 1st, a Brigade of the 37th Division relieved the 186th, which withdrew to Souastre and Henu, and next night the remainder of the 62nd Division (less Artillery) was relieved by the 37th, and moved back into the Reserve area.

It will be admitted that they had earned their relief. The Field Marshal's summary runs, under date March 27th : 'A series of strong attacks commenced all along our front from about Bucquoy to the neighbourhood of Hamelincourt, in the course of which the enemy gained possession of Ablainzevelle and Ayette' (which was re-taken by the 32nd Division on April 3rd). ' Elsewhere,' it continues, ' all his assaults were heavily repulsed by troops of the 62nd Division, under Command of Major-General W. P. Braithwaite, and of the 42nd and Guards Divisions.'[1] And, under date March 28th : ' The 42nd Division drove off two attacks from the direction of Ablainzevelle

[1] *Despatches*, page 208.

BUCQUOY: STREET.

BUCQUOY: MARKET PLACE.

[Face p. 178.

and the 62nd Division with an attached Brigade of the 4th Australian
Division also beat off a succession of heavy attacks about Bucquoy
with great loss to the enemy.'[1]   We have filled in some details in this
outline, which is sufficiently effective in its statement of duty done
and of local successes achieved.   If we go behind it at all, it is rather
to point to some lessons that were learned than to gild the laurels of
renown which the Division earned during those fiery days.

We have already mentioned the work of the newly-organized
Machine-Gun Battalion, and the comparative lack of Rifle bombs and
Stokes Mortars.   Another fact worth noting is the renewed confidence
reposed in the Rifle and the Lewis Gun.   In the face of effective
fire from these weapons the enemy never succeeded in pushing home
an attack across the open.   Communication between the Division
and Brigades was maintained with very little interruption, and the two
Brigade Headquarters being kept together enabled the admirable
Signal Service to devote all their attention to one main route.   Under
these novel conditions of open warfare, it was found that special training
was required for the Power Buzzer operations of Brigade Sections,
and in other technical details the experience at Bucquoy was to prove
valuable.

Most valuable of all was the knowledge that, with nearly all the
chances against them, they had fought the enemy to a standstill.
Despite a perilous gap in the thinned line of British troops, and despite
the delays in filling it, the enemy had not broken through.   The line
was threatened on March 25th.   It was constantly, almost continuously,
assailed from the East, and, where disclosed, from the South.   It
still held on March 31st.   Mistakes unavoidable in the medley were
heroically repaired.   Odd pockets of men, as we have seen—a thousand
from the 19th Division behind Hébuterne, another thousand from
the 41st about Gommecourt—showed incomparable resourcefulness.
Sudden orders were given in emergency, and were carried out un-
erringly under darkness.   Troops confidently expected in the afternoon
arrived short of their destination after nightfall, and the intervals of
time and place were filled up.   The whole story of these days is a
lesson in how not to yield, and the whole moral of it is contained in
the fact that the end of the first phase of the Second Battle of the
Somme was, at best, an incomplete German victory.   They had not
achieved what they had hoped, and, losing hope, they would lose all.

So, Bucquoy is a name that shines in the war record of the 62nd
Division.   We leave them now, at the beginning of April, in Divisional
Reserve, with their Headquarters at Pas, enjoying a well-earned
respite from active operations, though under two hours' notice to
move : and we turn next to another part of the wide field, where the
49th Division, the First Line of the West Riding Territorials, bore
its separate part in the grand defensive.

[1] *Ibid.*, page 212.

CHAPTER XIII

WITH THE 49TH IN THE VALLEY OF THE LYS

I.—FIRST PHASE

WE reach a confused tract of warfare, punctuated, as ever, by noble deeds, through which we must strike a careful trail.

In an Order, issued by Major-General Cameron, Commanding the 49th Division, and reviewing the period from April 10th to May 5th, 1918, upon which we are now to enter, the General drew attention to the fact that his Division had not been fighting as a whole. 'In some ways it is sad,' he wrote ; ' but the fact that we have been separated for a great part of the time has in no way diminished the credit of your achievements. Every part of the Division in its own sphere of action has done exceptionally well, and every part has earned high praise from Commanders outside the Division.'

Partly, then, the confusion arises from the distribution of the Troops to outside Commands. But the mere fact of this distribution is itself evidence to the difficulty of responsible leadership in those days ; and, before we attempt to draw a table of the activities of the Division in place and time during the period covered by that Order, a brief survey may be made from a more general point of view. 'Every part earned high praise from Commanders outside the Division': we are concerned, then, with outside Commands and with a wider outlook than the 49th Division's.

We are concerned with Ludendorff's point of view, so far as we are at liberty to re-construct it. On a previous page we tried to show how the German mind in March was divided between two strategic plans, one of which pointed to Paris and the other to the Channel ports. Both were pursued in turn, and even to some extent simultaneously, and either, if successful, would have inflicted an almost irreparable blow on the Allied forces of France and Britain. The point is, that neither quite succeeded : the union of those Forces under Foch and the response of the British Armies to Haig's summons on April 13th, 'WITH OUR BACKS TO THE WALL, AND BELIEVING IN THE JUSTICE OF OUR CAUSE, EACH OF US MUST FIGHT TO THE END,' were to prove incalculably more effective than all the odds combined against them. But the initiative in April was with the Germans. So soon as one plan miscarried, or was left standing, or was conveniently broken off, they were able to call the other plan, and to make a new push with fresh Troops. The initiative was theirs, and the superiority was theirs, in numbers and (by the offensive) in surprise. 'The possibility of a German attack North of the La Bassée Canal had been brought to my notice,' wrote Sir Douglas Haig, ' prior to the 21st March. Indications that preparations for a hostile attack in this sector were nearing completion had been observed in the first days of April.'[1]   But no observations, however accurate, and no prevision, however acute, could organize fifty-eight Divisions to fight battles in two sectors at one time.   Forty of the fifty-eight Divisions had been engaged in the Second Battle of the Somme, and ' the steps which I could take,' he continued, ' to meet a danger which I could foresee were limited by the fact that, though the enemy's progress on the Somme had for the time being been stayed, . . . [he] was in a position to take immediate advantage of any weakening of my forces in that area.'[2] And to initiative, numbers and surprise was added the fortune of the weather.   The early spring had been 'unseasonably fine,' and the low-lying ground in the Lys Valley dried up in time for the Germans to anticipate a relief of the Portuguese, who were holding the front to the South of Armentières, and who had been in the line for several months.   A shattering German assault fell suddenly (April 9th) on this thin-spread Portuguese Division, already overdue for relief ; and 'no blame,' we instinctively know, 'can be attached to inexperienced troops who gave way to so terrific a blow, which would have been formidable to any soldiers in the world.'[3]

Such, then, in the broadest outline, was the strategic situation, when Ludendorff, leading the *Kaiser-schlacht*, which had opened on March 21st, left the fate of Amiens hanging in the precarious balance to which it had been fought in ten days, and sought to add terror to exhaustion by renewing his thrust at the Channel ports.

When this underlying principle is seized, and Sir Douglas Haig's problem is imagined, what ensued may briefly be recounted to the date of the engagement of units of the 49th.   We are not now to consider the biggest aspect : the point of view of the War Council at Versailles.   The facts that Americans were coming, and that British reinforcements would be poured in, did not illumine the darkness in Flanders in the middle of the second week of April.   Nor is it immediately to the point, that, when Sir Frederick Maurice saw Marshal Foch on April 16th, and the Germans seemed ' well on the road to Calais and Boulogne, . . . Foch had himself measured accurately both the German strength and the endurance of the British Army. . . . " The battle in Flanders is practically over," he said ; " Haig will not need any more troops from me."   Not even the loss of Kemmel a few days later ruffled him.   He was right, and the battle in Flanders ended in a complete repulse of the second German effort to break through.'[4]   No.   We should thank heaven, fasting, for the Marshal's masterly imperturbability.   It won the war, among many

[1] *Despatches*, page 218.

[2] *Ibid*, page 220.

[3] Sir A. Conan Doyle, *op. cit.*, page 227.

[4] *The Last Four Months*, page 59.

claimants for that boon.   But the great leader himself would admit, that his estimate of ' the endurance of the British Army ' had been calculated to the last ounce of its worn strength, and that ' the loss of Kemmel a few days later ' (on April 25th, to be precise) imposed a well-nigh intolerable strain.

We are to contract our horizon on those days : to forget, what were then invisible, the dots and spots on the Atlantic, which marked the precious troopships bringing help from the New World to the Old ; to forget the set will of Paris, raided from the air by night and day, and nearly within gunshot as well ; to forget the last effort of England, and how, in a room at the War Office, all was ready to call out the Volunteers, the final arm of Home Defence ; and we are to try to piece together events in Flanders from early morning on April 9th, when the brave Portuguese were overrun, till the confidence of the French Marshal was justified at the end of the battle on May 8th. Throughout that month, we are to remember the superb generalship of Sir Douglas Haig, splendidly backed as he was by Generals Sir H. Horne, Commanding the First, and Sir Herbert Plumer, Commanding the Second Army.   Through all ranks of the heroic forces which they commanded, whether tired veterans from the hills and valleys of the Somme, or new drafts of young soldiery from home, and in all arms of the Service, one spirit prevailed : to obey, at whatever personal cost, the supreme call of their Commander-in-Chief, which was issued on the fourth day of the Flanders battle, and the pith of which we quoted above.   The enemy's objects, they were told, 'are to separate us from the French, to take the Channel ports, and destroy the British Army.'   He had, as yet, 'made little progress towards his goals.'   Time, they were reminded, was on their side, not necessarily as individuals but as Englishmen : 'Victory will belong to the side which holds out the longest.'   And then followed the stern command : 'There is no other course open to us but to fight it out.   Every position must be held to the last man : there must be no retirement.   With our backs to the wall, and believing in the justice of our cause, each one of us must fight to the end.   The safety of our homes and the freedom of mankind depend alike upon the conduct of each one of us at this critical moment.'

So we come to the 49th Division, which has been in the Ypres area all that year, performing necessary and at times exacting duties on a front which was never immune from Artillery attacks and sudden raids, and to its response, through its various units, to the call to stand fast and die.

The German advance on April 9th between Armentières and the La Bassée Canal had bulged in the line by that evening to a distance of three to five miles.   Next day, the attack was extended North of Armentières to Wytschaete and Hollebeke, and the enemy gains were extended.   The 34th Division in Armentières, though not yet attacked

[Face p. 182.

Ypres
49th Divisional Headqrs
in the Ramparts:—Winter. 1917—18.

on their own front, had their two flanks dangerously exposed, and were withdrawn in a North-westerly direction, reaching a stopping-place at Nieppe. If we follow this action a little further, we shall be able to fit in more intelligibly the narrative of the 49th Division. On April 11th the advance was pressed in the direction of Nieppe and Neuve Église, and in the afternoon there was fierce fighting about Messines, now in enemy occupation. These losses pinched the 34th out of their temporary foothold at Nieppe. The withdrawal on this day did not cease in that particular area till about a thousand yards

East of Neuve Église and Wulverghem, involving the abandonment of Hill 63. Next day, an assault in great strength was launched due westwards between Merville and Steenwerk, and affected our line below Bailleul, which looks down through Nieppe to Armentières. On the same day and the following (the 13th) Neuve Église was hotly involved, and fell before midnight on the 14th. Another twenty-four hours and Bailleul had suffered the same fate. There was now a very perilous salient in this stricken northerly region, and on the night of April 15th/16th the decision was taken to withdraw from the

Passchendaele Ridge, the scene of so much bloodshed in the previous summer ; and, consequently, to close in nearer to Ypres.   These retirements, as may be seen on a map, brought the Kemmel sector into prominence, and the German capture on April 16th of Meteren and Wytschaete, at the two extremes of that front, was developed next morning (17th) into a determined attack on Kemmel Hill.

Recalling now from page 46 above, and from an earlier April 17th, the geographical significance of Ypres, noting that this significance was not diminished by the improvement in German heavy Artillery, as shown by the guns trained on Paris, and observing that a sentimental value had accrued to Ypres in those middle years almost bigger than its geographical significance, we are now better qualified to measure the anxiety of the British Command during the crucial week, April 9th to 16th, 1918.   Would Ypres fall ?   Would the Channel ports follow, with all their accumulated stores, and G.H.Q. be driven to the sea ?   Could the hard-pressed Troops of the Second Army hold out to perform their allotted task, since 'the constant and severe fighting in the Lys battle front, following so closely on the tremendous struggle South of Arras, had placed a very serious strain upon the British forces ' ?   'Many British divisions,' continued their Commander, 'had taken part in the northern and southern battles, while others had been engaged almost continuously from the outset of the German offensive.'[1]   We know the answer to these questions. It is time now to see in one area how those answers were dictated.

Take, first, in the 49th Division, the 147th Infantry Brigade, which moved on the night of April 9th/10th to join the 34th near Armentières with the following Group Details : 'A' Company of the Machine Gun Corps, a Light Trench Mortar Battery, a Field Company (57) Royal Engineers, a Field Ambulance (1/2nd West Riding), and No. 3 Company, 49th Divisional Train.   On April 10th, the 1/4th Duke of Wellington's were engaged at Erquinghem, covering a crossing of the Lys.   That night, the Brigade was defending Nieppe, in support of the 34th Division in its withdrawal from Armentières.   On the night of the 11th/12th, they carried out a skilful rearguard action, covering a further withdrawal.   From the 12th to 14th, they maintained their position, despite repeated attacks, in the southern outskirts of Bailleul. A few hours' rest, and on the evening of the 15th the Brigade was again in the front line, in consequence of Bailleul's fall.   On April 16th and 17th, they were successfully holding their own on the slopes to the North-west of Bailleul, and taking heavy toll of the enemy. 'In this action,' we read, 'all units of the Brigade Group greatly distinguished themselves.'   On the 19th, they moved into the 34th Divisional Reserve, and two days later they rejoined their own Division in and around Poperinghe.   Thus, this Group is inserted into the fighting which we summarized just now ; and, before taking the

[1] *Despatches*, page 229.

other Groups in order, or expanding the narrative of this, we may fitly interpolate the praises which it won from Major-General C. L. Nicholson, Commanding the 34th Division :

'The G.O.C. 34th Division wishes to place on record his great appreciation of the services rendered by the 147th Infantry Brigade during the period it has been attached to the Division under his Command.   The action of the 4th Battalion Duke of Wellington's, South of the Lys on 10th April, the skilful rearguard fighting under cover of which the Division withdrew from the Nieppe position, the stubborn defence of the right of the Division at Steam Hill (South of Bailleul), and the complete defeat of a whole German Regiment on the 16th April, are exploits of which the Brigade may well be proud.

'Throughout the period, the steadiness, gallantry and endurance of all ranks has been worthy of the highest traditions of British Infantry, and the G.O.C. 34th Division is proud to have had such Troops under his Command.'

Or these praises bestowed on a gallant Regiment may be tested by the record of one man : No. 24066, Pte. Arthur Poulter, of the 1/4th Battalion, Duke of Wellington's (West Riding), who was awarded the Victoria Cross for his action on April 10th, commemorated in the following terms in the *London Gazette* of June 28th :

'For most conspicuous bravery when acting as a stretcher-bearer.   On ten occasions Pte. Poulter carried badly wounded men on his back to a safer locality, through a particularly heavy artillery and machine-gun barrage.   Two of these were hit a second time whilst on his back.   Again, after a withdrawal over the river had been ordered, Pte. Poulter returned in full view of the enemy who were advancing, and carried back another man who had been left behind wounded.   He bandaged up over forty men under fire, and his conduct throughout the whole day was a magnificent example to all ranks.   This very gallant soldier was subsequently seriously wounded when attempting another rescue in the face of the enemy.'

A Group, similarly constituted, of the 148th Infantry Brigade was sent on April 10th to Neuve Église, which was plainly threatened on that day, under orders to move at half an hour's notice.   The same night, its 1/5th York and Lancasters became attached to the 74th Brigade (25th Division) where it was drawn into the fighting near Steenwerk, to the South of Nieppe, and rendered valuable service, remaining in attachment until April 16th.   Next day (11th), in the morning, the 1/4th Battalion of the same Regiment was detailed to counter-attack on a line West of Ploegsteert Wood, where the rest of the 25th Division was engaged.   Hill 63 is situated immediately North of the North-west corner of that Wood, and Neuve Église lies about two miles to its North-west.   We shall have to come back

to the gallant record of this unit, and of the 1/4th King's Own Yorkshire Light Infantry, and of others in the Group, during the struggle for
Neuve Église, which lasted till the night of April 14th/15th.   It is a
record of desperate valour against overwhelming odds ; and, when,
weary but undaunted, the Brigade was withdrawn to Poperinghe
on April 19th, it had thoroughly earned the encomium of Major-
General Sir E. G. T. Bainbridge, Commanding the 25th Division :

> ' Will you thank the 148th Infantry Brigade for all they
> did in holding on to Neuve Église ?   It is, of course, greatly
> due to them that the place was held as long as it was.'

Similar praises were bestowed by the Brigadier-General Commanding the 74th Brigade (25th Division) on the Battalion of the 148th
Brigade, which had been under his orders.   He placed on record,

> 'his great appreciation of the services rendered by the 5th Battalion
> York and Lancaster Regiment during the time it was attached
> to the Brigade under his Command.   The gallantry and en-
> durance of all ranks throughout the operations are worthy of the
> highest traditions of the British Army, and it was a pleasure to
> the B.G.C. to have such Troops under his Command.   He was
> much impressed by the dashing manner in which the Battalion
> carried out the attack on Cabaret du Saule on 11th April, and
> by its stubborn resistance on 14th April on Mont de Lille.'

We come, last in this summary, to the 146th Infantry Brigade
(49th Division).

On April 10th, it was in line in the Ypres salient, under the orders
of the 21st Division.

Next day, very early in the morning, its 1/7th Battalion, West Yorkshire Regiment, became attached to the 62nd Infantry Brigade, which
had been detached from the 21st Division and placed under the orders
of the 9th (Scottish) Division, commanded by Major-General G. H.
Tudor.   That Division (the 9th), we may note, in anticipatory compensation for its terrible losses in this area in April, was to have the
honour on July 19th of capturing Meteren with great *éclat*.   This
reversal of misfortune lay in the future.   To-day the situation was
very grave, and the part played by the 1/7th West Yorkshires, in
attachment to the attached Brigade, may best be told, in advance of the
more detailed narrative, in the Report of the Brigadier-General
Commanding the 62nd Brigade, which was transmitted by General
Tudor to General Cameron (49th Division).   It was dated April
20th and ran as follows :—

> 'I should like also to draw attention to the very gallant be-
> haviour of the 1/7th Battalion West Yorkshire Regiment, of
> the 146th Infantry Brigade.

> 'On the critical afternoon of the 11th April, when the Brigade
> holding the Messines Sector was driven back, leaving my right
> flank perilously exposed, the 1/7th West Yorkshire Regiment

was moved up at very short notice from Parret Camp to form a defensive flank on the Bogaert Farm-Pick Wood Spor, and to fill the gap on our right.

'Under very heavy shelling the Battalion moved forward splendidly, and their steadiness undoubtedly saved the situation. From that evening until the morning of the 16th the Battalion held the right sub-sector of the Brigade front from Bogaert Farm to Pick Wood ; on the night of the 15/16th they handed over from Bogaert Farm to Scott Farm to the 1st Battalion, Lincolnshire Regiment, and took over to Spanrock-Molen inclusive.   On an extended front they encountered the full force of the enemy attack on the morning of the 16th, and fought most gallantly until overwhelmed by superior numbers.   As in the case of other Battalions the mist placed them at an enormous disadvantage, and deprived them of the full use of their fire power.'

Major-General Cameron, in communicating this message to the Brigadier of the 146th, added the expression of his 'great hope, that you will find that you have sufficient old hands remaining to carry on the spirit which has animated the 146th Brigade, and infuse it into the new drafts which I hope to see joining you soon, in order that the name of the 146th Brigade may live for ever.   Please let your Battalions know that I feel deeply proud of them.'

The Battalion had rejoined its own unit on April 18th.   Its casualties between the 11th and 16th had been eleven Officers and four hundred and forty-two other ranks.

Noting that Parret Camp, referred to in the above message, lay a mile and a quarter to the North-west of Kemmel, and that the 1/7th West Yorkshires were supposed to be already tired out when they marched there in high fettle in the early hours of April 11th, we return on that date to the rest of the 146th Brigade.   The Group units were established in the defences of Kemmel Hill, which, though not immediately in the front line, formed a position, as we are aware, of supreme prospective importance.   The Command was entrusted to Lt.-Col. H. D. Bousfield, of the West Yorkshire Regiment, a supernumerary Lieutenant-Colonel at the time, who came under the orders of the 49th Division up to April 13th, of the 19th Division on that date, and, on April 19th, of the 28th French Infantry Division.   To the final assault on the Hill under its French Commander we shall presently come back.

This outline-sketch of the activities of units of the 49th Division in their places in the Valley of the Lys may be supplemented with one or two details, before we pass to the second and worse phase of the battle in that area of fire.

Take, for instance, the struggle about Neuve Église, in which the 148th Brigade bore itself so gallantly, in the grim days, April 12th to 14th.   A glance at the map will show that Neuve Église lies almost midway between Messines and Steenwerk, but (in a narrow area, of course) some way to the West of either.   Thus, its capture, besides re-acting on the hard-pressed 34th Division below, would enable the Germans to round back on the 19th above, where Major-General G. D. Jeffreys would be caught in the rear.   Accordingly, here, as much as anywhere (we should say 'worse than elsewhere,' but no comparison could be sustained), the command to hold out to the last man was imperative and binding.   And right well this Brigade of the 49th supported the valorous efforts of various bodies of brave troops, including a mixed lot of a thousand, whom Brigadier-General Wyatt, formerly Commanding the 1/4th York and Lancs., had collected from anywhere to do everything.   General Wyatt's old Battalion and a sister-Battalion in the Brigade, the 1/4th King's Own Yorkshire Light Infantry, had already done stiff service in the defence of Neuve Église, where, on April 13th, the assault broke out again with added fierceness.   At 7 a.m. on that day, the enemy entered the village.   At 8-30, counter-attacks were launched of their own initiative by all available units of the Brigade, and were pushed with courage and determination.   In this action, Major Jackson, M.C. (of the 458th Field Company, Royal Engineers), Captain J. F. Wortley, M.C., and Lieut. Gifford, M.C., (both of the 1/4th York and Lancs.), were specially mentioned in the Brigadier's message to the Battalion. A big bag of prisoners was made, and the village was cleared of Germans.   We are told that, about this time (the afternoon of April 13th), the Troops were still cheerful and in good heart, but that the continuous strain and want of sleep were beginning to tell.   Unfortunately, they told in vain.   On the night of 13th/14th, the enemy came on again, and forced a way into the village.   Captain Wortley was killed in an attempt to establish a line about the Church, though that line was subsequently held by small parties of the 4th York and Lancs. and of the 9th Highland Light Infantry (Glasgow Highlanders). We read that 'these plucky men refused to obey the order to withdraw, and were eventually cut off completely by the enemy, and there is little doubt that they died fighting to the last.'   To lose Neuve Église under such conditions was to win imperishable renown.

Or take a difficult little operation by two Companies of the 1/5th West Yorkshires (146th Brigade), which was not less difficult because it proved successful.   On the night of April 15th/16th, a partial withdrawal, as we saw above, was made perforce in the Ypres salient. These two Companies, under the Command of Major Foxton, were left to hold posts in the Corps line across the Menin Road about three miles East of Ypres.   They did their job very thoroughly.   By moving dummy carrying parties about the tracks, and keeping six men in the front line, right away till broad noon on that day, and by other manœuvres, they deceived the enemy so completely that no approach to our old front line was attempted till 3-30 p.m.

Meteren : Ap: 1918:

Bailleul
(Meteren Road)
Ap. 1918.

[Face p. 188.

We need not expand the account of the exploits of the 1/7th West Yorkshires during their hard days of service with the 62nd Brigade. We know by now that a situation could be 'saved,' in the expressive word endorsed by General Tudor, only by endurance of a kind corresponding to the call of the British Commander-in-Chief on the 13th.   We prefer to conclude on a quieter note.   These few, casual illustrations of a week's fighting, as desperate as it was heroic, for the ultimate safety of the Channel ports, would convey a false impression if they painted no scene but 'death or glory.'   It was hard going all the time, and the conditions told, as we have seen.   But the grit of the Yorkshiremen was not unequal to the incessant demands. We read nearly always of a cheerful spirit, of a line which seemed 'good' by comparison with other lines which they had known worse, of refreshing snatches of rest, of the welcome arrival of the limbered wagons with rations, and similar incidents of the kind, which helped to ease what had to be endured.   We read, too, in an Officer's diary, such a characteristic entry as the following : 'Next morning, there was light shelling, but about 1-30 p.m. the Boche started a heavy bombardment, and attacked at 3 o'clock from the South-west.   *This was his usual time-table all through these operations.*' (The italics are ours). And, again, a page or two later on : 'The Boche programme continued : a heavy bombardment 1 p.m.—3 p.m.'   They had taken the measure of their Boche.   It was all very frightful and terrible, and good men were falling every hour ; but frightfulness 'according to plan,' as Macbeth discovered in his day, contains an antiseptic element, which is related to the sense of humour in the British soldier.   If it is too much to say that this sense would always enhearten him, at least it stood him in good stead, and even inspired him with good hope, when Hollbeke, Messines, Ploegstreet, Neuve Église and Bailleul had been left behind the German front, and the salient round Ypres had been retracted, and the storm was about to burst on Kemmel Hill.

II.—SECOND PHASE

THERE were four or five more or less calm days in the sector North of the Lys.   The battle-fury surged a little South on a front from Merville to Givenchy, extending along the La Bassée Canal, and it broke out afresh in the Somme Valley, on the slopes just East of Amiens, where the village of Villers Bretonneux changed hands twice in two days (April 24th, 25th), remaining the second time in British possession.   The interval in the Northern area, though used for rest and re-organization, so far as circumstances allowed, was less an interval than a breathing-space, in which both sides were awaiting the call of ' Time ! '   A renewed attack was obviously impending.   The enemy would want to exploit his gains, and to make that push for Ypres and Dunkirk, which had haunted his day-dreams for four years.   The blow fell on April 25th, at about 5 o'clock in the morning, when a very violent bombardment along the whole line from Hollbeke to Bailleul announced the commencement of the second phase of the sanguinary Battle of the Lys.

If we look once more at the familiar map, we shall see the Allied line stretching from North-east to South-west.   British troops were holding the line from a point on the Ypres-Commines Canal just above St. Eloi to a point about a mile below Wytschaete.   The 21st Division was on the Canal, with a composite Brigade of the 39th; the 9th Division held the Wytschaete Ridge, with three units of the

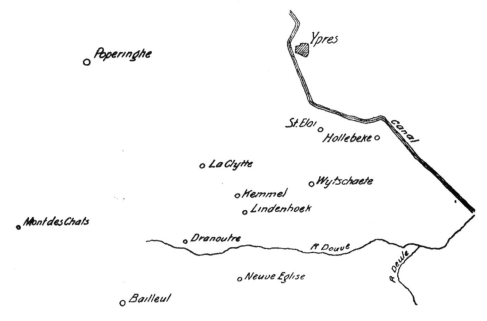

21st and 49th (chiefly the 146th Infantry Brigade).   The rest of the line was French.   Immediately below our 9th Division was the 28th French Division, in Command of the Kemmel Defences; next below, at Dranoutre, came the 154th, in face of an enemy assault from Neuve Église.   Then came the French 34th, and their 138th at St.-Jans-Cappel.   Behind the line, two Brigades of our 49th (the 147th and 148th) were in Corps Reserve in and around Poperinghe, and one Brigade each of the 30th and 31st were located between Poperinghe and the front line.   Our 25th Division was in Reserve, a little behind the two Brigades of the 49th.

Against these worn and weary Troops, so lately withdrawn from the positions from which they were now to be assailed, and so hardly re-organized or recruited, the enemy launched nine Divisions, 'of which five were fresh Divisions and one other had been but lightly engaged.'[1]

[1] *Despatches*, page 232.

Their direct objective was Kemmel Hill, an important point of observation in that country of low-lying flats, and important, too, as a jumping-off place for Ypres ; their subsidiary purpose was to separate the British from the French forces by a flanking movement below Wytschaete.   Accordingly, the weight of the attack fell first on the French 28th and the British 9th Divisions, with the two Brigades attached to the latter.   Dealing first, with the British sector, we are not surprised to learn, in Sir A. Conan Doyle's temperate narrative, that 'the 9th Division in the north was forced to fall back upon the line of La Clytte [behind Kemmel], after enduring heavy losses in a combat lasting nine hours, during which they fought with their usual tenacity, as did the 64th and 146th Brigades, who fought beside them.'[1] It is rather the details which surprise us, and help to make this 'tenacity' real.   At 2-30 a.m. on April 25th, this Brigade of our 49th Division had to endure a two hours' bombardment with heavy gas-shells and smoke.   It was followed by half an hour of the greatest intensity with High Explosives.   At 5 o'clock, in the inevitable mist, which enhanced the difficulty of the defence, the Infantry attack was launched, but was held on the Brigade front.   At 6-45, a Company of the 1/6th West Yorkshires was reported to be fighting a rearguard action under Captain Sanders, V.C.   This gallant Officer was seen rallying his men from the top of a pill-box, and, though wounded, he continued firing with his revolver at point blank range until he fell.   No news came from the front line Companies, but all the evidence goes to show that they fought and died at their posts.   We need not follow the retirement of what was left of these Battalions, first, to Vierstraat Cross Roads and then to Ouderdom.   The evidence of casualties is more pertinent.   In the West Yorkshire Regiment, on these two days (April 25th, 26th),[2] the 1/5th's casualties amounted to eighteen Officers and five hundred and fifty-seven other ranks ; the 1/6th's to twenty-two and four hundred and sixty-one, and the 1/7th's to five and one hundred and thirty-nine respectively.   The Trench Mortar Battery of the Brigade was engaged on Kemmel Hill during this battle, and none of those in action returned.   We may add here, that, at Ouderdom on April 27th, some Brigade remnants were formed into a composite Battalion, under Major R. Clough, of the 1/6th West Yorkshires, and were placed in Divisional Reserve at the call of the 147th Brigade, the rest being withdrawn into a back area.

Turning now to the action on the French front, and to the German assault on Kemmel Hill,[3] and observing that St. Eloi and Dranoutre, to the East and West of the position, fell at an early hour into the enemy's

[1] *Op. cit.*, page 301.

[2] The 9th Division, after its tremendous fighting, for which it was thanked by both Army Commanders, was withdrawn on April 26th, when Major-General Cameron, of the 49th, took Command of the sector.

[3] The assailants brought up an Alpine Division (among three others), trained especially for hill fighting.

hands, we have to record that by 10 a.m. on April 25th Kemmel Village
and Hill had both been lost.   It will be recalled from our summary
of this fighting that Lt.-Col. Bousfield, Commanding some units of
the 49th Division (146th Brigade) had been left in Command on Kemmel
Hill on April 11th, and handed over to the French Divisional Commander on the 19th.   He and his fellow Yorkshiremen continued
the defence till the last moment with conspicuous courage and devotion.
On April 26th, at 3 a.m., counter-attacks were made by the French
and British in combination, in which Troops from the 49th Division,
attached to the 25th, again bore themselves gallantly.   But the
position then was irretrievable, at least in its main aspects, and the
line in the salient was further re-adjusted during the night of April
26th/27th.

This brief account of a big event (the darkest hour of the Flemish
battle, it has been called) might be extended into the local fighting
which marked the course of the next few days.   But an extract from
one Officer's diary may suffice as a sample of what was happening :
we have trusted his judgment before, and his first and last sentences
are decisive.   He writes on April 28th :

'The Germans were not ready to profit by their success at
Kemmel.   During the next three days there was a good deal
of shelling by long-range guns, but no attacks, and the Battalion
[it was in the 148th Brigade] was able to improve the line greatly,
with Lewis gun posts pushed well forward to command the valley
in front.   A French cart stranded in No Man's Land was found
to be full of excellent signalling equipment, which improved
our communications.

'29th April.—On April 29th the Germans made what proved
to be their last attempt on the Ypres front.   Their plan was to
attack on the whole front from Dranoutre to Voormezeele, and
so pierce the line to the South of the city.   A heavy bombardment
with shells of the heaviest calibre opened and continued unceasingly from 3 a.m. to 4 p.m.   It was probably the heaviest bombardment the Battalion has had to face, and casualties were many,
including some of the finest fighters of the Battalion.   At 4, the
Germans attacked.   On the 7th Battalion front, where there
was dead ground, the Germans got into the line, and were only
driven out by successive bayonet charges.   On the 6th Battalion
front, the forward posts could see the Germans descending
Kemmel, and with Lewis gun and Rifle fire stopped them dead
with great loss.   Before dark, the attack had definitely failed
along the line : the Germans had played their last card.'

This conclusion agrees with Sir F. Maurice's : 'The gain of
Kemmel proved to be the enemy's undoing ' ; and with that of all
competent authorities, reviewing the battles of March and April,

1918, with the knowledge acquired since the war was ended.   Ludendorff could not exploit his successes, for in no sector was any of them complete.   The failure to break through in the north 'was hardly less important in its effect on the campaign than that which the Germans had suffered on March 28th, and these two triumphs of our defence over the enemy's attack went far in preparation for the victories which came later in the year.'[1]

So, the darkest hour gave place to the dawn.

Congratulatory messages, couched in the highest terms, reached the 49th Division in its time of merited relief.

General Sir Herbert Plumer, Commanding the Second Army, conveyed, on April 29th, the following message from Field-Marshal Sir Douglas Haig, Commander-in-Chief of the British Armies :

' I desire to express my appreciation of the very valuable and gallant service performed by Troops of the 49th (West Riding) Division since the entry of the 146th Infantry Brigade into the Battle of Armentières.   The courage and determination shown by this Division have played no small part in checking the enemy's advance, and I wish to convey to General Cameron and to all Officers and Men under his Command my thanks for all that they have done.'

On May 2nd, the IXth Corps Commander, Lieut.-General Sir A. Hamilton Gordon, sent the following message :

'Heartiest congratulations on the splendid fight you put up on 29th April.'

Throughout this period (April 10th to May 2nd), the 49th Divisional Artillery had been serving with the 21st Division, and they received from Major-General Campbell the following letter of thanks :

'Before handing over Command of the 49th Divisional Artillery, I wish to express to all ranks my thanks and appreciation of the excellent work done since it has been under my Command. No Commander could have been better served in every possible way.   The splendid fighting spirit shown by all ranks has been beyond all praise.'

We may add here that the 49th Division were no whit less appreciative of the gallant and efficient help which they had received from C.R.A., 9th Division, in Command of the following Artillery Brigades : 50th, 51st, 148th, 156th and 162nd R.F.A. Brigades and 30th Heavy Artillery Brigade.

D.D.M.S., XXIInd Corps, wrote to A.D.M.S., 49th Division, to congratulate him on 'the extraordinarily efficient manner in which casualties have been evacuated from your area under the recent trying conditions.   I have never seen the work more speedily and successfully carried out'; and truly Major-General Cameron might say to his 'Comrades of the 49th Division ' :

[1] *The Last Four Months*, page 52.

O

'The reputation which you have won for courage, determination and efficiency, during recent operations, has its very joyous aspect, and it is deeply precious to us all.'

The name of Ypres is inscribed in English history : like Khartoum, Kandahar, Trafalgar, and other names in older times, it has been adopted in the title of a British Commander.   It belongs, by the same token, to the 49th Division, whom, twice in the course of the War, in the Spring of 1915 and of 1918, we have seen defending its trenches or fighting in the open for its safety, and to whom a Memorial is dedicated on its site.   They had well earned the praises bestowed upon them.   To them, with very gallant comrades, including our Belgian Allies, fell the part of guarding the approaches to the vital line of the Channel ports.   On April 9th, 1918, when the course of the *Kaiser-schlacht* was diverted from the Southern to the Northern front, Sir Herbert Plumer's Second Army formed our last line of defence in Flanders.   That line held at the end of April, after three weeks' shattering blows, unsurpassed in impetus and severity ; and, throughout those weeks, the 49th were in the line.

CHAPTER XIV

THE YEOMANRY

THE pace was too fast to be kept up. The Germans could not be doing it all the time, and pauses, lengthening in duration as the fury of the attacks increased, were bound to be interposed between one onslaught and the next. Here, again, as on previous occasions, the official German historians of the war will be able to correct the impression which their daily bulletins sought to create, and will tell an attentive world how the desperate courage of the invader broke on the final factor which no resources of science can permanently disguise—fighting men's physical exhaustion.

Such a pause, partly filled, as we shall see, by a transfusion of bloodshed to another area, occurred at the height of that darkest hour, which we followed in the last chapter ; and, before pursuing our account of the West Riding Infantry Divisions through the last hundred days of the war, we may fitly utilize this interval to narrate, necessarily a little summarily, the fortunes and the disappointments of some of the West Riding Mounted Troops. For they, too, as Earl Haig has testified, 'came forward at the beginning of the war to serve their country in the hour of need,' and 'performed their duty under all circumstances with thoroughness and efficiency.'

These words occur in an Order, dated September 9th, 1917, and addressed by the Field-Marshal to the 1/1st Yorkshire Hussars Yeomanry. 'The Army Council,' the Order starts, 'has found it necessary to dismount certain Special Reserve and Yeomanry Regiments, and to utilize the services of Officers and other Ranks in other branches of the Service.' Here we see the meaning of 'under all circumstances,' and the cause of the disappointments to which we have referred.

That the war was not a Cavalry war, and that its 'circumstances' did not often call for the special faculties furnished by Mounted Troops, are facts that enhance, rather than diminish, the praise of the 'thoroughness' and 'efficiency' with which the duties falling on the Yeomanry were discharged. Officers, N.C.O.'s and men adapted themselves with conspicuous cheerfulness to the shifting needs of the day's work, and became fitted to the uses which were made of them. But no keenness, military or moral, could turn the war into *their* war. The war in South Africa was their war, the next war may be their war again ; 'but the circumstances of the late war gave them few chances of doing the work for which they were intended, and their chief claim to credit lies in the fact, that, whatever work they were given to do, they carried out to the best of their ability, and to the complete satisfaction of the authorities under whom they worked.'[1]

How complete that satisfaction was, may be judged by one or two letters, which we are privileged to quote, and which it is appropriate to produce in advance of such narrative as may prove available of the miscellaneous duties which the Yeomanry actually performed. Thus, when 'B' Squadron of the Yorkshire Hussars left the 46th Division in May, 1916 (the particulars of this move will be found below), Major-General E. J. Montague Stuart-Wortley wrote to their Commanding Officer, Lieut.-Col. W. G. Eley :

' Many thanks for your letter. It was a great blow to me to find on my return from leave, that your Squadron had left the Division, and that our very pleasant connection had come to an end.

'I can assure you that it has been the greatest pleasure to me to have had your Squadron under my command ; and I should be very much obliged if you would tell all your Officers, N.C.O.'s and men how deeply I appreciate all the good work they have done whilst with this Division. They have frequently been called upon to do work which was quite outside of what Cavalry are trained to perform ; and on every occasion, they have carried it out with zeal and efficiency which has been deserving of all praise.

'You will be glad to have the whole Regiment together again ; I shall watch all you do with the greatest interest ; I know that all you are called upon to do, will be done well.'

Again, in 1917, when the same Yeomanry Regiment left the XVIIth Corps, in consequence of the decision of the Army Council, notified in the Field-Marshal's Order as above, to dismount them and utilize them 'in other branches of the Service,' Lieut.-General Sir Charles Fergusson, Bt., Commanding the Corps, wrote to Lieut.-Col. Eley :

'On the departure of the Regiment from the XVIIth Corps I wish to express to you and to the Officers and men under your command my thanks for the loyalty and assistance which has invariably been given by the Regiment during the period of its connection with the Corps.

'Its smartness, discipline, and soldierly spirit have been conspicuous ; and no matter what the work has been, it has always been carried out in accordance with the best traditions of the Regiment and of the Service.

'I know that Officers and men will continue to live up to these traditions, and that no matter where duty and the service

---

[1] From a Memorandum on the Yorkshire Dragoons, prepared for the purposes of this history by Lieut.-Col. W. Mackenzie Smith, D.S.O., in Command, 1914, of which full use has been made in the present chapter.

of the country call them, they will never forget that the reputation and good name of the Regiment remain in their hands. Whether as a unit or as individuals the spirit of the Regiment will remain ; and when the time comes for it to be re-united, the knowledge that they have done their duty under all circumstances will add to the pride and satisfaction with which Officers and men will look back to their record in the war.

'I wish goodbye and good luck to all ranks.'

Again, in 1919, when the Yorkshire Dragoons left the Rhine (these particulars, too, will be found below), Lieut.-General Sir C. W. Jacob, K.C.B., Commanding the IInd Corps of the Second Army, addresses the following letter to Major-General the Earl of Scarbrough, in his capacity as Hon. Colonel of the Regiment :

'The Yorkshire Dragoons are leaving very shortly for England on reduction to cadre, and as you are the Hon. Colonel of the Regiment, I thought you would like to hear how well the Regiment has done all the time that it has been with the IInd Corps.

'You know that at first the Regiment was split up and its squadrons distributed among various Divisions. In the early part of 1916 it was decided to take away from Divisions their Cavalry Squadrons, and to have a Cavalry Regiment at the headquarters of every Army Corps. The three squadrons of the Yorkshire Dragoons were thus brought together and formed into a Regiment again, and in May, 1916, became the Cavalry Regiment of the IInd Corps. It was in that month, too, that I took over command of the IInd Corps.

'From the time the Yorkshire Dragoons came to the IInd Corps till hostilities ceased on the 11th November, 1918, their work has been excellent all through. They have had strenuous times, but have always shown themselves equal to the occasion.

'Yorkshire has given many thousands of splendid soldiers to the British Army, and I place the Yeoman of the Yorkshire Dragoons high up in the list. They have responded to every call made on them, and have fought magnificently.

'In October, 1917, the regiment was taken away from the IInd Corps for work with the Cavalry Corps. Later on, owing to the shortage of horses in the army, it was decided to dismount the Yeomanry Regiments and to turn them into machine-gun or cyclist units. The Yorkshire Dragoons were formed into a Cyclist Regiment, and came back to the IInd Corps as such. It was naturally a disappointment to them to be dismounted, but they accepted the situation in the right spirit and very soon became the best cyclist unit in the British Army.

'I cannot speak too highly of their work in the final phase of the war, when they took part in the attack from Ypres in

September, 1918, and when the Germans were driven clean
out of Belgium.

' The Regiment has been fortunate in its Officers. They
were first of all commanded by Lieut.-Col. Mackenzie Smith,
D.S.O., up to the time they were dismounted. Since then
they have been commanded by Lieut.-Colonel R. Thompson,
D.S.O. Both these officers have been first-class, and I cannot
speak too highly of the latter. Lieut.-Colonel Thompson is a
first-rate leader, and he has been backed up by an excellent lot
of junior officers.

' I regret very much to have to part with the Regiment, but
their turn for demobilisation has come round. They have earned
the gratitude of their country and county in the way they have
worked and fought all through the war, and have made a name
for themselves which will never be forgotten.'

General Jacob's letter (May 27th, 1919) epitomizes clearly, six
months after the Armistice, the successive stages of organization
through which the Mounted Troops had passed. Between the lines
of the various decisions therein recorded ('to take away from the
Divisions their Cavalry Squadrons,' to take away the Cavalry Regiments
from the Corps, 'to dismount the Yeomanry Regiments and to turn
them into machine-gun or cyclist units '), we may read the meaning
of some remarks occurring in earlier letters : ' They have frequently
been called upon to do work which was quite outside of what Cavalry
are trained to perform ' (General Stuart-Wortley) ; ' No matter what
the work has been, it has always been carried out in accordance with
the best traditions of the Regiment and the Service ' (General
Fergusson), and ' their chief claim to credit lies in the fact, that,
whatever work they were given to do, they carried out to the best
of their ability ' (Col. Mackenzie Smith). The time never quite came
to employ the Cavalry. They never really came into their own. But
it was not till a late period in the war, when the shortage of horses
in the Army and the skrinkage of man-power and shipping at home
compelled the authorities to drastic action, that the repeatedly disappointed hope of employing them at last in their right capacity was
finally abandoned. Accordingly, their history in the Great War
is a history of partially fulfilled renown, in relation to their pre-war
training and to their anticipations on mobilization. ' It must be
admitted,' we read, 'that the Yorkshire Dragoons never felt either
pride or affection for their bicycles. The one thing to be said for them
was that they were more easily cleaned than horses, and never had
to be exercised or fed.' In this sense, 'their chief claim to credit,'
in the words of Lieut.-Col. Mackenzie Smith,[1] may be stated in the

---

[1] Col. Smith relinquished his Command of the Dragoons at this date, since in its new form
it was only a Major's Command, to Major, afterwards, Lieut.-Col. R. Thompson,
D.S.O.

highest terms as a claim to the credit of subordinating their own desires, and the ambition appropriate to their Arm of Service, to the needs of the Army and the Empire as a whole.

We may follow these changes more precisely.

Originally, both Yeomanry Regiments, after coast defence and other work at home, went out to France as Divisional Cavalry. The Hussars arrived at Havre in April, 1915, and were posted as follows :

'A' Squadron to the 50th (Northumbrian) Division,

'B' Squadron to the 46th Division, and

'C' Squadron to the 49th (West Riding) Division.

The Dragoons arrived in August, and were posted :

'A' Squadron to the 17th Division,

'B' Squadron to the 37th Division, and

'C' Squadron to the 19th Division,

all in General Plumer's Second Army, to which, under General Jacob's Command, they were to return later on as a Cyclist Corps.

Their time as Divisional Cavalry lasted till May, 1916, but was not as full as they had hoped. 'Our work,' writes an Hussar Officer in a personal letter, 'was very miscellaneous. We fetched up remounts, dug trenches, buried wires, supplied M.M.P. and orderlies to the Divisional Staff, and observation posts to the Infantry in the front line;' and Col. Smith, of the Dragoons, writes in much the same vein : 'They did many dull, but arduous and necessary fatigues. But they took an especial interest in the Divisional observation posts, the management of which was entrusted to them by the Division,' and which proved, as he says in another place, 'a definite speciality of the Regiment, and earned them considerable credit.'

The first organic change is explained in a letter from G.H.Q., dated May 2nd, 1916, and addressed to the Third Army Commander. We cite here the salient extracts :

'In consequence of the growth of the Army and the development of the Corps Organisation, much of the independence of action and movement formerly belonging to the Division has passed to the Corps. It has been found necessary, therefore, to reconsider the organization and distribution of the Mounted Troops hitherto allotted to Divisions.

'The allotment of these troops was originally made with a view to providing the Divisional Commander with a small mobile force under his immediate control for reconnaissance, protective and escort duties ; and on the assumption (originally correct) that the Division would be moving either independently, or with one or more roads allotted to its exclusive use.

'These conditions are unlikely to recur ; any future movement will be by Corps, marching and fighting in depth on a comparatively narrow front. The mounted troops belonging to the Corps must, therefore, be assembled under the direct

control of the Corps Commander, and organized as Corps units.
'The Commander-in-Chief has accordingly decided—

'(a) to convert the Squadrons of Divisional Cavalry into Corps
Cavalry Regiments, composed of a Headquarters and Three
Squadrons each; one Regiment being allotted to each
Corps.

'(b) to withdraw the Cyclist Companies from Divisions, to
reconstitute them into Battalions of Three Companies each,
and to allot one Battalion to each Corps.

'(c) to allot one Motor Machine-Gun Battery to each Corps.
This battery will normally be attached to the Cyclist
Battalion.'

The following Table shows how the foregoing provisions were
applied to the Squadrons of Yorkshire Dragoons and Yorkshire
Hussars :

Transferred	From			To	
Squadron	Div.	Corps	Army	Corps	Army
'A' Squadron 1/1st Yorkshire Dragoons ...	17	II	Second	II	Second
H.Q. & 'B' Squadron 1/1st Yorkshire Dragoons	37	VII	Third		
'C' Squadron 1/1st Yorkshire Dragoons ...	19	XI	First		
'A' Squadron 1/1st Yorkshire Hussars ...	50	V	Second	XVII	Third
'B' Squadron 1/1st Yorkshire Hussars ...	46	XVII	Third		
'C' Squadron 1/1st Yorkshire Hussars ...	49	X	Fourth		

Thus, the Divisional Cavalry were transferred, and each Corps
now received a Squadron of Cavalry, a Battalion of Cyclists, and a
Battery of Motor Machine-Guns. At this time the training of the
Cavalry in France was inspired mainly by General Gough, who
subsequently commanded the Fifth Army ; and the rôle devised for
Corps Cavalry Regiments was summed up, as he said, in the one
word ' "Security" : that is, the protection of the Infantry with
which it is working.' These were the days, it will be remembered
from earlier chapters of the present volume, in which a break-through
was still hoped for, when the Corps Mounted Troops would have
followed the five Divisions of Regular Cavalry through the 'gap'
to be made in the German line, and would become immediately
responsible for the protection of the Infantry Reserve and for general
Advance Guard duties.

But events did not fall out as had been expected. ' During the
summer and autumn of 1916 there were several occasions,' we are
told, 'on which the Higher Command had hopes of a Cavalry situation,

. . . but these hopes never materialized.' The main work of the Regiment in these months—and very important work it proved—was to maintain observation posts in forward areas, and it was true that opportunities occurred, and were seized with gallant alacrity, to win the Military Cross and the Military Medal for special acts of reconnaissance and daring. In less forward areas the duties were more laborious, but were not less cheerfully performed. Traffic control, unloading ammunition trains, helping at hospitals and burying the dead; the maintenance of communications in winter mud, when the Infantry were roped together in order to go into the front line, and casualties by drowning were almost as numerous as those caused by the enemy: these, with training, and the care of horses, and the usual Regimental sports, were among the functions substituted in reality for the purpose cherished by the Corps Cavalry. In March, 1917, at the time of the German retreat, the IInd Corps Cavalry had the chance, of which they fully availed themselves, of proving their mettle in mounted action, and the D.S.O. awarded to Lieut.-Col. Mackenzie Smith was a recognition of his wise insistence on a constant high level of training efficiency. The disappointment of his Mounted Troops at Cambrai in November, 1917, was their final grief before the Order for dismounting.'

We shall not follow in detail the dismounted history either of the Dragoons or the Hussars in the miscellaneous duties to which they were called. We may note, however, that, in the battles of 1918, good fighting work was done by both Regiments, and that, early as October 20th in that year, Lieut.-Col. Thompson received his D.S.O. as an immediate award, in recognition of his gallantry at the crossing of the River Lys. General Jacob's letter to Lord Scarbrough, quoted on an earlier page, refers particularly to this Officer, and to the part taken by his cyclists 'when the Germans were driven clean out of Belgium.'

So the Yeomanry, too, before war's end, had their fill of fighting in the front line, and, alike in honours and casualties, through all the phases of their experience, as Divisional Cavalry, as Corps Cavalry, and as Dismounted Troops, they bore themselves with conspicuous bravery and with not less conspicuous self-sacrifice. They were content to do the task set before them, when, owing to causes beyond control, they could not do the task for which they had been trained, and neither in the West Riding nor beyond it will their splendid record be allowed to fade. Not inappropriately it happened that the IInd Corps of the Second Army[1] was chosen to form part of the Army of the Rhine. The Yorkshire Dragoons were detailed to act as Advance Guard to the Infantry of the 9th, 29th and 41st Divisions; and 'consequently,' we read, 'in most of the towns and villages through which they passed, they were the first British troops which the

[1] See Table, above.

inhabitants saw. The march through Belgium was a triumphal progress.'

But we must not anticipate the day of triumph, amply as the Yeomen had contributed to it. The battles of 1918 have still to be won, and we return at this point to the interval called by exhaustion after the First Battle of the Lys.

CHAPTER XV

THE LAST HUNDRED DAYS
I.—THE SECOND BATTLE OF THE MARNE

THE force of the German onslaughts of March 21st and April 9th, 1918, had been spent beyond hope of renewal on the fronts in which they occurred. On the Lys, as, a month earlier, on the Somme, and more necessarily because of the further month's exhaustion, time had to be taken to reorganize, to recuperate, and to recommence; and the time taken by the enemy was time given to the Allies.

How admirably they employed it in May, June and the first part of July does not fall within the province of the present chronicler. It happened that it was not till July 20th that the Territorial Infantry from the West Riding entered into action since May on any considerable scale. Accordingly, we may pass over the interval. We may pass over the dispatch of the IXth Corps, commanded by Sir A. Hamilton Gordon, and consisting of the 8th, 21st, 25th and 50th Divisions, all of which had had their full share of fighting, to join the Sixth French Army on the Aisne. The intention was, to give them a chance of rest in a section unlikely to be busy ; the effect was to give them a worse experience in the sudden battles about Reims than they had endured on the Somme or on the Lys. How they acquitted themselves is best told in the noble language of the French Army Commander, General Maistre, in his farewell letter (July 3rd) to General Hamilton Gordon :

> 'Avec une ténacité, permettez-moi de dire, toute anglaise, avec les débris de vos divisions décimées, submergées par le flot ennemi, vous avez reformé, sans vous lasser, des unités nouvelles que vous avez engagées dans la lutte, et qui nous ont en fin permis de former la digue où ce flot est venu se briser. Cela aucun des témoins français ne l'oubliera.'

Immediately after this disaster, which had brought the Germans within forty miles of Paris, and Paris within range of their 'freak' gun, Marshal Foch withdrew from Flanders his force of about eight Divisions, and transferred them southwards to the French front. Next, he asked that four British Divisions might be moved down to the Somme, so as to ensure the connection between the French and British forces about Amiens ; and, 'after carefully weighing the situation,' wrote Sir Douglas Haig, 'I agreed to this proposal.' But the Generalissimo's resources still fell short of the plans he was maturing. 'On the 13th July a further request was received from Marshal Foch that these four British Divisions might be placed unreservedly at his disposal, and that four other British Divisions might be dispatched to take their places behind the junction of the Allied Armies.   This request,' wrote the British Commander-in-Chief, 'was also agreed to, and the 15th, 34th, 51st and 62nd British Divisions, constituting the XXIInd Corps, under Command of Lieut.-General Sir H. Godley, were accordingly sent down to the French front.'[1]

We resume our chronicle, therefore, with the record of the 62nd Division in the counter-offensive by Marshal Foch, which he launched on July 18th, and which, by repeated hammer-strokes, increasing in strength and velocity, was to bring the war to its appointed end. Exactly a hundred days elapsed between July 18th and October 26th, when Ludendorff's resignation was accepted, and he left German Army Great Headquarters. Before resuming it, however, for the space of those hundred days, a word, though not strictly within our province, may be said about Haig's decision on July 15th. We are to recall that the Allies had been defeated three times in less than four months, and had given up far more ground than was ever contemplated in the previous winter Councils. A German gun had found the range of Paris, and might find the range of the Channel ports. The secrets of the autumn of victory were locked up in the harvester's brain ; yet he asked for four *plus* four Divisions to be moved from the British to the French front. We should leave the matter there : all the papers have not yet been published ; but perhaps we may quote at this point the reasoned opinion of Major-General Sir F. Maurice :

'Haig, being responsible to his Government for the safety of his army and the ports, felt that he must obtain their concurrence in this last step, though he was quite ready to take the responsibility upon himself of advising them to concur. It does honour to Foch, to Mr. Lloyd George and to Sir Douglas Haig that in this critical time they all agreed. Both the British Government and the British Commander-in-Chief supported Foch, decided to back his judgment, and to accept the danger of weakening the British forces in the north, and he was thus enabled to mature his plans for the defeat of Ludendorff. . . It required great courage and determination to make that attack as it was made. The Germans had still a superiority of more than 250,000 Infantry on the Western front, and Foch, as well as Mr. Lloyd George and Sir Douglas Haig, had to take risks.'[2]

So, we march with General Braithwaite's Yorkshire lads to the Valley of the Ardre, where for the next ten days (July 20th to 30th) they played a glorious part in the Second Battle of the Marne, after which there was no turning back.

The River Ardre rises due south of Reims, in the forest called

[1] *Despatches*, pp. 254-55.
[2] *The Last Four Months*, pages 71, 97.

after that city. It flows in a north-westerly direction through richly-timbered and hilly country, which afforded every facility for the cunning nests of machine-guns in which the enemy excelled. We have two or three descriptions of the lie of the land from a military point of view. The valley, we read, 'is bounded on each side by high ridges and spurs, the crests of which are heavily wooded : those on the north by the Bois de Reims, on the south by the Bois de Coutron and the Bois d'Eclisse. The villages of Marfaux and Chaumuzy in the bottom of the valley, also the dominating height of the Montagne de Bligny (some seven thousand yards from the line of departure) afforded the enemy three successive *points d'appui* of great strength.

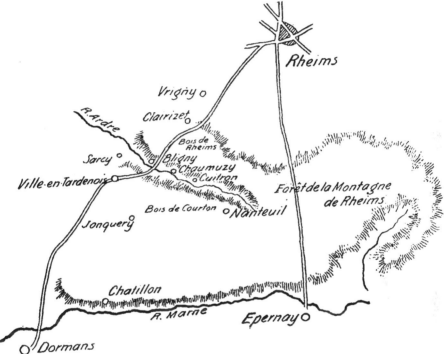

These centres of defence were further strengthened by natural buttresses formed by the hamlets of Cuitron (North), Espilly, Les Haies and Nappes (South), all perched high up on the abrupt slopes and spurs running down into the valley below. So steep are some of these slopes that the light French Tanks (*Chars d'Assaut*) were unable to operate upon them in places, and the Tanks' activities were further restricted by stretches of soft and marshy ground on either bank of the Ardre. Standing crops in the undulating valley, the vineyards on the slopes, and the dense woods on the ridges, concealed the hostile positions from view, whilst sunken roads and banks running at right angles to the direction of attack provided ready-made positions for a stubborn defence.'

In this large, dense wood of summer foliage, on slopes running down to marshy ground, we are to remember that the 'stubborn defence' was now the business of the Germans.   The conditions of the war in the West had changed in several important aspects. Not merely was the enemy on the defensive, to the huge enheartenment of the Allied Forces, but this account of the natural features is necessary because the fighting was now in the open, and no longer in a too familiar entrenched area.   To these changes in tactics and terrain, at once so novel and so inspiriting, was added the fresh experience of fighting side by side with new friends.   General Godley's Corps, we remember, was sent at Marshal Foch's request right away from the British northern sector into the area of the French Command. There it found the 1st Italian Division, the 14th and the 120th French Divisions, and the 1st Colonial French Corps ; and we are told that, in this War of Positions, 'the transference to a sector with its natural obstacles, the novel situation of passing through Italian Troops to attack side by side with our French Allies in the attempt to oust enemy forces (enjoying all the advantages that the possession of the initiative and positions of great natural strength would give them) presented problems to all Arms which had hitherto been met with only in theory.'   The practical problem of language was the least.   Education authorities will learn with pleasure, though some of their critics may be surprised, that 'there were far fewer French Officers with any working knowledge of English than British Officers with a working knowledge of French, and French was the language generally used.' Whether it was the French of Stratford-atte-Bow, or the French of the British private, 'Tout-de-suite, and the tooter the sweeter,' our information does not reveal ; but it is satisfactory to know that the 'working knowledge' aimed at in our schools answered a test which experts might not have satisfied.   Of other details, such as entraining and 'embussing,' this is not the place to speak : certain differences in practice were found, and were solved with good will on both sides.   We may add here, in this list of new conditions, that the 62nd Division now included the 2/4th Hampshire Regiment, recently arrived in France, and the 1/5th Devons, lately from Egypt. On August 2nd, Major-General Braithwaite wrote to the County Territorial Associations, at Southampton and Exeter respectively, to express his high sense of their several distinguished services ; and he wrote at the same time to the Durham Association, in connection with the 9th Durham Light Infantry, the Pioneer Battalion of the Division, to say that it has been necessary to employ them in this Second Battle of the Marne as a fighting Battalion, and that 'they fought magnificently, as Durham men always do.'

The assembly of the Troops for the battle was not an easy matter. Long marches were entailed ; the roads were strange and crowded ; exact positions on the night of 19th/20th were difficult to ascertain, and it was not till after daybreak on July 20th that the Brigades were in position upon the base of departure. Briefly, the River Ardre formed the dividing-line between Divisions, with the 62nd (West Riding) on the right and the 51st (Highland) on the left.[1] The two Divisional Headquarters remained together throughout the operations, an arrangement which they found of incalculable value. On July 31st, we may note, Generals Braithwaite and Carter-Campbell exchanged letters, expressing in the most cordial terms the pleasure each Division had derived from serving side by side with the other.

A start was made on the right at 8 a.m. on July 20th, under an artillery barrage, the leading Brigades being the 187th (right) and 185th (left), with the 186th in Divisional Reserve, to leap-frog and capture the second objective. As may be judged from the nature of the country and the advantages offered to its defenders, progress was slow and casualties were heavy, and the deadly nests of German machine-gunners proved very stubborn to rout out. Now in one part and now in another, the combined advance was temporarily held up ; small groups went too far forward ; detachments tried to work a way round ; till, through the standing grain or wooded undergrowth, little streams of prisoners trickled out, vocal witnesses to the prowess of the attackers. It was obvious at the end of the first day that a part of the Bois de Reims between Courmas and Cuitron, especially a strong point located on a timbered spur south-west of the Bois du Petit Champ, would have to be thoroughly cleared before the operations could be successful, and at 10-30 on July 21st, the 187th Brigade was detailed for this work. As one result of this day's heavy fighting, in which the 9th Durham Light Infantry and the 2/4th York and Lancs. may particularly be mentioned, the 103rd and 123rd German Divisions had to be completely withdrawn, and replaced by Regiments of the 50th German Division. Thus, the 62nd had fought two enemy Divisions out of the field.

On July 22nd, the capture and clearance of the obstructive Bois du Petit Champ was entrusted to the 186th Brigade (Brig.-General Burnett), and was successfully carried out with great dash and initiative by the 5th Duke of Wellington's. Initiative, indeed, was the key to a very trying and tricky situation. The undergrowth in places was found to be as thick as in a tropical jungle, and machine-gun crews hidden in the thickets had evidently been trained to fire in the direction of sound. It was necessary to attack at close range, with casualties increasing as the range shortened. Two companies of the 5th Devons arrived to reinforce their Yorkshire comrades, and to assist in capturing a strong point of eight machine-guns and their garrison. It was a very gallant little enterprise, in which the front company of the Left Column was surrounded after hard hand-to-hand

[1] These Divisions, it will be recalled, had fought together at Cambrai in November, 1917. See page 148, above.

fighting, and its position rendered untenable by the superior numbers of the enemy. Captain Cockhill, M.C., cleverly withdrew his few remaining men, and two Officers and six other ranks fought their way out to the posts of the rear company. By nightfall, the whole of the area was cleared, with the exception of a strong pocket of the enemy situated in the centre of the wood, and very difficult to locate, who were captured next day ; and this example of a single, small action in a tight corner of a wood, down south of the long front line, serves to show with what gallantry and courage the invader was driven out of France.

The prisoners' bag of July 22nd was two Officers and two hundred and six other ranks of the 53rd Infantry Regiment, 50th German Division, together with forty-one machine-guns. On the 23rd, the clearance of the Bois enabled progress to be made all along the northern front of the Ardre, and eight French 75 m.m. guns, re-captured from the enemy, were included in an excellent day's haul.

Passing over the intervening period, with its daily tale of prisoners and gains, though accompanied by very heavy losses, we come to July 28th, when the 8th West Yorkshire Regiment, supported by the 5th Devons, made a particularly brilliant assault on the Montagne de Bligny, north-west of the Bois de Reims. They started at 4 o'clock in the morning, and, aided by the half-light of a late July dawn, succeeded in reaching the foot of the steep slopes of the mountain before they attracted hostile fire. This surprise, combined with the dash displayed by the assaulting Troops, who, in spite of serious casualties, succeeded in rushing the hill, resulted in the capture of a position of great tactical importance.

How important, in the opinion of the best judges, may be gathered from the following extract from the Minutes of the West Riding Territorial Force Association, held at York on October 28th, 1918 :

'MAJOR CHADWICK asked if any information could be given as to whether the French Government had awarded the *Croix de Guerre* to the 8th Battalion, West Yorkshire Regiment (Leeds Rifles).

'LORD HAREWOOD replied : The *Croix de Guerre* has been offered to the Battalion of the Leeds Rifles referred to, but whether or not the War Office will allow the Battalion to accept it I do not know.'

The Fifth French Army Commander's Order on the subject, dated October 16th, was worded as follows :

'Le 8th Bataillon du West Yorkshire Rgt.

' Bataillon d'élite ; sous le commandement énergique du Lieutenant-Colonel Norman Ayrton, England, a participé brillamment aux durs combats du 20 au 30 Juillet, qui ont valu la conquête de la Vallée de l'Andre. Le 23 Juillet, 1918, après s'être frayé un chemin dans les fourres épais du Bois du Petit

Champ, s'est emparé d'une position importante malgré un feu nourri des mitrailleuses ennemies. Le 28 Juillet, 1918, dans un brio magnifique, a enlevé la Montagne de Bligny, fortement défendue des forces ennemies supérieures en nombre, s'y est maintenu malgré les pertes subies, et les efforts désespérés de l'adversaire pour réprendre la position.'

It was a great and almost a unique compliment ; and, as we shall presently see, the 8th West Yorkshires enjoyed at a later date another striking opportunity of proving their gallantry in action.

July 29th, to return to our recital, was a comparatively quiet day. On the 30th, the 2/5th West Yorks. successfully carried out a small attack to complete the capture of the Mount Bligny, and, meanwhile, the remaining Troops of both Divisions had reached their final objectives.

We subjoin the official account of these ten days' ' continuous fighting of a most difficult and trying nature. Throughout this period,' runs the statement, 'steady progress was made, in the face of vigorous and determined resistance. Marfaux was taken on the 23rd July, and on the 28th July British Troops retook the Montagne de Bligny, which other British Troops had defended with so much gallantry and success two months previously. In these operations, throughout which French Artillery and Tanks rendered invaluable assistance, the 51st and 62nd Divisions took one thousand two hundred prisoners from seven different German Divisions, and successfully completed an advance of over four miles.'[1] The total casualties for the period in the 62nd Division alone amounted to 4,126 :

	Killed.	Wounded.	Missing.
Officers	28	108	10
Other Ranks	521	3,063	406

Apart from the victory which was gained, the whole operation, as shown above, afforded very useful lessons in the new conditions of warfare, and it was utilized to the full in this sense. Particular attention may, perhaps, be drawn to the experiment of Machine-Gun Battalions, which was found to have more than justified the change of system. The M.G. Battalion of the 62nd Division had now fought in two battles : in a defensive battle in the previous March, and now in an offensive battle on the Marne, and the improvement in the Machine-Gun service was estimated at sixty per cent. at least. Partly, its success might be ascribed to the fact that the Commanding Officer of the Battalion was not selected for expert gunnery, but was a good Infantry Officer, with an eye for country, a knowledge of tactics, and a power of command.

But where all units and Commanders did so well, it is invidious to select one Arm. We may more fitly close this section of the Second

[1] *Despatches*, page 255.

P

Battle of the Marne with some extracts from the congratulatory messages earned by General Braithwaite's Division. There was, of course, the new fact of a close *liaison* between British and French Troops, which caused more than common punctiliousness in the preparation and dispatch of these epistles ; but the tone is exceptionally cordial, the sentiments are extraordinarily sincere, and the praises were very thoroughly deserved. General Bertholot, Commanding the Fifth French Army, published an Order of the Day, dated July 30th, of which the following is a translation :

'Now that the XXIInd British Corps has received orders to leave the Fifth Army, the Army Commander expresses to all the thanks and admiration which its great deeds, just accomplished, deserve.

'On the very day of its arrival, the XXIInd Corps, feeling in honour bound to take part in the victorious counter-attack, which had just stopped the enemy's furious onslaught on the Marne, and which had begun to hurl him back in disorder towards the north, by forced marches and with minimum opportunity for reconnaissance, threw itself with ardour into the battle.

'By constant efforts, by harrying and driving back the enemy for ten successive days, it has made itself master of the Valley of the Ardre, which it has so freely watered with its blood.

'Thanks to the herioc courage and proverbial tenacity of the British, the continued efforts of this brave Army Corps have not been in vain.

'Twenty-one Officers and more than one thousand three hundred other ranks taken prisoners, one hundred and forty machine-guns and forty guns captured from an enemy, four of whose Divisions were successively broken and repulsed ; the upper Valley of the Ardre, with its surrounding heights to the north and south reconquered ; such is the record of the British share in the operations of the Fifth Army.

'Highlanders, under the Command of General Carter-Campbell, Commanding the 51st Division ; Yorkshire lads, under the Command of General Braithwaite, Commanding the 62nd Division ; Australian and New Zealand Mounted Troops ; all Officers and men of the XXIInd Army Corps, so brilliantly commanded by General Sir A. Godley—you have added a glorious page to your history.

'Marfaux, Chaumuzy, Montagne de Bligny—these famous names may be inscribed in letters of gold in the annals of your Regiments.

'Your French comrades will always remember with emotion your splendid valour and perfect fellowship as fighters.'

It was well and generously said.

The XXIInd Corps Commander specially conveyed through

Major-General Braithwaite his high appreciation of the Divisonal Artillery : 'The way in which Batteries worked with Battalions, and Brigades with Brigades of Infantry, in open warfare, must have been a source of enormous satisfaction to all Officers, Non-Commissioned Officers and men, and the way in which it was done is worthy of the best traditions of the Royal Regiment.' Other letters and orders were published, and the memory of the Marne was added to that of Bucquoy, Cambrai and Havrincourt in the tradition of the 62nd Division.

II.—THE FINAL OFFENSIVE.

EVENTS moved quickly from this date, more quickly, indeed, than they were divined except in the swift mind of the great Marshal, and more quickly than they can be conveniently followed in a day-to-day narrative of two Divisions. The greatest battle in all history was planned, and fought, and won, between August 8th and September 9th, 1918, the period described by Sir Douglas Haig as 'the opening of the final British offensive.' It is the word 'final' which signifies. So definite, in fact, was the issue, that Ludendorff described August 8th as 'the black day of the German Army in the history of this war,' and proffered his resignaton a few days later. This was not accepted at the time, but at a Council held on August 14th he expounded the situation to the Kaiser and to the ruling German statesmen, with the result that Prince Max of Baden was subsequently appointed Imperial Chancellor with a view to paving the road to peace. These developments, not quite obscurely hinted at in a Note issued by Sir Douglas Haig on the eve of the Battle of Bapaume (August 21st to September 1st), must inevitably dominate our review of the 'great series of battles, in which, throughout three months of continuous fighting, the British Armies advanced without a check from one victory to another.'[1] The autumn fighting of 1918 differed from that of previous years, in that there was no fifth winter to the war. We have not to follow our Divisions over the top of their trenches, and back again, when the weather failed, into the monotony of trench life. They did not fully know that they were fighting the last battles : it would be difficult to fix the exact date when this was revealed even to Marshal Foch and Sir Douglas Haig. They did not welcome the Armistice with the joy with which it was acclaimed in London : 'the news of the cessation of hostilities was received by the fighting Troops,' writes an Officer of the 62nd Division who was 'in at the kill,' ' without any of the manifestations of excitement that marked the occasion at home ' ; it was just an incident of the day's work, and a sign that the work had been done well. But an effect of increasing speed, of the accelerated progress of Titanic forces, directed irresistibly to one end, cannot but be felt during this period. Amiens was disengaged

[1] *Despatches*, page 257.

after August 8th, partly by a brilliant feint in Flanders, which deceived even the King of the Belgians. Thiepval Ridge, with its graves of 1916, Pozières, Martinpuich, Mory (by the 62nd Division) were re-taken in the fourth week of August, and on August 29th Bapaume fell. On September 1st, the Australians took Péronne, and Bullecourt and Hendecourt fell the same day. Meanwhile, the Channel ports were safe at last, for the enemy had no Troops with which to threaten them, and he partly withdrew and was partly driven from the Lys salient. Merville, Bailleul, Neuve Église, Kemmel Hill, Hill 63 : all the tragic places of the previous spring were once more in rightful hands in September. There followed the Battle of the Scarpe, and the storming of the Drocourt-Quéant Line, by the results of which, on the British front, in the centre, we were brought right in face of the main German defences known as the Hindenburg Line. The question was, whether to attack it now or later. On September 9th, Sir Douglas Haig had been in London, and had indicated that the end might be near. He wrote, after weighing all the chances : ' I was convinced that the British attack was the essential part of the general scheme, and that the moment was favourable. Accordingly, I decided to proceed with the attack, and all preparatory measures were carried out as rapidly and as thoroughly as possible.'[1] A great month, and a grand decision.

So, we return at this point to the services of the Troops from the West Riding, and shall fit them in to the concluding battles, where they occurred.

At the end of August (25th to 27th), the 62nd Division drove the Germans out of Mory, situated in country which they knew, about four miles north of Bapaume. Excellent work there was achieved, among other units, by the 2/4th and 5th King's Own Yorkshire Light Infantry and by the 2/4th York and Lancs. 'D' Company Commander in that Battalion led a charge against a nasty position in an awkward little hold-up, and personally accounted for the machine-gun team with his revolver. Many prisoners, including a Battalion Commander, were captured by the Division in these three days.

There was still hard fighting for the Division before it was withdrawn for a few days' rest, and the height of efficiency it had reached may fitly be judged by a single instance, extracted from the *London Gazette*, December 26th, 1918. Therein is recorded the award of the coveted Victoria Cross to Sec.-Lieut. James Palmer Huffam, of the 5th (attached, 2nd) West Riding Regiment (T.F.), in the following circumstances :

'For most conspicuous bravery and devotion to duty on August 31st, 1918.

'With three men he rushed an enemy machine-gun post, and put it out of action. His post was then heavily attacked,

[1] *Ibid.*, page 278.

and he withdrew fighting, carrying back a wounded comrade. Again, on the night of August 31st, 1918, at St. Servin's Farm, accompanied by two men only, he rushed an enemy machine-gun, capturing eight prisoners and enabling the advance to continue. Throughout the whole of the fighting from August 29th to September 1st, 1918, he showed the utmost gallantry.'

Meanwhile, on August 27th, Major-General Walter Braithwaite was appointed to the Command of the IXth Corps, with the rank of Lieutenant-General, when a Knight Commandership of the Bath was conferred upon him in recognition of his services with the 62nd. It will be recalled that he succeeded Sir James Trotter in Command of the 62nd Division in December, 1915.[1] He took the Division over to France, and led it with conspicuous gallantry till the very eve of its final bout of victory. His affection for his brave 'Yorkshire lads' was fully reciprocated by his subordinate Officers, Non-Commissioned Officers and men, who were all sensible of the constant care and fine, soldierly qualities of their Commander. Sir Walter Braithwaite has taken every opportunity, in subsequent meetings with, or references to, the Division, to testify to his pride and pleasure in that office : 'I look back,' he wrote to the Secretary of the West Riding Association (November 3rd, 1918), 'on the time spent in Command of that heroic Division as one of the proudest terms of years in my life. . . . I don't think I can be accused of partiality in saying that there is no Division in the B.E.F. with a prouder record of continued success than the 62nd.' He was succeeded now by Major-General Sir R. D. Whigham, K.C.B., D.S.O., who took over at a most responsible time and who saw the war out and the peace in.

The grand decision referred to above, and concerted early in September between Marshal Foch and Sir Douglas Haig, found the Division in the Gomiecourt area, where they had been withdrawn on September 3rd, in order to rest and train. On the 8th, Lieut.-General Sir J. A. L. Haldane, Commanding the VIth Corps in the Third Army (General Sir Julian Byng), called on Major-General Whigham to explain the part to be taken by the 62nd in the impending operations. It was to attack and capture the village of Havrincourt, and 'Z' day was subsequently appointed for September 12th. We may recall from page 150 above, the first capture of Havrincourt by this Division on November, 1917. We may recall, too, how on September 9th, 1919, almost on the anniversary of its second capture, it was announced at a Divisional Dinner that a Memorial to the Division was to be erected in Havrincourt Park. We are now to see how it was won on the second occasion.

There was this difference between the second and the first. In the battle of 1917, the break-through on the Cambrai front did not close with a permanent advance. Owing partly, as we now know,

[1] See page 74, above.

to the diversion of some Divisions to Italy, the brilliant design, so
courageously supported, could not be completely carried out.   This
time, there was no going back.   It was the Hindenburg Line which
was to be captured, on the road from the River Marne to the River
Meuse.

The Hindenburg Line, so called by our Troops, was neither
Hindenburg nor a Line.   As described and pictured by great generals,[1]

it consisted of a series of defences, including many defended villages,
and forming a belt, or fortified area, varying in depth from seven to
ten thousand yards.   It stretched from Lille to Metz, and among
its extensions, or switches, was the famous 'Drocourt-Quéant Switch,'
which had held up our advance more than once.   Within this system
of barriers, running through a stratum of deep cuttings, the enemy

[1] See, particularly, *Despatches*, pp. 278 *ff*, and Sir F. Maurice, *The Last Four Months*, pp. 133 *ff*.

had prepared elaborate dug-outs, shelters, and gun-emplacements, all heavily fortified and wired. The luxurious appointments of some of them, which so much astonished beholders, need not detain us here. The importance of these extraordinary entrenchments to their assailants in the autumn of 1918 lay, first, in their genuine strength, to which German engineers had devoted all the ingenuity of their craft, and, next, in the almost legendary awe with which time and sentiment had invested them. This effect was carried out in their native names. Working from north-west to south-east, they were known in the German Army and behind it as Wotan, Siegfried (supported by Herrmann), Hundung (Hagen), Brunehilde (Freya), Kriemhilde and Michel ; and we may well believe that, at the back of the front, until such time as the front broke, German opinion was obstinately convinced that their tutelary heroes must protect the Fatherland from invasion.

It was the task of the 62nd Division to break into this line through Havrincourt, and, by breaking it, to shatter the illusion. For, at last, on the Western front, we were fighting not only positions but ideas.

The operation (September 12th to 15th) proved a complete success. It was carried out on the left by the 187th, and on the right by the 186th Infantry Brigade, with the 9th Durham Light Infantry (Pioneers) attached to the latter as an assault Battalion. One company of the 62nd Machine-Gun Battalion was allotted to each attacking Brigade, and eight Brigades of Field Artillery and three Groups Heavy Artillery were in position to support. The plan of attack entailed a change of direction from north to east, in order to obviate the difficulties of the terrain, and the consequent complication of the Artillery barrage had to be very carefully worked out. In contrast to the attacks in November, no Tanks were employed in this action, but it bore in another respect a superficial resemblance to the First Battle of Havrincourt, insomuch as the first day's work 'could not have been bettered, but again there was to be a second chapter, a chapter of hard fighting, in very difficult circumstances, fought to the end, and crowned with success.' We shall not follow it in detail, save to note that, an hour after Zero (5-30 a.m.) on September 12th, 'large batches of prisoners were coming back,' and that four Officers and eighty men of these had been captured at a strong point which 'offered little resistance, owing to the great gallantry of Sergt. Laurence Calvert,[1] of the 5th King's Own Yorkshire Light Infantry.' His great gallantry won the Victoria Cross, in circumstances officially described as follows :

'For most conspicuous bravery and devotion to duty in attack, when the success of the operation was rendered doubtful owing

---

[1] It should be observed that Sergt. L. Calvert, V.C., was enlisted in the 1/5th K.O.Y.L.I., 49th Division. This Battalion was amalgamated in February, 1918, with the 2nd Line unit, and became the 5th K.O.Y.L.I., 187th Brigade, 62nd Division.

to severe enfilade machine-gun fire. Alone and single-handed, Sergt. Calvert, rushing forward against the machine-gun team, bayoneted three and shot four. His valour and determination in capturing single-handed two machine-guns and killing the crews therefore enabled the ultimate object to be won. His personal gallantry inspired all ranks.'

All ranks were inspired to good purpose ; or, more precisely, the inspiration of all ranks found its typical expression in the brave act of this gallant N.C.O. The Division's team-work, now as always, was exemplary ; and, whether judged by casualties or captures,[1] the result of the Second Battle of Havrincourt was a great triumph for General Whigham in his new Command.

For Havrincourt looked to the east. It looked through the intricate defences, in which the German people still believed, to Cambrai and St. Quentin, and beyond. Thus it formed one of those 'formidable positions,' which, as Sir Douglas Haig wrote, 'had to be taken before a final attack on the Hindenburg Line could be under-taken.' By its capture, and that of others, 'our line advanced to within assaulting distance of the enemy's main line of resistance.'[2] And General Whigham, in a letter of October 9th, addressed to the Secretary of the Association at York, said, in almost identic terms : 'On September 12th, the Division was called upon to repeat its former feat of capturing the village of Havrincourt. This village stands on very commanding ground, and formed a most formidable position in the Hindenburg front line. Its capture was essential to the development of the great offensive south of Cambrai, in which we have latterly been engaged. . . Without the possession of Havrincourt, the grand attack of September 27th could not have been successfully launched.'

So, we come to that 'grand attack,' in which, as the General went on to say, 'the Division has once more added fresh lustre to its fame.' On this occasion they were engaged to the south of the scenes of their exploit in November. Graincourt now fell to the 63rd Division, Anneux to the 57th, Bourlon and Bourlon Wood to the 4th and 3rd Canadian Divisions. The 3rd Division moved forward with the Guards, forcing the crossings of the Canal, by capturing Ribécourt and Flesquières (the objective of the 51st in the previous November). To the 62nd was allotted the task of following up the attack, and of securing the crossings of the Canal at Marcoing. Once more, we have the high privilege of illustrating the nature of the operations by a single typical example of the spirit which animated all ranks. The *London Gazette* of December 14th, 1918, announced

---

[1] The figures were : *Killed*, 8 Officers, 199 other ranks ; *Wounded*, 34 Officers, 1,068 other ranks ; *Missing*, 228 other ranks ; *Total*, 42 Officers, 1,495 other ranks.
   Captured : *Prisoners*, 18 Officers, 866 other ranks ; *Field Guns*, 4 ; *Trench Mortars*, 12 ; *Machine Guns*, 46.

Despatches, page 276.

the award of the Victoria Cross to Private Henry Tandey, D.C.M., M.M., of the 5th Duke of Wellington's, in the following circumstances :

'For most conspicuous bravery and initiative during the capture of the village and the crossings at Marcoing, and the subsequent counter-attack on September 28th, 1918.

'When, during the advance on Marcoing, his platoon was held up by machine-gun fire, he at once crawled forward, located the machine-gun, and, with a Lewis gun team, knocked it out.

'On arrival at the crossings he restored the plank bridge under a hail of bullets, thus enabling the first crossing to be made at this vital spot.

'Later in the evening, during an attack, he, with eight comrades, was surrounded by an overwhelming number of Germans, and, though the position was apparently hopeless, he led a bayonet charge through them, fighting so fiercely that thirty-seven of the enemy were driven into the hands of the remainder of his company.

'Although twice wounded, he refused to leave till the fight was won.'

No defences made by man, certainly none made by German, could withstand courage of this kind.

In a Special Order of the Day, issued on October 1st, by Major-General Sir R. Whigham, Commanding the 62nd Division, he addressed his gallant Troops as follows :

'The capture of Havrincourt on 12th September was essential to the success of the operations south of Cambrai, in which the 62nd Division has been engaged during the last four days.

'As a sequel to that brilliant achievement, the Division has now captured Marcoing, Masnières, and the high ground north of Crèvecoeur, thus establishing a bridgehead over the Canal de St. Quentin, which is vital to the further successful prosecution of the campaign.

'The Field Marshal Commanding-in-Chief visited Divisional Headquarters to-day, and desired me to convey to all ranks of the Division his congratulations and high appreciation of their splendid courage and endurance.

'For myself, I give you all my warmest thanks for the unfailing cheerfulness with which you have carried out the most arduous tasks, often in conditions of great hardship and discomfort.

'It will ever be to me a pride to have commanded so magnificent a Division.'

Yet one more word about Marcoing. On an earlier page we remarked that we should have occasion to come back to the 8th Battalion of the West Yorkshire Regiment, the *Bataillon d'élite* of a French Army Order. This occasion occurred on September 27th, when two companies of that Battalion earned from the VIth Corps

Commander (Lieut.-General Sir A. Haldane) the following striking encomium, dispatched through the 62nd Divisional Commander:

'Please convey to the survivors of the two companies 8th West Yorkshire Regiment my high appreciation and admiration of their initiative, dash and gallantry in pushing up to the outskirts of Marcoing yesterday [September 27th], in spite of all obstacles. It is by resolution and bravery such as they displayed that great victories have been won in the past history of the British Army.

'I heartily congratulate the whole Battalion, yourself, and your splendid Division on the inspiring incident in front of Marcoing.'

Major-General Whigham, in publishing this letter, for the information of all ranks of the Division, showed how well the action of the two Companies illustrated the principle of pressing an advantage, whenever gained.

'The great and critical assaults, in which, during these nine days of battle [September 27th to October 5th], the First, Third and Fourth Armies stormed the line of the Canal du Nord and broke through the Hindenburg Line, mark the close of the first phase of the British offensive. The enemy's defence in the last and strongest of his prepared positions had been shattered. The whole of the main Hindenburg defences has passed into our possession, and a wide gap had been driven through such rear trench systems as had existed behind them. The effect of the victory upon the subsequent course of the campaign was decisive.'[1]

So far, Sir Douglas Haig, with his usual modesty and brevity. In Flanders now, King Albert of the Belgians, leading his nation at last in victory, as he had led it so gallantly in defeat, entered Ostend on October 16th. The Second Battle of Le Cateau in the previous week had driven the last German out of Cambrai; and about this date, as Sir Frederick Maurice writes, 'The revulsion of feeling and the collapse of confidence were such that no enthusiasm could be aroused for a war of endurance in defence of the Fatherland. Even in an autocratic country it is not possible to deceive all the people all the time, and the German people knew in October, 1918, that the victory which had been promised to them could never be obtained '[2]

In these circumstances, the battles still ahead, in which the Divisions from the West Riding were to take part, need not detain us long. The 49th were engaged in October (11th to 17th) at Villers-en-Cauchie and Saulzoir, on the road running eastward out of Cambrai between Douai and Le Cateau. They fought with all their accustomed gallantry, especially in the capture of Saulzoir, which was

[1] *Despatches*, page 285.
[2] *The Last Four Months*, page 203.

RHONELLE RIVER CROSSING (Nov. 1st, 1918).

[Face p. 218.

defended by Machine-Guns and Tanks. When the obstinate resistance had been overcome, an Officer of the 1/6th Duke of Wellington's found the houses full of civilians, who had taken refuge in their cellars, and who welcomed the arrival of the British Troops with offerings of cognac and coffee. The Division fought again below Valenciennes on November 1st and 2nd, and, with the 5th and 61st Divisions, crossed the Rhonelle River and captured the villages of Préseau and Maresches. Lieut.-General Sir A. Godley, Commanding the XXIInd Corps, conveyed to Major-General Cameron the expression of his appreciation of these exploits in the following complimentary terms :

'I wish to heartily congratulate you and your Division on the successful capture of all your objectives and the heavy losses inflicted on the enemy as the result of your two days' hard and gallant fighting.

'All three Infantry Brigades, your Artillery, and Engineers, have added another page to the distinguished record of the Division.'

The 62nd Division, on October 19th and 20th, had the task of capturing Solesmes, and of driving the enemy from the line east of the River Selle, to which he had retired a few days before, partly as a result of the operations in which the 49th had borne themselves so gallantly. This further assault on the German positions, directed ultimately at Le Quesnoy, was to be a surprise, without preliminary bombardment. It was carried out 'according to plan,' with very conspicuous success. Twelve Officers and six hundred and eighty-seven other ranks, seventy-one machine-guns, thirteen trench mortars and five guns were captured at the cost of a casualty list of fifty-seven other ranks killed, ten Officers and three hundred and seventy other ranks wounded. The River Selle was crossed by wading, the water being in many places waist-high. The ground to be traversed proved difficult, with dense hedges and barbed-wire fencing, and in Solesmes itself the street-fighting was serious and severe. But the fine leadership of Platoon Commanders and the excellent spirit of the men carried all obstacles before them ; and, once more, and now for the last time, we have the advantage of illustrating these qualities by an extract from the *London Gazette* (January 6th, 1919), announcing the award of the supreme decoration of the Victoria Cross to Corpl. (A/Sergt.) John Brunton Daykins, of the 2/4th York and Lancaster Regiment, 187th Infantry Brigade, 62nd Division, in the following circumstances :

'For conspicuous bravery and initiative at Solesmes on October 20th, 1918, when, with twelve remaining men of his Platoon, he worked his way most skilfully, in face of heavy opposition, towards the Church. By prompt action, he enabled his party to rush a machine-gun, and during subsequent severe hand-to-hand fighting he himself disposed of many of the enemy,[1] and secured his objective ; his party, in addition to heavy casualties inflicted, taking thirty prisoners.

'He then located another machine-gun, which was holding up a portion of his Company. Under heavy fire he worked his way alone to the post, and shortly afterwards returned with twenty-five prisoners, and an enemy machine-gun, which he mounted at his post.

'His magnificient fighting spirit and example inspired his men, saved many casualties, and contributed very largely to the success of the attack.'

The war's end on November 11th at 11 o'clock in the morning found the bulk of the 49th Division resting on its well-earned laurels in the neighbourhood of Douai. The Gunners, the Royal Engineers

and the Pioneer Battalion went forward in the final stages of the advance, and the Artillery had the distinction of finishing at a point further east than any other Divisional Artillery engaged. The 62nd Division ended in the Valley of the Sambre. If we draw an irregular quadrilateral, dipping a bit on the southern side, with its north-west angle at Valenciennes, its south-west at Le Quesnoy, and its north-east and south-east angles at Mons and Maubeuge respectively, we shall be able to prick in the places of the Division's stout advance between November 4th and 11th (Orsinval, Frasnoy, Obies, Hautmont, Louvroil : it is at this end that the line dips towards Avesnes), by the help of which, as Sir Douglas Haig wrote : 'On the 9th November the enemy was in general retreat on the whole front of the British

---

[1] A Battalion record gives the number as seven.

Douai.
The Belfry

Armies. The fortress of Maubeuge was entered by the Guards Division, and the 62nd Division (Major-General Sir R. D. Whigham), while the Canadians were approaching Mons.'[1]

And Mons, as we know, is the last word of the war on the Western front.

On November 18th, 1918, the 62nd Division started to march to Germany, where it formed part of the British Army of Occupation in the Rhine Province of the Kingdom of Prussia. As a Division of the IXth Corps of the Second Army, it had the luck to come under the command of its former Divisional Commander, Lieut.-General Sir W. P. Braithwaite, K.C.B., then commanding that Corps, who, accordingly, saw the Pelican at last put down his foot on German soil.

[1] *Despatches*, page 297.

APPENDIX I.

TERRITORIAL FORCE.
WEST RIDING OF YORK COUNTY ASSOCIATION.

List of Members and Permanent Officials : 1908 *to* 1920.

Name, etc.	Representation.	Period.
Adair, Lt -Col. T. S., M B., T. D., 3rd W. Riding F.A. (T.F.)	Military Member	1912/13
Allen, Col. Sir C., Kt., V.D., 3rd W. Riding R.F.A.	,, ,,	1908/10
d Anderson, Lt.-Col. F. H., V.D., 5th W. Yorks. Regt.	,, ,,	1908/10
d Armytage, Sir G., Bt., D.L.	Co-opted Member	1908/13
Atkinson, Lt.-Col. H. S., 4th W. Riding Regt.	Military Member	1912/15
Bateman, Lt.-Col. C. M., D.S.O., 6th W. Riding Regt.	,, ,,	1919 to present date
Beadon, Lt.-Col. F. W., V.D., late 7th V.B. W. Riding Regt.	,, ,,	1908/10
Bewicke-Copley, Brig.-Gen. Sir R. C. A. B., K.B.E., C.B.	Co-opted Member Vice-Chairman	1914 to present date 1914 to present date
d Bingham, Col. Sir J. E., Bt., V.D....	Military Member	1908/15
Bingham, Lt.-Col. Sir A. E., V.D., W. Riding Div. R.E.	,, ,,	1908/15
Birch, Col. de B., C.B., M.D., V.D., Admin. Med. Off. W.R. Div.	,, ,,	1908/12
Birkbeck, Lt.-Col. J.	,, ,,	1913/15
T.F. Res.	,, ,,	1918/19
Blakey, J., Esq.	County Borough	1918 to present date
d Bodington, Sir N., Kt., LL.D. (Leeds)...	University	1908/11
Bottomley, Lt.-Col. R. A. A., 6th W. Yorks. Regt.	Military Member	1908/10
Bousfield, Lt.-Col. H. D., C.M.G., D.S.O., T.D., 7th W. Yorks Regt.	,, ,,	1919 to present date
Bower, Capt. H. M., 5th W. Yorks. Regt.	,, ,,	1916/19
d Braithwaite, Major W., V.D., late 3rd V.B. W. Yorks. Regt.	,, ,,	1916/17
Boyd-Carpenter, Capt. A.B.	Asst. Secretary	1914/15
Branson, Col. G. E., V.D., 4th York and Lancs. Regt.	Military Member	1908 to present date
Broadley, A., Esq. (Halifax)...	County Borough	1918 to present date
Brook, Lt. C., Yorks. Dns. Yeomanry ...	Military Member	1908/13
Brooksbank, Sir Edward, Bart., J.P., ...	County Council	1918 to present date
Brown, Col., J. W. H., T.D.	Military Member	1913/15
Northern Command Tel. Cos. R.E.	Military Member	1919 to present date
Brown, Capt. and Ald. A. W., M.B.E., J.P. (Bradford)	County Borough	1919 to present date
Buckle, J., Esq.	Co-opted Member	1908/13
Campbell, Rev. W. O. F. (Chaplain 2nd Class—attd. W. R., R.G.A.)	Military Member	1916 to present date
Carr, J. R., Esq. (Dewsbury)	County Borough	1918/19
Cass, Major C. P., T.D., 6th W. Riding Regt.	County Council	1915/19
Chadburn, Col. A. W., V.D., late W. Riding Div. R.E.	Military Member Co-opted Member	1908/13 1914 to present date
Chadwick, Major G. W., T.D., late 7th W. Yorks. Regt.	Military Member	1916/19

List of Members and Permanent Officials—continued.

Name, etc.	Representation.	Period.
Chambers, Lt.-Col. J. C., C.B., V.D. ...	Military Member	1908/15
T.F. Res.		1918/19
	Co-opted Member	1919 to present date
Chappell, A., Esq., J.P.	County Council	1908/13
	Co-opted Member	1914/to present date
Clark, Lt.-Col., E.K., T.D., T.F. Reserves	,, ,,	1908/13
	Military Member	1914/15
	,, ,,	1919 to present date
Clayton, Lt.-Col. W. K., C.M.G., Yorks.	Co-opted Member	1911
Mtd. Field Amb., R.A.M.C., T.F.	Military Member	1912/15
Clegg, Sir W. E., Knt.	Vice-Chairman	1908/15
	Co-opted Member	1908/15
Clifford, Lt.-Col. C., C.M.G., V.D., 3rd W.	Military Member	1908/15
Riding Bde., R.F.A.		1919 to present date
Clough, Major T. C., V.D., T.F. Res. ...	Co-opted Member	1908 to present date
Clough, Lt.-Col. R., M.C., T.D., 6th Bn.	Military Member	1919 to present date
W. Yorks. Regt.		
Coghlan, Col. C., C.B., V.D., D.L. ...	,, ,,	1908/10
	Co-opted Member	1911/19
Collins, Major E. A.D., T.D., Yorks. Hrs.	Military Member	1918/19
Yeo.		
Connell, Bt.-Col. A. M., F.R.C.S. (Edin.),	,, ,,	1916/19
(late A. Medical Services T.F.)		
Copley, see under Bewicke		
d Cooke-Yarborough, C.B., Esq., D.L., J.P.	Co-opted Member	1908-09
Dalton, Major-Gen., J. C., J.P., Retired	,, ,,	1913 to present date
Pay p.s.c. (R.).		
Dawson, Lt.-Col. W. S., T.D., late 4th W.	Military Member	1910/19
Riding Bde. R.F.A.		
Dawson, Major J. M.	County Council	1919 to present date
Deramore, Lt.-Col. R. W., Lord, Yorks.	Military Member	1919 to present date
Hrs. Yeo.		
Dobson, Major J. F., M.B., F.R.C.S., 2nd	,, ,,	1913-15
N. General Hosp.		
Duncan, Lt.-Col. K., D.S.O., 4th W.	,, ,,	1919 to present date
Riding Bde. R.F.A.		
Duncombe, Col. C. W.E., C.B.E., T.D.,	,, ,,	1909/13
Yorks. Hrs. Yeo.	,, ,,	1915
	County Director	1916/19
Durnford, W. A., Esq.	County Council	1918 to present date
d Fawcett, J. E., Esq., (Bradford)	County Borough	1908/18
Firth, Lt.-Col. B. A., V.D., T.F. Res. ...	Military Member	1914/19
Fitzwilliam, Lt.-Col. W. C. de M., Earl,	Co-opted Member	1908/10
K.C.V.O., C.B.E., D.S.O., W.R.,	Military Member	1911/15
R.H.A.	,, ,,	1919 to present date
Foster, Lt.-Col. E. H., T.D., 2nd W. Riding	,, ,,	1908/15
Bde. R.F.A.		
d Foster, E. H., Esq.	County Council	1908/16
d Foster, H. A., Esq., J.P.	Co-opted Member	1908/09
Foster, Lt.-Col. L. P., V.D., late 1st V.B.	County Borough	1915/17
W. Rid. Regt. (Halifax)		
Fox, Lt.-Col. C., T.D., T.F. Res.	Military Member	1915
	,, ,,	1918 to present date
d Franklin, G., Esq. (Sheffield)	University	1908
Freeman, Col. C. E., V.D., late 2nd V.B.	Military Member	1916/19
W. Riding Regt.		
Garnett, R., Esq.	County Council	1919 to present date
Garstang, W., Esq., M.A., D.Sc. (Leeds) ...	University	1915/19
Gascoigne, Col. R. F. T., D.S.O., late Yorks.	Military Member	1908
Hrs. Yeo.	,, ,,	1916/19
Gaskell, Major E. M., D.L., Yorks. Dns. Yeo.	County Council	1908/17

List of Members and Permanent Officials—continued.

Name, etc.	Representation.	Period.
Goodyear, Major H. S., V.D., late 1st V.B. K.O. Yorks. L.I.	Military Member	1916/19
Gordon, Professor G. S. (Leeds)	University	1919 to present date
Graham, Major W., W. Rid., R.G.A. ...	Military Member	1914/15
Green, Lt.-Col. F. W., late Yks. Dns. Yeo. ...	,, ,,	1915/19
d Greenwood, A., Esq.	Co-opted Member	1908/09
Hardaker, D., Esq., J.P.	County Council	1908/19
Hartley, Lt.-Col. J. E., 4th W. Rid. R. ...	Military Member	1909/10
Harewood, Col. H. U., Earl of, K.C.V.O., T.D., A.D.C.	President	1908 to present date
Haslegrave, Lt.-Col. H. J., C.M.G., T.D., 4th Bn. K.O. Yorks. L.I.	Military Member	1914-15
	,, ,,	1918 to present date
Hastings, Lt.-Col. J. H., D.S.O., 6th Bn. W. Yorks. Regt.	,, ,,	1911/12
Haywood, Lt.-Col. R. B., W.R. Dnl. R.E.	,, ,,	1919 to present date
Hepworth, Lt.-Col. W., V.D., 8th Bn. W. Yorks. Regt.	,, ,,	1911/17
Hickson, Lt.-Col. J. L., W. Rid. Vol. Regt.	Co-opted Member	1918/19
Hind, Col. E., V.D., 4th K.O. Yks. L.I. ...	Military Member	1908/13
	Co-opted Member	1914/17
	,, ,,	1919 to present date
Hirst, Lt.-Col. E. A., C.M.G., T.D., 1st W.R. Bde., R.F.A. (Leeds)	County Borough	1908/17
	Co-opted Member	1919 to present date
Hirst, T. J., Esq., J.P.	,, ,,	1908 to present date
Hobson, A. J., Esq.	,, ,,	1908/19
Hobson, C., Esq.	,, ,,	1908/13
Hoskin, J., Esq.	,, ,,	1908/09
d Howard, Major J. B., 4th W. Rid. Regt. ...	Military Member	1911
d Hoyle, Lt.-Col. C. F., Northern Com. Tele. Cos., R.E.	,, ,,	1908/12
Hoyle, Lt.-Col. E., O.B.E., W.R. Motor Volunteers	Co-opted Member	1919 to present date
d Hughes, Col. H., C.B., C.M.G., V.D., Ret. T.F.	Military Member	1908/16
Husband, Lt.-Col. J. C. R., V.D., late 5th Bn. W. Yorks. Regt.	,, ,,	1908/12
	,, ,,	1918/19
Ingham, Major H. O., T.D., late W. Rid. R.G.A., Vols.	,, ,,	1916/19
Ingilby, Major J. U. M., O.B.E.	Asst. Secretary	1908
	County Council	1914/19
Jackson, Lt.-Col. Hon. F. S., late 3rd Bn. R. Lancs. Regt.	Co-opted Member	1911/17
Jones, F. L., Esq.	,, ,,	1908/13
Jonas, J., Esq. (Sheffield)	County Borough	1908
Knight, Major J. E., T.D. (Rotherham) ...	,, ,,	1908 to present date
Land, Col. W. H., C.B.E., T.F. Res. ...	Military Member	1908
Lane-Fox, Major G. R., M.P., T.F. Res. ...	Co-opted Member	1910/19
Lee, Col. E., V.D., T.F. Res.	Military Member	1913/19
Liddell, Lt.-Col. J., V.D., J.P., late 2nd V.B. W. Rid. Regt. (Huddersfield) ...	County Borough	1914 to present date
Lister, Capt. A. E., 5th Bn. W. Rid. Regt.	Military Member	1916/17
Littlewood, Col. H., C.M.G., F.R.C.S., 2nd N. General Hospital	,, ,,	1916/19
Lockwood, H., Esq.	County Council	1919 to present date
Lucey, Lt.-Col. W. F., C.M.G., D.S.O., 1st W. Rid. Bde., R.F.A.	Military Member	1919 to present date
Lumsden, Major G., V.D., late 5th Bn. W. Yorks. Regt. ...	,, ,,	1916-19
Lupton, F. M., Esq., J.P.	Co-opted Member	1908/19
Lyons, Lt.-Col. F. W., 4th Bn. K.O.Y.L.I.	Military Member	1918/19
Mackinnon, Lt.-Col. J., D.S.O., 3rd W.R. Field Ambce. R.A.M.C., T.F.	,, ,,	1919 to present date

List of Members and Permanent Officials—continued.

Name, etc.	Representation.	Period.
Marsh, H. P., Esq., J.P. (Sheffield) ...	County Borough	1909 to present date
Marsden, Lt.-Col. J., V.D., 5th W.R. Regt.	Military Member	1909/11
Mason, Major A. W., V.D., F.R.C.S. ...	,, ,,	1908/11
Metcalfe, Capt. A. W., M.D., W.R.R.G.A.	,, ,,	1915-16
Mends, Brig.-Gen. H. R., C.B., ret. pay ...	Secretary	1908 to present date
Mildren, Capt. W., M.B.E., T.F. Res. ...	Asst. Secterary	1915 to present date
Mitchell, Col. T. W. H., V.D., 5th Bn. York & Lancs. Regt.	Military Member ,, ,,	1909/14 1918 to present date
d Morrell, Lt.-Col. A. R., V.D., 5th W. Yks. Regt.	Military Member	1913
Moxon, Lt.-Col. C. C., C.M.G., D.S.O., T.D., 5th Bn. K.O. Yorks. L.I.	,, ,,	1914-15
Norton, Lt.-Col. G. P., D.S.O., 5th Bn. W. Riding Regt.	,, ,,	1919 to present date
Oddie, Lt.-Col. W., D.S.O., T.D., 5th Bn. W. Yorks. Regt.	,, ,,	1919 to present date
Parkin, Lt.-Col. F. L., D.S.O., 5th Bn. K.O. Y.L.I.	,, ,,	1919 to present date
Paul, Lt.-Col. J. A., T.D., 1st W.R. Bde. R.F.A.	,, ,, ,, ,,	1908/11 1916/19
Pawlett, Vet. Major F. W., Yorks. Hrs. Yeo.	,, ,,	1908
Pearson, Capt. W. A., V.D., J.P. (York) ...	County Borough	1908 to present date
Pickering, Lt.-Col. E. W., D.S.O., M.P., 2nd W. Riding Bde., R.F.A.	Co-opted Member	1919 to present date
Pilkington, Col. Sir T. E., M.S.	,, ,,	1918/19
Porter. Major M. L., O.B.E.	Asst. Secretary	1909/13
d Priestley, Major F. N., R.F.A. (T.F.) ...	Military Member	1915/18
Raley, J.P., Esq. (Barnsley)	County Borough	1918 to present date
Ratcliffe, G., Esq., J.P. (Leeds)	,, ,,	1918 to present date
d Rowe, Lt.-Col. G. H., V.D., 8th W. Yorks. Regt.	Military Member	1908/10
Ruck-Keene, Lt.-Col. H. L., D.S.O. ...	Co-opted Member	1919 to present date
Rudgard, Major W. D., T.D., T.F. Res. ...	Military Member ,, ,,	1911/13 1916/19
Sadler, Sir M. E., K.C.S.I., C.B., M.A., LL.D. (Leeds)	University	1913/14
Scarborough, Major-General A. F. G. B., Earl of, K.C.B., T.D., A.D.C.	Chairman and Military Member	1908 to present date
Senior, Col. A., V.D., 2nd Y. & L. Regt.	,, ,,	1908
Shann, Lt.-Col. F., V.D., 5th W. Yks. Regt.	,, ,,	1908-15
Sharp, Col. A. D., C.B., C.M.G., F.R.C.S., Admin. Med. Off., W.R. Divn.	,, ,,	1919 to present date
d Shaw, Col. J. R., 5th Bn. K.O. Yorks. L.I. ...	County Council	1908/16
Smith, Lt.-Col. W. McK., D.S.O., T.D., Yorks. Dns. Yeo.	Military Member	1914/15
Smithett, Major H. C. E.	Asst. Secretary	1914
Somerville, Col. S. E., V.D., late Y.L.I. ...	Military Member ,, ,,	1908/13 1916/19
Sowerby, Major R. J., late 1st V.B. West Riding Regt.	,, ,,	1916/19
Speight, Major C. H., V.D., late 2nd V.B. West Yorks. Regt.	,, ,,	1916/17
Stamer, A. C., Esq.	Co-opted Member	1911/13
Stanyforth, Lt.-Col. E. W., D.L., T.D., T.F. Res.	Military Member	1908 to present date
Stead, Lt.-Col. J. W., V.D., 7th W. Yks. R.	,, ,,	1908/15
Stephenson, Lt.-Col. H. K., D.S.O., V.D., M.P., J.P., T.F. Res. (Sheffield)	University	1909 to present date
Sutcliffe, Major H. (Halifax)	County Borough	1908/14
Sugden, Lt.-Col. R. E., D.S.O., T.D., 4th Bn. W. Riding Regt.	Military Member	1919 to present date

List of Members and Permanent Officials—continued.

Name, etc.	Representation.	Period.
d Sykes, J., Esq. (Huddersfield)	County Borough	1908/13
Talbot, E., Esq.	County Council	1918 to present date
Tanner, Major G., D.S.O., 7th W.R. Regt.	Military Member	1916/17
	,,　　　,,	1919 to present date
d Tannett-Walker, Col. F. W., late 7th W. Yorks. Regt.	,,　　　,,	1908/10
Tetley, Lt.-Col. C. H., D.S.O., T.D., 7th Bn. West Yorks. Regt.	,,　　　,,	1919 to present date
Thomson, W. F. H., Esq., J.P.	Co-opted Member	1908 to present date
Tighe, Lt.-Col. F. A., 1st W.R. Bde., R.F.A.	Military Member	1912-13
Treble, Col. G. W., C.M.G., 7th W.R. Regt.	,,　　　,,	1911/15
d Trevelyan, Lt.-Col. E. F., M.D., 2nd N. Gen. Hosp.	,,　　　,,	1911
d Vickers, Col. T. E., C.B., V.D., 4th Bn. York & Lancs. Regt.	Military Member	1908/09
Wade, Lt.-Col. H. O., C.M.G., T.D., 6th Bn. W. Yorks. Regt.	,,　　　,,	1913/15
Walker, Lt.-Col. J., D.S.O., 4th Bn. W. Riding Regt.	,,　　　,,	1919 to present date
Walker, Major P. B., V.D., J.P., 4th Bn. K.O. Yorks. L.I. (Dewsbury)	Co-opted Member / County Borough	1910/13 / 1914 to present date
d Walker-Tannett (see Tannett).		
Wear, Col. A. E. L., C.M.G., M.D., T.D., W.R. Cas. Clearing Station	Military Member	1919 to present date
Welch, Major W., T.D.	,,　　　,,	1916/19
Wharncliffe, Commander F., Earl of, D.L., J.P., Ret. R.N.	Co-opted Member	1908/10 / 1914 to present date
White, Col. W. A., V.D., J.P., late 1st V.B. W. Yorks. Regt.	Military Member	1908 to present date
White, Lt.-Col. J. S., M.D., F.R.C.S., 3rd N. Gen. Hosp. R.A.M.C. (T.F.)	,,　　　,,	1911/13
Whitley, Col. E. N., C.B., C.M.G., D.S.O., T.D. 2nd W.R. Bde., R.F.A.	,,　　　,,	1919 to present date
Wilberforce, Lt.-Col. H. H., D.S.O., W.R. Divnl. R.A.S.C (T.F.)	,,　　　,,	1919 to present date
Wilkinson, Major E. W., T.D., 4th Bn. York & Lancs. Regt.	,,　　　,,	1919 to present date
Williamson, Col. E. R., V.D., 6th W. Riding Regt.	,,　　　,,	1908/12 / 1914/17
d Wilson, Sir M. A., Bt., J.P.	County Council	1908/13
Wilson, Lt.-Col. H., 5th W. Riding Regt....	Military Member	1914/15
Wood, Lt.-Col. C. E., V.D., C.M.G., T.F. Res.	,,　　　,,	1915 / 1918/19
d Yarborough (see Cook-)		
Young, Lt.-Col. W. McG., M.D., 2nd W. Riding F. Ambce., R.A.M.C. (T.F.).	,,　　　,,	1914/15

APPENDIX II.

(A). SUMMARY OF HONOURS AND AWARDS OBTAINED BY 49TH (W.R.) DIVISION.

V.C.	5
C.B.	8
C.M.G.	17
O.B.E.	4
D.S.O.	79
D.S.O. and 1 Bar	6
D.S.O. and 2 Bars	1
M.C.	393
M.C. and Bar	34
D.C.M.	336
D.C.M. and Bar	2
M.M.	1,501
M.M. and Bar	62
M.M. and 2 Bars	2
M.S.M.	94
Foreign Orders, etc.	96
TOTAL	2,640

LIST OF HONOURS AND AWARDS OBTAINED BY 49TH (W.R.) DIVISION

HEADQUARTER STAFF

Regtl. No.	Rank.	Name.	Award.
	MajGen. ...	Perceval, E. M.	C.B. D.S.O. Belgian Order of St. Leopold, with Swords Russian Order of St. Vladimir, 4th Class, with Swords.
	MajGen. ...	Cameron, N. J. G.	C.B. C.M.G.
	Lt.-Col.... ...	Scobell, S. J. P.	D.S.O.
	Lt.-Col.... ...	Legge, W. K.	D.S.O.
	Lt.-Col.... ...	Henley, A. M.	D.S.O.
	Lt.-Col.... ...	Preston, Sir E. H., Bart. ...	D.S.O. M.C.
	Lt.-Col.... ...	Scaife, W. E.	D.S.O.
	Major	Bingham. C. H. M.	D.S.O.
	Major	Duckworth, R.	D.S.O.
	Major	Beddows, W. J.	M.C.
	Captain ...	Nicholl, N. J.	D.S.O.
	Captain ...	Forty, H. J.	M.C.
TS/19008	S.S.M. ...	Hopkins, M. E.	M.S.M.
S/249817	S.Q.M.S. ...	Green, G.	M.S.M.
305294	C.Q.M.S. ...	McBretney, A. C.	M.S.M.
S/24644	S. Sgt. ...	Pagett, S.	M.S.M.
200646	Sgt.	Lawrence, G. L.	M.S.M.
4593	Cpl.	Calvert, H.	M.S.M.

DIVISIONAL ARTILLERY HEADQUARTERS

	Br.-Gen. ...	Caulfield, C. T.	C.M.G.
	Br.-Gen. ...	Kaye, W. H.	D.S.O.
	Br.-Gen. ...	Forman, A. B.	C.M.G. D.S.O.
	Major	Lewer, L. W.	D.S.O.
	Major	Allen, C.	D.S.O.
	Captain ...	Peters, J. C.	M.C.
	Lieut.	Morgan, D.	French Croix de Guerre.
312072	R.S.M.	Uttley, G.	M.S.M.
900732	Cpl.	Walder, F. H.	M.S.M.

HEADQUARTERS 146TH (1ST W.R.) INFANTRY BRIGADE

	Br.-Gen. ...	Macfarlan, F. A.	C.B.
	Br.-Gen. ...	Goring-Jones, M. D. ...	C.M.G. D.S.O.
	Br.-Gen. ...	Rennie, G. A. P.	C.M.G. D.S.O. Command Crown of Roumania.
	Major	Hunt, T. E. C.	M.C.
	Captain ...	Muller, J.	M.C.

HEADQUARTERS 146TH (1ST W.R.) INFANTRY BRIGADE—*continued*

Regtl. No.	Rank.	Name.	Award.
	Captain ...	Watson, F. L.	M.C.
	Captain ...	Green, D.	M.C.
	Lieut.	Tempest, S. V.	D.S.O.
	Rev.	Whincup, R.	M.C.
T4/249840	Q.M.S. ...	Longfield, H. P.	M.S.M.
S4/253925	Sgt.	Watson, A.	M.S.M.
255041	2/Cpl.	Young, N. A.	M.M. Bar to M.M.
241553	L.-Cpl. ...	Wilson, J.	M.M.
266170	L.-Cpl.	Hunter, J.	M.M.
59080	Pte.	Wilson, A.	M.M.
200206	Pte.	Marshall, G. H.	M.M.
241391	Pte.	Mason, H.	M.M.
242958	Pte.	Wagstaffe, S.	M.M.
305173	Pte.	Wilkinson, T.	M.M.
265637	Rfm.	Kirk, H.	M.M.

HEADQUARTERS 147TH (1ST W.R.) INFANTRY BRIGADE

Regtl. No.	Rank.	Name.	Award.
	Br.-Gen. ...	Brereton, E. F.	C.B. D.S.O.
	Br.-Gen. ...	Lewis, C. G.	C.M.G. D.S.O.
	Major	Stanton, H. A. S.	D.S.O.
	Captain ...	Whitaker, F.	M.C.
	Captain ...	Prior, G. E. R.	M.C. Bar to M.C.
	Captain ...	Tetlow, J. L.	M.C.
	Lieut.	Stalman, A. C.	M.C.
	Lieut.	Spencer, T. S.	M.C.
	2/Lieut. ...	Addenbrooke, H. S. W. ...	M.C.
	Rev.	Jones, J. C.	M.C.
305128	Q.M.S.	Smeath, H.	M.S.M.
2462	Sgt.	Lumb, F. E.	D.C.M.
200201	Sgt.	Thornton, A. L.	D.C.M.
265045	Sgt.	Woods. W.	M.M.
200599	Cpl.	Tyson, W. H.	M.S.M.
242133	Cpl.	Bottomley, E.	M.M.
482235	Cpl.	Pitcher, W. H.	M.M.
482103	L.-Cpl.	Cooks, J. E.	D.C.M. M.M. Bar to M.M.
66576	Sapr.	Bird, G. F.	M.M.
72205	Sapr.	Shaw, J.	M.M.
482117	Sapr.	Tyas, A.	M.M. Bar to M.M.
26255	Pioneer	Hart, V.	M.M.
316322	Pioneer	Morris, C. J.	M.M.
200536	Pte.	Heeliwell, B.	M.M.
201473	Pte.	Pearson, B.	M.M.
201595	Pte.	Briggs, W.	M.M.
201943	Pte.	Bailey, W.	M.M.
240241	Pte.	Tetley, T.	M.M.
240827	Pte.	Timmins, E. B.	M.M.
307182	Pte.	Haddon, F. J.	M.M.
307870	Pte.	Copley, G.	M.M.
307871	Pte.	Fawcett, J. S.	M.M.
365613	Pte.	Sanderson, O.	M.M.

HEADQUARTERS 148TH (1ST W.R.) INFANTRY BRIGADE

Regtl. No.	Rank.	Name.	Award.
	Br.-Gen. ...	Dawson, R.	C.B.
	Br.-Gen. ...	Adlercrow, R. L.	C.M.G.
			D.S.O.
	Br.-Gen. ...	Green Wilkinson, L. F. ...	C.M.G.
	Major	Pickering, C. J.	D.S.O.
	Major	Kaye, H. S.	M.C.
			D.S.O.
	Captain ...	Heson, F. P.	M.C.
	Captain ...	Moxsy, A. R.	M.C.
	Lieut.	Peal, A. F. H.	M.C.
	Rev.	Edgood, H. F.	M.C.
200226	R.Q.M.S. ...	Deakin, M. H.	M.S.M.
240018	C.S.M. ...	Lumb, G.	D.C.M.
482006	Sgt.	Ardern, A. W.	M.M.
1894	Cpl.	Meadows, H.	M.M.
23021	Cpl.	Hobson, H.	M.M.
47743	Sapr.	Eusch, A. R.	M.M.
478505	Sapr.	Iliffe, G. K.	M.M.
482088	Sapr.	Lumley, H.	M.M.
1708	Pte.	Jeanes, H.	M.M.
200496	Pte.	Hough, H.	M.M.
200846	Pte.	Wilcox, J. S.	M.M.
201774	Pte.	Wilson, P.	M.M.
203504	Pte.	Stephenson, J.	M.M.
			Bar to M.M.
240372	Pte.	Duncan, J.	M.M.
242310	Pte.	Heppinstall, C.	M.M.
242360	Pte.	Abbott, R. E.	M.M.
242708	Pte.	Escott, W. C.	M.M.
260604	Pte.	Whallery, G.	M.M.
	Pte.	Ganton, W. H.	M.M.

245TH (1ST W.R.) BRIGADE R.F.A.

Lt.-Col. ...	...	Hirst, E. A.	C.M.G.
Major	...	Lucey, W. F.	C.M.G.
			D.S.O.
			Croix de Guerre.
Major ...	...	Butler, B. H.	M.C.
Major ...	...	Horsfield, R. M.	D.S.O
Major ...	...	Petrie, P. C.	D.S.O
			M.C.
Major ...	...	Dean, W. H.	M.C.
			Bar to M.C.
Major ...	...	Bullock, R. L.	D.S.O.
Captain	...	Gordon, C. F.	M.C.
Captain	...	Wood, W. L. R. (R.A.M.C.) ...	M.C.
Captain	...	Lupton, A. M.	M.C.
Captain	...	Fowler, G. N.	M.C.
Captain	...	Day, R.	M.C.
Captain	...	Middleton, J. H.	M.C.
Lieut. ...	...	Hudson, E. C.	M.C.
Lieut. ...	...	Gordon, A. McD.	M.C.
Lieut. ...	...	Barran, H. B.	M.C.
Lieut. ...	...	Lawson, E. A. C.	M.C.
Lieut. ...	...	Stewart, H. D.	M.C.
Lieut. ...	...	Collins, C. V.	M.C.
Lieut. ...	...	Lord, R. H.	M.C.
2/Lieut.	...	Butler, S. R.	M.C.

245TH (1ST W.R.) BRIGADE R.F.A.—*continued*

Regtl. No.	Rank.	Name.	Award.
	2/Lieut. ...	Hattersley, T. G.	M.C.
	2/Lieut. ...	Rowland, J. G.	M.C.
860	S.M.	Abbott, H. C.	D.C.M. Medaille Militaire.
14	B.S.M. ...	Brown, M.	Bronze Medal for Military Valour. M.M.
1420	B.S.M. ...	Band, J.	D.C.M.
15009	B.S.M. ...	Laws, A. H.	M.M.
776113	B.S.M. ...	Dwyer, E.	Belgian Croix de Guerre
775101	B.Q.M.S. ...	Wales, A. J.	M.S.M.
776835	B.Q.M.S. ...	Duffy, J.	Belgian Croix de Guerre
776899	Far.-Sgt. ...	Sellars, A.	M.S.M.
776139	Far.-Sgt. ...	Wilkinson, F.	M.S.M.
515	Sgt.	Plumer, F. H.	D.C.M.
664	Sgt.	Hartley, C.	D.C.M.
180	Sgt.	Nolan, M. M.	M.M.
942	Sgt.	Hemsley, J. A.	M.M.
931	Sgt.	Norfolk, N. A. N.	M.M.
561	Sgt.	Robinson, W.	M.M.
870	Sgt.	Holgate, H.	M.M.
776116	Sgt.	Gaines, S.	M.M.
776883	Sgt.	Price, A.	M.M.
775224	Sgt.	Smith, H.	D.C.M. M.M.
776896	Sgt.	Stubbs, G. H.	M.M.
253860	Sgt.	Smith, A.	M.M.
775262	Sgt.	Kilburn, G.	M.M.
10601	Sgt.	Holdsworth, W.	M.M.
776900	Sgt.	Smith, H.	D.C.M.
795739	Sgt.	Redgrave, J.	Croix de Guerre
1842	Cpl.	Nelson, G. O.	D.C.M. M.S.M.
570	Cpl.	Askin, T. S.	D.C.M. M.M.
1013	Cpl.	Smith, J.	M.M.
676	Cpl.	Kirby, G. H.	M.M.
735755	Cpl.	Bonnell, W. F.	M.M.
776122	Cpl.	Newton, D. P.	M.M.
776042	Cpl.	Haith, J.	M.M.
775078	Cpl.	Wood, H.	Belgian Croix de Guerre
775095	Cpl.	Shires, C. W.	D.C.M. Croix de Guerre
1221	Bdr.	Elliott, T.	D.C.M.
775307	Bdr.	Home, W.	M.M.
776382	Bdr.	Dalton, P.	D.C.M.
776097	Bdr.	Booth, J.	M.M.
735655	Bdr.	Dombavand, H.	M.M.
775136	Bdr.	Musgrove, F.	M.M.
775194	Bdr.	Thornton, W.	M.M.
775321	Bdr.	Wright, J. W.	M.M.
775408	Bdr.	Oldfield, H.	M.M.
L/26405	Bdr.	Brightmore, W.	M.M.
1059	Gnr.	Mortimer, J.	D.C.M.
783	Gnr.	Booth, F. V.	D.C.M.
1382	Gnr.	Clarke, A.	M.M.
939	Gnr.	Malone, F. A.	M.M.
371	Gnr.	Fitzpatrick, E.	M.M.

245TH (1ST W.R.) BRIGADE R.F.A.—*continued*

Regtl. No.	Rank.	Name.	Award.
879	Gnr.	Driver, A.	M.M.
1168	Gnr.	Ackroyd, H.	M.M.
1699	Gnr.	Long, H.	M.M.
2505	Gnr.	Stockdale, H.	M.M.
4148	Gnr.	Reaney, J.	M.M.
4364	Gnr.	Walker, E. H.	M.M.
667	Gnr.	Sunderland, A.	M.M.
775315	Gnr.	Thompson, R.	M.M.
835893	Gnr.	Francis, F. T.	M.M.
77684	Gnr.	Freeman, E.	M.M.
775327	Gnr.	Clarke, T.	M.M.
776210	Gnr.	Asquith, E.	M.M.
26561	Gnr.	Liversedge, T.	M.M.
775984	Gnr.	Gee, A.	M.M.
1528	Dr.	Murgatroyd, A.	M.M.
1402	Dr.	Hinslay, C.	M.M.
1177	Dr.	Collins, W.	M.M.
1440	Dr.	Halton, E.	M.M.
1441	Dr.	Teare, A. M.	M.M.
76029	Dr.	Sargeant, H.	D.C.M
775129	Dr.	Matthews, E.	M.M.
276937	Dr.	Garratt, B.	M.M.
275146	Dr.	Marston, S.	Medaille Barbatie si Credinta, 3rd Class
479945	Sapr.	Sugden, H.	M.M.
247370	Sapr.	Paterson, W.	M.M.

246TH (2ND W.R.) BRIGADE R.F.A.

Regtl. No.	Rank.	Name.	Award.
	Lt.-Col.... ...	Whitley, C. N.	C.B. C.M.G. D.S.O.
	Lt.-Col.... ...	Hon. Stanley, O. H. ...	D.S.O. Croix de Guerre
	Major	Bullock, R. L.	D.S.O.
	Major	Pickering, E. W.	D.S.O.
	Major	Fowler, G. N.	M.C. Bar to M.C.
	Major	Shaw, R. M.	D.S.O.
	Surg.-Major ...	Peck, E. G.	D.S.O.
	Captain ...	Shaw, R. M.	M.C.
	Captain	Allen, W. B. (R.A.M.C.) ...	V.C.— D.S.O. M.C.
	Captain ...	Duncan, H. S.	M.C.
	Captain ...	Stowell, T.	M.C.
	Captain ...	Lord, A.	M.C.
	Captain ...	Walker, P. H.	M.C. Bar to M.C.
	Lieut.	de St. Paer, L. E.	M.C.
	Lieut.	Howarth, G. B.	M.C.
	Lieut.	Whitworth, R. B.	M.C.
	Lieut.	Colson, A. F. D.	M.C.
	Lieut.	Maufe, F. W. B.	M.C.
	2/Lieut. ...	Kerr, A. A.	M.C.
	2/Lieut. ...	Wilson, H. McD.	M.C.
	2/Lieut. ...	Longbottom, H.	M.C.
	2/Lieut. ...	Ryland-Whitaker, J.	M.C.
	2/Lieut. ...	Daniels, V. C. T.	M.C.
	Rev.	Jenkyn, C. W. O.	M.C.

246TH (2ND W.R.) BRIGADE R.F.A.—*continued*

Regtl. No.	Rank.	Name.	Award.
146	B.S.M. ...	Long, W.	D.C.M.
781677	B.S.M. ...	Hudson, W.	D.C.M.
780037	B.Q.M.S. ...	Healas, H.	M.S.M.
781787	B.Q.M.S. ...	Raynor, G.	D.C.M.
			Bar to D.C.M.
780203	B.Q.M.S. ...	Rinder, J.	M.S.M.
780375	Sgt.-Fitter ...	Noble, H.	M.M.
1155	Sgt. ...	Marshall, A. C.	D.C.M.
781080	Sgt.	Byard, S. G.	D.C.M.
780042	Sgt.	Bailey, H.	M.M.
781038	Sgt.	Wise, A.	M.M.
780336	Sgt.	Mitchell, C. W.	M.M.
			Belgian Croix de Guerre
780024	Sgt.	Sharp, H.	M.M.
781759	Sgt.	Long, H.	M.S.M.
780967	Sgt.	Shaw, C.	D.C.M.
780472	Sgt.	Sherwin, F.	M.M.
			Bar to M.M.
			2nd Bar to M.M.
780045	Sgt.	Quinn, W.	Croix de Guerre
971	Cpl.	Armitage, G.	D.C.M.
1039	Cpl.	Lee, H.	D.C.M.
857	Cpl.	Lee, C.	M.M.
780248	Cpl.	Knowles, C.	M.M.
780958	Cpl.	Matthews, B.	M.M.
849	Bdr.	Dennison, E.	D.C.M.
1258	Bdr.	Eastwood, T.	M.M.
3144	Bdr.	Briggs, C.	M.M.
1325	Bdr.	Leatham, H.	D.C.M.
1079	Bdr.	Mellor, L.	M.M.
951	Bdr.	Oldroyd, W.	M.M.
795842	Bdr.	Bennett, G.	M.M.
52873	Bdr.	Betts, H.	M.M.
780112	Bdr.	Briggs, W.	M.M.
797075	Bdr.	Campbell, G. G.	M.M.
1426	Gnr.	White, S. S.	D.C.M.
			M.M.
1100	Gnr.	Schofield, W.	M.M.
1053	Gnr.	Mitchell, C. A.	M.M.
			Bar to M.M.
1117	Gnr.	Firth, F. P.	M.M.
			Bar to M.M.
1736	Gnr.	Blakesley, E.	M.M.
619	Gnr.	Clarke, C.	M.M.
			Bar to M.M.
1106	Gnr.	Cockcroft, H.	M.M.
2011	Gnr.	Pennington, W.	M.M.
6057	Gnr.	Todd, A. S.	M.M.
1629	Gnr.	Muscroft, A.	M.M.
1114	Gnr.	Thornton, C.	M.M.
3455	Gnr.	Petty, W. F.	M.M.
2291	Gnr.	Gregson, H.	M.M.
1779	Gnr.	Henstler, H.	M.M.
1206	Gnr.	Hesslewood, H.	M.M.
741	Gnr.	Tankard, J. W.	M.M.
846	Gnr.	Rushworth, A. B.	M.M.
781797	Gnr.	Smith, F.	M.M.
781795	Gnr.	Stewart, W. H.	D.C.M.
125580	Gnr.	Davidson, J.	M.M.
781487	Gnr.	Harrison, F.	M.M.

246TH (2ND W.R.) BRIGADE R.F.A.—*continued*

Regtl. No.	Rank.	Name.	Award.
1227	Dr.	Triffitt, E. W.	M.M.
780385	Dr.	Gully, J. A.	M.M.
781327	Dr.	Allen, J. H.	M.M.
780292	Dr.	Page, E. C.	M.M.
26296	Dr.	Howard, J.	M.M.
780226	Dr.	Bland, N.	M.M.
780643	Dr.	Spencer, W. B.	M.M.
162878	Dr.	Green, S.	M.M.
780913	Dr.	Heald, H.	M.M.
229280	Dr.	Blenston, T.	M.M.
702142	Dr.	Kindlaw, H.	M.M.
881	Tmptr.	Eddington, H.	M.M.

247TH (3RD W.R.) BRIGADE R.F.A.

Regtl. No.	Rank.	Name.	Award.
	Lt.-Col.... ...	Clifforrd, C.	C.M.G.
	Major	Howson, W.	M.C.
	Major	Clifford, E. C.	M.C.
	Major (A.V.C.)	Abson, J. (F.R.C.V.S.) ...	D.S.O.
	Captain ...	Lovegrove, J.	M.C.
	Captain ...	Earnshaw, S. E.	M.C.
	Captain ...	Dust, F. W.	M.C.
	Captain ...	Tenison, W. P. C.	D.S.O.
	Lieut. ...	Benson, R. C.	M.C.
	Lieut. ...	Armitage, G.	M.C.
	2/Lieut. ...	Ibbetson, T. R.	M.C.
1177	B.Q.M.S. ...	Brooker, H.	M.S.M.
L/19824	Sgt.	Ullyott, D.	M.M.
779	Cpl.	Cooper, H.	D.C.M.
773	Cpl.	Askew, L.	M.M.
1426	Cpl.	Driver, H.	M.S.M.
889	Cpl.	Webster, W.	M.M.
1873	Cpl.	Burnett, A. G.	M.M.
1517	Bdr.	Holland, A. H....	D.C.M.
1511	Bdr.	Tinton, J. W.	M.M.
946	Bdr.	Houlden, W.	M.M.
1213	Gnr.	Smith, C.	D.C.M.
1073	Gnr.	Kisley, A. P.	M.M.
1051	Gnr.	White, T. A.	M.M.
1467	Gnr.	Hall, J. W.	M.M.
1202	Gnr.	Battersby, R. L.	M.M.
1272	Gnr.	Roberts, H.	M.M.
2510	Dr.	Spirrett, H.	M.M.

148TH (4TH W.R.) BRIGADE R.F.A.

Regtl. No.	Rank.	Name.	Award.
	Lt.-Col.... ...	Duncan, K.	D.S.O. Bar to D.S.O.
	Major	Petrie, P. C.	M.C.
	Captain ...	Greene, J. (R.A.M.C.) ...	M.C.
	Captain ...	Shaw, R. M.	M.C.
	Lieut. ...	Eddison, J. W.	M.C.
	Lieut. ...	Whittaker, V.	M.C.
	2/Lieut. ...	Dean, W. H.	M.C.
	2/Lieut. ...	Pashley, J.	M.C.
84152	R.S.M. ...	Seymour, T.	M.C.
1191	B.S.M. ...	Cotton, A.	D.C.M.
544	B.Q.M.S. ...	Dwyer, E.	M.M.

148TH (4TH W.R.) BRIGADE R.F.A.—*continued*

Regtl. No.	Rank.	Name.	Award.
228	Arm. S.M. ...	Alexander, E. F. (A.O.D.) ...	D.C.M.
549	Bdr.	Whitfield, E.	D.C.M.
778	Bdr.	Rhodes, J. R.	D.C.M.
619	Bdr.	Clarke, G. C.	M.M.
777	Bdr.	King, P. J.	M.M.
535	Bdr.	Goode, A.	M.M.
825	Bdr.	McDormell, J.	M.M.
			Bar to M.M.
439	Bdr.	Brayshaw, C. E.	M.M.
			Bar to M.M.
879	Gnr.	Driver, A.	D.C.M.
616	Gnr.	Tennant, N.	D.C.M.
1246	Gnr.	Snoxell, F. N.	M.M.
1596	Gnr.	Green, C.	M.M.
2886	Gnr.	Smithwaite, S. E.	M.M.
511	Gnr.	Towll, C. E.	M.M.
1942	Dr.	Russell, W. L.	M.M.
528	Dr.	Moorhouse, A.	D.C.M.
8150	Dr.	Smith, D.	M.M.

49TH (W.R.) DIVISIONAL AMMUNITION COLUMN

Regtl. No.	Rank.	Name.	Award.
	Lt.-Col.... ...	Stephenson, H. K.	D.S.O.
	Lt.-Col.... ...	Middleton, F.	D.S.O.
	2/Lieut. ...	Pashley, J.	M.C.
			Bar to M.C.
92678	R.S.M.	Byrne, C.	M.S.M.
795292	B.S.M. ...	Stott, C.	M.S.M.
795443	Sgt.	Nicholson, J. W.	M.M.
740063	Sgt.	Waite, J.	M.S.M.
795438	Sgt.	Atack, O.	M.S.M.
262	Cpl.	Hunter, J. A.	D.C.M.
795029	Cpl.	Woffendale, A.	M.M.
200	Bdr.	Timmins, G.	M.M.
795717	Bdr.	Hepworth, H.	M.M.
777117	Gnr.	Ratcliffe, F. G.	M.M.
797167	Gnr.	Allen, E.	M.M.
796302	Dr.	Lockwood, W.	M.M.
796394	Dr.	Topliss, J. W.	M.M.
796242	Dr.	Turner, W.	M.M.
796013	Dr.	Womersley, F.	M.M.
796227	Dr.	Fletcher, R.	M.M.

49TH (W.R.) DIVISIONAL TRENCH MORTAR BATTERIES

Regtl. No.	Rank.	Name.	Award.
	Captain ...	Walker, R. F.	M.C.
	Captain ...	Pike, W. L.	M.C.
	Captain ...	Hein, M. H.	M.C.
	Lieut.	Trippett, R. H.	M.C.
	2/Lieut. ...	Shiel, G. L.	M.C.
49063	Sgt.	Surtees, J.	Belgian Croix de Guerre.
2953	Sgt.	Reed, H.	M.M.
265043	Sgt.	Woods, W.	M.S.M.
365105	Sgt.	Hartley, R.	Croix de Guerre.
35202	Cpl.	Drew, T.	M.M.
47010	Cpl.	Williams, W.	M.M.
795703	Cpl.	Bate, A.	M.M.

49TH (W.R.) DIVISIONAL TRENCH MORTAR BATTERIES—*cont.*

Regtl. No.	Rank.	Name.	Award.
1455	Cpl.	Thornton, L.	M.M.
203278	Cpl.	Wallis, J. H.	M.S.M.
40	L.-Cpl.	Storrell, E.	D.C.M.
2160	L.-Cpl.	Springs, F.	M.M.
201437	L.-Cpl.	Ellis, J. A.	M.M.
407	Bdr.	Butler, J.	M.M.
48444	Bdr.	Coursh, W.	M.M.
57168	Bdr.	Guy, M.	D.C.M.
48779	Gnr.	Brunton, W.	M.M.
416	Gnr.	Mason, N.	M.M.
48110	Gnr.	Pelan, W.	D.C.M.
1947	Gnr.	Leighton, T.	D.C.M.
436	Gnr.	Gelder, S. M.	D.C.M.
2556	Gnr.	Fry, E.	M.M.
795825	Gnr.	Bishop, G.	M.M.
7107	Gnr.	Clark, W.	M.M.
201434	Pte.	Grayson, J.	M.M.
2039	Pte.	Cartwright, T.	M.M.
1734	Pte.	Bowker, W.	M.M.
305646	Pte.	Haigh, H.	D.C.M.
242594	Pte.	Brown, F.	M.M.
240743	Pte.	Thornhill, H.	Belgian Croix de Guerre.
203345	Pte.	Lilley, G.	M.M.
203544	Pte.	Johnson, G. D.	M.M.

49TH (W.R.) DIVISIONAL R.E.

	Rank.	Name.	Award.
	Lt.-Col.	Ogilvy, D.	D.S.O.
	Major	Digby-Jones, O. G.	M.C.
	Major	Neill, F. A.	D.S.O. French Croix de Guerre.
	Major	Hobson, A. F.	D.S.O.
	Major	Lund, F. N.	M.C.
	Major	Jackson, E.	D.S.O
	Captain ...	Humphreys, E. W.	M.C.
	Captain ...	Turner, R. A.	M.C.
	Captain ...	Yule, G. N.	D.S.O.
	Captain ...	Whitten, F. R.	M.C.
	Captain ...	Williams, C. V. Moiner ...	M.C.
	Captain ...	Wever, R. O.	M.C.
	Captain ...	Ward, E. A. N.	M.C.
	Captain ...	Fincham, E.	M.C.
	Captain ...	Best, E.	M.C.
	Captain ...	Walls, F. R.	M.C.
	Lieut.	McLean, L. J.	M.C.
	Lieut.	Rhodes, H.	M.C.
	Lieut.	Butterworth, H. L.	M.C.
	Lieut.	Paul, R. B.	M.C.
	Lieut.	Scott, T. I.	M.C.
	2/Lieut. ...	MacDonald, D. H.	Silver Medal for Military Valour.
	2/Lieut. ...	Glover, E. P.	M.C.
	2/Lieut. ...	Mills, D. L. C. L.	M.C.
	2/Lieut. ...	McGregor, D. H.	M.C.
	2/Lieut. ...	Bell, L. C.	M.C.
	2/Lieut. ...	Wise-Barnes, T.	M.C.
	C.S.M.	Ellis, H. C.	Croix de Guerre (French)

49TH (W.R.) DIVISIONAL R.E.—*continued*

Regtl. No.	Rank.	Name.	Award.
19206	C.S.M.	Giles, J.	M.M.
20575	C.S.M.	Ritchie, J.	D.C.M.
10957	C.Q.M.S.	Sharp, R.	M.S.M.
			Belgian Croix de Guerre.
399	C.Q.M.S. ...	Black, R. H.	D.C.M.
476332	Sgt.	Baynes, J. F.	M.S.M.
23950	Sgt.	Peck, G.	M.M.
20921	Sgt.	Fear, E.	M.M.
24208	Sgt.	Wright. J.	M.M.
666	Sgt.	Boom, H.	M.M.
478127	Sgt.	Mason, J. H.	M.M.
478011	Sgt.	Littlewood, F. A.	M.S.M.
1422	Sgt.	Morrill, C.	D.C.M.
1465	Sgt.	McKenney, J. W.	D.C.M.
1481	Sgt.	Lowe, C. E.	M.M.
1711	Sgt.	Sunners, H.	M.M.
476294	Sgt.	Dolby, H.	M.M.
476221	Sgt.	Totty, C.	Belgian Decoration Militaire.
545	Sgt.	Horner, E. M.	M.M.
482229	Sgt.	Andrews, F.	M.M.
479950	Sgt.	Bownass, F.	D.C.M.
479958	Sgt.	Peers, R.	M.S.M.
20898	Sgt.	Atkinson, W. A.	D.C.M.
			M.M.
17971	Sgt.	Stanford, D.	M.S.M.
444086	Sgt.	Toothill, R.	M.M.
478128	Sgt.	Croydon, L.	M.M.
200460	Sgt.	Hatton, F.	M.M.
37856	Sgt.	Young, S. H.	M.S.M.
1336	Sgt.	Webster, F.	M.M.
482201	Sgt.	Scorah, L.	M.S.M.
16985	Sgt.	Dobson, E.	Medaille d'Honneur Avec Glavies, en Argent.
12058	Cpl.	Oke, F.	D.C.M.
15394	Cpl.	Leach, W.	M.M.
			Bar to M.M.
			2nd Bar to M.M.
24094	Cpl.	Neary, C. F. W.	M.M.
24214	Cpl.	Jacobs, S. T.	M.M.
1359	Cpl.	Chambers, W. B.	D.C.M.
1375	Cpl.	Trudore, W.	M.M.
			Medaille Militaire
1022	Cpl.	North, E. J.	M.M.
478057	Cpl.	Beaumont, H.	M.M.
478112	Cpl.	Ellis, B.	M.M.
478150	Cpl.	Thompson, C. J.	M.M.
478536	Cpl.	Wildgoose, W. J.	M.M.
1433	Cpl.	Overall, P.	D.C.M.
1578	Cpl.	Lees, J. T.	D.C.M.
1609	Cpl.	Ainsley, F.	M.M.
1518	Cpl.	Creek, C. P.	M.M.
476735	Cpl.	Riley, F.	M.M.
476264	Cpl.	Hillman, F.	M.M.
			Bar to M.M.
478159	Cpl.	Fawcett, H.	M.M.
476248	Cpl.	Marshall, A. E.	M.M.
476237	Cpl.	Stones, J.	M.M.
476311	Cpl.	Westwood, A.	M.M.

49TH (W.R.) DIVISIONAL R.E.—*continued*

Regtl. No.	Rank.	Name.	Award.
476076	Cpl.	Litchfield, W.	French Croix de Guerre
1854	Cpl.	Osborne, H.	D.C.M.
676	Cpl.	Booth, J. M.	M.M.
1818	Cpl. ·... ...	Whitehurst, G.	M.M.
1873	Cpl.	Burnett, A. G.	M.M.
1323	Cpl.	Beeston, A.	M.M.
482228	Cpl.	Wilburn, F.	D.C.M.
478059	Cpl.	Beverley, L.	M.M.
552751	Cpl.	Hayes, L.	M.M.
476735	Cpl.	Riley, F	D.C.M. M.M.
482537	Cpl.	Pholl, S.	M.M.
482204	Cpl.	Smith, N.	M.M.
482055	Cpl.	Beevers, F. W.	M.M.
482511	Cpl.	Hawkesworth, H. C.	M.M.
54380	Cpl.	Holmes, F. G.	M.S.M.
1392	2/Cpl.	Ellis, A....	M.M.
482202	2/Cpl.	Pinder, P.	M.M.
255041	2/Cpl.	Young, N. A.	M.M.
482072	2/Cpl.	Clarke, F.	Italian Bronze Medal for Military Valour.
94238	2/Cpl.	Kenton, H.	M.M.
16175	2/Cpl.	Hancock, A.	M.M.
476263	L.-Cpl.	Moore, W.	Belgian Croix de Guerre
1852	L.-Cpl.	Morris, G. R.	M.M.
482222	L.-Cpl.	Wordsworth, A. C.	M.M.
476318	L.-Cpl.	Tinker, J.	M.M.
479952	L.-Cpl.	White, S. S.	D.C.M. Bar to D.C.M.
1115	L.-Cpl.	Owen, W. B.	D.C.M.
16050	Sapr.	Donald, J. C.	M.M.
3373	Sapr.	Hoyland, J.	M.M.
854	Sapr.	Ashmore, W.	M.M.
3512	Sapr.	Hydes, W.	M.M.
831	Sapr.	Gordon, C.	M.M.
478032	Sapr.	Hutton, H.	M.M.
478552	Sapr.	Hawley, F.	M.M.
478250	Sapr.	Rowley, C. W.	M.M. Bar to M.M.
478067	Sapr.	Orwin, A.	M.M.
478651	Sapr.	Mounsley, C. E.	M.M.
1336	Sapr.	Webster, F.	M.M.
482538	Sapr.	Wilkinson, J.	M.M.
93649	Sapr.	Meanwell, F.	M.M.
482220	Sapr.	Westmoreland, A.	M.M.
247370	Sapr.	Paterson, W.	M.M.
479956	Sapr.	Beaston, A.	M.M.
482212	Sapr.	Brown, W. H.	M.M.
25257	Sapr.	Ashton, W.	M.S.M.
134015	Sapr.	Smith, T. C.	M.M.
542457	Sapr.	Male, G.	M.M.
482445	Sapr.	Grant, H. E.	M.M.
267748	Sapr.	Richardson, J.	M.M.
151784	Sapr.	Portch, A. B.	M.M.
482085	Sapr.	Demming, S. A.	M.M.
482255	Sapr.	Stockley, J. R.	M.M.
504257	Sapr.	Thomas, S. G. F.	M.M.
1105	Sapr.	Jennett, A.	D.C.M.
247382	Sapr.	Holland, R. W.	M.M.

49TH (W.R.) DIVISIONAL R.E.—*continued*

Regtl. No.	Rank.	Name.	Award.
441908	Sapr.	Connolly, J. E....	M.M.
217540	Sapr.	Barker, T. E.	M.M.
1036	Sapr.	Packard, G.	D.C.M.
1857	Pioneer	Norris	M.M.
34808	Pioneer	Sillence, E.	M.M.
1714	Dr.	Wright, W.	M.M.
478050	Dr.	France, C.	M.M.
23689	Dr.	Akers, W.	Medaille Barbatie si Credinta, 3rd Class

1/5TH WEST YORKS. REGIMENT

Regtl. No.	Rank.	Name.	Award.
	Lt.-Col. ...	Wood, C. E.	C.M.G.
	Lt.-Col. ...	Oddie, W.	D.S.O. Bar to D.S.O.
	Captain ...	Williamson, P. G.	M.C.
	Captain ...	Sowerby, G.	M.C.
	Captain ...	Pinder, J. (R.A.M.C.) ...	M.C.
	Captain ...	Freeman, W. H.	M.C. Bar to M.C.
	Captain ...	Ablett, B. E.	M.C. Bar to M.C.
	Captain ...	Wycherley, R. B.	M.C. Bar to M.C.
	Captain ...	Green, D.	M.C.
	Captain ...	Heaton, H. F.	M.C.
	Captain ...	Peters, J. C.	M.C.
	Lieut. ...	Jameson, J. L.	M.C.
	Lieut. ...	Mackay, K.	M.C.
	Lieut. ...	Birbeck, L. S.	M.C.
	Lieut. ...	Rushforth, J. W.	M.C.
	2/Lieut. ...	Shillaker, E. C. H.	M.C.
	2/Lieut. ...	Gilesnan, T. D. C.	M.C. Croix de Guerre
	2/Lieut. ...	Saxby, F.	M.C.
	2/Lieut. ...	Wallace, D. W.	M.C.
	2/Lieut. ...	Parker, J. W.	M.C.
	2/Lieut. ...	Irish, H.	M.C.
	2/Lieut. ...	Hardwick, T. W.	M.C.
	2/Lieut. ...	King, B. A.	M.C.
	2/Lieut. ...	Wilson, M.	M.C.
	2/Lieut. ...	Jones, S. L.	M.C.
	2/Lieut. ...	Berghoff, H.	M.C.
	2/Lieut. ...	Todd, G. L.	M.C.
4713	R.S.M. ...	Raynor, F.	D.C.M.
2210	C.S.M. ...	Nicholson, J. C.	D.C.M.
1931	C.S.M. ...	Lund, G.	D.C.M.
200593	C.S.M. ...	Pattison, H.	D.C.M. Medal Militaire
2816	C.Q.M.S. ...	Ronder, R.	M.M.
200025	C.Q.M.S. ...	Calder, G.	M.S.M.
1470	Sgt.	Morton, M. C....	D.C.M.
1161	Sgt.	Tolley, G.	D C.M.
1643	Sgt.	Broughton, W.	M.M.
900	Sgt.	Kitchen, G.	D.C.M.
203143	Sgt.	Thornhill, R.	M.M.
200049	Sgt.	Thompson, J. W.	M.M.
200620	Sgt.	Hewson, A.	M.M
6494	Sgt.	Emerson, J.	D.C.M.
200610	Sgt.	Willis, A.	M.M.

1/5TH WEST YORKS. REGIMENT—*continued*

Regtl. No.	Rank.	Name.	Award.
200875	Sgt.	Ledgond, E.	D.C.M.
202272	Sgt.	Waind, W. F.	Belgian Croix de Guerre
200510	Sgt.	Henderson, J.	D.C.M.
200065	Sgt.	Whinn, J. D. P.	M.S.M.
201063	Sgt.	Long, A.	M.M. Bar to M.M.
200221	Sgt.	Light, R. ... ••• ...	M.M.
201114	Sgt.	Ingleby, A.	M.M.
265375	Sgt.	Kavanagh, P.	D.C.M.
202817	Sgt.	Wilson, T.	M.M.
200788	Sgt.	McQuade, J. C.	D.C.M.
200350	Sgt.	Akers, J.	M.S.M.
2623	Sgt.	Dracup, J.	M.M.
1441	Cpl.	Richardson, J. W.	M.M.
1780	Cpl.	Metcalf, A.	M.M.
201125	Cpl.	Radbank, E.	M.M.
200789	Cpl.	Raftery, J.	M.M.
200794	Cpl.	Baldison, C. H.	D.C.M. M.M.
2629	Cpl.	Tomlinson, H. A.	M.M. Bar to M.M.
4616	Cpl.	White	M.M.
200575	Cpl.	Lee, R. J.	M.M.
1799	Cpl.	Foster, R. J.	M.M.
26285	Cpl.	Buckroyd, J.	M.M.
2372	Cpl.	Emmott, G.	M.M.
203042	Cpl.	Cairns, E. ... ••• ...	M.M.
1540	Cpl.	Grice, E. W.	D.C.M.
1488	L.-Cpl.	Atkinson, J.	D.C.M.
5968	L.-Cpl.	Pascol, N.	D.C.M.
2755	L.-Cpl.	Smith, F. ... ••• ...	M.M. Bar to M.M.
2379	L.-Cpl.	Haynes, H.	M.M.
7733	L.-Cpl.	Benson, W.	M.M.
202721	L.-Cpl.	Carney, T.	M.M.
201172	L.-Cpl.	Wilson, H.	M.M.
21/394	L.-Cpl.	Rastrick, W.	M.M. Bar to M.M.
66507	L.-Cpl.	Wellington, H. H.	M.M.
62512	L.-Cpl.	Avery, S. G.	M.M.
16/1553	L.-Cpl.	Butterfield, F.	M.M. Bar to M.M.
241408	L.-Cpl.	Marriott, C.	M.M. Bar to M.M.
54171	L.-Cpl.	Payne, A. H.	M.M.
3727	L.-Cpl.	Simpson, W.	M.M.
202714	L.-Cpl.	Uttley, A.	M.M.
3501	L.-Cpl.	Sutcliffe, W.	M.M.
306670	L.-Cpl.	India, J.	M.M.
3091	L.-Cpl.	Airey, M. S.	M.M.
62503	L.-Cpl.	Green, E.	M.M.
1247	L.-Cpl.	Corke, A.	M.M.
1790	Pte.	Cook, A. W.	D.C.M.
2168	Pte.	Usher, H.	D.C.M.
2158	Pte.	Beech, N. W.	D.C.M.
1817	Pte.	Allen, A. J.	M.M.
1666	Pte.	Brown, F.	M.M.
2552	Pte.	Dixon, F. W.	M.M.
3928	Pte.	Brooks, A.	M.M.
1709	Pte.	Trousdale, L.	M.M. Bar to M.M.

1/5TH WEST YORKS. REGIMENT—*continued*

Regtl. No.	Rank.	Name.	Award.
6517	Pte.	Chadwick, G.	M.M. Bar to M.M.
201221	Pte.	Twineham, G.	M.M. Bar to M.M.
3402	Pte.	Farnhill, A.	D.C.M.
2688	Pte.	Shillits, J. W.	M.M.
2518	Pte.	Butler, B.	M.M.
2583	Pte.	Maw, T. V.	M.M.
2220	Pte.	McAndrew, B.	M.M.
1289	Pte.	Clark, J. W.	M.M.
36959	Pte.	Carr, H.	D.C.M.
202759	Pte.	Lockwood, L.	M.M.
202967	Pte.	Padgett, H.	M.M.
41282	Pte.	Pickard, S.	M.M.
202162	Pte.	Mitchell, C.	M.M.
200946	Pte.	Bland, R.	M.M.
202152	Pte.	Shepherd, W.	M.M.
200670	Pte.	Blanshard, J.	M.M.
200726	Pte.	Rogers, N.	M.M.
200703	Pte.	Kitson, I. R.	M.M.
203134	Pte.	Wilson, J. W.	M.M.
18/411	Pte.	Howarth, H.	M.M.
18/1288	Pte.	Pickles, H.	M.M.
203003	Pte.	O'Connor, G.	M.C.
235031	Pte.	Fawcett, H.	M.M.
983	Pte.	Jowett, W. H.	M.M.
54131	Pte.	Holeford, J. T.	M.M.
62513	Pte.	Chandler, A. J.	M.M.
58951	Pte.	Drake, W. H.	M.M.
240888	Pte.	Watson, W.	M.M. Bar to M.M.
54901	Pte.	Miller, J.	M.M.
22185	Pte.	Dickens, F.	M.M.
9457	Pte.	Birbeck, J.	M.M.
63020	Pte.	Harrison, W.	M.M.
307593	Pte.	Mackay, A.	Belgian Croix de Guerre.
2485	Pte.	Gatenby, W. A.	M.M.
310	Pte.	Marshall, A. T.	M.M.
2292	Pte.	Moss, C. E.	M.M.
4231	Pte.	Greenwood, W.	M.M.
3506	Pte.	Smith, C.	M.M.
201434	Pte.	Grayson, J.	M.M.

1/6TH WEST YORKS. REGIMENT

	Lt.-Col.... ...	Wade, H. O.	D.S.O.
	Lt.-Col.... ...	Wistance, W.	M.C. D.S.O.
	Major	Clough, R.	M.C.
	Major	Hornshaw, F. G.	M.C.
	Captain ...	Sanderman, G. R.	M.C.
	Captain ...	Fawcett, R. A.	M.C.
	Captain ...	Armistead, T. E.	M.C.
	Captain ...	Fawcett, W. L.	M.C.
	Captain ...	Gordon, J. S.	M.C.
	Captain ...	Weighill, W. C. S.	M.C.
	Captain ...	Mossop, W. N.	M.C.
	Captain ...	Sanders, G., V.C.	M.C.
	Captain ...	Rees, G. F. G.	M.C.

R

1/6TH WEST YORKS. REGIMENT—*continued*

Regtl. No.	Rank.	Name.	Award.
	Captain ...	Stansfield, E. D.	M.C. Bar to M.C.
	Captain ...	Hill, W. H.	M.C.
	Captain ...	Muller, J.	M.C.
	Lieut.	Mitchell, H.	M.C.
	Lieut.	MacLusky, W. B.	M.C. Bar to M.C.
	2/Lieut. ...	Scales, W. A.	M.C.
	2/Lieut. ...	Speight, G. H.	M.C.
	2/Lieut. ...	Tempest, E. V.	M.C.
	2/Lieut. ...	Hick, B.	M.C.
	2/Lieut. ...	Greenwood, L.	M.C.
	2/Lieut. ...	Illingworth, J.	M.C.
9	R.S.M.	Barker, H.	M.C. D.C.M.
11572	R.S.M.	Sugden, A.	D.C.M. M.S.M.
229	C.S.M.	Walmsley, W.	Croix de Guerre.
240037	C.S.M.	Moorhouse, W.	Belgian Croix de Guerre.
260007	C.S.M.	Padgett, C.	M.M.
240144	C.S.M.	Wallace, A.	M.M.
298	Q.M.S.	Paisey, J. L.	D.C.M.
1809	C.Q.M.S.	Woodhead, C.	M.S.M.
1147	Sgt.	Meckosha, S.	V.C.
1140	Sgt.	Kelly, J. W.	D.C.M.
1773	Sgt.	Simpson, C. G.	D.C.M.
2626	Sgt.	Sayers, J.	D.C.M.
79	Sgt.	Banks, H.	D.C.M.
1259	Sgt.	Stanton, W.	M.M.
2623	Sgt.	Dracup, J.	M.M.
3539	Sgt.	Bradley, E.	D.C.M. Cross of St. George 4th Class.
324	Sgt.	King, H. R.	M.M.
2450	Sgt.	Sunter, T.	M.S.M.
1706	Sgt.	McIvor, R. G.	M.M.
2044	Sgt.	Fairbank, F. E.	M.M.
241048	Sgt.	Browne, W.	D.C.M.
240980	Sgt.	Powell, F.	M.M.
240398	Sgt.	Ward, J.	M.S.M.
240197	Sgt.	Chapman, S.	M.S.M.
241856	Sgt.	Cheer, R.	M.M.
9230	Sgt.	Bagnall, T.	M.M.
242634	Sgt.	Sharp, B.	M.S.M.
1165	Cpl.	Smith, A.	D.C.M.
2474	Cpl.	Ellison, W.	D.C.M.
1799	Cpl.	Foster, R. J.	M.M.
4616	Cpl.	White, W.	M.M.
2372	Cpl.	Emmott, G.	M.M.
1908	Cpl.	Mee, H.	M.M.
1500	Cpl.	Hutchinson, W.	M.M.
241215	Cpl.	Davies, J.	M.M.
241764	Cpl.	Bradley, G.	M.M.
242637	Cpl.	Brown, A. P.	D.C.M.
240143	Cpl.	Turton, H.	M.M.
72577	Cpl.	Clacey, E.	M.M.
240883	Cpl.	Stott, W.	M.M.
1140	Cpl.	Kelly, J. W.	D.C.M.
1266	L.-Cpl. ...	Wilkinson, E. J.	D.C.M.
3225	L.-Cpl. ...	Johnson, E.	D.C.M.

1/6TH WEST YORKS. REGIMENT—*continued*

Regtl. No.	Rank.	Name.	Award.
3727	L.-Cpl.	Simpson, W.	M.M.
1249	L.-Cpl.	Corke, A.	M.M.
2091	L.-Cpl.	Airey, N. G.	M.M.
3301	L.-Cpl.	Sutcliffe, W.	M.M.
372	L.-Cpl.	Simpson, W. G.	D.C.M.
1360	L.-Cpl.	Wilcock, H.	D.C.M.
4539	L.-Cpl.	Silverwood, A.	M.M.
241126	L.-Cpl.	O'Donnell, G.	M.M. Bar to M.M.
241394	L.-Cpl.	Hird, W.	M.M.
242770	L.-Cpl.	Thomas, D.	M.M.
242490	L.-Cpl.	Middleton, W.	M.M.
240737	L.-Cpl.	Woolham, H.	M.M.
242864	L.-Cpl.	Poole, E. P.	M.M.
20/37	L.-Cpl.	Smithies, D.	M.M.
42398	L.-Cpl.	Shepherd, G. F.	M.M.
62922	L.-Cpl.	Smythe, C. G.	M.M.
54179	L.-Cpl.	Rough, C. E.	M.M.
372	L.-Cpl.	Simpson, W. G.	D.C.M.
2424	Pte.	Preston, E.	D.C.M.
2315	Pte.	Francis, W.	D.C.M.
2190	Pte.	Kenmore, E. M.	D.C.M.
1418	Pte.	Hodgson, G. H.	M.M.
2292	Pte.	Moss, E.	M.M.
3107	Pte.	Marshall, A. T.	M.M.
4274	Pte.	Greenwood, W.	M.M.
3506	Pte.	Smith, C.	M.M.
4539	Pte.	Silverwood, A.	D.C.M.
31822	Pte.	Nicholson, W.	D.C.M.
1263	Pte.	Cooke, B.	M.M.
3808	Pte, ...	Cawthra, M.	M.M.
1756	Pte.	Bradley, T.	M.M.
1608	Pte.	Coupland, A.	M.M.
2503	Pte.	Dawson, J. H.	M.M.
242747	Pte.	Howe, A. G.	M.M.
241548	Pte.	Marton, E.	M.M.
242878	Pte.	Horner, A. J.	M.M.
242826	Pte.	Charlton, W.	M.M.
242614	Pte.	Sweet, J	M.M.
240344	Pte.	Cassarley, V.	M.M.
240910	Pte.	Walker, J.	M.M.
211568	Pte.	Thistlethwaite, L.	M.M.
240787	Pte.	Woddiwiss, C. B.	M.M.
240174	Pte.	Hainsworth, A.	M.M.
242520	Pte.	Hirst, W.	M.M.
242897	Pte.	Dodds, C.	M.M.
62974	Pte.	Swinton, A. R.	M.M.
54181	Pte.	Rawding, H. T.	M.M.
62911	Pte.	Porte, A. D.	M.M.
18104	Pte.	King, H.	D.C.M.
240180	Pte.	Evans, H.	D.C.M.
202059	Pte.	Hanson, R.	M.M.
16/1532	Pte.	Dalby, H.	M.M.
15/1622	Pte.	Pawson, R.	M.M.
62621	Pte.	Hitman, A. J.	M.M.
238233	Pte.	Hawkins, E. T.	M.M.
50749	Pte.	Johnson, T. J.	M.M.
63690	Pte.	Hardy, D.	M.M.
62611	Pte.	Reed, G. W.	M.M.
21717	Pte.	Butler, D.	M.M.
15887	Pte.	Pickles, B.	M.M.

1/7TH WEST YORKS. REGIMENT

Regtl. No.	Rank.	Name.	Award.
	Lt.-Col....	Bousfield, H. D.	C.M.G.
			D.S.O.
			Belgian Croix de Guerre
	Lt.-Col....	Tetley, C. H.	D.S.O.
	Major ...	Braithwaite, W. H.	M.C.
	Captain	Redmayne, J. B.	M.C.
	Captain	Walling, E.	M.C.
			French Croix de Guerre
	Captain	Foulds, C. L.	M.C.
	Captain	Booth, G. L.	M.C.
	Lieut. ...	Noone, W. J. S.	M.C.
	Lieut. ...	Haydon, P. M....	M.C.
	Lieut. ...	Desprez, L. W.	M.C.
	Lieut. ...	Swift, A. E.	M.C.
	Lieut. ...	Smith, C. J. B.	M.C.
	2/Lieut.	Glazebrook, A. R.	M.C.
	2/Lieut.	Baldwin, F. J.	M.C.
	2/Lieut.	Feather, N.	M.C.
	2/Lieut.	Dickinson, T. E.	M.C.
265012	R.S.M. ...	Stembridge, F....	D.C.M.
265001	R.Q.M.S.	Rhodes, H.	M.S.M.
25	C.S.M. ...	Lodge, H.	D.C.M.
1610	C.S.M. ...	Fenton, H.	D.C.M.
			M.M.
267579	C.S.M. ...	Allerton, A.	D.C.M.
265703	C.S.M. ...	Cushworth, G.	D.C.M.
			Belgian Croix de Guerre
265079	C.S.M. ...	Peacock, H. E.	M.S.M.
305665	C.S.M. ...	Turner, W.	D.C.M.
433	C.Q.M.S.	Wilkinson, F. ...	D.C.M.
566	Sgt. ...	Coates, J.	D.C.M.
			Croix de Guerre
1931	Sgt. ...	Elliott, J. H.	M.M.
3203	Sgt. ...	Sanders, G.	V.C.—
773	Sgt. ...	Denbigh, P.	M.M.
2032	Sgt. ...	Chaplin, A.	M.M.
1370	Sgt. ...	Chickley, H.	M.M.
266906	Sgt. ...	Sanderson, S. ...	D.C.M.
			M.M.
265069	Sgt. ...	Bourne, H.	M.M.
266959	Sgt. ...	Lightfoot, H. ...	M.M.
265437	Sgt. ...	Yeadon, E.	Belgian Croix de Guerre
266654	Sgt. ...	McNichol, M. ...	D.C.M.
268855	Sgt. ...	Train, J.	M.M.
266627	Sgt. ...	Ibbitson, G.	M.M.
265005	Sgt. ...	Wortley, R.	M.S.M.
265556	Sgt. ...	Guchrie, G. H.	Croix de Guerre
2953	Sgt. ...	Read, N.	M.M.
1601	L.-Sgt.	Cawgill, J.	D.C.M.
265534	L.-Sgt.	Beevers, C.	M.M.
307880	L.-Sgt.	Cross, S.	M.M.
3017	Cpl. ...	Bentley, J.	D.C.M.
2625	Cpl. ...	Makin, W.	D.C.M.
4137	Cpl. ...	Cook, L.	Bronze Medal for Military Valour
265816	Cpl. ...	Dennison, E.	M.M.
266121	Cpl. ...	Moss, J.	D.C.M.

1/7TH WEST YORKS. REGIMENT—*continued*

Regtl. No.	Rank.	Name.	Award.
268080	Cpl.	Fryer, E.	M.M.
265590	Cpl.	Stothard, W.	M.M.
2991	L.-Cpl.	Ingleby, H.	M.M.
2050	L.-Cpl.	Anderson, J.	M.M.
3176	L.-Cpl.	Pickles, P.	M.M.
2103	L.-Cpl.	Fawcett, A.	M.M.
3000	L.-Cpl.	Kirk, L.	M.M.
1847	L.-Cpl.	Moss, J. C.	D.C.M.
265470	L.-Cpl.	Vince, F.	M.M.
2330	L.-Cpl.	Beanland, C.	Croix de Guerre
267752	L.-Cpl.	Pullan, F. H.	M.M.
265658	L.-Cpl.	Craker, C. W.	M.M.
268059	L.-Cpl.	Turner, E.	M.M.
367846	L.-Cpl.	Newson, A.	M.M.
265321	L.-Cpl.	Metcalf, J.	M.M.
265311	L.-Cpl.	Strickland, G. H.	M.M.
265864	L.-Cpl.	Smith, G.	M.M.
265948	L.-Cpl.	Sheard, A.	M.M.
267772	L.-Cpl.	Hart, G. A.	M.M.
267581	L.-Cpl.	Hawkins, A.	M.M.
59616	L.-Cpl.	Kinsman, J. W.	M.M.
266235	L.-Cpl.	Schofield, W.	M.M.
265233	L.-Cpl.	Agar, T. W.	M.M.
1971	Rfm.	Garrity, M.	D.C.M.
1215	Rfm.	Waters, L.	D.C.M.
2154	Rfm.	Worth, J.	D.C.M.
1966	Rfm.	Emmett, H.	M.M.
4487	Rfm.	Hawland, W.	M.M.
2775	Rfm.	Blackburn, G. W.	Medal St. George 4th Class
2036	Rfm.	Evans, G. H.	M.M.
266684	Rfm.	Dickinson, A.	M M.
265924	Rfm.	Musgrove, J. W.	M.M.
268037	Rfm.	Smith, H.	M.M.
265771	Rfm.	Millson, H.	M.M.
267859	Rfm.	Lincoln, H.	M.M.
267950	Rfm.	Hall, N A.	M.M.
241714	Rfm.	Duckworth, W.	M.M.
267787	Rfm.	Goggin, J.	M.M.
307675	Rfm.	Dinsdale, G.	M.M.
266897	Rfm.	Woodcock, E.	M.M.
201234	Rfm.	Exilby, T.	M.M.
242583	Rfm.	Haylock, G.	M.M.
62762	Rfm.	Lyons, J.	M.M.
236366	Rfm.	Watkin, J. W.	M.M.
242336	Rfm.	Bottomley, J.	M.M.
268041	Rfm.	Lindsell, J. W.	M.M.
266763	Rfm.	Smith, H.	M.M.
62708	Rfm.	Craddock, J. W.	M.M.
54405	Rfm.	Hart, L.	M.M.
39620	Rfm.	Smith, S. L.	M.M.
265771	Rfm.	Wilson, H.	M.M.
266958	Rfm.	Conlon, H.	M.M.
3017	Rfm.	Bentley, J.	D.C.M.
1512	Pte.	Cooper, J. W.	M.M.
268534	Pte.	Hudson, D.	D.C.M.
265616	Pte.	Capp, A. H.	D.C.M.
307876	Pte.	Chapman, H. W.	M.M.
307898	Pte.	Rudder, J.	M.M.

1/8TH WEST YORKS. REGIMENT

Regtl. No.	Rank.	Name.	Award.
	Lt.-Col. ...	Alexander, J. W.	D.S.O.
	Major ...	Hudson, R. A.	D.S.O.
	Major ...	Sykes, S. S. ...	M.C.
	Major ...	Longbottom, T.	D.S.O.
	Captain ...	Brooke, W. H.	M.C.
	Captain ...	Burke, H. J. (R.A.M.C.)	M.C.
	Lieut. ...	Lupton, H. R.	M.C.
	2/Lieut.	Allexander, J. C. K. ...	M.C.
	2/Lieut.	Wilkinson, E. F.	M.C.
	2/Lieut.	Smith, F. W.	M.C.
	2/Lieut.	Worsley, W. E.	M.C.
	2/Lieut.	Kemp, W. G. ...	M.C.
268228	R.S.M. ...	Hemmingway, H.	D.C.M.
305509	R.Q.M.S.	Pickersgill, F. ...	M.S.M.
305126	C.S.M. ...	Spence, C. C. ...	D.C.M.
22501	C.Q.M.S.	Smith, F. T. ...	M.M.
721	Sgt. ...	Fretwell, C. N.	D.C.M.
559	Sgt. ...	Pearson, A.	D.C.M.
2505	Sgt. ...	Coulson, C. ...	D.C.M.
2063	Sgt. ...	Archer, H.	M.M. Bar to M.M.
305601	Sgt. ...	Flockton, J.	D.C.M.
307153	Sgt. ...	Inglis, A.	M.M.
1983	Cpl. ...	Green, E.	D.C.M.
306198	Cpl. ...	Pearson, E.	Belgian Croix de Guerre
132	L.-Cpl. ...	Thackray, H. ...	D.C.M.
2970	L.-Cpl. ...	Wright, H.	D.C.M.
3377	L.-Cpl. ...	Cunliffe, E.	M.M.
1757	L.-Cpl. ...	Blaizmire, G. A.	M.M.
2503	Rfm. ...	Dodd, A.	D.C.M.
1266	Rfm. ...	Clough, J.	D.C.M.
2634	Rfm. ...	Benson, A.	D.C.M.
2229	Rfm. ...	Stead, W.	D.C.M.
4320	Rfm. ...	Smith. J.	D.C.M.
2750	Rfm. ...	Webster, F.	M.M.
268178	Rfm. ...	Talbot, H.	M.M.
305096	Rfm. ...	Nicholson. E. O.	M.M.
13569	Rfm. ...	Bateman, W.	M.M.
307706	Rfm. ...	Webb, E.	M.M.
305888	Rfm. ...	Grant, J.	M.M.
307180	Rfm. ...	Culley, A.	M.M.

1/4TH WEST RIDING REGIMENT

	Lt-Col. ...	Sugden, R. E.	D.S.O. Bar to D.S.O.
	Lt.-Col....	Mowat, A. L. ...	M.C. Bar to M.C. D.S.O.
	Major ...	Stanton, H. A. S.	D.S.O.
	Captain ...	Sykes, E. E. ...	M.C.
	Captain ...	Greaves, S. S. (R.A.M.C.)	M.C.
	Captain ...	Mowat, J. G.	M.C.
	Captain ...	Fenton, W. C.	M.C. Bar to M.C.
	Captain ...	Marshall, E. N.	M.C.
	Captain ...	Geldard, N.	M.C.
	Captain ...	Farrar, N. T. ...	M.C.
	Captain ...	Luty, A. M. ...	M.C.

1/4TH WEST RIDING REGIMENT—*continued*

Regtl. No.	Rank.	Name.	Award.
	Captain ...	Kirk, A.	M.C.
	Lieut.	Everitt, W. N.	M.C.
	Lieut.	King, M. H.	M.C.
	Lieut.	Blakey, E. V.	M.C.
	Lieut.	Mackie, W. G.	M.C.
	Lieut.	Bales, P. G.	M.C.
	Lieut.	Irish, F.	M.C.
	2/Lieut. ...	Innes, F. A.	M.C.
	2/Lieut. ...	Blackwell, F. V.	M.C.
	2/Lieut. ...	Ackroyd, H. H.	M.C.
	2/Lieut. ...	Gumby, L.	M.C.
	2/Lieut. ...	Huggard, B. H.	M.C.
	2/Lieut. ...	Newman, N. R.	M.C.
	2/Lieut. ...	Jessop, T. E.	M.C.
	2/Lieut. ...	Lumb, J. W.	M.C.
83	R.Q.M.S. ...	Lee, W....	M.C.
2353	C.S.M.	Stirzaker, A.	D.C.M.
2350	C.S.M.	Stirzaker, F. P.	M.C.
200441	C.S.M.	Medley, W.	M.C. Medal Militaire.
235227	C.S.M.	Brooke, N.	D.C.M.
200598	C.S.M.	Parkinson, J.	D.C.M.
200135	C.S.M.	Haigh, H.	D.C.M. M.M.
235524	C.S.M.	Yates, J. C.	M.M.
2040	Sgt.	Clarke, T. H.	D.C.M.
5793	Sgt.	Johnson, F.	M.M.
2413	Sgt.	Sheard, J. S.	M.M.
6750	Sgt.	Moscrop, C.	D.C.M.
1485	Sgt.	Hodgson, A. M.	M.M.
73	Sgt.	Moran, P.	M.M.
2364	Sgt.	Wilson, J.	M.M.
1002	Sgt.	Flather, J. N.	M.M.
601	Sgt.	McNulty, A.	M.M.
30	Sgt.	Crossley, J. W.	M.M.
200192	Sgt.	Smith, H.	M.M.
235519	Sgt.	Binns, W.	D.C.M.
200064	Sgt.	Naylor, C.	Belgian Croix de Guerre.
200688	Sgt.	Jones, E.	M.S.M.
200483	Sgt.	Firth, F.	M.S.M.
200298	Sgt.	Brown, F. J.	D.C.M. M.M.
200453	Sgt.	Bancroft, J.	D.C.M. M.M.
203229	Sgt.	Mann, J.	D.C.M.
200653	Sgt.	Brunt, R. G.	M.M.
200055	Sgt.	Flitcroft, S.	D.C.M. M.M.
242567	Sgt.	Smith, A.	M.M.
200763	Sgt.	Whittaker, A.	M.M.
203305	Sgt.	Wilson, R.	D.C.M.
15805	Sgt.	Loosemoor, A.	V.C. D.C.M.
203336	Sgt.	Bolt, A. A.	M.M.
13014	Sgt.	Thompson, W.	M.M.
200101	Sgt.	Turner, E.	M.M.
201125	Sgt.	Chilton, T.	M.M.
201178	Sgt.	Knowles, J.	M.M.
201191	Sgt.	Wood, F.	D.C.M. M.M.

1/4TH WEST RIDING REGIMENT—*continued*

Regtl. No.	Rank.	Name.	Award.
203252	Sgt.	Foster, W. D.	D.C.M.
242274	Sgt.	Redpath, J.	D.C.M.
			M.M.
10737	Sgt.	Kay, S.	M.M.
16075	Sgt.	Widdop, J.	M.M.
306365	Sgt.	Barnes, W.	M.M.
200143	Sgt.	Downes, N.	D.C.M.
201219	L.-Sgt.	Jessop, S.	M.M.
200396	L.-Sgt.	Maskimmon, A.	M.M.
203349	L.-Sgt.	Field, F. J.	D.C.M.
201012	L.-Sgt.	McHugh, P.	M.M.
1495	Cpl.	Landale, C.	D.C.M.
855	Cpl.	Ashworth, E.	D.C.M.
3060	Cpl.	Bancroft, W.	D.C.M.
1605	Cpl.	Bailey, G. A.	M.M.
1747	Cpl.	Jackison, E.	D.C.M.
			M.M.
1535	Cpl.	Walker, J.	Bronze Medal for Military Valour.
201186	Cpl.	Taylor, V.	M.M.
201295	Cpl.	Wilson, B.	M.M.
200204	Cpl.	Wainwright, H.	M.M.
242371	Cpl.	Brown, W.	D.C.M.
			M.M.
200127	Cpl.	Gledhill, R.	M.M.
203217	Cpl.	Brice, A.	M.M.
240168	Cpl.	Spring, F.	M.M.
			Bar to M.M.
238031	Cpl.	Varley, J. W.	M.M.
200681	Cpl.	Mitchell, W. H.	M.M.
200153	L.-Cpl.	Mortimer, C.	M.M.
200096	L.-Cpl.	Barker, S.	M.M.
			Bar to M.M.
201013	L.-Cpl.	Mitchell, A. R.	M.M.
203285	L.-Cpl.	Kam, R.	D.C.M.
			M.M.
			Bar to M.M.
202664	L.-Cpl.	Jennings, B.	M.M.
202042	L.-Cpl.	Brook, E.	M.M.
200053	L.-Cpl.	Beverley, A.	M.M.
200146	L.-Cpl.	Ennis, J.	M.M.
			Bar to M.M.
200130	L.-Cpl.	Lancaster, J.	M.M.
			Bar to M.M.
203351	L.-Cpl.	Moon, A.	D.C.M.
202936	L.-Cpl.	Hudson, R. A.	D.C.M.
220539	L.-Cpl.	Whiteley, H.	M.M.
			Bar to M.M.
201886	L.-Cpl.	Birkinshaw, G.	M.M.
26498	L.-Cpl.	Barber, G. W.	M.M.
203371	L.-Cpl.	North, G.	M.M.
201893	L.-Cpl.	Bolton, C.	M.M.
			Croix de Guerre.
200134	L.-Cpl.	Ryder, J. W.	M.M.
267198	L.-Cpl.	Driver, H.	M.M.
203285	L.-Cpl.	Fane, N.	M.M.
202746	L.-Cpl.	Rhodes, F.	M.M.
202042	L.-Cpl.	Booth, E.	M.M.
202787	L.-Cpl.	Broadbent, G.	M.M.
3406	Pte.	Sykes, H.	M.M.
1063	Pte.	Murray, W.	M.M.

1/4TH WEST RIDING REGIMENT—*continued*

Regtl. No.	Rank.			Name.				Award.
1889	Pte.	...	...	Royals, S.	...	...	...	M.M.
6606	Pte.	...	...	Swinburne, R.		...	...	M.M.
6520	Pte.	...	...	Metcalf, W.	...	...	...	M.M.
6598	Pte.	...	...	Bowers, J.	...	...	...	M.M.
1645	Pte.	...	...	Knox, R.	...	...	...	M.M.
1715	Pte.	...	...	Bibby, H.	...	...	...	M.M.
203177	Pte.	...	...	Brabben, S. R.		...	...	M.M.
202120	Pte.	...	...	Conroy, T.	...	...	...	M.M.
203649	Pte.	...	...	Dewar, J.	...	...	...	M.M.
201923	Pte.	...	...	Meneghan, T. ...		...	...	M.M.
203480	Pte.	...	...	Hookham, F.	...	...	...	M.M.
201879	Pte.	...	...	Gallow, J.	...	...	...	M.M.
200172	Pte.	...	...	Dennis, N.	...	...	...	M.M.
203188	Pte.	...	...	Lowth, H.	...	...	...	M.M.
235253	Pte.	...	...	Green, G.	...	...	...	M.M.
201689	Pte.	...	...	Naylor, J. H. ...		...	...	M.M.
203551	Pte.	...	...	Howker, W.	...	...	...	M.M.
201687	Pte.	...	...	Howarth, F.	...	...	...	M.M.
200320	Pte.	...	...	Walsh, C.	...	...	...	M.M.
203178	Pte.	...	...	Berridge, J. T.		...	...	M.M.
203595	Pte.	...	...	Beckley, W.	...	...	...	M.M.
203193	Pte.	...	...	Pearson, G.	...	...	...	M.M.
200488	Pte.	...	...	Lee, O.	...	...	...	M.M.
203728	Pte.	...	...	Haggas, E.	...	...	...	M.M.
16465	Pte.	...	...	Binns, H.	...	...	...	M.M.
202433	Pte.	...	...	Burfoot, T.	...	...	...	M.M.
202149	Pte.	...	...	Taylor, J. W.	...	...	...	M.M.
203390	Pte.	...	...	Scales, F.	...	...	...	M.M.
203513	Pte.	...	...	Foster, G. A. ...		...	...	M.M.
203650	Pte.	...	...	Denham, H.	...	...	...	M.M.
203072	Pte.	...	...	Inman, W.	...	...	...	M.M.
202888	Pte.	...	...	Scruton, W. A.		...	...	M.M.
203441	Pte.	...	...	Atkinson, J. H.		...	...	M.M.
242371	Pte.	...	...	Tibb, J....	...	...	...	M.M.
201336	Pte.	...	...	Pettit, F.	...	...	...	M.M.
203352	Pte.	...	...	Nichols, T.	...	...	...	M.M. — 5
24066	Pte.	...	...	Poulter, A.	...	...	...	V.C. — 5
203517	Pte.	...	...	Hurtley, T.	...	...	...	M.M.
203501	Pte.	...	...	Atkinson, J. T. N.		...	...	M.M.
26515	Pte.	...	...	Cresswell, A. ...		...	...	M.M.
235120	Pte.	...	...	Witts, F.	...	...	...	M.M.
201883	Pte.	...	...	Sutcliffe, A.	...	...	...	M.M.
26010	Pte.	...	...	Bishop, A.	...	...	...	M.M.
200504	Pte.	...	...	Limb, J.	...	...	...	M.M.
242821	Pte.	...	...	Firth, P.	...	...	...	M.M.
242874	Pte.	...	...	Emmett, R.	...	...	...	M.M.
202410	Pte.	...	...	Brookes, J. W.		...	...	M.M.
203315	Pte.	...	...	Hinchecliffe, B.		...	...	M.M.
34005	Pte.	...	...	Wall, A.	...	...	...	M.M. Bar to M.M.
34007	Pte.	...	...	Webster, H.	...	...	...	M.M.
202669	Pte.	...	...	North, T.	...	...	...	M.M.
202647	Pte.	...	...	Dawson, H.	...	...	...	M.M.
242202	Pte.	...	...	Ryder, G.	...	...	...	M.M.
12682	Pte.	...	...	Henderson, H.	...	...	...	M.M.
202579	Pte.	...	...	Brooksbank, N.		...	...	M.M.
306873	Pte.	...	...	Proctor, T.	...	...	...	M.M.
33014	Pte.	...	...	Johnson, J. E.		...	...	M.M.
26524	Pte.	...	...	Davies, H. S. ...		...	...	M.M.
203451	Pte.	...	...	Dobson, V. T.	...	...	...	M.M.
32897	Pte.	...	...	Sambrooks, E.	...	...	...	M.M.

1/4TH WEST RIDING REGIMENT—*continued*

Regtl. No.	Rank.	Name.	Award.
238181	Pte.	Lowe, W.	M.M.
26271	Pte.	Young, J.	M.M.
200471	Pte.	Andrews, C.	M.M.
201353	Pte.	Firth, C.	M.M.

1/5TH WEST RIDING REGIMENT

Regtl. No.	Rank.	Name.	Award.
	Lt.-Col.... ...	Norton, G. P.	D.S.O.
	Lt.-Col.... ...	Walker, J.	D.S.O. Belgian Croix de Guerre
	Major	Crosland, G. W. K.	D.S.O.
	Major	Rendall, F. H. S.	D.S.O.
	Captain ...	Sykes, K.	M.C.
	Captain ...	Cockhill, J. B.	M.C. Bar to M.C.
	Lieut.	Golding, H. C.	M.C.
	Lieut.	Mollett, B.	M.C.
	Lieut.	Broadbent, A. V.	M.C.
	2/Lieut. ...	Browning, H. O.	M.C.
2418	R.S.M.	Columbine, T. W. O.... ...	M.C.
	R.S.M.	Baster, R.	D.C.M.
183	C.S.M.	Sykes, H. J.	D.C.M.
4	C.S.M.	Tiffany, C. E.	M.C.
240358	C.S.M.	Fisher, W.	Belgian Croix de Guerre D.C.M. Bar to D.C.M.
1644	Sgt.	Fuller, G. A.	D.C.M.
2672	Sgt.	Cox, C.	M.M.
2923	Sgt.	Lee, C.	M.M.
2664	Sgt.	Gardner, C. H.	M.M.
2873	Sgt.	Goldsborough, A.	M.M. Bar to M.M.
2249	Sgt.	Ellis, W.	M.M.
6813	Sgt.	Bull, A. H. J.	M.M.
1117	Sgt.	Rogers, J.	M.M.
1434	Sgt.	Whiteley, L. I.... ...	M.M.
2743	Sgt.	Lamb, J.	M.M.
242879	Sgt.	Hazle, R.	M.M.
242548	Sgt.	Kenyon, A.	M.M.
240525	Sgt.	Callins, E.	M.S.M.
2670	L.-Sgt.	Convoy	D.C.M.
1553	L.-Sgt.	Holdsworth, F. E.	M.M.
2806	L.-Sgt.	Blackburn, H.	M.M.
2331	Cpl.	Black, D.	D.C.M. Croix de Guerre
2107	Cpl.	Ferguson, A.	M.M.
2201	Cpl.	Schofield, G. A.	M.M.
2123	Cpl.	Allen, W. B.	M.M.
2533	Cpl.	Broughton, J. T.	M.M.
3513	Cpl.	Warner, S.	Medaille Militaire
2578	Cpl.	Faulkes, H.	M.M.
241337	Cpl.	Siswick, B.	D.C.M.
240112	Cpl.	Wilkinson, G. E.	M.M.
240088	Cpl.	Meeriman, H. S.	M.M.
240076	Cpl.	Lee, S. H.	D.C.M.
1776	L.-Cpl.	Sheard, H. L.	D.C.M.
3610	L.-Cpl.	Smith, N.	M.M.
2380	L.-Cpl.	Caine, F.	M.M.

1/5TH WEST RIDING REGIMENT—*continued*

Regtl. No.	Rank.	Name.	Award.
6579	L.-Cpl.	Kerwyn, J.	M.M.
240368	L.-Cpl.	Halstead, T.	M.M.
4150	Pte.	Thomas, H.	M.M.
5958	Pte.	Rowlandson, A.	M.M.
7122	Pte.	Short, J.	M.M.
53972	Pte.	Pearson, W.	M.M.
3136	Pte.	Mitchell, G. H.	M.M.
2298	Pte.	Lancaster, H.	M.M.
3291	Pte.	Kaye, E.	M.M.
3594	Pte	Garside, J.	M.M.
4246	Pte.	Smith, R. S.	M.M.
3451	Pte.	North, A.	M.M.
6769	Pte.	Thomas, W.	M.M.
6829	Pte.	Saunders, W.	M.M.
6826	Pte.	Chilvers, E. B.	M.M.
6775	Pte.	Flowers, F.	M.M.
6834	Pte.	Turner, H. L.	M.M.
6822	Pte.	Wasey, E.	M.M.
6818	Pte.	Legget, V. S.	M.M.
3251	Pte.	Armitage, A.	M.M.
2159	Pte.	Swain, W. H.	M.M.
241325	Pte.	Hinchliffe, F.	M.M.
242871	Pte.	Hey, W.	M.M.
242896	Pte.	Balmforth, M.	M.M.
242488	Pte.	Taxley, R. T.	M.M.
242136	Pte.	Blakeborough, P.	M.M.
241432	Pte.	Schofield, H.	M.M.
240274	Pte.	Archer, W.	M.M.
242408	Pte.	Sykes, F.	M.M.
240521	Pte.	Woodcock, R.	M.M.
242391	Pte.	Bradbury, A.	M.M.
240433	Pte.	Crossland, W. D.	M.M.
242070	Pte.	Lilley, H. S.	D.C.M.
204126	Pte.	Whittaker, W. C.	D.C.M.
242454	Pte.	Arnold, V. A.	M.M.
24960	Pte.	Brummett, S.	M.M.
242628	Pte.	Matthews, S.	M.M.
242455	Pte.	Frost, F.	M.M.
242034	Pte.	Castle, F.	M.M.
240514	Pte.	Taylor, J. W.	M.M.
240176	Pte.	Hynes, H.	M.M.
240310	Pte.	Graham, H.	M.M.
242439	Pte.	Raistrick, T.	M.M.
268495	Pte.	Bell, E. E.	M.M.
242063	Pte.	McMinney, T. H.	M.M.
240510	Pte.	Taylor, G. H.	M.M.
240743	Pte.	Thornhill, H.	Croix de Guerre

1/6TH WEST RIDING REGIMENT

	Lt.-Col. ...	Bateman, C. M.	D.S.O.
			Bar to D.S.O.
	Major	Clarkson, A. B.	D.S.O.
			M.C.
	Captain ...	Chaffers, W. B.	M.C.
	Captain ...	Smith, F. L.	M.C.
	Captain ...	Clough, S. H.	M.C.
	Captain ...	Buxton, B. G.	M.C.
			Bar to M.C.
	Captain ...	Smith, A. P.	M.C.

1/6TH WEST RIDING REGIMENT—*continued*

Regtl. No.	Rank.	Name.	Award.
	Captain	Stoker, S. P. ...	M.C.
	Captain	Marriner, S. F. ...	M.C.
	Lieut. ...	Proctor, J. N. W. A. ...	M.C.
	Lieut. ...	Hart, J. ...	M.C.
	Lieut. ...	Lowther, C. H. E. ...	M.C.
	Lieut. ...	Hopwood, H. ...	M.C.
	2/Lieut.	Denison, J. W. ...	M.C.
	2/Lieut.	Whitehead, A. M. ...	M.C.
	2/Lieut.	Farrar, H. ...	M.C.
	2/Lieut.	Spratt, W. ...	M.C.
2879	R.S.M. ...	Buckley, O. ...	M.C.
265015	R.S.M. ...	Richardson, T....	D.C.M.
838	C.S.M. ...	Robinson, W. J. ...	D.C.M.
265080	C.S.M. ...	Wiseman, E. ...	D.C.M.
265413	C.S.M. ...	Limmer, T. W. ...	M.C. M.M.
265661	C.S.M. ...	McDermott, O. ...	D.C.M. Belgian Croix de Guerre
265991	C.Q.M.S.	Thompson, B. ...	M.S.M.
265037	C.Q.M.S.	Norton, J. ...	M.S.M.
2663	Sgt. ...	Garrett, P. H. ...	D.C.M.
2308	Sgt. ...	Bury, J. ...	D.C.M. M.M.
2337	Sgt. ...	Hartley, H. ...	M.M.
3370	Sgt. ...	Whiteley, J. ...	M.M.
32	Sgt. ...	Webster, J. ...	M.M.
2165	Sgt. ...	Limmer, G. W. ...	M.M.
1560	Sgt. ...	Watson, J. ...	M.M.
2002	Sgt. ...	Bateson, J. ...	M.M.
33	Sgt. ...	Field, P. ...	M.M.
266611	Sgt. ...	Partridge, H. ...	M.M.
268394	Sgt. ...	Pass, W. ...	M.M.
265626	Sgt. ...	Cryer, F. ...	M.M.
265642	Sgt. ...	Rachy, C. ...	M.M.
265395	Sgt. ...	Harding, C. ...	M.M.
265113	Sgt. ...	Driver, H. ...	D.C.M.
265676	Sgt. ...	Broom, J. J. ...	D.C.M.
265270	Sgt. ...	Crawshaw, C. ...	M.M.
300029	Sgt. ...	Laycock, H. ...	M.M.
300131	Sgt. ...	Godwin, G. E. ...	M.M.
267914	Sgt. ...	Sykes, A. ...	D.C.M.
268650	Sgt. ...	Rosenthal, E. ...	D.C.M.
265433	Sgt. ...	Calvert, G. E. ...	D.C.M. M.M.
265988	Sgt. ...	Turner, F. ...	M.M.
266791	Sgt. ...	Reeder, D. ...	M.M.
24601	Sgt. ...	Cuerer, W. ...	M.M.
265595	Sgt. ...	Burns, J. ...	M.M.
2631	L.-Sgt. ...	Hepworth, J. S. ...	M.M.
265851	L.-Sgt. ...	Bailey, J. ...	M.M. Bar to M.M.
265527	L.-Sgt. ...	Calvert, J. ...	D.C.M.
265484	L.-Sgt. ...	Green, T. ...	D.C.M.
265883	Cpl. ...	Emmett, W. ...	M.M.
265239	Cpl. ...	Crook, C. ...	M.M.
265115	Cpl. ...	Driver, G. ...	D.C.M.
265253	Cpl. ...	Fredrickson, E. ...	D.C.M. M.M.
268056	Cpl. ...	Joynes, E. ...	M.M.
265067	Cpl. ...	Bryden, H. ...	M.M.

1/6TH WEST RIDING REGIMENT—*continued*

Regtl. No.	Rank.	Name.	Award.
265264	Cpl.	Page, G.	M.M.
265178	Cpl.	Gibson, W.	D.C.M.
265694	Cpl.	Barton, P.	M.M.
266534	Cpl.	Midgley, A.	M.M. Croix de Guerre.
267498	Cpl.	Barrett, H.	M.M.
265195	Cpl.	Swindon, H.	D.C.M.
265663	Cpl.	Chapman, J.	M.M.
265447	Cpl.	Kennedy, H.	D.C.M.
16519	Cpl.	Hansford, G. H.	M.M.
26597	Cpl.	Swift, W.	M.M. Bar to M.M.
200191	Cpl.	Woodhead, J. A.	M.M.
267465	Cpl.	Fisher, S.	M.M.
49680	Cpl.	Culclough, E.	M.M.
315323	Cpl.	Roebuck, A.	M.M.
265962	Cpl.	Best, W. H.	M.M.
265556	Cpl.	Jones, L.	Medaille Militaire.
2930	L.-Cpl.	Bailey, E.	M.M.
2618	L.-Cpl.	Brassington, T. W.	M.M.
2066	L.-Cpl.	Hicks, W.	M.M.
265588	L.-Cpl.	Grainger, C.	M.M.
265086	L.-Cpl.	Dixon, V.	M.M.
265086	L.-Cpl.	Wimblett, H.	M.M. Bar to M.M.
269276	L.-Cpl.	Hartley, C.	M.M.
267892	L.-Cpl.	Scarff, J. W.	M.M.
23464	L.-Cpl.	Varley, J.	M.M.
266453	L.-Cpl.	Smale, R.	M.M.
265095	L.-Cpl.	Williams, L.	M.M.
267433	L.-Cpl.	Ames, W. G.	M.M.
265695	L.-Cpl.	Edwards, F.	M.M.
265595	L.-Cpl.	Kaye, H.	M.M.
2367	Pte.	Bracewell, F.	D.C.M.
2524	Pte.	Crook, R.	M.M.
3360	Pte.	Pickup, J. E.	D.C.M.
2026	Pte.	Scott, A. B.	M.M.
2304	Pte.	Scott, J.	M.M.
3050	Pte.	Falshaw, J.	M.M.
4122	Pte.	Pilkington, L.	M.M.
2106	Pte.	Rhodes, C.	M.M.
3128	Pte.	Snowdon, R.	M.M.
3376	Pte.	Brook, T.	M.M.
3358	Pte.	Harrison, G.	M.M.
2249	Pte.	Bradley, J. E.	M.M.
266478	Pte.	Dickinson, F.	M.M.
204463	Pte.	Bloom, J.	M.M.
265940	Pte.	Smith, J. W.	M.M.
266505	Pte.	Bibby, J.	D.C.M.
266789	Pte.	Smith, J.	M.M.
265237	Pte.	Hook, G.	M.M.
267840	Pte.	Field, E.	M.M.
266375	Pte.	Metcalf, J.	M.M.
265171	Pte.	Caulfield, J.	M.M.
267516	Pte.	Hirst, W. R.	M.M.
266877	Pte.	Nelson, J.	M.M.
267410	Pte.	Cole, W. C.	M.M.
266498	Pte.	Oversby, E.	M.M.
267615	Pte.	Boocock, H. A.	M.M.
268237	Pte.	Fawcett, E.	M.M.
266994	Pte.	Lord, J. C.	M.M.

1/6TH WEST RIDING REGIMENT—*continued*

Regtl. No.	Rank.	Name.	Award.
267901	Pte.	Batley, J. F.	M.M.
267536	Pte.	Flatt, G.	M.M.
204646	Pte.	Trollope, G. R.	M.M.
266763	Pte.	Nichol, B.	M.M.
26129	Pte.	Law, T.	M.M.
268523	Pte.	Lawson, J.	D.C.M.
12515	Pte.	Jefferson, J.	M.M.
267596	Pte.	Richardson, J. H.	M.M.
265611	Pte.	Maude, G.	M.M.
			Bar to M.M.
267936	Pte.	Walker, F. M.	M.M.
267498	Pte.	French, H.	M.M.
267501	Pte.	Emmett, N.	M.M.
268027	Pte.	Stephenson, J. W.	M.M.
			Bar to M.M.
233889	Pte.	Garside, J.	M.M.
6098	Pte.	Holden, L.	M.M.
266104	Pte.	Burnley, H.	M.M.
23726	Pte.	Ballam, P.	M.M.
31731	Pte.	Buckley, P.	M.M.
33948	Pte.	Vine, A.	M.M.
34147	Pte.	Hickman, W.	M.M.
265475	Pte.	White, E.	M.M.
41203	Pte.	Shippey, R.	M.M.
263019	Pte.	Copeman, F. W.	M.M.
265209	Pte.	Riley, E.	M.M.
242623	Pte.	Lund, J. W.	M.M.
34052	Pte.	Adams, C.	M.M.
47321	Pte.	Sinkinson, S.	M.M.
267359	Pte.	Bills, A.	M.M.
266993	Pte.	Wright, H.	M.M.
267828	Pte.	Graham, J.	M.M.
267498	Pte.	Dennison, H.	M.M.
241781	Pte.	Crabtree, C.	M.M.
33946	Pte.	Vickers, A. A.	M.M.
266885	Pte.	Puttergill, G.	M.M.
1708	Pte.	Panes, H.	M.M.
265780	Pte.	Lang, A.	M.M.
242594	Pte.	Brown, F.	M.M.

1/7TH WEST RIDING REGIMENT

	Lt.-Col.	Parkin, F. L.	D.S.O.
	Major	Bennett, V. L.	M.C.
			Bar to M.C.
	Major	Tanner, G.	D.S.O.
	Captain ...	Harris, L. G. R.	M.C.
	Captain ...	Rapp, T. C.	M.C.
	Captain ...	Pedlow, W. L.	M.C.
	(R.A.M.C.)		
	Captain ...	Lupton, B. C.	M.C.
	Captain ...	Conyers, H. F.	M.C.
			Bar to M.C.
	Captain ...	Lawton, C.	M.C.
	Captain ...	Reilly, M. F.	M.C.
	Captain ...	Crabtree, N.	M.C.
	Captain ...	Burbery, B. T.	M.C.
	Lieut.	Brierley, J.	M.C.
	Lieut.	Netherwood, H. S.	M.C.
	Lieut.	Rothery, L.	M.C.

1/7TH WEST RIDING REGIMENT—*continued*

Regtl. No.	Rank.	Name.	Award.
	Lieut.	Bamforth, B.	M.C.
	Lieut.	Howcroft, G. B.	M.C.
	Lieut.	Dacre, A.	M.C.
	Lieut.	Whalley, A. H.	M.C.
	Lieut.	Wood, H. E.	M.C.
	2/Lieut. ...	Haslam, F.	M.C.
	2/Lieut. ...	Aspinall, K. I.	M.C.
	2/Lieut. ...	Davy, W. H.	M.C.
	2/Lieut. ...	Wilson, E. H.	M.C.
	2/Lieut. ...	de Maine, H. C.	M.C.
	2/Lieut. ...	Waddington, H.	M.C.
	2/Lieut. ...	Hutchon, N. R.	M.C.
308015	R.S.M. ...	Lynn, J.	D.C.M. M.M. Belgian Croix de Guerre.
308012	C.S.M. ...	Lindsell, J.	M.M. Bar to M.M.
307350	C.S.M. ...	Clarke, F.	D.C.M.
307007	C.S.M. ...	Elliott, J. T.	M.M. Decoration Militaire (Belgium)
421	Sgt.	Warwick, W.	D.C.M.
2176	Sgt.	Irvine, W.	D.C.M.
2076	Sgt.	Muff, F.	M.M.
220	Sgt.	Brook, A.	M.M.
934	Sgt.	Kinnan, A.	D.C.M.
1038	Sgt.	Hitchman, F.	M.M.
1502	Sgt.	Gaynor, W.	M.M.
25	Sgt.	Gledhill, F.	M.M.
446	Sgt.	Senior, A.	M.M.
305070	Sgt.	Leach, E.	M.M.
306340	Sgt.	Horton, R.	M.M.
305649	Sgt.	Rhodes, R.	M.M.
305479	Sgt.	Foster, W.	M.M.
305631	Sgt.	Pollard, W.	M.S.M.
307341	Sgt.	Wilson, L.	D.C.M. M.M.
307747	Sgt.	Hirst, H.	M.S.M. M.M.
305241	Sgt.	Haigh, F.	D.C.M.
305569	Sgt.	Parker, L.	M.M.
235318	Sgt.	Sherwood, T.	D.C.M.
235768	Sgt.	Sutton, R.	M.M.
307923	Sgt.	Alderson, A.	M.M.
309923	Sgt.	Fryer, F.	M.M.
305260	Sgt.	Jackson, F.	Croix de Virtute Militaire, 2nd Class
1795	Cpl.	Barrow, H.	M.M.
1618	Cpl.	Hodgkinson, H.	M.M.
1211	Cpl.	Godley, J.	M.M.
268646	Cpl.	Hall, L.	D.C.M.
10883	Cpl.	Chadwick, A.	M.M.
111856	Cpl.	Suggett, L.	M.M.
305744	Cpl.	Taylor, B.	M.M.
307861	Cpl.	Wilkinson, H.	M.M.
307307	Cpl.	Oldroyd, S.	M.M.
10888	Cpl.	Chadwick, A.	D.C.M.
241373	Cpl.	Turner, P.	D.C.M.
305341	Cpl.	Robinson, T.	M.M.
305749	Cpl.	Harris, C.	M.M.

1/7TH WEST RIDING REGIMENT—*continued*

Regtl. No.	Rank.	Name.	Award.
306156	Cpl.	Kenyon, S.	M.M.
307507	Cpl.	Stilling, J.	M.M.
328001	Cpl.	Clarke, W. J.	M.M.
2094	L.-Cpl.	Shaw, J. S.	D.C.M.
5649	L.-Cpl.	France, L.	M.M.
3031	L.-Cpl.	Garlick, J.	M.M.
307287	L.-Cpl.	Lister, H.	M.M.
305423	L.-Cpl.	Heppenstall, S.	M.M.
305228	L.-Cpl.	Hobson, E.	M.M.
307668	L.-Cpl.	Moseley, H.	M.M. Bar to M.M.
305589	L.-Cpl.	Waddington, F.	M.M.
307454	L.-Cpl.	Mellor, T.	M.M.
307932	L.-Cpl.	Booth, H.	M.M.
302100	L.-Cpl.	Jones, H.	M.M.
307795	L.-Cpl.	Adamson, A.	M.M.
23767	L.-Cpl.	Moscrop, J.	M.M.
305464	L.-Cpl.	Emms, W.	M.M.
1457	Pte.	Rowlands, J. E.	D.C.M.
1067	Pte	Blakey, W.	D.C.M.
305291	Pte.	Robinson, J.	M.M. Bar to M.M.
1216	Pte.	Wright, H.	M.M.
5405	Pte.	Williams, W. H.	M.M.
1970	Pte.	Kirkpatrick, G.	M.M.
2756	Pte.	Mellor, F.	M.M.
5461	Pte.	Kelling, J.	M.M.
5589	Pte.	Nutt, W.	M.M.
7125	Pte.	Gibb, T.	M.M.
1320	Pte.	Haigh, H.	M.M.
1616	Pte.	Wood, L.	M.M.
3904	Pte.	Chamberlain, E.	M.M.
7062	Pte.	Ainsley, E.	M.M.
1482	Pte.	Waterhouse, F.	M.M.
2195	Pte.	Shaw, J.	M.M.
2497	Pte.	Walsh, J.	D.C.M.
2185	Pte.	Marlow, G.	M.M.
305937	Pte.	Cartwright, F.	M.M.
307945	Pte.	Baker, W.	M.M.
305579	Pte.	Nelson, S.	M.M.
307873	Pte.	Rounding, J.	M.M.
307367	Pte.	Metcalf, G.	M.M.
305481	Pte.	Settle, H.	M.M.
308107	Pte.	Lisle, H.	M.M.
307365	Pte.	Mason, G.	M.M.
306102	Pte.	Crampton, H.	M.M.
268609	Pte.	Bell, J.	D.C.M.
22960	Pte.	Alves, J.	M.M.
23997	Pte.	Mennell, W.	M.M.
307570	Pte.	Wilson, J.	M.M.
340283	Pte.	Berry, J.	M.M.
33857	Pte.	Cable, G.	M.M.
307691	Pte.	Atkins, J.	M.M.
306205	Pte.	Mellor, J. W.	M.M.
305166	Pte.	Robinson, W.	M.M.
12890	Pte.	Russell, C.	M.M.
305537	Pte.	Parkin	M.M.
306146	Pte.	Eryland, J.	M.M.
307537	Pte.	Kaye, J. A.	M.M.
305961	Pte.	Hett, H.	D.C.M.
307240	Pte.	Barker, S.	M.M. Bar to M.M.

1/7TH WEST RIDING REGIMENT—*continued*

Regtl. No.	Rank.	Name.	Award.
307127	Pte.	Plume, G.	M.M.
16524	Pte.	Walker, F.	M.M.
205104	Pte.	Appleby, A. L.	M.M.
267320	Pte.	Hardcastle, C.	M.M.
240214	Pte.	Hellewell, C.	M.M.
305829	Pte.	Smith, F.	M.M.
269079	Pte.	Shaw, S.	M.M.
308009	Pte.	Odrell, J. J.	M.M.
307119	Pte.	Efford, J.	M.M.
307943	Pte.	Land, W.	M.M.
33114	Pte.	Bowles, J. J.	M.M.
306167	Pte.	Manton, J.	M.M.
33770	Pte.	Toomer, C.	M.M.
269204	Pte.	Limbach, L.	M.M.
33838	Pte.	Allsop, A.	M.M.
305435	Pte.	Bottomley, J.	M.M.
267320	Pte.	Hardcastle, C.	M.M. Bar to M.M.
266835	Pte.	Williams, J.	M.M. Bar to M.M.
34823	Pte.	Farnell, W.	M.M.
269131	Pte.	Armitage, A.	M.M.
305769	Pte.	Dyson, J.	M.M.
307466	Pte.	Sunderland, H.	M.M.
307071	Pte.	Grange, H.	M.M.
24865	Pte.	Boothroyd, G.	M.M.
25454	Pte.	Stones, F.	M.M.
33102	Pte.	Bradford, A.	M.M.
305236	Pte.	Shepherd, W.	M.M.

1/4TH K.O. YORKSHIRE LIGHT INFANTRY

	Rank.	Name.	Award.
	Lt.-Col. ...	Haslegrave, H.	C.M.G.
	Lt.-Col. ...	Fraser, H. G.	D.S.O. M.C.
	Lt.-Col. ...	Brierley, S. C.	D.S.O.
	Major ...	Moorhouse, H.	Legion of Honour D.S.O.
	Captain ...	Taylor, L. M.	M.C.
	Captain ...	Creswick, W. B.	M.C.
	Captain ...	Edwards, A. C. (R.A.M.C.) ...	M.C.
	Captain ...	Thomson, G.	M.C.
	Captain ...	Moorhouse, R. W. ...	M.C.
	Captain ...	Chadwick, T.	M.C.
	Captain ...	Stiebel, C. A.	M.C.
	Captain ...	Brice-Smith, H. F. ...	M.C.
	Captain ...	Hindle, W. J.	M.C.
	Captain ...	Fearn, C. A.	M.C.
	Captain ...	Mackay, F. W.	M.C.
	Lieut. ...	Muirhead, J. J.	M.C.
	Lieut. ...	Brook, G. H.	M.C.
	Lieut. ...	Massie, F. E.	M.C.
	Lieut. ...	Lamb, J. W.	M.C.
	2/Lieut. ...	Greenhough, E. E.	M.C.
	2/Lieut. ...	Ricketts, G. A. Mac G. ...	M.C.
	2/Lieut. ...	Burkinshaw, W. L. ...	M.C.
	2/Lieut. ...	Hodgkinson, J.	M.C.
	2/Lieut. ...	Boot, W. E.	M.C.
	2/Lieut. ...	Appleton, J.	M.C.
	2/Lieut. ...	Battiland, J.	M.C. Bar to M.C.

1/4TH K.O. YORKSHIRE LIGHT INFANTRY—*continued*

Regtl. No.	Rank.	Name.	Award.
	2/Lieut. ...	Shorton, H.	M.C.
	2/Lieut. ...	Pierce, S. E.	M.C.
4504	R.S.M. ...	Trott, H. G.	D.C.M.
52	R.S.M.	Grice, J.	M.C.
200084	R.S.M.	Alderson, W.	Medaille Barbatie si Credinta, 1st Class. Chevalier de l'Orde Leopold II. Belgian
200325	R.Q.M.S. ...	Milner, H.	M.S.M.
885	C.S.M.	Hemingway, C. F.	D.C.M.
200489	C.S.M.	Barraclough, J....	D.C.M.
200301	C.S.M.	Gledhill, H. G.	D.C.M.
200474	C.S.M.	Jones, F.	Belgian Croix de Guerre. D.C.M.
2627	Sgt.	Best, T....	D.C.M.
2342	Sgt.	Hunt, G. M.	D.C.M.
2371	Sgt.	Henson, H.	M.M.
1174	Sgt.	Cropper, J.	M.M.
2486	Sgt.	Paterson, M. W.	M.M.
2688	Sgt.	Stainthorpe, G.	M.M.
2507	Sgt.	Wallace, W.	D.C.M.
2510	Sgt.	Moon, F.	M.M.
203430	Sgt.	Ogle, H. C.	M.M.
203293	Sgt.	Redmore, W.	M.M.
200084	Sgt.	Alderson, W.	M.M.
203006	Sgt.	Clark, H.	M.M.
202045	Sgt.	Rylah, E.	M.M.
240719	Sgt.	Maskill, H.	M.M.
200054	Sgt.	Litchfield. H.	M.M.
200205	Sgt.	Smith, J.	M.M.
200269	Sgt.	Ray, I.	M.M.
200037	Sgt.	Preece, C. J.	D.C.M. M.M.
35351	Sgt.	Johnstone, J.	M.M.
201944	Sgt.	Simpson, W. H.	M.M.
11270	Sgt.	Clark, F.	M.M.
220768	Sgt.	Daley, W.	M.M.
203417	Sgt.	Stobie, J. W.	M.M. Bar to M.M.
200468	L.-Sgt.	Hatton, F.	M.M.
240067	L.-Sgt.	Kirby, F.	M.M.
2481	Cpl.	Gudgin, H. W.	M.M.
36044	Cpl.	Mackenzie, T.	D.C.M.
33088	Cpl.	Lees, J. P.	M.M.
200231	Cpl.	Farrar, H.	M.M.
36406	Cpl.	Hudson, D. C.	M.M.
200115	Cpl.	Stringer, J.	M.M.
36889	Cpl.	Hustwaite, J.	M.M.
25437	Cpl.	Guy, G.	D.C.M.
13050	Cpl.	Downing, H.	M.M.
16794	Cpl.	Mitchell, G.	M.M.
2611	L.-Cpl.	Berry, A.	M.M.
2403	L.-Cpl.	Musgrave, T.	M.M.
2639	L.-Cpl.	Field, J. W.	M.M. Medal St. George 3rd Class.
1833	L.-Cpl.	Hatton, J.	M.M.
2717	L.-Cpl.	Archer, J.	D.C.M.
200119	L.-Cpl.	Beaumont, H.	M.M. Bar to M.M.

1/4TH K.O. YORKSHIRE LIGHT INFANTRY—*continued*

Regtl. No.	Rank.	Name.	Award.
203228	L.-Cpl.	Greasby, S.	M.M.
202031	L.-Cpl.	Thompson, M.	M.M.
201353	L.-Cpl.	Moorhouse, E.	M.M.
200420	L.-Cpl.	Pilbrow, J.	M.M.
36043	L.-Cpl.	Martin, R.	M.M.
4/125	L.-Cpl.	Oldroyd, W.	M.M.
36035	L.-Cpl.	Dixon, W. E.	M.M.
201056	L.-Cpl.	Gowland, I.	M.M.
47468	L.-Cpl.	Kitching, H.	M.M.
203346	L.-Cpl.	Sadler, T.	M.M.
200125	L.-Cpl.	Jagger. G.	M.M.
34383	L.-Cpl.	Wilkinson, H.	M.M.
203337	L.-Cpl.	Chockham, W....	M.M.
203718	L.-Cpl.	Norfolk, F.	D.C.M.
995	Pte.	Atha, E. R.	D.C.M.
2056	Pte.	Gill, J.	D.C.M.
2648	Pte.	Hooper, W. F.	D.C.M.
1625	Pte.	Gibbs J. A.	D.C.M.
1403	Pte.	Heptonstall, A.	D.C.M.
2662	Pte.	Naylor, W.	M.M.
1361	Pte.	Brook, S.	M.M.
1869	Pte.	Leonards, G.	M.M.
7049	Pte.	Pennie, A.	M.M.
7064	Pte.	Milburn, W.	M.M.
4429	Pte.	Rose, E.	M.M.
7193	Pte.	Dowie, J.	M.M.
6600	Pte.	Edwards, J.	M.M.
20946	Pte.	Fearnley, E.	D.C.M.
30844	Pte.	Mills, W.	M.M.
201375	Pte.	Green, W. E.	M.M.
203360	Pte.	Woodall, C. V.... ...	M.M.
203447	Pte.	Scott, R.	M.M.
22168	Pte.	Rennison, W. H.	M.M.
200858	Pte.	Hill, F.	M.M.
203398	Pte.	Lavender, R. H.	M.M.
24192	Pte.	Crelly, —.	M.M.
20085	Pte.	Arundel, T.	M.M.
47502	Pte.	Langford, G.	M.M.
45238	Pte.	Chadwick, F.	D.C.M.
36026	Pte.	Snaith, H.	M.M.
36090	Pte.	Curtis, A.	M.M.
36411	Pte.	Haycock, T. H.	M.M.
36015	Pte.	Kew, J. H.	M.M.
203204	Pte.	Baristow, H.	M.M.
201339	Pte.	Todd, A.	M.M.
235105	Pte.	Campbell, A.	M.M.
14506	Pte.	Fox, F.	M.M. Bar to M.M.
6227	Pte.	Timms, R. W.	M.M.
38356	Pte.	Sykes, W.	M.M.
27861	Pte.	Johnstone, F.	M.M.
36512	Pte.	Collins, W.	M.M.
203291	Pte.	Graves, L.	M.M.
42219	Pte.	Gibson, S.	M.M.
62271	Pte.	Thornton, W. E.	M.M.
201974	Pte.	Heald, J.	M.M.
240764	Pte.	Griffen, J.	M.M.
203026	Pte.	Platts, F.	M.M.
6035	Pte.	Coulson, B. S.	M.M.

1/5TH K.O. YORKSHIRE LIGHT INFANTRY

Regtl. No.	Rank.	Name.	Award.
	Lt.-Col. ...	Moxon, C. C.	C.M.G. D.S.O.
	Major ...	Bradley, C. G.	D.S.O.
	Captain ...	Sullivan, G. K.	M.C.
	Captain ...	Mackenzie, T. G.	M.C.
	Captain ...	Bentley, P.	M.C.
	Captain ...	Campbell, Q. H.	M.C.
	Captain ...	Simpson, M. N.	M.C.
	Captain ...	Linley, J. S.	M.C.
	Captain ...	Shirley, J.	M.C.
	Lieut. ...	Clayton-Smith, H. E. H. ...	M.C.
	Lieut. ...	Sandford, C. R. F.	M.C.
	2/Lieut. ...	Short, A. G.	M.C.
	2/Lieut. ...	Hobbs, F. G.	M.C.
3232	R.S.M.	Mathews, H.	M.C.
240015	R.S.M.	Hellewell, J.	D.C.M.
240028	R.Q.M.S. ...	Roughton, J. W.	M.S.M.
240158	C.S.M.	Sutherland, W.	D.C.M.
240321	C.S.M.	Wright, W.	D.C.M.
175	Sgt.	Livesey, T.	D.C.M.
2534/240349	Sgt.	Fletcher, J. T.	M.M.
3357	Sgt.	Raikes, J. D.	D.C.M.
240182	Sgt.	Blakey, W.	M.M.
240351	Sgt.	Elliott, J.	D.C.M.
242161	Sgt.	Quirk, W. E.	M.M.
241014	Sgt.	Wootten, H.	M.M. Belgian Croix de Guerre.
240119	Sgt.	Walker, J. W.	M.M.
241337	L.-Sgt.	Andrews, R.	M.M.
4045	Cpl.	Lappin, W.	D.C.M.
1710	Cpl.	Caton, G.	M.M.
240574	Cpl.	Brain, A.	D.C.M.
240620	Cpl.	Taylor, T. W.	D.C.M.
242582	Cpl.	Langton, A.	D.C.M.
130	L.-Cpl.	Pacey, W.	D.C.M.
2414	L.-Cpl.	Steel, W.	D.C.M.
3270	L.-Cpl.	Leadbeater, T.	D.C.M.
242344	L.-Cpl.	Kynman, H.	M.M.
2639	L.-Cpl.	Field, J. W.	M.M.
1781	Pte.	Raynell, C.	D.C.M.
2222	Pte.	Williams, P.	D.C.M.
2559	Pte.	Loving, F. H.	M.M.
3699	Pte.	Davy, A.	M.M.
3064	Pte.	Addy, W. H.	M.M.
3175	Pte.	Rosewarne, B. J.	D.C.M.
2880	Pte.	Short, S.	D.C.M.
2914	Pte.	Wilson, G. E.	D.C.M.
25320	Pte.	Smith, J.	D.C.M. M.M.
4699	Pte.	Brook, H.	Bronze Medal for Military Valour.
242448	Pte.	Bear, E....	M.M. Bar to M.M.
240498	Pte.	O'Neill, M.	M.M.
242661	Pte.	Dawson, W.	M.M.
240599	Pte.	Jackson, J.	M.M.
241914	Pte.	Goodwin, H.	M.M.
242561	Pte.	Gittings, A.	M.M.
242584	Pte.	Mercer, W.	M.M.
242880	Pte.	Padgett, J.	M.M.

1/5TH K.O. YORKSHIRE LIGHT INFANTRY—*continued*

Regtl. No.	Rank.	Name.	Award.
242631	Pte.	Leighton, N.	M.M.
242694	Pte.	Tempest, W.	M.M.
240415	Pte.	Taylor, J.	M.M.
240286	Pte.	Fenwick, E.	M.M.
242111	Pte.	Constantine, H.	M.M.

1/4TH YORK AND LANCS. REGIMENT

Regtl. No.	Rank.	Name.	Award.
	Lt.-Col.	Wyatt, L. J.	D.S.O.
	Lt.-Col.	Branson, D. S.	D.S.O. Bar to D.S.O. 2nd Bar to D.S.O. M.C.
	Major	Unsworth, G.	M.C.
	Captain	Williams, R. N.	M.C.
	Captain	Barber, H. G.	M.C.
	Captain	Bernard, C. A.	M.C.
	Captain	Johnson, P. N.	M.C.
	Captain	Wilson, R. E.	M.C. Bar to M.C.
	Captain	Holmes, E. M.	M.C.
	Captain	Brooke, S.	M.C.
	Captain	Wortley, J. F.	M.C.
	Captain	Grant, D. P.	M.C.
	Captain	Wilkinson, R. M.	M.C.
	Captain	Ryan, W.	M.C.
	Captain	Elvington, M.	M.C.
	Lieut.	Johnson, L. W.	M.C.
	2/Lieut.	Christmas, E. S.	M.C.
	2/Lieut.	Warburton, S. E.	M.C.
	2/Lieut.	Gifford, W. D. G.	M.C. Bar to M.C.
	2/Lieut.	Payne, H.	M.C.
	2/Lieut.	Wilson, R. E.	M.C.
	2/Lieut.	Hope, C. R.	M.C.
200433	R.S.M.	Immison, G.	D.C.M. M.M. Belgian Croix de Guerre
200588	R.Q.M.S.	Thickett, H.	M.S.M.
173	C.S.M.	Hutchinson, W.	D.C.M.
692	C.S.M.	Pemberton, W.	D.C.M. M.M.
200077	C.S.M.	Wagg, W.	D.C.M.
200485	C.S.M.	Wood, W.	D.C.M. M.M. Belgian Croix de Guerre
200121	C.S.M.	Cadman, W.	D.C.M.
200208	C.S.M.	Pearson, G.	D.C.M.
	C.S.M.	Mount, F.	D.C.M.
7583	C.S.M.	Nash, E.	M.M.
390	Sgt.	Clarke, A. W.	D.C.M.
2102	Sgt.	Dodd, W. R.	M.M.
2187	Sgt.	Warburton, S.	M.M.
2278	Sgt.	Shute, G. A.	D.C.M.
1986	Sgt.	Breaves, E.	M.M.
1629	Sgt.	Kay, J.	M.M.
250	Sgt.	Brown, G. A.	M.M.

1/4TH YORK AND LANCS. REGIMENT—*continued*

Regtl. No.	Rank.	Name.	Award.
1435	Sgt.	Cartwright, T. W.	M.M.
201421	Sgt.	Beedham, G. H.	D.C.M.
203129	Sgt.	Jones, W.	D.C.M.
200144	Sgt.	Megson, L.	D.C.M.
200570	Sgt.	Lawless, L.	D.C.M.
201986	Sgt.	Warren, J. E.	M.M.
14/992	Sgt.	Firth, C.	D.C.M.
200054	Sgt.	White, E.	M.S.M.
200642	Sgt.	Baker, F.	M.M.
33591	Sgt.	Davison, J.	D.C.M.
201010	Sgt.	Bingham, A.	M.M. M.M.
200311	L.-Sgt.	Galley, W. D.	M.M.
33591	L.-Sgt.	Davidson, J.	D.C.M.
200405	L.-Sgt.	Crossland, F.	M.M.
1797	Cpl.	Eaton, A.	M.M.
2057	Cpl.	Wilkinson, H.	D.C.M.
3271	Cpl.	Hayes, T. F.	M.M.
203777	Cpl.	Green, H.	M.M.
203006	Cpl.	Luton, F.	M.M.
200766	Cpl.	Fell, S.	M.M.
201744	Cpl.	Hudson, G.	M.M.
8/16306	Cpl.	Waters, A.	M.M.
202951	Cpl.	Oldfield, H.	M.M.
1569	L.-Cpl.	Biggins, J. W.	D.C.M.
670	L.-Cpl.	Crapper, C.	D.C.M.
1099	L.-Cpl.	Leggatt, F.	D.C.M.
672	L.-Cpl.	Porter, H.	M.M.
2420	L.-Cpl.	Levesley, H.	M.M.
2807	L.-Cpl.	Bathe, H.	M.M.
2386	L.-Cpl.	Brady, J.	M.M.
1832	L.-Cpl.	Freeman, G.	M.M.
4253	L.-Cpl.	Coote, W. T.	D.C.M.
2533	L.-Cpl.	Tarlton, A. P.	M.M.
6173	L.-Cpl.	Scarbrooke, A. G.	M.M.
2206	L.-Cpl.	Brown, C.	M.M.
200	L.-Cpl.	Fell, W.	M.M.
1580	L.-Cpl.	Lindley, G.	M.S.M.
300888	L.-Cpl.	Bower, E. C.	M.M.
200527	L.-Cpl.	Hall, T.	M.M.
201478	L.-Cpl.	Jackson, M.	D.C.M.
200279	L.-Cpl.	Ogden, C.	M.M.
203206	L.-Cpl.	Lawrence, C.	M.M.
8/13315	L.-Cpl.	York, F.	M.M. Bar to M.M.
33344	L.-Cpl.	Foster, A.	M.M.
201897	L.-Cpl.	Leaver, H.	M.M.
11527	L.-Cpl.	Eyre, J. W.	D.C.M.
200268	L.-Cpl.	Ramsden, H.	M.M. M.M.
40404	L.-Cpl.	Davies, W. E.	M.M.
1892	L.-Cpl.	Marton, H.	D.C.M.
273	Pte.	Cowlishaw, J.	D.C.M.
2343	Pte.	Thickett, T.	D.C.M.
2500	Pte.	Morton, A.	M.M.
6551	Pte.	Jelly, J.	M.M.
6576	Pte.	Gray, E.	M.M.
3636	Pte.	Ibbotson, S.	M.M.
6035	Pte.	Cordson, B. S.	M.M.
4157	Pte.	Lymer, F.	M.M.
6249	Pte.	Vernon, A.	M.M.

1/4TH YORK AND LANCS. REGIMENT—*continued*

Regtl. No.	Rank.			Name.			Award.
202033	Pte.	...	...	McAvoy, T. E.	...	...	M.M.
201720	Pte.	...	...	Smith, J. T. ...	...	...	M.M.
202544	Pte.	...	...	Tyler, W.	...	...	M.M.
200567	Pte.	...	...	Longdon, J. ...	...	...	M.M.
202518	Pte.	...	...	Marshall, W. E.	...	...	M.M.
203547	Pte.	...	...	Mackie, R.	...	...	M.M.
203426	Pte.	...	...	Wilson, J. K. ...	...	...	M.M.
300742	Pte.	...	...	Jenkinson, P. ...	...	...	M.M.
203426	Pte.	...	...	Downes, G. ...	...	...	M.M.
203349	Pte.	...	...	Lockwood, F. ...	...	...	M.M.
203245	Pte.	...	...	Rodgers, V. ...	...	...	M.M.
201702	Pte.	...	...	Dungworth, C.	...	...	M.M.
9/15317	Pte.	...	...	Barron, L.	...	...	M.M.
13/29301	Pte.	...	...	Dale, F.	...	...	M.M.
14264	Pte.	...	...	Adly, A.	...	...	M.M.
203419	Pte.	...	...	Peart, H.	...	...	M.M.
203380	Pte.	...	...	Hopkinson, H.	...	...	M.M. Bar to M.M.
17511	Pte.	...	...	Turtle, C.	...	...	M.M.
201839	Pte.	...	...	Jeffrey, H.	...	...	M.M.
17690	Pte.	...	...	Clark, J.	...	...	M.M.
1277	Pte.	...	...	Cahill, A. E. ...	...	...	M.M.
203221	Pte.	...	...	Neve, A. H. ...	...	...	M.M.
241229	Pte.	...	...	Wharton, F. W.	...	...	M.M.
201996	Pte.	...	...	Sissons, F. W.	...	...	M.M.
10/40481	Pte.	...	...	May, P.	...	...	M.M.
15/28153	Pte.	...	...	Thickett, G. ...	...	...	M.M.
202304	Pte.	...	...	Andrews, J. ...	...	...	M.M.
13/3	Pte.	...	...	Atkinson, H. ...	...	...	M.M.
202838	Pte.	...	...	Bennett, A. ...	...	...	M.M.
200800	Pte.	...	...	Peat, A.	...	...	M.M.
3/877	Pte.	...	...	Winter, R.	...	...	M.M.
47093	Pte.	...	...	Gunn, A.	...	...	M.M.
46678	Pte.	...	...	Jennings, J. H.	...	...	D.C.M.
46711	Pte.	...	...	Hurd, J.	...	...	M.M. Bar to M.M.
1746	Pte.	...	...	Jow, G. F.	...	...	M.M.
202057	Pte.	...	...	Baker, S.	...	...	M.M.
47267	Pte.	...	...	Nichols, A. ...	...	...	M.M.
46682	Pte.	...	...	Davies, E.	...	...	M.M.
203486	Pte.	...	...	Holder, W. R. ...	...	...	M.M.
235152	Pte.	...	...	Wolmersley, G. H.	...	...	M.M.
46639	Pte.	...	...	Bennett, T. E. ...	...	...	M.M.
44926	Pte.	...	...	Tate, T.	...	...	M.M.

1/5TH YORK AND LANCS. REGIMENT

	Rank.		Name.			Award.
	Lt.-Col.	...	Parkinson, T. W.	...	...	D.S.O.
	Lt.-Col.	...	Rhodes, S. ...	...	...	D.S.O.
	Captain	...	Johnson, E. D. C.	...	...	M.C.
	Captain	...	Fisher, J. M. ...	...	...	M.C.
	Captain	...	Roberts, G. G....	...	...	M.C.
	Captain	...	Morrell, H. H.	...	...	M.C.
	Captain	...	Baker, A.	...	...	M.C.
	Captain	...	Briffault, R. (R.A.M.C.)	...		M.C. Bar to M.C.
	Captain	...	Glenn, C. E. ...	...	...	M.C. Bar to M.C.
	Captain	...	Melly, E. E. ...	...	...	M.C. Bar to M.C.

1/5TH YORK AND LANCS. REGIMENT—*continued*

Regtl. No.	Rank.	Name.	Award.
	Captain ...	Price, E. V.	M.C. Bar to M.C.
	Captain ...	Jennison, R.	M.C.
	Captain ...	Pitt, H. P.	M.C.
	Lieut. ...	Southern, V. G.	M.C.
	Lieut. ...	Cattle, E. S.	M.C.
	Lieut. ...	Marshall, J. F.	M.C.
	Lieut. ...	Wilson, J.	M.C. Bar to M.C.
	Lieut. ...	Dunkerton, E. L. H.	M.C. Bar to M.C.
	Lieut. ...	Hill, J. J.	M.C. Bar to M.C.
	Lieut. ...	Bennett, G. W.	M.C. Bar to M.C.
	Lieut. ...	Clyne, C.	M.C. Bar to M.C.
	Lieut. ...	Clayton, B.	M.C.
	Lieut. ...	Grogan, V. L. de L.	M.C.
	2/Lieut. ...	Haigh, J. J.	M.C.
	2/Lieut. ...	Elliott, G. R.	M.C.
	2/Lieut. ...	Beaumont, J. W.	M.C.
	2/Lieut. ...	Storm, W. G.	M.C.
	2/Lieut. ...	Shires, J.	M.C.
	2/Lieut. ...	Bagnall, A. E.	M.C.
	2/Lieut. ...	Fairbairn, W. F.	M.C.
	2/Lieut. ...	Redshaw, F. W.	M.C. M.M.
	2/Lieut. ...	Revill, H. H.	M.C.
	2/Lieut. ...	Wood, W. A.	M.C.
	2/Lieut. ...	Naylor, J. A.	M.C.
	2/Lieut. ...	Goodier, V. R.	M.C.
	Rev. ...	Partington, E. F. E.	M.C. Bar to M.C.
240429	R.Q.M.S. ...	Holmes, J. H. T.	M.S.M.
1432	C.S.M.	Parkes, W.	D.C.M.
5106	C.S.M.	Nowlan, S. C.	D.C.M.
240467	C.S.M.	Calvert, A.	M.C.
240241	C.S.M.	Murtagh, B.	D.C.M.
2349	Sgt.	Calvert, A.	D.C.M.
2067	Sgt.	Yate, J.	D.C.M.
68	Sgt.	Jessop, F.	D.C.M.
210	Sgt.	Inman, P.	D.C.M. M.M.
217	Sgt.	Medlock, J.	D.C.M.
2423	Sgt.	Crummock, E. E.	D.C.M. Medal St. George and Cross.
2153	Sgt.	Teece, G.	M.M. Bar to M.M.
2126	Sgt.	Poxon, H.	M.M.
2093	Sgt.	Inman, E. E.	M.M.
1402	Sgt.	Roadhouse, G. H.	M.M.
242444	Sgt.	Gedney, G.	D.C.M.
241759	Sgt.	Hipkin, A. P.	M.M.
240717	Sgt.	Gledhill, E.	M.M.
200288	Sgt.	Steeples, J.	M.M.
242141	Sgt.	O'Kelly, G. C.	M.M.
240059	Sgt.	Parkin, G. H.	D.C.M.
240407	Sgt.	Hall, R. W.	M.M. D.C.M.

1/5TH YORK AND LANCS. REGIMENT—*continued*

Regtl. No.	Rank.	Name.	Award.
240073	Sgt.	Weatherill, F.	D.C.M.
203878	Sgt.	Lees, E. V.	M.M.
242471	Sgt.	Johnson, J.	D.C.M. Medaille Militaire (French).
2174	L.-Sgt.	Urquhart, G.	M.M.
2186	Cpl.	Grinnette, A.	D.C.M.
1792	Cpl.	Murtagh, B.	M.M.
2334	Cpl.	Semley, A.	M.M.
2918	Cpl.	Hague, A. L.	M.M.
1872	Cpl.	Wright, S.	D.C.M.
240673	Cpl.	Lord, B.	M.M. Bar to M.M.
242487	Cpl.	Smelt, J.	M.M.
2619	Cpl.	Wilson, D.	D.C.M.
241489	Cpl.	Hines, H.	M.M. Bar to M.M.
240919	Cpl.	Berry, I.	M.M.
241438	Cpl.	Johnson, F.	M.M.
240160	Cpl.	Royston, F. R.	M.M.
240100	Cpl.	Yeal, A....	M.M.
240211	Cpl.	Frost, C.	M.M.
20443	Cpl.	Wilson, J.	M.M.
58244	Cpl.	Reach, C.	D.C.M.
42150	Cpl.	Stephenson, F....	M.M.
240385	Cpl.	Gamble, J. T.	M.S.M.
5076	L.-Cpl.	Stockley, P. H.	M.M.
2357	L.-Cpl.	Galloway, F.	M.M.
2604	L.-Cpl.	Cooper, T.	M.M.
241453	L.-Cpl.	Goodwin, J.	M.M. Bar to M.M.
242445	L.-Cpl.	Duckett, F.	D.C.M.
204754	L.-Cpl.	Henry, A.	M.M.
240298	L.-Cpl.	Harris, G. S.	D.C.M.
240175	L.-Cpl.	Childs, J. R.	D.C.M.
241226	L.-Cpl.	Scott, J.	M.M.
235806	L.-Cpl.	Collier, A.	M.M.
11974	L.-Cpl.	Porter, W. H.	M.M.
242850	L.-Cpl.	Anisworth, W.	M.M.
201726	L.-Cpl.	Greaves, H.	M.M.
240392	L.-Cpl.	Hepstinstall, B.	M.M.
2446	Pte.	Clements, C.	D.C.M.
1119	Pte.	Gray, A.	M.M.
2317	Pte.	Wilde, J.	M.M.
2173	Pte.	Whitworth, T.	M.M. D.C.M.
3923	Pte.	Barker, H.	M.M.
2432	Pte.	Hatton, H.	M.M.
2361	Pte.	Heppinstall, G.	M.M. Bar to M.M.
1539	Pte.	Robinson, J. W.	M.M.
5142	Pte.	Puan, J.	M.M.
2509	Pte.	Cooper, O.	M.M.
6181	Pte.	Milburn, P. S.	D.C.M.
240465	Pte.	Jackson, G.	M.M.
242272	Pte.	Freeman, C. P.	M.M.
240698	Pte.	Spurr, C.	M.M.
240022	Pte.	Billington, J.	M.M.
240014	Pte.	Slock, J. G.	M.M.
242335	Pte.	Clements, F. W.	M.M.
240617	Pte.	Pilkington, J.	M.M.

1/5TH YORK AND LANCS. REGIMENT—*continued*

Regtl. No.	Rank.	Name.	Award.
242346	Pte.	Small, J.	M.M.
240231	Pte.	Wing, A.	M.M.
240522	Pte.	Hunt, J. W.	Belgian Croix de Guerre
3771	Pte.	Golicher, J.	M.M.
31906	Pte.	Coleman, T.	M.M.
240697	Pte.	Nadin, J.	M.M.
40446	Pte.	Owen, J. V.	M.M.
242237	Pte.	Potter, I.	M.M.
1466	Pte.	Mansfield, B. ...	M.M.
242080	Pte.	Pheasants, E. W.	M.M.
38867	Pte.	Pilbrow, H.	M.M.
240089	Pte.	Moon, F.	M.M.
42276	Pte.	Padley, M.	M.M.
242215	Pte.	Exon, W.	M.M.
31907	Pte.	Grainger, S.	M.M.
240624	Pte.	Quinn, L.	M.M.
241509	Pte.	Cox, H.	M.M.
31924	Pte.	Dennis, A.	M.M.
377	Pte.	Godfrey, F.	M.M.
247375	Pte.	Swift, H.	M M.
240206	Pte.	Watson, A.	M.M.
47288	Pte.	Smith, C. R.	M.M.
57790	Pte.	Bolton, H.	M.M.
27859	Pte.	Haigh, W.	M.M.
12/111	Pte.	Geldert, S.	M.M.
742	Pte.	Whitfield, F.	M.M.
205605	Pte.	Sivett, J.	M.M.
17502	Pte.	Lakin, P.	M.M.
11015	Pte.	Jackson, G. F.	M.M.
47146	Pte.	Hedgeman, W. W.	M.M.
38321	Pte.	Williamson, T....	M.M.
44772	Pte.	Clamp, T.	M.M.
240005	Pte.	Parkin, C.	Medaille d'Honneur Avec Glavies en Bronze.

19TH LANCASHIRE FUSILIERS *(Pioneer Bn.)*

	Lt.-Col. ...	Graham, J. M. A., D.S.O. ...	Bar to D.S.O.
	Lt.-Col. ...	Smith, J. H.	Croix de Guerre
	Major ...	Wade-Gery, H. T.	M.C.
	Captain ...	Hibbert, G.	M.C.
	Captain ...	Palk, S. A.	M.C.
	Captain ...	Whittles, N.	M.C.
	Captain ...	Musker, H.	M.C.
	Captain ...	Edden, R. P. S.	O.B.E., 5th
	Lieut. ...	Moxsy, A. R.	M.C.
	2/Lieut. ...	Macfarlane, D. M.	M.C.
	2/Lieut. ...	Norman, R. B.	M.C.
27239	R.S.M. ...	Garner, W.	D.C.M. Croix de Guerre
17781	R.Q.M.S. ...	Timperley, W.	M.S.M.
18570	C.S.M.	Taylor, W.	D.C.M.
17392	C.S.M.	Cheney, A.	M.S.M.
17779	C.Q.M.S. ...	Moulson, J.	M.M.
17989	Sgt.	Baguley, J.	M.M.
18600	Sgt.	Banham, A.	M.M. Bar to M.M.

19TH LANCASHIRE FUSILIERS—*continued*

Regtl. No.	Rank.	Name.	Award.
17497	Sgt.	Magee, T.	M.M.
15125	Sgt.	Lewis, J. W.	M.M.
1420	Sgt.	Johnson, C.	M.M.
17362	Sgt.	Hickinbotham, G.	M.M.
18914	Sgt.	Haynes, F. J.	D.C.M.
17431	Sgt.	Pierce, T.	D.C.M.
1586	Sgt.	Rossey, A.	M.S.M.
17655	Sgt.	Jackson, J. F.	D.C.M.
36888	Sgt.	Osmond, E. F.	M.M.
235663	Sgt.	Atkinson, T.	Croix de Guerre
17387	Sgt.	Mathews, J.	M.S.M. Medaille d'Honneur avec Glavies en Argent
17583	L.-Sgt.	Brennan, J.	M.M.
18673	Cpl.	Smith, J.	M.M.
36820	Cpl.	Jones, W.	M.M.
36442	Cpl.	Hird, G.	M.M.
17357	Cpl.	Fennd, A.	M.M.
17572	Cpl.	Mayell, F.	M.M.
36637	L.-Cpl.	Foreman, E. J.	M.M.
202606	L.-Cpl.	Hitchen, J.	M.M.
34928	L.-Cpl.	Chadwick, F.	M.M.
49469	L.-Cpl.	Gear, H.	M.M.
238153	L.-Cpl.	Wainwright, W.	M.M.
34941	L.-Cpl.	Warburton, S.	M.M.
49513	L.-Cpl.	Davies, J.	M.M.
49534	L.-Cpl.	Potter, H. M.	M.M.
17866	Pte.	Taylor, E.	M.M.
27577	Pte.	Settle, J.	M.M.
18911	Pte.	Christian, L.	Croix de Guerre
18595	Pte.	Bradbury, T.	M.M.
23544	Pte.	Leech, E.	M.M.
36706	Pte.	Pooley, A. G.	M.M.
45935	Pte.	Fisher, V.	M.M.
17916	Pte.	Milligan, F.	M.M.
36909	Pte.	Prosser, T. J.	M.M.
202378	Pte.	Booth, W. H.	M.M.
25058	Pte.	Fogell, G.	M.M.
5320	Pte.	Wolfenden, A.	D.C.M.
203188	Pte.	Thomas, C. W. J.	Croix de Guerre

3RD MONMOUTH REGIMENT

Regtl. No.	Rank.	Name.	Award.
	Captain	Steel, O. W. D. (R.A.M.C.)	M.C.
	Captain	Gattie, K. F. D.	M.C.
135	S.M.	Gravenoe, G. A.	D.C.M. Croix de Guerre
1920	Sgt.	Jenkins, B.	D.C.M.
2172	Sgt.	Sketchley, G. W.	D.C.M.
675	Cpl.	Hoare	D.C.M.
1425	L.-Cpl.	Dixon, W.	D.C.M.
1511	L.-Cpl.	Leonard,	D.C.M.
1814	L.-Cpl.	Andrews, L.	M.M.
2440	Pte.	Skidmore. J.	D.C.M.
1343	Pte.	Moore. J. J.	D.C.M.
1317	Pte.	Powell G.	M.M.

49TH MACHINE-GUN BATTALION

Regtl. No.	Rank.	Name.	Award.
	Major	Sproulle, W. J. M.	M.C.
	Major	Rideal, J. G. E.	D.S.O.
	Major	Hanson, H. W.	M.C.
	Major	Boxer, H. T.	French Croix de Guerre
	Major	Milne, W.	French Croix de Guerre
	Captain ...	Bain, C. W. C....	M.C.
	Lieut. ...	Thresh, A. E.	M.C.
	2/Lieut. ...	Bellerby, J. R.	M.C.
	2/Lieut. ...	Ratcliff, W.	M.C.
	2/Lieut. ...	Bain, J.	M.C.
	2/Lieut. ...	Durlacher, P. A.	M.C.
	2/Lieut. ...	Hawes, W. A.	M.C.
	2/Lieut. ...	Jones, D. T.	M.C.
	2/Lieut. ...	Bentley, A. E.	M.C.
	2/Lieut. ...	Wood, S. F. H.	M.C.
	2/Lieut. ...	Steel, A. K.	M.C.
	2/Lieut. ...	Nathan, L. G....	M.C.
	2/Lieut. ...	Scott, R. C.	M.C.
	2/Lieut. ...	Dudley, F.	M.C.
	2/Lieut. ...	Marshall, W.	M.C.
	2/Lieut. ...	Barker, N. P.	M.C.
1669	Sgt.	Stembridge, E....	D.C.M.
24616	Sgt.	Thompson, R. S.	M.S.M.
16023	Sgt.	Maule, H. J.	D.C.M. M.M.
24270	Sgt.	Stancliffe, F.	M.M.
15664	Sgt.	Luffrum, A. H.	D.C.M. M.S.M.
1962	Sgt.	Bradley, A.	M.M.
2385	Sgt.	Brignell, A. E.	M.M.
1971	Sgt.	Binney, E.	M.M.
2207	Sgt.	Berry, C.	D.C.M.
23588	Sgt.	Craw-haw, G.	M.M.
23636	Sgt.	Jakeman, T. C.	D.C.M.
23655	Sgt.	Linton, C.	M.M.
9848	Sgt.	Morris, ...	M.M.
46118	Sgt.	Stafford, P. H.	M.M.
9285	Sgt.	Fewell, C. W.	M.M.
44626	Sgt.	Kennedy, J. J.	D.C.M.
24612	Sgt.	Walker, A.	D.C.M.
20247	Sgt.	Jackson, F. J.	D.C.M. M.M.
16761	Sgt.	Burkett, J.	D.C.M.
23658	Sgt.	Collumbine, A. C.	M.M. M.S.M.
23587	Sgt.	Lowe, J. E.	M.M.
23056	Sgt.	Sainsbury, A. L.	M.S.M.
24764	Sgt.	Garside, H.	M.S.M.
67534	Sgt.	Crockett, D.	D.C.M.
1242	L.-Sgt.	Dibb, D.	M.M.
1927	L.-Sgt.	Naigh, H.	M.M.
34885	Cpl.	Fogarty, T.	M.M.
19271	Cpl.	Smoothy, F.	M.M.
72533	Cpl.	Turner, F.	M.M.
1605	Cpl.	Micklethwaite, J.	M.M.
23603	Cpl.	Stevenson, W. J.	M.M.
11942	Cpl.	Barratt, T.	M.M.
36711	Cpl.	Godfrey, L.	M.M.
36466	Cpl.	Wood, J.	M.M.

49TH MACHINE-GUN BATTALION—*continued*

Regtl. No.	Rank.	Name.	Award.
81329	L.-Cpl.	Willis, T. C.	M.M.
102862	L.-Cpl.	Precious, A. M.	M.M.
59214	L.-Cpl.	Barratt, C.	D.C.M.
36740	L.-Cpl.	Deadman, T.	M.M. Bar to M.M.
10288	L.-Cpl.	Walton, H.	M.M.
70626	L.-Cpl.	White, W. H.	M.M.
5259	L.-Cpl.	Toon, A.	M.M.
55721	L.-Cpl.	White, A. J.	M.M.
1240	Pte.	Creyke, R.	D.C.M.
60482	Pte.	Mason, F.	M.M.
20738	Pte.	Start, S.	M.M.
24620	Pte.	Harris, L.	Belgian Croix de Guerre
73432	Pte.	Banson, J.	M.M.
24693	Pte.	Field, G. E.	M.M.
24688	Pte.	Bolton, G.	Belgian Croix de Guerre
1925	Pte.	Spurr, P.	M.M.
2251	Pte.	Wallace, J.	D.C.M.
85656	Pte.	Biddle, A. E.	M.M.
12700	Pte.	Ditchfield, J.	M.M.
16270	Pte.	Mason, L.	M.M.
7945	Pte.	Middleton, A. R.	M.M.
24752	Pte.	O'Neill, J.	M.M.
147840	Pte.	Ramsden, J.	M.M.
60493	Pte.	Maplethorpe, S.	M.M.
108125	Pte.	Byrne, G. H.	M.M.
139628	Pte.	Frost, E. D.	M.M.
139630	Pte.	Walker, F.	M.M.
136591	Pte.	Polwin, W.	M.M.
142701	Pte.	Kitchen, E.	M.M.
137524	Pte.	Price, G.	M.M.
139627	Pte.	Rawson, E.	M.M.
24684	Pte.	Spavin, L.	M.M.
45587	Pte.	Chidgey, R. J.	M.M.
87801	Pte.	Barincoat, R. H.	M.M.
28754	Pte.	Colley, H. C.	Croix de Guerre
57445	Pte.	Griffin, E.	M.M.
71584	Pte.	Spinks, A.	M.M.

49TH DIVISIONAL R.A.S.C.

Regtl. No.	Rank.	Name.	Award.
	Lt.-Col. ...	Chambers, J. C.	C.B.
	Lt.-Col. ...	Haigh, B.	D.S.O.
	Major ...	Montgomery, C. E.	M.C.
	Major ...	Butler, H. B. B.	O.B.E. 4th
	Captain ...	Milner, J.	M.C.
	Captain ...	Pearson, R. T.	M.C.
	Captain ...	Mills, G. H.	O.B.E. 4th
T4/249822	S.S.M. ...	Welburn, A. E.	M.S.M.
S4/072024	S. Sgt. ...	Jacques, H.	M.S.M.
M/2/164229	Q.M.S. ...	Telfor, W.	M.S.M.
T4/250989	S.Q.M.S. ...	Leng, J. R.	M.S.M.
S4/249596	Sgt.	Elsworth, C.	M.S.M.
T4/250904	Sgt.	Keighley, J. E.	Medaille Barbatie si Credinta, 2nd Class.
MS/1401	Sgt.	Ridley, W.	M.S.M.
T/232	Cpl.	Kay, J. S.	M.M.

49TH DIVISIONAL R.A.S.O.—*continued*

Regtl. No.	Rank.	Name.	Award.
T/3008	Dr.	Liversedge, F.	D.C.M. Croix de Guerre.
T/418	Dr.	Styles, J.	M.M.
T4/25101	Dr.	Hook, E.	M.M.
T4/250886	Dr.	Robinson, A.	M.M.
T4/251948	Dr.	Olford, A.	M.M.
T4/252278	Dr.	Smith, N. B.	Medaille d'Honneur Avec Glavies en Bronze.

HEADQUARTERS R.A.M.C.

Regtl. No.	Rank.	Name.	Award.
	Colonel ...	Sharp, A. D.	C.M.G. C.B.
	Major	Turner, A. C.	D.S.O.
107	Q.M.S.	DeBarr, S. G.	M.S.M.
403556	Sgt.	Cox, A.	M.S.M.

1/1st WEST RIDING FIELD AMBULANCE

Regtl. No.	Rank.	Name.	Award.
	Lt.-Col. ...	Whalley, F.	D.S.O.
	Major	Goode, H. N.	M.C. Bar to M.C.
	Captain ...	Partridge, H. R.	M.C. Bar to M.C.
	Captain ...	Metcalfe, J. C.	M.C.
	Captain ...	Pinder, J.	M.C.
	Revd.	McGuinness, E.	M.C.
401417	S. Sgt.	Wood, A. E.	M.S.M.
1670	Sgt.	Robson, F. W.	M.M.
175	Sgt.	Turner, C. S.	M.M.
596	Sgt.	Johnston, J. W.	M.M.
1735	Sgt.	Maury, P.	M.M.
401452	Sgt.	Beevers, F.	D.C.M. M.M.
M/2/076141	Sgt. (A.S.C. Attd.)	Routh, J.	M.M.
401039	Sgt.	Daniels, A.	M.M.
401330	Sgt.	Slater, F. H.	M.M.
401004	Sgt.	Pawson, F.	M.S.M.
401234	L.-Sgt. ...	Kew, A.	M.M.
M2/005122	Cpl. (A.S.C. Attd.)	Beale, H. C.	Belgian Croix de Guerre.
401090	Cpl.	Harvey, P.	M.M.
123	L.-Cpl.	Fisher, G. H.	M.M.
45	L.-Cpl.	Wiles, H.	M.M.
401205	L.-Cpl.	Ibbetson, J. W.	M.M.
401194	L.-Cpl.	Vaughan, R.	M.M.
128	Pte.	Brown, B.	M.M.
279	Pte.	Dibbs, E.	M.M.
1603	Pte.	Middleton, E.	M.M.
1550	Pte.	Robinson, W.	M.M.
206	Pte.	Gott, A.	M.M.
28	Pte.	Castlelow, F.	M.M.
594	Pte.	Hinchcliffe, T. J.	M.M.
401436	Pte.	Johnson, H.	M.M.
401325	Pte.	Adams, H. V.	M.M.
92903	Pte.	Mackie, A. J. G.	M.M.

1/1st WEST RIDING FIELD AMBULANCE—*continued*

Regtl. No.	Rank.	Name.	Award.
401024	Pte.	Haley, T. B.	M.M. Bar to M.M.
401491	Pte.	Dickinson, A.	M.M.
M2/076128	Pte.	Jackson, F.	M.M.
M2/073631	Pte.	Thorn, W.	M.M.
401340	Pte.	Daniels, J.	M.M.
401033	Pte.	Ormsby, G.	M.M.
401334	Pte.	Hursley, J. T.	M.M.
401047	Pte.	Tillotson, J.	M.M.
403634	Pte.	Peckett, L. V.	M.M.
405169	Pte.	Hague, J.	M.M.
405445	Pte.	Welsh, R.	M.M.
405424	Pte.	Treddwell, W. H.	M.M.

1/2nd WEST RIDING FIELD AMBULANCE

Regtl. No.	Rank.	Name.	Award.
	Lt.-Col. ...	Collinson, H.	D.S.O.
	Lt.-Col. ...	Dobson, F. G.	D.S.O.
	Major	Smith, C. N.	M.C. Bar to M.C.
	Captain	Foxton, H.	M.C.
	Revd. ...	Jarvis, E. C.	M.C.
403033	S.M. ...	Moss, H. C.	M.S.M.
T4/253975	S.S.M. ...	Norris, G. H.	M.S.M.
176	Sgt. ...	Bland, G.	D.C.M.
	Sgt. ...	Holdsworth, W. E.	D.C.M.
M2/055497	Sgt. ...	Culmane, J.	M.M.
407	Sgt. ...	Hind, J. F.	M.M.
845	Sgt. ...	Earl, V.	M.M.
403067	Sgt. ...	Wilkinson, E.	M.M.
403243	Sgt. ...	Hind, J. F.	D.C.M.
403576	L.-Sgt. ...	Geavins, A. J. E.	M.M.
368046	Cpl. ...	John, A. E.	M.M.
137	L.-Cpl. ...	Knight, H.	M.M.
403550	L.-Cpl. ...	Turner, H. H.	M.M.
403564	L.-Cpl. ...	Cooper, R. J.	M.M.
403549	L.-Cpl. ...	Hill, C. H.	M.M.
403338	L.-Cpl. ...	Todd, P. R.	M.M.
364	Pte. ...	Todd, M. W.	M.M.
72	Pte. ...	Linley, A.	M.M.
385	Pte. ...	Bradley, E. N.	M.M.
1590	Pte. ...	Waters, S.	M.M.
198	Pte. ...	Partridge, J. N.	M.M.
403111	Pte. ...	Bottomley, R.	M.M.
403203	Pte. ...	Newton, H.	Belgian Croix de Guerre.
403582	Pte. ...	Arnold, D.	M.M.
M2/073659	Pte. ...	Somerville, J. M.	M.M.
403591	Pte. ...	Kellett, W.	M.M.
403163	Pte. ...	Bolton, R. E.	M.M.
403446	Pte. ...	Booker, J. H.	M.M.
403425	Pte. ...	Lickess, H.	M.M.
403575	Pte. ...	Haigh, K. C.	M.M.
403134	Pte. ...	Kirby, W.	M.M.
403534	Pte. ...	Dellar, H.	French Croix de Guerre.
405267	Pte. ...	Carter, H.	M.M.

1/3RD WEST RIDING FIELD AMBULANCE

Regtl. No.	Rank.	Name.	Award.
	Lt.-Col....	Mackinnon, J. ...	D.S.O.
	Major ...	Allen, (V.C.), W. B. ...	D.S.O.
			M.C.
			Bar to M.C.
	Captain	Stark, R. A. ...	M.C.
			Bar to M.C.
	Captain	Carr, G. F. ...	M.C.
	Captain	Partridge, H. R. ...	M.C.
837	Sgt. ...	Brookes, W. ...	Medaille Militaire
476	Sgt. ...	Oliver, H. ...	D.C.M.
903	Sgt. ...	Brownhill, E. H. ...	M.M.
			Bar to M.M.
405160	Sgt. ...	Crofts, H. E. ...	M.M.
			Bar to M.M.
405244	Sgt. ...	Pickering, F. ...	M.M.
405120	Cpl. ...	Bollard, G. W. ...	M.M.
405247	Cpl. ...	Bower, H. ...	M.M.
405272	Cpl. ...	Briggs, W. ...	M.M.
M2/053961	Cpl. ...	Davies, F. C. ...	M.M.
180	L.-Cpl. ...	Needham, G. H. ...	D.C.M.
405267	L.-Cpl. ...	Carter, H. ...	M.M.
			Bar to M.M.
405109	L.-Cpl. ...	Dent, F. ...	M.M.
			M.S.M.
M2/073647	Dr. ...	Lewis, W. ...	M.M.
173	Pte. ...	Northend, E. ...	M.M.
405195	Pte. ...	Harvey, B. ...	M.M.
405114	Pte. ...	Bradshaw, H. ...	M.M.
405079	Pte. ...	Hoyland, L. B. ...	M.M.
83339	Pte. ...	Marshall, W. F. ...	M.M.
405424	Pte. ...	Tradewell, W. H. ...	M.M.
405027	Pte. ...	Emmerson, J. W. ...	French Medaille Militaire
405133	Pte. ...	Hayward, A. C. ...	M.M.
405152	Pte. ...	Gregory, E. ...	M.M.
405199	Pte. ...	Marris, H. ...	M.M.
405147	Pte. ...	Jenkinson, J. H. ...	M.M.
405039	Pte. ...	Lockington, J. E. ...	M.M.
405451	Pte. ...	Hilliam, J. H. ...	M.M.
405485	Pte. ...	Richards, A. R. ...	M.M.

UNITS ATTACHED TO 49TH (W.R.) DIVISION

M.M. POLICE.

Regtl. No.	Rank.	Name.	Award.
P/4816	Sgt. ...	Ryan, J. F. ...	M.M.
			Bar to M.M.
P/868	Sgt. ...	Lewendon, G. ...	M.M.
P/4812	Sgt. ...	Beveridge, G. O. H. ...	M.S.M.
P/2871	L.-Cpl. ...	Hignett, R. ...	M.S.M.
P/4760	L.-Cpl. ...	Joel, H. M. ...	M.M.
P/4890	L.-Cpl. ...	Till, J. ...	M.M.
P/4824	L.-Cpl. ...	Parker, J. ...	M.M.
P/7661	L.-Cpl. ...	Tokins, A. ...	M.M.
P/1365	L.-Cpl. ...	Agar, G. ...	M.S.M.

3RD SOUTH LANCS. 243RD EMPLOY. COY.

Regtl. No.	Rank.	Name.	Award.
118154	Pte. ...	Furniss, O. ...	M.M.

UNITS ATTACHED TO 49TH (W.R.) DIVISION—*continued*

Regtl. No.	Rank.	Name.	Award.
		R.A.O. CORPS.	
S/6351	S. Condtr.	...| Young, J. E. ... ...|	M.S.M.
S/4976	S. Condtr.	...| Stagg, F. G. ... ...|	M.S.M.
	S. Condtr.	...| Parker, W. ... ...|	M.S.M.
		CHAPLAIN.	
	Revd. ...	...| Barnes, S. R. ... ...|	O.B.E., 4th
	Revd. ...	...| Goodwin, H. F. ... ...|	M.C.
		34TH T.M. BATTERY.	
	2/Lieut.	...| Whittaker, O. ... ...|	M.C.
62376	Gr. ...	...| Raynor, W. ... ...|	D.C.M.
		ATTACHED TO A.P.M.	
S/243106	L.-Cpl. ...	...| Haigh, H. ... ...|	M.S.M.
		DIVISIONAL GAS OFFICER.	
	Lieut. ...	...| Stott, O. ... ...|	M.C.
		ARMY VETERINARY CORPS.	
	Captain	...| Keir, D. ... ...|	M.C.
TT/03171	Sgt. ...	...| Heveringham, A. G. ... ...|	M.S.M.
TT/03216	Sgt. ...	...| Taylor, F. J. S. ... ...|	M.S.M.
TT/33338	Sgt. ...	...| Wilks, J. ... ...|	M.S.M.
		NEW ZEALAND FIELD ARTILLERY.	
11/2074	Sgt. ...	...| Davis, C. H. ... ...|	M.M.
		NEW ZEALAND DIVISIONAL AMMUNITION COLUMN.	
2/651	Sgt. ...	...| Burt, O. C. H. ... ...|	M.M.
2/2221	Cpl. ...	...| MacGibbon, D. A. ... ...|	M.M.
10622	Bdr. ...	...| Malone, D. ... ...|	M.M.
10597	Dr. ...	...| Henry, G. E. ... ...|	M.M.
13/2846	Dr. ...	...| Mason, S. ... ...|	M.M.
		1/1ST FIELD COY. NEW ZEALAND ENGINEERS.	
4/1227a	Cpl. ...	...| Duggan, J. W. ... ...|	M.M.
4/1978	2nd Cpl.	...| McKinlay, W. D. ... ...|	M.M.
4/126a	Sapr. ...	...| Ramsey, J. K. ... ...|	M.M.
4/1207	Sapr. ...	...| Walker, J. ... ...|	M.M.
		1/3RD FIELD COY. NEW ZEALAND ENGINEERS.	
4/2112	Sapr. ...	...| McMillan, H. ... ...|	M.M.

APPENDIX II

(B). SUMMARY OF HONOURS AND AWARDS OBTAINED BY 62ND (W.R.) DIVISION.

V.C.	5
C.M.G.	4
M.B.E.	1
D.S.O.	61
Bar to D.S.O.	6
M.C.	402
Bar to M.C.	49
2nd Bar to M.C.	3
3rd Bar to M.C.	1
D.C.M.	169
Bar to D.C.M.	6
M.M.	1,754
Bar to M.M.	97
2nd Bar to M.M.	3
M.S.M.	68
Foreign Orders, etc.	26
Total	2,655

LIST OF HONOURS AND AWARDS OBTAINED BY 62ND (W.R.) DIVISION.

HEADQUARTERS 62ND (W.R.) DIVISION.

Regtl. No.	Rank.	Name.	Award.
	Maj.-Gen. ...	Braithwaite, Sir W. P. (C.B.)...	K.C.B.
	Maj.-Gen. ...	Whigham, Sir R. D. (K.C.B.)	K.C.M.G.
			D.S.O.
	Br.-Gen. ...	Foot, R. M. (C.M.G.)... ...	D.S.O.
	Br.-Gen. ...	Gillam, —.	D.S.O.
	Lt.-Col.... ...	Newman, C. R. (D.S.O.) ...	C.M.G.
			Legion d'Honneur
			(Chevalier)
	Major	Bissett, F. W.L.	D.S.O.
			M.C.
	Major	Lindsett, W. G. (M.C.) ...	D.S.O.
	S.S.M.	Preston, —.	M.S.M.

185TH INFANTRY BRIGADE.

Regtl. No.	Rank.	Name.	Award.
	Bt.-Major ...	O'Connor, E. N.	D.S.O.
	Captain ...	Lloyd, W. A. C.	M.C.
	Captain ...	Harter, J. F.	M.C.
	2/Lieut. ...	Freer, E. H.	M.C.
48214	Sgt.	Ellis, H.	M.M.
			Bar to M.M.

186TH INFANTRY BRIGADE.

Regtl. No.	Rank.	Name.	Award.
	Brig.-General ...	Burnett, J. L. G.	C.M.G.
			D.S.O.
	Major	Boyd, J. D. (D.S.O.) ...	Bar to D.S.O.
	Major	Wright, W. O.	D.S.O.
	Captain ...	Wingfield-Stratford, G. E. ...	Croix de Guerre.
	Sgt.	Hirst, H.	D.C.M.
S269578	Sgt.	Robertshaw, W. G.	M.S.M.

187TH INFANTRY BRIGADE.

Regtl. No.	Rank.	Name.	Award.
	Brig.-General ...	Reddie, A. J.	C.M.G.
			D.S.O.
	Captain ...	Manley, M. A.	M.C.
			Bar to M.C.
	Captain ...	Impson, —.	M.C.
			M.B.E.

229TH INFANTRY BRIGADE.

Regtl. No.	Rank.	Name.	Award.
	Brig.-General ...	Thackeray, F. S.	D.S.O.
			M.C.

310TH BRIGADE, R.F.A.

Regtl. No.	Rank.	Name.	Award.
	Major	Currie, J. M.	Croix de Guerre.
	Major	Foot, E. C.	M.C.
	Major	Jephson, E. W. F.	M.C.
			Bar to M.C.
	Major	Lockhart, J. F. K.	D.S.O.
	Captain ...	Archer, D. de B.	M.C.
	Captain ...	Robinson, J. G.	M.C.

310TH BRIDAGE R.F.A.—*continued.*

Regtl. No.	Rank.	Name.	Award.
	Lieut.	Abrahams, F.	M.C.
	Lieut.	Mills, J.	M.C.
	Lieut.	Holt, W. P.	M.C.
	Lieut.	Morgan, R. G.	M.C.
	2/Lieut. ...	Gane, L. C.	M.C.
	2/Lieut. ...	Murray, A. C.	M.C.
	2/Lieut. ...	Nowill, J. C. F.	M.C.
	2/Lieut. ...	Parkinson, E.	M.C.
	Lieut. ...	Hess, N.	M.C.
255022	B.S.M. ...	Salmon, J. P.	M.M. Bar to M.M.
77638	B.Q.M.S. ...	Woolf, E.	M.S.M.
786097	Sgt.	Stradling, C. H.	M.M. Bar to M.M. Medaille Militaire.
775421	Sgt.	Bentley, J. A.	M.M.
776389	Sgt.	Clements, L. D. J.	D.C.M. M.M.
03191	Sgt.	Mollett, T. A.	M.M.
776403	Sgt.	Stapley, A. H.	M.M.
50531	Sgt.	Eggot, G. H.	M.M.
968755	Sgt.	Darling, G.	M.M.
03221	Sgt.	Daniels, G. W. (A.V.C.) ...	M.M.
776674	Sgt.	Rider, H.	M.M. D.C.M.
40915	Sgt.	Chamberlain, C.	M.M. Bar to M.M.
775542	Sgt.	Waide, E. H.	M.S.M.
119305	Sgt.	Parker, J.	M.M.
776671	Sgt.	Harrison, H.	M.M.
796614	Sgt.	Moseley, W.	M.M.
775909	Cpl.	Chapman, A.	M.M.
776418	Cpl.	James, T. E.	M.M.
686809	Cpl.	Mitchell, J.	M.M.
775025	Cpl.	Clarke, F.	M.M.
776679	Cpl.	Harrison, A.	M.M.
780184	Cpl.	Settle, W.	M.S.M.
797096	Cpl.	Schofield, H. H.	M.M.
479756	Cpl.	Swithenbank, H. L.	M.M.
775811	Cpl.	Othen, P.	M.M.
775071	Cpl.	Howard, A.	M.M.
49163	Cpl.	Bourne, F. H.	M.M.
479751	L.-Cpl. ...	Clarke, F. W.	M.M.
776421	Bdr.	Kirk, J.	M.M.
776689	Bdr.	Aspinall, C.	M.M. Bar to M.M.
776686	Bdr.	McCart, J.	M.M.
775526	Bdr.	Pawsey, O.	M.M.
776629	Bdr.	Simpson, J.	M.M.
149519	Bdr.	Gerrard, F. B.	M.M.
785747	Bdr.	Jow, G. R.	M.M.
775809	Bdr.	Preston, J.	M.M.
686749	Bdr.	Blakeley, J.	M.M.
775228	Bdr.	Naylor, C. B.	M.M.
57500	Bdr.	Heard, J.	M.M.
776659	Gnr.	Wood, F.	M.M.
776440	Gnr.	Slater, F.	M.M.
170024	Gnr.	Hales, H. E.	M.M.
775175	Gnr.	Fender, M.	M.M.
776435	Gnr.	Pearce, H. E.	M.M.
14383	Gnr.	Cooper, S.	M.M.

310TH BRIGADE R.F.A.—*continued.*

Regtl. No.	Rank.	Name.	Award.
776595	Gnr.	Charlesworth, G.	M.M.
776518	Gnr.	Eshelby, J.	M.M.
777007	Gnr.	Foster, E.	M.M.
40813	Gnr.	Johnson, W. L.	M.M.
26073	Gnr.	Wendrop, E.	M.M.
796216	Gnr.	Fisher, R.	M.M.
765565	Gnr.	Walker, H.	M.M.
73649	Gnr.	Champton, M. F.	M.M.
534665	Spr.	Stockwell, A. W.	M.M.
526246	Spr.	Page, W.	M.M.
775859	Sgnr.	Milnes, N.	M.M.
154325	Sgnr.	Thornton, S. W.	M.M.
775451	Sgnr.	Doolan, J.	M.M.
247749	Sgnr.	Courtney, H.	M.M.
775873	Dr.	Simpson, A.	M.M.
775729	Dr.	Fincham, G.	M.M.
4317	Dr.	Smart, G.	M M

312TH BRIGADE R.F.A.

Regtl. No.	Rank.	Name.	Award.
	Major	Elston, A J.	Croix de Guerre.
	Bde.-Major ...	Fitzgibbon, F.	D.S.O.
			Croix de Guerre.
	Major	Swain, G. A.	M.C.
	Major	Fleming, G. R.	Croix de Chevalier (French).
	Major	Arnold Foster, F. A.	D.S.O.
	Captain ...	Senior, A.	M.C.
	Lieut.	Yore, P.	M.C.
			Bar to M.C.
	Lieut.	Bennett, A. G.	M.C.
	Lieut.	Watson, H. S.	M.C.
	Lieut.	Ness, N.	M.C.
			Bar to M.C.
	Lieut.	Boden, J. B.	M.C.
			Bar to M.C.
	Lieut.	Smith, H.	M.C.
	Lieut.	Lloyd, E. S.	M.C.
	Lieut.	Swain, G. A.	Croix de Guerre. (French).
	2/Lieut. ...	Latter, H. A.	M.C.
	2/Lieut. ...	Nelson, H. G.	M.C.
	2/Lieut. ...	Dowden, H. J.	M.C.
	2/Lieut. ...	Douett, C. F. M.	M.C.
	2/Lieut. ...	Alderton, B.	M.C.
	2/Lieut. ...	Lintern, E. E. C.	M.C.
	2/Lieut. ...	Lee. A. G.	M.C.
	2/Lieut. ...	Reynolds, J. L. T.	M.C.
	2/Lieut. ...	Gooch, F. E.	M.C.
	2/Lieut. ...	Smart, E.	M.C.
	2/Lieut. ...	Ellis, G. A.	M.C.
			Bar to M.C
	2/Lieut. ...	Nicholson, K. B.	M.C.
	2/Lieut. ...	Furlong, P. C.	M.C.
	2/Lieut. ...	Williams, E. T.	M.C.
240004	B.S.M. ...	Brown, J. D.	M.M
5341	B.S.M. ...	Turner, G.	M.M.
73925	B.S.M. ...	Hodges, J. W.	M.M.
785528	B.S.M. ...	Bowden, G. F.	D.C.M.
			M.M.

312TH BRIGADE R.F.A.—*continued.*

Regtl. No.	Rank.	Name.	Award.
90174	Sgt.	Wild, T.	M.M.
785264	Sgt.	Brothwell, T.	M.M.
781817	Sgt.	Butcher, W. T.	M.M.
786046	Sgt.	Lupton, W.	M.M.
39688	Sgt.	Anson, A. E. J.	D.C.M. M.M.
78621	Sgt.	Firth, H.	M.M.
785292	Sgt.	Buchanan, H.	M.M.
786257	Sgt.	Sweeney, A.	M.M.
786145	Sgt.	Penny, A.	M.M.
786788	Sgt.	Simpson, T.	M.M.
786051	Sgt.	McGowen, H.	M.M.
70957	Sgt.	Stevenson, W.	M.M.
786071	Sgt.	Parr, G.	M.M.
	Sgt.	Whittaker, F.	D.C.M.
62908	Sgt.	Yates, J.	M.M.
785248	Sgt.	Hebblethwaite, —.	M.M.
686744	Sgt.	Black, J.	M.M.
786705	Sgt.	Kettlewell, J.	M.M.
785538	Sgt.	Roper, F.	D.C.M.
786449	Cpl.	Jeffrey, W.	D.C.M.
786191	Cpl.	Pollard, F.	M.M.
785989	Cpl.	Bland, C.	M.M.
786041	Cpl.	Jeffrey, H.	M.M.
786087	Cpl.	Smith, J. A.	M.M.
786714	Cpl.	Worshop, C.	M.M.
785268	Cpl.	Steele, A.	M.S.M.
117895	Bdr.	Roberts, R.	M.M.
786581	Bdr.	Orme, O.	D.C.M.
786289	Bdr.	Stobart, G.	M.M.
786186	Bdr.	Tweed, A.	M.M.
785655	Bdr.	Davis, H.	M.M.
786597	Bdr.	Brears, B.	M.M.
81459	Gnr.	Mellor, T. H.	M.M.
90085	Gnr.	Head, W.	M.M.
811015	Gnr.	Fellows, A.	M.M.
68531	Gnr.	Brackfield, E.	M.M.
947529	Gnr.	Glass, A.	M.M.
786570	Gnr.	Hollyhead, G.	M.M.
165323	Gnr.	Holmes, T.	M.M.
786409	Gnr.	Leaf, E.	M.M.
786176	Gnr.	Noble, J.	M.M.
785544	Gnr.	Clapton, G.	M.M.
786216	Gnr.	Heaton, R.	M.M.
686672	Gnr.	Potts, J.	M.M.
785507	Gnr.	Heslam, W.	M.M.
14394	Gnr.	Friend, F.	M.M.
78372	Gnr.	Austin, E. J.	M.M.
786188	Gnr.	Wakefield, E.	M.M.
178962	Gnr.	Gething, H.	M.M.
155862	Sgnr.	Hill, F.	M.M.
403491	Pte.	Yates, C.	M.M.
786267	S.-Smith ...	Wilthew, L.	M.M.
775441	Dr.	Marsden ,W.	M.M.
795579	Dr.	Marks, H.	M.M.
785515	Dr.	Ames, L.	M.M.
670	Dr.	Morgan, D. E.	M.M.
786427	Dr.	Whitaker, S.	M.M.
786321	Dr.	Howard, G.	M.M.
796698	Dr.	Taylor, E.	M.M.
216999	Dr.	Willis, W.	M.M.

312TH BRIGADE R.F.A.—*continued.*

Regtl. No.	Rank.	Name.	Award.
786277	Dr.	Cartwright, M.	M.M.
786245	Dr.	Utley, F. A.	M.M.
786012	Dr.	Ellis, W.	M.M.
785652	Dr.	Wheatley, G.	M.M.
786070	Dr.	Parkinson, T.	M.M.
11390	Dr.	Slater, B.	M.M.
796529	Dr.	Edwards, H.	M.M.
47715	Dr.	O'Reilly, M.	M.M.
479981	Spr.	Butcher, C.	M.M.
490257	Spr.	Fisher, H.	M.M.
354350	Spr.	Starding, E.	M.M.

293RD BRIGADE R.F.A.

Regtl. No.	Rank.	Name.	Award.
48262	Sgt.	Mackrill, S. W.	D.C.M.
52069	Sgt.	Rae, W.	M.M.
781506	Cpl.	Burton, E.	D.C.M.
606140	Gnr.	Evans, J.	M.M.

WEST RIDING DIVISIONAL AMMUNITION COLUMN.

Regtl. No.	Rank.	Name.	Award.
	Captain ...	Long, V. H. S.	Croix de Guerre.
	Lieut.	House, W. H.	M.C.
796450	Sgt.	Mather, W.	M.M. Bar to M.M.
795060	Sgt.	Mallinson, G.	M.M.
795531	Sgt.	Lacey, W.	M.M.
796760	Bdr.	Bawn, A. S.	M.M.
795487	Bdr.	Hattersley, J. W.	M.M.
795655	Bdr.	Firth, A.	M.M.
795432	Gnr.	Scott, E.	M.M.
795519	Gnr.	Simmons, F. W.	M.M.
68968	Dr.	Bain, W.	M.M.
795469	Dr.	Wheater, T. W.	M.M.
796096	Dr.	Morley, T. H.	M.M.
745725	Dr.	Green, T. J.	M.M.
796893	Dr.	Marton, W. J.	M.M.

62ND TRENCH MORTAR BATTERY.

Regtl. No.	Rank.	Name.	Award.
	Captain ...	Bate, R. E. de B.	M.C. Bar to M.C.
	Lieut.	Schofield, H. O.	M.C.
	Lieut.	Wilson, E.	M.C.
	Lieut.	Gaulder, C. W. E.	M.C.
	2/Lieut. ...	Hart, P. H.	M.C.
	2/Lieut. ...	Doig, K. H.	M.C.
786598	Cpl.	Firth, E.	M.M.
781506	Cpl.	Burton, E.	D.C.M. M.M.
775751	Cpl.	Smith, H.	M.M.
775939	Cpl.	Arundel, J. W.	M.M.
781904	Cpl.	Adams, E.	M.S.M.
776494	Bdr.	Mornan, J.	M.M.
776523	Bdr.	Malhom, A.	M.M.
26073	Gnr.	Windrop, E.	M.M. Bar to M.M.
190884	Gnr.	Newby, M. D.	M.M.
200961	Dr.	Metcalf, J. F.	D.C.M.

62ND (W.R.) DIVISIONAL ROYAL ENGINEERS.

Regtl. No.	Rank.	Name.	Award.
	Lt.-Col.... ...	Chenevix-Trench, L.	C.M.G.
			D.S.O.
	Major	Montgomery, R. V.	M.C.
	Major	Paul, A. F. B.	M.C.
	Major	Walthew, E. J.	M.C.
	Major	Seaman, W. A.	M.C.
	Captain ...	Phillips, C. K.	M.C.
	Lieut.	Stranger, J. R.	M.C.
			Bar to M.C.
	Lieut.	Cooper, D. E.	M.C.
	Lieut.	Pearce, H. J.	M.C.
	Lieut.	O'Dowda, B. F.	M.C.
	Lieut.	Collins, A. B. C.	M.C.
	Lieut.	Howard, A. H....	M.C.
	2/Lieut. ...	Shannon, J. A.	M.C.
	2/Lieut. ...	Smith, S. A.	M.C.
	2/Lieut. ...	Clarson, C. L....	M.C.
	2/Lieut. ...	Froggatt, W.	M.C.
	2/Lieut. ...	Graham, M. R.	M.C.
480031	C.S.M.	Neale, R. C.	M.M.
			M.S.M.
428181	C.Q.M.S. ...	Alexander. E. T.	M.S.M.
482140	Sgt.	Ellis, H.	D.C.M.
			M.M.
482147	Sgt.	Anstwick, G. H.	M.M.
			Bar to M.M.
482032	Sgt.	McNeille, J. L.	M.M.
482310	Sgt.	Laxton, T. J.	M.M.
482134	Sgt.	Marples, N.	D.C.M.
			M.M.
482182	Sgt.	Barker, G. R.	M.M.
484141	Sgt.	Dawson, H.	D.C.M.
			M.M.
482119	Sgt.	Harrington, W. J.	M.S.M.
482348	Sgt.	O'Neill, J.	M.S.M.
480057	Sgt.	Wood, T.	M.M.
480070	Sgt.	Proctor, E.	M.M.
			M.S.M.
480098	Sgt.	Williams, J. H.	M.S.M.
480316	Sgt.	Bruins, F.	M.M.
480315	Sgt.	Bailey, W.	M.M.
			M.S.M.
478021	Sgt.	Chapman, F.	M.M.
476246	Sgt.	Fox, W.	M.M.
476404	Sgt.	Edwards, C.	M.M.
476392	Sgt.	Whitehead, J.	M.M.
			Bar to M.M.
476425	Sgt.	Elliott, E.	M.M.
476433	Sgt.	Henry, J.	M.M.
482190	Cpl.	Lodge, A.	M.M.
482037	Cpl.	North, G. H.	M.M.
			Bar to M.M.
458759	Cpl.	Doyle, T.	M.M.
482341	Cpl.	Squires, A.	M.M.
481804	Cpl.	Bilton, W. H.	M.M.
482353	Cpl.	Rogers, J.	M.M.
482170	Cpl.	King, S.	M.M.
482409	Cpl.	Mallinson, B.	M.M.
482347	Cpl.	Spencer, R. H....	M.M.
482180	Cpl.	North, H.	M.M.
482135	Cpl.	Goodsir, T. B.	M.M.
			Bar to M.M.

62ND (W.R.) DIVISIONAL ROYAL ENGINEERS—*continued.*

Regtl. No.	Rank.	Name.	Award.
482136	Cpl.	Marshall, W.	M.M.
482138	Cpl.	Wallace, W.	M.M. Bar to M.M.
482124	Cpl.	Maxfield, T.	M.M.
482421	Cpl.	Groocock, A. W.	M.M.
479979	Cpl.	Blair, S.	M.M.
552167	Cpl.	Ashby, S.	M.M.
480443	Cpl.	Smith, B.	M.M.
430042	Cpl.	Tyldesley, E.	M.M.
476432	Cpl.	Field, L.	M.M.
470888	Cpl.	Reay, G.	M.M.
498457	Cpl.	Wilson, E.	M.M.
482256	L.-Cpl.	Oven, H. G.	M.M. Bar to M.M.
482419	L.-Cpl.	Borthwick, T. D.	M.M. Bar to M.M.
282422	L.-Cpl.	Draycott, G.	M.M.
482375	L.-Cpl.	Yeadon, L. W.	M.M.
316723	L.-Cpl.	Piggott, E. C. C.	M.M.
482271	L.-Cpl.	Lake, F. E.	M.M.
482125	L.-Cpl.	Dixon, L.	M.M.
492533	L.-Cpl.	Trueman, H.	M.M.
37010	L.-Cpl.	Hearne, W.	M.M. Bar to M.M.
32675	L.-Cpl.	Randall, H.	M.M.
482301	L.-Cpl.	Wallace, A.	M.M.
482176	L.-Cpl.	Ebbatson, A.	M.M. Bar to M.M.
259377	L.-Cpl.	Williams, M. A.	M.M. Bar to M.M.
400195	L.-Cpl.	Craig, R.	M.M.
476397	L.-Cpl.	Pettifer, W.	M.M.
498404	L.-Cpl.	Arnold, G.	M.M.
400622	L.-Cpl.	Nairn, J.	M.M.
62366	Spr.	Read, D. W.	M.M.
482385	Spr.	Adamson, —.	M.M. Bar to M.M.
268251	Spr.	Arch, J. C.	M.M.
479989	Spr.	Wilson, H.	M.M.
142357	Spr.	Gishy, S.	M.M.
482169	Spr.	Meeks, —.	M.M.
482239	Spr.	Beeley, A.	M.M.
266449	Spr.	Lyle, J. A.	M.M.
282274	Spr.	Steedman, A.	M.M.
508141	Spr.	Hooper, G.	M.M.
428148	Spr.	Marshall, E. H.	M.M.
482313	Spr.	Pycock, E.	M.M.
482131	Spr.	Snowden, W. H.	M.M.
479981	Spr.	Butcher, C.	M.M. Bar to M.M.
322132	Spr.	Connelly, F. G.	M.M.
548448	Spr.	Pearce, J.	M.M.
325997	Spr.	Pitts, B.	M.M.
482343	Spr.	Holmes, F. H. W.	M.M.
166287	Spr.	Justice, W. C.	M.M.
48049	Spr.	Middleton, J. A. R.	M.M.
480641	Spr.	Green, J.	M.M.
480637	Spr.	Goodrum, E.	M.M.
476579	Spr.	Cross, J.	M.M.
183791	Spr.	Critchley, F. D.	M.M.
482130	Pnr.	Jackson, W. H.	M.M. Bar to M.M.

62ND (W.R.) DIVISIONAL ROYAL ENGINEERS—*continued*.

Regtl. No.	Rank.	Name.	Award.
325692	Pnr.	Hayton, H. W....	M.M.
			Bar to M.M.
221657	Pnr.	Watton, F. G.	M.M.
166154	Pnr.	Wright, E.	M.M.
259599	Pnr.	Douglas, E. R.	M.M.
267573	Pnr.	Douglas, H.	M.M.

2/5TH WEST YORKSHIRE REGIMENT.

	Lt.-Col.... ...	Josselyn, J.	D.S.O.
	Lieut.	Skirrow, G.	Croix de Guerre (French).
	Lieut.	Green, A. E.	D.S.O.
	Lieut.	Smith, A. W. L.	M.C.
	Lieut.	Sawyer, E. C.	M.C.
	Lieut.	Airey, J. C.	M.C.
	Lieut.	Riley, B. M.	M.C.
	Lieut.	Bardsley, E. H.	M.C.
	Lieut.	Anderson, J. M.	M.C.
	2/Lieut. ...	Bailey, R.	M.C.
	2/Lieut. ...	Tewson, H. V.	M.C.
	2/Lieut. ...	Veal, L. T.	M.C.
	2/Lieut. ...	Simpson, J. H....	Croix de Guerre.
	2/Lieut. ...	Kermode, E. M.	M.C.
			Bar to M.C.
			D.S.O.
	2/Lieut. ...	Donkersley, R.	M.C.
	2/Lieut. ...	Gwynn, A. J.	M.C.
	2/Lieut. ...	McKintoch, W. J.	M.C.
	Lieut. & Q.M....	Riley, T.	M.C.
200372	R.Q.M.S. ...	Richmond, W. E.	M.M.
200026	C.Q.M.S. ...	Pope, A.	M.M.
200783	Sgt.	Abbott, J.	M.M.
201195	Sgt.	Rathke, W. E.	D.C.M.
201129	Sgt.	Pearson, H. A.	M.M.
201012	Sgt.	Huggins, J. W	M.M.
4252	Sgt.	Symonds, W.	M.M.
201115	Sgt.	Irving, J.	M.M.
306966	Sgt.	Horner, J. W.	D.C.M.
238027	Sgt.	Campbell, R. W.	D.C.M.
201138	Sgt.	Wright, —.	M.M.
200950	Sgt.	Sigsworth, W.	M.M.
200047	C.Q.M.S. ...	Greaves, G. E.	M.M.
252897	L.-Sgt. ...	Priestley, H.	Bar to M.M.
42438	Cpl.	Moody, J. A.	M.M.
200436	Cpl.	White, J. H.	M.M.
200463	Cpl.	Hudson, T.	M.M.
200985	Cpl.	Cole, A.	M.M.
42436	Cpl.	Burdett, T. H.	M.M.
42120	Cpl.	Raw, J. R.	M.M.
4265	L.-Cpl. ...	Marston, T.	M.M.
3717	L.-Cpl. ...	Crust, J. W.	M.M.
305451	L.-Cpl. ...	Shepherd, H.	M.M.
42032	L.-Cpl. ...	Briggs, F.	M.M.
201126	L.-Cpl. ...	Bradley, J.	M.M.
			Bar to M.M.
201557	L.-Cpl. ...	Newbank, J.	M.M.
			Bar to M.M.
200094	L.-Cpl. ...	Lamb, C. W.	M.M.
265469	L.-Cpl. ...	Crowther, C.	M.M.
267154	L.-Cpl. ...	Brear, G. W.	M.M.

2/5TH WEST YORKSHIRE REGIMENT—*continued.*

Regtl. No.	Rank.	Name.	Award.
20166	L.-Cpl.	Falconer, J. S.	M.M.
202109	L.-Cpl.	Appleby, S. P.	M.M.
3700	L.-Cpl.	Plumb, F.	M.M.
5264	L.-Cpl.	Taylor, W.	M.M.
268521	L.-Cpl.	Keteley, J. C.	M.M.
201935	L.-Cpl.	Holliday, R.	M.M.
200162	L.-Cpl.	Waite, R.	M.M.
42044	L.-Cpl.	Damme, R.	M.M.
203581	L.-Cpl.	Stones, J.	Decoration Militaire (Belgian).
42028	L.-Cpl.	Bevens, G. H.	M.M.
202019	Pte.	Collinson, A. E.	M.M.
200858	Pte.	Foster, W. V.	M.M.
20476	Pte.	McGrigor, J.	M.M.
201361	Pte.	Grasby, J. W.	M.M.
200982	Pte.	Doe, C. ...	M.M.
11307	Pte.	Bell, S. D.	M.M.
202093	Pte.	Bingham, T.	M.M.
38216	Pte.	Rushworth, A.	M.M.
48379	Pte.	Haigh, W.	M.M.
52035	Pte.	Cope, R.	M.M.
203630	Pte.	Bryant, C. E.	M.M.
201202	Pte.	Smith, J.	D.C.M. M.M.
203773	Pte.	Beetham, H.	D.C.M.
57492	Pte.	Boult, J. R.	M.M.
41785	Pte.	Page, P....	M.M.
57460	Pte.	Ross, D. G.	M.M.
42016	Pte.	Allen, A. E.	M.M.
52004	Pte.	Aves, C. A.	M.M.
20484	Pte.	Platt, A. T.	M.M.
57191	Pte.	Plant, H. G.	M.M.
241936	Pte.	Allinson, W. B.	M.M.
53706	Pte.	Raynor, W.	M.M.
59207	Pte.	Cross, A.	M.M.
40973	Pte.	Dagg, J. T.	M.M.
201163	Pte.	Sheard, B.	M.M.
59588	Pte.	Johnson, J.	M.M.
20928	Pte.	Smith, H.	M.M.
201908	Pte.	Day, A.	M.M.
201906	Pte.	Broomfield, J.	M.M.

2/6TH WEST YORKSHIRE REGIMENT.

	Lt.Col. ...	Hastings, J. H....	D.S.O.
	Lt.-Col....	Hoare, C. H.	D.S.O. Bar to D.S.O.
	Major	Whiteaway, E. G. L.	M.C.
	Captain ...	Smith, H.	M.C.
	Lieut.	Ling, G. F. M.	M.C. Bar to M.C.
	Lieut.	Stewart, G. F.	D.S.O.
	Lieut.	Lawrence, F. C.	M.C.
	2/Lieut. ...	Frost, T.	M.C.
	2/Lieut. ...	Rhodes, H.	M.C.
	2/Lieut. ...	Bickerdike, R.	M.C.
	2/Lieut. ...	Humphries, E. B.	M.C.
	2/Lieut. ...	Allett, J. R.	M.C.
	2/Lieut. ...	Brookbank, G. E. J.	M.C.
	2/Lieut. ...	Hodgson, G. H.	M.C.

2/6TH WEST YORKSHIRE REGIMENT—*continued*.

Regtl. No.	Rank.	Name.	Award.
	2/Lieut. ...	Worth, J.	M.C.
	2/Lieut. ...	Moor, J.	M.C.
	2/Lieut. ...	Bonsor, G. F.	M.C.
	Lieut. & Q.M.	Welch, A.	M.C.
7840	R.S.M.	Brough, A.	M.C.
			D.C.M.
240730	C.S.M. ...	Silkstone, M.	D.C.M.
241831	Sgt.	Huggins, W.	D.C.M.
201284	Sgt.	Banfield, H.	D.C.M.
240954	Sgt.	Robinson, A.	M.M.
240788	Sgt.	Aldrid, E.	M.M.
241047	Sgt.	Pickles, H.	M.M.
242062	Sgt.	Taylor, J. R.	M.M.
202528	L.-Sgt. ...	Piper, A.	D.C.M.
242001	Cpl.	Binnington, R.	D.C.M.
241043	Cpl.	Sadler, F. N.	M.M.
4995	Cpl.	Heart, A.	M.M.
201126	Cpl.	Bradley, J.	M.M.
241356	Cpl.	Ellis, E.	M.M.
240069	Cpl.	Lawford, J.	M.M.
241246	Cpl.	Westerman, A. W.	M.M.
241718	Cpl.	Speight, E.	M.M.
12078	Cpl.	Moore, J.	D.C.M.
			Bar to D.C.M.
241124	L.-Cpl. ...	Sellers. H.	M.M.
240105	L.-Cpl. ...	Sellars, E.	M.M.
241744	L.-Cpl. ...	Boyle, T.	D.C.M.
40152	L.-Cpl. ...	Gamble, R.	M.M.
240132	L.-Cpl. ...	Healey, H.	M.M.
306068	L.-Cpl. ...	Hudson, W. H.	M.M.
200971	L.-Cpl. ...	Andrews, W.	M.M.
24183	L.-Cpl. ...	Garbett, S.	M.M.
2746	Pte.	Pickthall, W.	M.M.
242987	Pte.	Russell, E.	M.M.
240931	Pte.	Haseltine, L.	M.M.
203744	Pte.	Hobson, J. A.	M.M.
203487	Pte.	Allinson, J. H.	M.M.
266968	Pte	Hird, S.	M.M.
306624	Pte.	Wright, A.	M.M.
41950	Pte.	Matthews, L. G.	M.M.
242462	Pte.	Mosley, A.	M.M.
21529	Pte.	Self, R.	M.M.
203058	Pte.	Brown, F.	M.M.
41981	Pte.	Hambleton, F.	M.M.
241211	Pte.	Benn, W.	M.M.
17682	Pte.	Emmett, G.	M.M.
240203	Pte.	Hard, S. H.	M.M.
241866	Pte.	Busfield, J. H.	M.M.
203442	Pte.	Gelby, W.	M.M.
41973	Pte.	Johnson, A.	M.M.

2/7TH WEST YORKSHIRE REGIMENT.

Regtl. No.	Rank.	Name.	Award.
	Lt.-Col. ...	James, C. K.	D.S.O.
			Bar to D.S.O.
	Captain ...	Cooper, S. R.	M.C.
	Lieut. ...	Hannam, C. D.	M.C.
	Lieut. ...	Hamilton, J. S.	D.S.O.
	Lieut. ...	Raven, G. E.	M.C.
	2/Lieut. ...	Chance, J.	M.C.
			D.C.M.

2/7TH WEST YORKSHIRE REGIMENT—*continued.*

Regtl. No.	Rank.	Name.	Award.
	2/Lieut.	Swaney, L. T.	M.C.
	2/Lieut.	Hall, J. ...	M.C.
	2/Lieut.	Ling, G. F. M.	M.C.
	2/Lieut.	Mowen, C. H.	M.C.
	2/Lieut.	Jones, L. R.	M.C.
	2/Lieut.	Sagar-Musgrave, C. L.	M.C.
	2/Lieut.	Fane, F. L.	M.C.
	2/Lieut.	Bazley-White, J.	M.C.
	2/Lieut.	Edwards, C. G.	D.S.O.
	2/Lieut.	Brown, W. R.	M.C.
	2/Lieut.	Rugh, W.	M.C.
	2/Lieut.	Donne, P.	M.C.
	2/Lieut	Tillotson, J. E....	D.S.O. M.C.
238203	C.S.M. ...	Cropper, J.	D.C.M. M.M.
	C.S.M. ...	Sykes, T.	D.C.M.
	Sgt.	Smith, A.	D.C.M.
267100	Sgt.	Wells, T.	D.C.M M.M. Bar to M.M.
202522	Sgt.	Lancaster, C. F.	M.M.
3508	Sgt.	McHugh, J.	M.M.
2929	Sgt.	Gavins, J.	M.M.
265747	Sgt.	Dean, T.	M.M.
267000	Sgt.	Holmes, H. E.	D.C.M.
265918	C.S.M. ...	Rosindale, H. ...	M.C.
303015	C.S.M. ...	Robson, J. M. ...	D.C.M.
265720	Sgt.	Burns, W.	M.M.
266033	Sgt.	Stead, H.	M.M.
3038	Sgt.	Cooper, C.	M.M.
267466	Sgt.	Smith, T.	M.M.
203478	L.-Sgt. ...	Bone, C.	M.M.
266385	Cpl.	Riley, O.	M.M.
266407	Cpl.	Elsworth, C.	M.M.
266325	Cpl.	Dutton, J.	M.M.
267136	Cpl.	Little, W.	M.M.
266165	L.-Cpl. ...	Yates, F.	M.M.
275830	L.-Cpl. ...	Dickinson, —. ...	Medaille Militaire (French).
365062	L.-Cpl. ...	Hirst, C.	M.M.
266131	L.-Cpl. ...	Child, J. A.	M.M.
39555	L.-Cpl. ...	Webb, H.	M.M.
43338	L.-Cpl. ...	White, G. E.	M.M.
16189	L.-Cpl. ...	Precious, G.	M.M.
22211	L.-Cpl. ...	Metcalf, T.	D.C.M.
39615	L.-Cpl. ...	Connor, T.	M.M.
266411	L.-Cpl. ...	Arnold, G. C.	M.M.
266418	L.-Cpl. ...	Izatt, R.	M.M.
4940	Rfm.	Wells, T.	M.M.
3443	Rfm.	Leach, A.	M.M.
267274	Rfm.	Walker, J. W. ...	M.M.
267313	Rfm.	Atkinson, H.	M.M.
267121	Rfm.	Walker, A.	M.M.
266124	Rfm.	Green, C.	M.M.
17331	Rfm.	Oates, S.	M.M.
403165	Rfm.	Bourn, W. O. H.	M.M.
52083	Rfm.	Lordan, D.	M.M.
52308	Rfm.	March, A.	M.M.
265714	Rfm.	Walgate, G.	M.M.
266240	Rfm.	Barker, W. W....	M.M.
51881	Rfm.	White, F.	M.M.

2/7TH WEST YORKSHIRE REGIMENT—*continued.*

Regtl. No.	Rank.	Name.	Award.
266494	Rfm.	Turner, E.	M.M.
26449	Rfm.	Trench, W.	M.M.
268661	Rfm.	Mortimer, R.	M.M.
267621	Rfm.	Tompofski, M.	M.M.
270176	Rfm.	Watson, C. H.	M.M.
586317	Rfm.	Coinllault, L. H.	M.M.
3–596	Rfm.	Leake, J. R.	M.M.
24178	Rfm.	Roberts, D.	M.M.
205542	Rfm.	Holmes, J.	M.M.

2/8TH WEST YORKSHIRE REGIMENT.

Regtl. No.	Rank.	Name.	Award.
	Lt.-Col.... ...	James, A. H.	D.S.O.
	Lt.-Col.... ...	England, N. A.	D.S.O.
	Major	Whiteaway, E. G. L.	M.C. Bar to M.C.
	Captain ...	Kinder, G. G.	M.C.
	Captain ...	Wall, D. L.	M.C.
	Captain ...	Hutchinson, B.	M.C.
	Captain ...	Reay, P. T.	M.C.
	Captain ...	Milligan, A.	M.C.
	Captain ...	Taft, C. F. T.	M.C.
	Captain ...	Hirst, G. M.	M.C.
	Capt. & Q.M. ...	Farrar, B.	M.C.
	Lieut. ...	Jowett, P.	M.C.
	Lieut. ...	Burrows, H. R.	M.C. Croix de Guerre.
	Lieut. ...	Graves, H. J.	M.C.
	Lieut. ...	Friend, C.	M.C.
	Lieut. ...	Pyman, J.	M.C.
	2/Lieut. ...	Nicholson, F.	M.C.
	2/Lieut. ...	Nethercot, R. P.	M.C.
	2/Lieut. ...	Crabtree, R. M.	M.C. Bar to M.C.
	2/Lieut. ...	Hartley, W. H.	M.C.
	2/Lieut. ...	Bullock, A.	M.C.
	2/Lieut. ...	Naylor, A.	M.C.
	2/Lieut. ...	Harrison, I. R. S.	M.C.
	2/Lieut. ...	Henderson, A.	M.C.
	2/Lieut. ...	Oates, A. H.	M.C.
	2/Lieut. ...	Monkman, G.	M.C.
	2/Lieut. ...	Foster, S.	M.C.
	2/Lieut. ...	Hauson, F.	M.C.
	2/Lieut. ...	McLintock, W. C.	Croix de Guerre.
	2/Lieut. ...	Clay, G. F.	M.C.
	Lieut.	Stead, C. V.	M.C.
306197	C.S.M.	Wheeler, W.	M.M.
7047	C.S.M.	Winters, H. E.	M.M.
	C.Q.M.S. ...	Leisham, J.	M.S.M.
18/209	C.Q.M.S. ...	Oliver, J.	M.M.
305674	Sgt.	Gowar, T. H.	M.M.
306265	Sgt.	Speight, H.	D.C.M.
306251	Sgt.	Andrews, W.	M.M.
303966	Sgt.	Horner, J.	M.M.
305374	Sgt.	Elliott, G. N.	M.M.
305960	Sgt.	Wilson, J.	M.M.
306144	Sgt.	Crymble, A.	M.M.
306795	Sgt.	Buttery, E. F.	M.M.
306238	Sgt.	Bryce, J.	M.M.
305700	Sgt.	Hutton, W. R.	D.C.M.
305621	Sgt.	Bullock, F. H. T.	M.S.M.

2/8TH WEST YORKSHIRE REGIMENT—*continued*.

Regtl. No.	Rank.	Name.	Award.
201685	Sgt.	Suffil, S. G.	M.S.M.
305958	Sgt.	Hipps, J.	M.M.
305213	Sgt.	Swarbeck, H.	M.M.
306413	Sgt.	Lockridge, W.	M.M.
306818	Sgt.	Stanhope, J.	M.M.
59618	Sgt.	Hubbard, C. F.	M.M.
305932	Sgt.	Richardson, J.	M.M.
235234	Sgt.	Mulrooney, H.	M.M.
265562	Sgt.	Trott, J. W.	M.M.
265422	Sgt.	Elsworth, R. J.	D.C.M.
306674	Sgt.	Booker, A.	M.M.
365685	Sgt.	Gough, H. T.	M.M.
305814	Sgt.	Threadgould, H.	M.M.
305804	Sgt.	Broadley, G.	D.C.M.
305904	Sgt.	Audsley, F.	M.M.
306209	L.-Sgt.	Wallis, T.	M.M.
42393	L.-Sgt.	Pamment, C.	M.M. Bar to M.M.
241935	L.-Sgt.	Hensey, R.	M.M.
305183	Cpl.	Elliott, D. W.	M.M.
305404	Cpl.	Dunant, E.	M.M.
42378	Cpl.	Brown, H.	M.M.
306280	Cpl.	Russell, F. T.	M.M.
305066	Cpl.	Latts, A.	M.M.
15760	Cpl.	Emms, F.	M.M.
305726	Cpl.	Webster, F.	M.M. Bar to M.M.
201025	Cpl.	Earl, H.	M.M.
24535	Cpl.	Stevenson, J.	M.M.
15–1744	Cpl.	West, W. B.	M.M.
52909	Cpl.	Briggs, T.	D.C.M.
240436	Cpl.	Hill, H.	M.S.M.
305949	L.-Cpl.	Athe, F.	M.M.
305208	L.-Cpl.	Markinson, J.	D.C.M. M.M.
236016	L.-Cpl.	Shepherd, H. R.	M.M.
18–158	L.-Cpl.	Garside, G. F.	M.M.
306898	L.-Cpl.	Sawyer, H.	M.M.
201997	L.-Cpl.	Kelly, J. H.	M.M.
37391	L.-Cpl.	Anderson, S.	M.M.
20166	L.-Cpl.	Falconer, J.	D.C.M. M.M.
3370	L.-Sgt.	Potts, W. E.	M.M.
4548	L.-Cpl.	Priestley, J.	M.M.
306240	L.-Cpl.	McCourt, E. P.	M.M.
13–383	L.-Cpl.	Emmett, S.	M.M. Bar to M.M.
241152	L.-Cpl.	Hollings, F.	M.M.
305209	L.-Cpl.	Wise, W.	M.M.
266418	L.-Cpl.	Izitt, R.	M.M.
46068	L.-Cpl.	Caset, T. M.	M.M.
15–1226	L.-Cpl.	Todd, J. E.	M.M.
265746	L.-Cpl.	Winn, W.	M.M.
307403	L.-Cpl.	McCready, T. R. V. ...	M.M.
20578	L.-Cpl.	Lewis, C.	M.M.
266208	L.-Cpl.	Wainwright, R.	M.M.
8171	L.-Cpl.	Carney, J.	M.M.
58777	L.-Cpl.	Keen, W.	M.M.
305223	L.-Cpl.	Slater, H.	M.M.
59164	L.-Cpl.	Youds, G.	M.M.
307755	L.-Cpl.	Sykes, A.	M.M.

2/8TH WEST YORKSHIRE REGIMENT—*continued.*

Regtl. No.	Rank.	Name.	Award.
60286	L.-Cpl.	Swynhoe, J.	M.M.
61028	L.-Cpl.	Leach, W.	M.M.
20442	L.-Cpl.	Booth, C. L.	M.M.
43397	Rfm.	Bird, W.	M.M.
305111	Rfm.	Pratt, D. C.	M.M.
42889	Rfm.	Stockdale, A.	M.M.
306774	Rfm.	Greenwood, L.	M.M.
8055	Rfm.	Cooper, F.	M.M.
205144	Rfm.	Lumbley, G.	M.M.
24144	Rfm.	Willoughby, J. H.	M.M.
27605	Rfm.	Clunie, A.	M.M.
58868	Rfm.	Hakey, J. H.	M.M.
205506	Rfm.	Harrison, R. E.	M.M.
205143	Rfm.	Collier, F.	M.M.
63934	Rfm.	Routledge, W.	M.M.
305447	Rfm.	Westerman, D.	M.M.
306092	Rfm.	Schofield, A.	M.M.
42440	Rfm.	Butler, W.	M.M.
61033	Rfm.	Cooper, G.	M.M.
60609	Rfm.	Dobson, G.	M.M.
306746	Rfm.	Owens, W.	M.M.
63912	Rfm.	Longbottom, E.	M.M.
13633	Rfm.	Taylor, A.	M.M.
60475	Rfm.	Reed, J. W.	M.M.
16–107	Rfm.	Grayson, A.	M.M.
2993	Rfm.	Preval, S.	M.M.
3730	Rfm.	Draycott, B.	M.M.
306873	Rfm.	Gough, W.	M.M.
308646	Rfm.	Sutton, P.	M.M.
306188	Rfm.	Harland, T.	M.M.
306362	Rfm.	Hirst, J.	M.M.
235247	Rfm.	McGowan, A.	M.M.
306202	Rfm.	Morton, T.	M.M.
307729	Rfm.	Schofield, J.	M.M.
306218	Rfm.	Wilby, A.	M.M.
39331	Rfm.	Ibbitson, J. H.	M.M.
267732	Rfm.	Ibbitson, W.	M.M.
307766	Rfm.	Rooney, J.	M.M.
14–13409	Rfm.	Lunn, A.	M.M.
57267	Rfm.	Jackson, A.	M.M.
306506	Rfm.	Russell, R.	M.M.
306113	Rfm.	Rawcliffe, H.	M.M.
306297	Rfm.	Hallas, H.	M.M.
306810	Rfm.	Gaunt, I.	M.M.
306864	Rfm.	Issitt, R.	M.M.
57449	Rfm.	Newrick, I. C.	M.M.
306274	Rfm.	Hutchinson, M. A.	M.M.
40210	Rfm.	Cross, S. L.	M.M.
39497	Rfm.	Harrison, J. J.	M.M.
61919	Rfm.	Marsh, G.	M.M.
266321	Rfm.	Gibson, H.	M.M.
			Bar to M.M.
53953	Rfm.	Eagin, S. E.	M.M.
61949	Rfm.	Robinson, W. E.	M.M.
307254	Rfm.	Wilkinson, T.	M.M.
305968	Rfm.	North, H.	M.M.
16–62	Rfm.	Beasley, J.	M.M.
58765	Rfm.	Shepherd, H.	M.M.
267455	Rfm.	Colman, G.	M.M.
60703	Rfm.	Barnett, C. H.	M.M.
267197	Rfm.	Goodall, A.	M.M.

2/8TH WEST YORKSHIRE REGIMENT—*continued.*

Regtl. No.	Rank.	Name.	Award.
27582	Rfm.	Bell, T.	M.M.
42815	Rfm.	Allan, G.	M.M.
40804	Rfm.	Palframan, J.	M.M.
62441	Rfm.	Smith, P.	M.M.
40633	Rfm.	Haywood, H.	M.M.
39440	Rfm.	Hirst, A.	M.M.
42395	Rfm.	Robinson, J. S.	M.M.
307108	Rfm.	Lax, T.	M.M.
52337	Rfm.	Smith, W. T.	M.M.
306703	Rfm.	Worrall, C. L.	M.M.
58787	Rfm.	Darlington, J. R.	M.M.
306731	Rfm.	Prentice, J. E.	M.M.
266112	Rfm.	Collinson, J.	M.M.
52471	Rfm.	Spurway, G.	M.M.
59620	Rfm.	Emms, G.	M.M.
305147	Rfm.	Mellor, J. L.	M.M.
53747	Rfm.	Tinker, W.	M.M.
38494	Rfm.	Hinchliffe, A.	M.M.
39356	Rfm.	Kermody, C.	M.M.
81373	Rfm.	Binns, J. H.	M.M.
39568	Rfm.	Fairlie, C.	M.M.
59620	Rfm.	Freeman, S.	M.M.
49515	Rfm.	Haw, H.	M.M.
305868	Rfm.	Curry, J.	M.M.
268038	Rfm.	Jeffrey, H.	M.M.
52146	Rfm.	Warrell, W.	M.M.
52119	Rfm.	Reading, F.	M.M.
236316	Rfm.	Carter, F.	M.M.
20366	Rfm.	Holdsworth, F.	M.M.
306294	Sglr.	Curnock, B.	M.M.
24323	Sglr.	Collephy, H.	M.M.
267658	Sglr.	Scott, H.	M.M.
63779	Bdsmn.	Clarke, J.	M.M.

2/4TH WEST RIDING REGIMENT.

	Rank.	Name.	Award.
	Lt.-Col. ...	Nash, H. E. P.	D.S.O.
	Captain ...	Smithson, W.	M.C.
	Captain ...	Stocks, J.	M.C.
	Captain ...	Lupton, B. C.	M.C.
			Bar to M.C.
	Captain ...	Threappleton, —.	Croix de Guerre.
	Lieut. ...	Sherrick, J. W. (U.S.) ...	M.C.
	Lieut. ...	Sayers, R. H.	M.C.
	2/Lieut. ...	Cordingley, L.	M.C.
	2/Lieut. ...	Knowles, W.	M.C.
	2/Lieut. ...	Castle, J. P.	D.S.O.
	2/Lieut. ...	Metcalf, H.	M.C.
	2/Lieut. ...	Irons, J. H.	M.C.
	2/Lieut. ...	Duckett, R.	M.C.
	2/Lieut. ...	Hully, M.	M.C.
	2/Lieut. ...	Dunnett, J. H.	M.C.
			Bar to M.C.
	2/Lieut. ...	Scott, B.	M.C.
			Bar to M.C.
	2/Lieut. ...	Potter, A. C.	M.C.
	2/Lieut. ...	Cram, J. E.	M.C.
	2/Lieut ...	Radcliffe, H.	M.C.
	2/Lieut. ...	Saunders, W.	M.C.
			M.M.

2/4TH WEST RIDING REGIMENT—*continued*.

Regtl. No.	Rank.	Name.	Award.
	2/Lieut. ...	Spafford, A. V.	M.C.
	2/Lieut. ...	Bilsbrough, H. J.	M.C.
	2/Lieut. ...	Marsden, F. K.	M.C.
	2/Lieut. ...	Walker. H. W.	M.C.
202940	R.Q.M.S.	Lowes, W. R.	M.S.M.
203174	C.S.M. ...	Wilcox, R. P.	D.C.M.
			Bar to D.C.M.
201254	C.S.M. ...	Taylor, L.	D.C.M.
265479	C.S.M. ...	Peacock, E.	M.M.
34578	C.S.M. ...	Elliott, J. J. S.	M.M.
			Bar to M.M.
200455	C.S.M. ...	Hoyle, W. H.	M.C.
10908	C.S.M. ...	Mann, J. H.	D.C.M.
201134	Q.M.S. ...	Furness, F.	M.M.
201170	C.Q.M.S.	Wood, A.	M.M.
201583	Sgt. ...	Kingham, S.	M.M.
201680	Sgt. ...	Spetch, J. R.	M.M.
200709	Sgt. ...	Beverley, G.	M.M.
201217	Sgt. ...	Heaton, H.	M.M.
305265	Sgt. ...	Garrod, G.	M.S.M.
201273	Sgt. ...	Harrison, E.	M.S.M.
201066	Sgt. ...	Hipwood, J.	M.M.
201458	Sgt. ...	Smith, W. H.	D.C.M.
			M.M.
202122	Sgt. ...	Haigh, A.	M.M.
200735	Sgt. ...	Greenwood, E....	M.M.
201000	Sgt. ...	Hay, H....	M.M.
306764	Sgt. ...	Redfearn, E.	M.M.
			Bar to M.M.
201649	Sgt. ...	Thompson, A.	D.C.M.
200707	Sgt. ...	Whitebread, F.	M.M.
202257	Sgt. ...	Crabtree, A.	M.M.
200798	Sgt. ...	Crossley, W.	D.C.M.
200897	Sgt. ...	Hoyle, E. H.	M.M.
263065	Sgt. ...	Clayton, F.	M.M.
235044	Sgt. ...	Madden, D.	D.C.M.
267261	Sgt. ...	Holmes, F.	M.M.
266173	Sgt. ...	Blackburn, A.	M.M.
201295	Sgt. ...	Nettleton, F.	M.S.M.
205610	L.-Sgt. ...	Scott, A.	M.M.
265081	L.-Sgt. ...	Scarborough, J. W. ...	M.S.M.
49839	Cpl. ...	Smith, E.	M.M.
201630	L.-Sgt. ...	Greenwood, H.	M.M.
265294	Cpl. ...	Falkingham, H.	D.C.M.
34628	Cpl. ...	Scotton, H.	D.C.M.
			M.M.
201774	Cpl. ...	Hanson, F.	D.C.M.
200708	Cpl. ...	Berry, K.	M.M.
266167	Cpl. ...	Rowley, C.	M.M.
306966	Cpl. ...	Kirton, C. W.	M.M.
201148	L.-Cpl. ...	Hanson, H.	M.M.
200800	L.-Cpl. ...	Foulds, W.	D.C.M.
			M.M.
22406	L.-Cpl. ...	Atkins, G.	M.M.
34721	L.-Cpl. ...	Cowell, A.	M.M.
201544	L.-Cpl. ...	Matthews, P.	M.M.
24981	L.-Cpl. ...	Waller, D.	M.M.
263171	L.-Cpl. ...	Mitchell, G.	M.M.
205531	L.-Cpl. ...	Hegarty, R.	M.M.
241737	L.-Cpl. ...	Freshwater, E.	M.M.
306026	L.-Cpl. ...	Haigh, G. A.	M.M.

2/4TH WEST RIDING REGIMENT—*continued.*

Regtl. No.	Rank.	Name.	Award.
265844	L.-Cpl.	Smith, W.	M.M.
202333	L.-Cpl.	Smith, S.	M.M.
202398	L.-Cpl.	Horner, R.	M.M.
3053	Pte.	Astin, W.	D.C.M.
8825	Pte.	Allen, S.	M.M.
202441	Pte.	Butterworth, S.	D.C.M.
201484	Pte.	Greenwood, H.	M.M.
200968	Pte.	Hind, S.	M.M.
3562	Pte.	Sunderland, E.	M.S.M.
201209	Pte.	Sutcliffe, W.	M.M.
202253	Pte.	Barrett, W.	M.M.
31910	Pte.	Calligan, S.	M.M.
201051	Pte.	Smith, W. H.	M.M.
202382	Pte.	Rawnsley, H.	M.M.
202305	Pte.	Cotton, T. J.	D.C.M.
238024	Pte.	Kershaw, A.	M.M.
201294	Pte.	Nutton, E.	M.M.
204069	Pte.	Hutchinson, N. B. ...	M.M.
202075	Pte.	Kelly, T.	M.M.
202017	Pte.	Walford, J.	M.M.
256394	Pte.	Marshall, W. A.	M.M.
245738	Pte.	Taylor, J.	M.M.
49796	Pte.	Shackleton, R.	M.M.
235728	Pte.	Heslop, W.	M.M.
307574	Pte.	Maude, H.	M.M.
35278	Pte.	Allen, A. V.	M.M.
49836	Pte.	Lister, H.	M.M.
44634	Pte.	Priest, F. C.	M.M.
34718	Pte.	Ash, A. C.	M.M.
201072	Pte.	Mitchell, B.	M.M.
202236	Pte.	Dumstead, A.	M.M.
22382	Pte.	Eastgate, S.	M.M.
235572	Pte.	Hall, H.	M.M.
202046	Pte.	Henley, C.	M.M.
22484	Pte.	Johnson, J.	M.M.
202066	Pte.	Ellis, C. H.	M.M.
202227	Pte.	Woodhead, H.	M.M.
350417	Pte.	Crabtree, W. H.	M.M.
34327	Pte.	Cleghorn, R.	M.M.
34720	Pte.	Cardon, J.	M.M.
22367	Pte.	Tranter, W.	M.M.
24135	Pte.	Rodgers, J.	M.M.
34860	Pte.	McGarvey, M.	M.M.
40086	Pte.	Reay, J. L. T.	M.M.
26318	Pte.	Bennett, F.	M.M.
267405	Pte.	Firth, H.	M.M.
267199	Pte.	Richardson, F. L. ...	M.M.
202133	Pte.	Massey, J. T.	M.M.
201540	Pte.	Woodhead, A.	M.M.
200620	Pte.	Jones, A.	M.M.
202472	Pte.	Sunderland, W.	M.M.
203564	Pte.	Shaw, H.	M.M.
306781	Pte.	Fox, H.	M.M.
267128	Pte.	Feather, E.	M.M.
201536	Pte.	Patchett, J. H.	M.M.
31749	Pte.	Hamer, J. A.	Croix de Guerre.
17491	Pte.	Mote, F. T.	M.M.
201239	Pte.	Patrick, A.	M.M.
11760	Pte.	Lipman, J.	M.M.
205560	Pte.	Robertshaw, P.	M.M.
203075	Pte.	Allison, J.	M.M.

2/4TH WEST RIDING REGIMENT—*continued.*

Regtl. No.	Rank.	Name.	Award.
46783	Pte.	Haines, E.	M.M.
			Bar to M.M.
9154	Pte.	Blythe, T.	M.M.
			Bar to M.M.
266273	Pte.	Cockerill, B.	M.M.
			Bar to M.M.
322103	Pte.	Dodd, J. A.	M.M.
22372	Pte.	Bailey, A.	M.M.
235711	Pte.	Robinson, A.	M.M.
201614	Pte.	Barber, V.	M.M.
22506	Pte.	Atkins, D.	M.M.
32836	Pte.	Bradley, A.	M.M.
308095	Pte.	Whitehouse, H.	M.M.
32417	Pte.	Hardcastle, F.	M.M.
33475	Pte.	Bennett, G. H.... ...	M.M.
257247	Pte.	Livesey, P.	M.M.
267774	Pte.	Cockerill, B.	M.M.
266273	Pte.	Broughton, A.	M.M.
308063	Pte.	Shannon, R.	M.M.
10504	Pte.	Massheder, J.	M.M.
			Bar to M.M.
242061	Pte.	North, S.	M.M.
202115	Pte.	Waterfield, C.	M.M.
32641	Pte.	Lockwood, A.	M.M.
26840	Pte.	Booth, G. R.	M.M.
25125	Pte.	Pindred, J. W.	M.M.
203844	Pte.	Hart, A. J.	M.M.
202310	Pte.	Blacks, S.	M.M.
265791	Pte.	Wood, T.	M.M.
26376	Pte.	Glading, A.	M.M.
266258	Dmr.	Lyons, F.	M.M.

2/5TH WEST RIDING REGIMENT.

Regtl. No.	Rank.	Name.	Award.
	Lt.-Col. ...	Best, T. A. D.	D.S.O.
			Bar to D.S.O.
	Lt.-Col. ...	Walker, J.	D.S.O.
	Captain ...	Jackson, H. S.	D.S.O.
	Captain ...	Robinson, W.	M.C.
	Captain ...	Goodall, T.	D.S.O.
	Captain ...	Moxon, C. S.	D.S.O.
	Captain ...	Sykes, K.	M.C.
			Croix de Guerre.
	Captain ...	Watkinson, P. J.	M.C.
	Captain ...	Tinker, G. L. ... ... •••	M.C.
	Captain ...	Cockhill, J. B.	D.S.O.
			M.C.
	Captain ...	Ellis, C. G. H....	D.S.O.
			M.C.
	Lieut.	Harris, E. W.	M.C.
	Lieut.	Bernay, G. V.	M.C.
	Lieut.	Black, D.	M.C.
	Lieut.	Tod, J. McK.	M.C.
	Lieut.	Mollett, B.	M.C.
			Bar to M.C.
	Lieut.	Yates, W.	M.C.
	Lieut.	Osincup, G. S....	M.C.
	Lieut.	Walte, H. F.	M.C.
	Lieut.	Ridley, P. R.	M.C.

2/5TH WEST RIDING REGIMENT—*continued.*

Regtl. No.	Rank.	Name.	Award.
	2/Lieut. ...	Jack, A. S.	M.C.
	2/Lieut. ...	Morton, T. R.	M.C.
	2/Lieut. ...	Dodd, G. M.	M.C.
	2/Lieut. ...	Chapman, F.	M.C.
	2/Lieut. ...	Barnes, P. R.	M.C.
	2/Lieut. ...	Machin, J. R.	M.C.
	2/Lieut. ...	Walker, L. F.	M.C.
	2/Lieut. ...	Hogan, J.	M.C.
	Revd.	Wright, A. B.	M.C.
9323	R.S.M.	Earle, B.	Italian Bronze Medal.
240139	C.S.M.	Hulse, W.	M.M.
240358	C.S.M.	Fisher, W.	D.C.M. M.M.
240101	C.S.M.	Schofield, H.	D.C.M.
240222	C.S.M.	Jones, G. V.	D.C.M.
340598	C.S.M.	Waterhouse, C. E.	D.C.M.
12275	C.S.M.	Handby, K.	D.C.M.
240957	C.S.M.	Dennis, W. H.	M.M.
240431	C.Q.M.S. ...	Pedley, J.	M.S.M.
240829	C.Q.M.S. ...	Airey, W.	M.S.M.
	C.S.M.	Wilkinson, W. S.	D.C.M.
241414	Sgt.	Priestley, E.	M.M.
240950	Sgt.	Mitchell, R.	M.M.
12391	Sgt.	Dean, F. E.	M.M.
240719	Sgt.	Eastwood, H. R.	M.M.
266035	Sgt.	Burrows, G.	M.M.
241337	Sgt.	Siswick, B.	D.C.M. Bar to D.C.M.
15807	Sgt.	Hamshaw, J.	M.M.
12886	Sgt.	Greaves, G. R....	M.M. Bar to M.M.
306308	Sgt.	McNay, W.	M.M.
242879	Sgt.	Hazle, R.	M.M. Bar to M.M.
202122	Sgt.	Haigh, A.	M.M. Bar to M.M.
240156	Sgt.	Ware, G. A. W.	M.M.
241704	Sgt.	Dyson, B.	M.M.
15002	Sgt.	Judson, M.	M.M.
240763	Sgt.	Hepworth, T.	M.M.
235755	Sgt.	Pearson, A.	M.M.
241596	Sgt.	Draper, F. N.	M.M.
240320	Sgt.	Micklethwaite, F.	M.S.M.
240076	Sgt.	Lee, S. H.	D.C.M. Bar to D.C.M.
240008	Sgt.	Merriman, H. S.	D.C.M. M.M. Bar to M.M.
240219	L.-Sgt.	Field, R.	M.M.
268050	L.-Sgt.	Spivey, F.	M.M. Bar to M.M.
306019	L.-Sgt.	Sykes, H.	M.M.
266170	L.-Sgt.	Southgate, H.	M.M.
240157	Sgt.	Allen, W. B.	M.M. Bar to M.M.
25069	Cpl.	Cockrane, J.	M.M.
203206	Cpl.	Gledhill, J.	M.M.
240970	Cpl.	Quarterman, R. C.	M.M.
241689	Cpl.	Parker, C. F.	M.M.
265094	Cpl.	Shires, H.	D.C.M.
11099	Cpl.	Williams, C.	M.M.

2/5TH WEST RIDING REGIMENT—*continued.*

Regtl. No.	Rank.	Name.	Award.
240832	Cpl.	Cox, A. F.	M.M.
267955	Cpl.	Pemberton, P.	M.M.
266325	Cpl.	Tillotson, S.	M.M.
267226	Cpl.	Simpson, H.	M.M.
308501	Cpl.	Hinchcliffe, J. T.	M.M.
242106	Cpl.	Whitterton, W.	M.M.
238190	Cpl.	Arnold, D.	M.M.
305152	Cpl.	Buckley, T.	D.C.M.
8397	L.-Cpl.	Priestley, H.	M.M.
241742	L.-Cpl.	Johnson, G.	M.M.
240981	L.-Cpl.	Eglinton, C.	M.M.
240971	L.-Cpl.	Halliwell, J.	M.M. Bar to M.M.
201484	L.-Cpl. ...	Greenwood, H.	M.M. Bar to M.M.
202472	L.-Cpl. ...	Sunderland, W.	M.M. Bat to M.M.
267064	L.-Cpl. ...	Bates, J.	M.M. Bar to M.M.
23773	L.-Cpl.	Chapman, J. G.	M.M.
240464	L.-Cpl.	Fawcett, C.	D.C.M.
306466	L.-Cpl.	Parker, A. E.	M.M.
241549	L.-Cpl.	Armitage, J.	M.M.
240954	L.-Cpl.	Nedderman, R. M.	M.M.
205353	L.-Cpl.	Wilkinson, E.	M.M.
241860	L.-Cpl.	Lockwood, H.	M.M.
11013	L.-Cpl.	Grogan, J.	M.M.
14870	L.-Cpl.	Watson, J.	M.M.
10664	L.-Cpl.	Fairburn, J.	M.M. Bar to M.M.
240604	L.-Cpl.	Ingram, G. E.	M.M.
240320	L.-Cpl.	Whiting, W.	M.M.
48495	L.-Cpl.	Bell, E. C.	M.M. Bar to M.M.
33488	L.-Cpl.	Ramsay, R. M.	M.M.
30106	L.-Cpl.	Healey, T. A.	M.M.
242979	L.-Cpl.	Keogh, J. W.	M.M.
34410	L.-Cpl.	Donkin, A. S.	M.M.
17016	L.-Cpl.	Chapman, J.	D.C.M.
240204	L.-Cpl.	Buckley, J.	M.M.
240205	L.-Cpl.	Shaw, L.	M.M.
266072	L.-Cpl.	Rowley, G.	M.M.
24726	L.-Cpl.	Ackroyd, J.	M.M. Bar to M.M.
49707	L.-Cpl.	Hall, R.	M.M.
238188	L.-Cpl.	Straker, R.	M.M.
240858	L.-Cpl.	Ball, E.	M.M.
241907	L.-Cpl.	Garbutt, J.	M.M.
241638	L.-Cpl.	Shoarsmith, E. W.	M.M. Bar to M.M.
241222	L.-Cpl.	Rhodes, C.	M.M.
235629	L.-Cpl.	Levey, J.	M.M.
34510	L.-Cpl.	Wild, F.	M.M.
268800	L.-Cpl.	Barker, W.	M.M.
241030	L.-Cpl.	Farrell, R. P.	M.M.
5100	Pte.	Chapman, C.	French Croix de Guerre.
263029	Pte.	Tipton, W. A.	M.M.
203949	Pte.	Tewlett, S.	M.M.
241049	Pte.	Moete, A.	M.M.
265782	Pte.	Walker, W.	M.M. Bar to M.M.

2/5TH WEST RIDING REGIMENT—*continued*.

Regtl. No.	Rank.			Name.				Award.
25078	Pte.	...	...	Ellis, W.	...	...	...	M.M.
241417	Pte.	...	...	Marsden, W.	...	...	...	M.M.
235092	Pte.	...	...	Slater, H.	...	...	...	M.M.
241688	Pte.	...	...	Robinson, G. G.		...	...	M.M.
								Bar to M.M.
242439	Pte.	...	...	Raistrick, T.	...	...	...	M.M.
								Bar to M.M.
242392	Pte.	...	...	Brook, H.	...	...	...	M.M.
								Bar to M.M.
205564	Pte.	...	...	Shaw, H.	...	...	...	M.M.
								Bar to M.M.
240750	Pte.	...	...	Squires, A.	...	...	...	M.M.
26337	Pte.	...	...	Glass, W.	...	...	...	M.M.
242367	Pte.	...	...	Raynard, J.	...	...	...	M.M.
242759	Pte.	...	...	Pearce, G. W.		...	...	M.M.
265891	Pte.	...	...	Butterfield, J.	...	...	...	M.M.
242466	Pte.	...	...	Wray, E. G.	...	...	...	M.M.
23901	Pte.	...	...	Holroyd, B.	...	...	...	M.M.
242859	Pte.	...	...	Ibbotson, P.	...	...	...	M.M.
								Bar to M.M.
29495	Pte.	...	...	Strafford, T.	...	...	...	M.M.
241978	Pte.	...	...	Hartley, F.	...	...	...	M.M.
25262	Pte.	...	...	Binsley, B.	...	...	...	M.M.
266187	Pte.	...	...	Wiltham, J. S.		...	...	M.M.
241045	Pte.	...	...	Dale, E.	...	...	...	M.M.
240742	Pte.	...	...	Tomlinson, R.		...	...	M.M.
22602	Pte.	...	...	Frank, T.	...	...	...	M.M.
240159	Pte.	...	...	Dobson, G. B.		...	...	M.M.
266281	Pte.	...	...	Ready, N.	...	...	...	M.M.
34506	Pte.	...	...	Tandy, H.	...	...	...	V.C. — 3
								D.C.M.
								M.M.
204703	Pte.	...	...	Appleyard, L.	...	...	...	M.M.
241663	Pte.	...	...	Simpson, J.	...	...	...	M.M.
241887	Pte.	...	...	Sutcliffe, S.	...	...	...	M.M.
24603	Pte.	...	...	Marshall, H.	...	...	...	M.M.
202639	Pte.	...	...	Gibbs, W.	...	...	...	M.M.
241465	Pte.	...	...	Bonner, C.	...	...	...	M.M.
204034	Pte.	...	...	Battye, H.	...	...	...	M.M.
242392	Pte.	...	...	Brook, H.	...	...	...	M.M.
241596	Pte.	...	...	Locking, A.	...	...	...	M.M.
24165	Pte.	...	...	Robinson, G. D.		...	...	M.M.
262472	Pte.	...	...	Baker, T.	...	...	...	M.M.
25101	Pte.	...	...	Lee, A. ...	...	...	...	D.C.M.
								M.M.
242683	Pte.	...	...	Beardsley, P.	...	...	...	M.M.
								Bar to M.M.
242607	Pte.	...	...	Taylor, R.	...	...	...	M.M.
203539	Pte.	...	...	Sykes, J. W.	...	...	...	M.M.
268909	Pte.	...	...	Denton, T. A. ...		...	...	M.M.
240433	Pte.	...	...	Crossland, W. D.		...	...	M.M.
								Bar to M.M.
203121	Pte.	...	...	Mackrell, S.	...	...	...	M.M.
268800	Pte.	...	...	Barker, W.	...	...	...	M.M.
34561	Pte.	...	...	Walker, H.	...	...	...	M.M.
34759	Pte.	...	...	McClintock, W.		...	...	M.M.
241691	Pte.	...	...	Cook, L. H.	...	...	...	M.M.
306313	Pte.	...	...	Stead, H. W.	...	...	...	M.M.
241048	Pte.	...	...	Taylor, F.	...	...	...	M.M.
								Bar to M.M.

2/5TH WEST RIDING REGIMENT—*continued.*

Regtl. No.	Rank.	Name.	Award.
242034	Pte.	Castle, F.	M.M. Bar to M.M.
236722	Pte.	White, H. J.	M.M.
201823	Pte.	Womersley, E.	M.M.
26204	Pte.	Harris, B.	M.M.
54426	Pte.	Hill, J.	M.M.
34499	Pte.	Peel, B.	M.M. Bar to M.M.
241669	Pte.	Asquith, H. O. K.	M.M.
34464	Pte.	Rider, A.	M.M.
16100	Pte.	Overend, J.	M.M.
34757	Pte.	Parkes, A.	M.M.
340623	Pte.	Dondaband, E.	M.M.
203562	Pte.	Armitage, H.	M.M.
235598	Pte.	Bashford, J. E.	M.M.
25098	Pte.	Jeffcott, H.	M.M.
240674	Pte.	Middleton, W.	M.M.
34588	Pte.	Williams, L.	M.M.
241857	Pte.	Cox, P.	M.M.
235593	Pte.	Bell, M.	M.M.
201575	Pte.	Birchenough, J.	M.M.
26327	Pte.	Bale, P.	M.M.
35158	Pte.	Charnock, W.	M.M.
26304	Pte.	Tippett, C. T.	M.M.
269234	Pte.	Laverock, W.	M.M.
269091	Pte.	Baldwin, R.	M.M.
34563	Pte.	Harrison, E.	M.M.
241184	Pte.	Swale, S.	M.M.
34552	Pte.	Snowden, J. W.	M.M.
240885	Pte.	Holroyd, G. W.	M.M.
34515	Pte.	Auton, T.	M.M.
203657	Pte.	Darlington, H.	M.M.
26663	Pte.	Cartledge, A.	M.M.
35639	Pte.	Johnson, T.	M.M.
266597	Pte.	Fletcher, C. H.	M.M.
307334	Pte.	Talbot, N.	M.M.
34408	Pte.	Dewhirst, J.	M.M.
202065	Pte.	Ellis, E. D.	M.M.
33500	Pte.	Gracie, D.	M.M.
33754	Pte.	Pallett, A.	M.M.
305187	Pte.	Hollingworth, H. ...	M.M.
203297	Pte.	Daft, C.	M.M.
263016	Pte.	Fox, A.	M.M.
17112	Pte.	Wilson, G.	M.M.
205420	Pte.	Drake, B.	M.M.
241352	Pte.	Haywood, H.	M.M.
235653	Pte.	Ward, T.	M.M.
34488	Pte.	Key, C.	M.M.
240883	Pte.	Jennings, R.	M.M.
306037	Pte.	Shaw, H.	M.M.
14367	Cpl.	Roberts, G.	M.M.
17052	Dmr.	Moran, P.	M.M.

2/6TH WEST RIDING REGIMENT.

	Captain ...	Somervell, A.	M.C.
	Captain ...	Geldard, N.	D.S.O. M.C.
	2/Lieut. ...	Luckman, W. F.	M.C.

2/6TH WEST RIDING REGIMENT—*continued*.

Regtl. No.	Rank.	Name.	Award.
	2/Lieut. ...	Thompson, J.	M.C.
	2/Lieut. ...	Barraclough, G. W.	M.C.
6872	C.S.M.	Gartside, C. H.	M.C.
265530	C.S.M.	Maude, J.	D.C.M.
265926	Sgt.	McLeod, J. T....	D.C.M.
265690	Sgt.	Mason, R.	M.M.
240661	Sgt.	Davies, W.	M.M.
265835	Sgt.	Smith, A.	M.M.
266926	Sgt.	Garnett, T. H.	M.M.
10921	L.-Sgt.	Rigg, G.	M.M.
266961	Cpl.	Constantine, T.	M.M.
267272	Cpl.	Egan, M.	M.M.
266956	Cpl.	Caton, W.	M.M.
265828	Cpl.	Bowman, G.	M.M.
265664	Cpl.	Metcalf, G.	M.M.
26640	Cpl.	Carey, A.	M.M.
266475	Cpl.	Midgley, J.	M.M.
266876	L.-Cpl.	Hodkinson, A.	M.M.
266022	L.-Cpl.	Patterson, J.	M.M.
5107	Pte.	Nussey, J. T.	M.M.
4564	Pte.	Williams, J.	M.M.
267064	Pte.	Bates, J.	M.M.
266338	Pte.	Birkett, J.	M.M.
266771	Pte.	Mills, A. E.	M.M.
266766	Pte.	Robinson, A. V.	M.M.
266966	Pte.	Bateson, R.	M.M.
266356	Pte.	Stevens, R.	M.M.
267043	Pte.	Hodges, S.	M.M.
300077	Pte.	Standish, A.	M.M.
11628	Pte.	Devannie, F.	M.M.
267279	Pte.	Cooks, H.	M.M.
267212	Pte.	Simpson, B.	M.M.
269304	Pte.	Mokes, W. H.	M.M.

2/7TH WEST RIDING REGIMENT.

Regtl. No.	Rank.	Name.	Award.
	Major	Cockburn, G. E.	D.S.O.
	Captain ...	Miller, G. W. M.	M.C.
	Captain ...	Shearne, F. E.. C.	M.C.
	Lieut. ...	Hayward, S. P.	M.C.
	Lieut. ...	Hopper, H. L.	M.C.
	2/Lieut. ...	Furniss, H.	M.C.
	2/Lieut. ...	Tanner, E.	M.C.
	2/Lieut. ...	Vaughan, J.	M.C.
	2/Lieut. ...	Gloag, A. F.	M.C.
	2/Lieut. ...	Muff, F.	M.C.
	2/Lieut. ...	Pepper, F. G. W.	M.C.
	2/Lieut. ...	Buckley, J.	M.C.
	2/Lieut. ...	Hardaker, H.	M.C. Bar to M.C.
305815	Sgt.	Robinson, B.	D.C.M.
306155	Sgt.	Cooper, W.	M.M.
305362	Sgt.	Holroyd, A.	M.M.
305158	Sgt.	Hitchcock, A.	M.M.
266285	Sgt.	Golding, G.	M.M.
305544	Sgt.	Allen, H.	M.M.
305852	Cpl.	Walton, G.	M.M.
11826	Cpl.	Neatby, E.	M.M.
306271	Cpl.	Holden, J.	M.M.
265487	Cpl.	Alton, E.	M.M.

2/7TH WEST RIDING REGIMENT—*continued*.

Regtl. No.	Rank.	Name.	Award.
306015	Cpl.	Baxter, E.	M.M.
26695	Cpl.	Nutter, R.	M.M.
			Bar to M.M.
305907	Cpl.	Blakeley, J. E.	M.M.
19370	Cpl.	Ramsden, T. V. C.	D.C.M.
306568	L.-Cpl.	Heaton, H.	M.M.
15005	L.-Cpl.	Robinson, E.	M.M.
7302	L.-Cpl.	Wooley, R.	Bar to M.M.
306779	L.-Cpl.	Marshall, H.	M.M.
267177	L.-Cpl.	Hay, A.	M.M.
10926	L.-Cpl.	Holmes, J.	M.M.
306861	Pte.	Crowther, F.	M.M.
25139	Pte.	Smith, R.	M.M.
28041	Pte.	Turnbull, G.	M.M.
305946	Pte.	Hoyle, M.	M.M.
306908	Pte.	Barron, B.	M.M.
306231	Pte.	Jackson, J. M.	M.M.
16300	Pte.	Crombie, A.	M.M.
17275	Pte.	Tunney, M.	M.M.
306811	Pte.	Smith, H.	M.M.
306625	Pte.	Thornton, J.	M.M.
25140	Pte.	Taylor, J.	M.M.
91541	Pte.	Blythe, T.	M.M.
305944	Pte.	Sykes, J.	M.M.
16842	Pte.	Graham, W.	M.M.
33484	Pte.	Smith, J.	M.M.
23624	Pte.	Dyson, F.	M.M.
266932	Pte.	Smales, —.	M.M.
			Bar to M.M.
306659	Pte.	Hainsworth, L.	M.M.
305283	Pte.	Fisher, H. B.	M.M.
267054	Pte.	Horner, T. M.	M.M.
25336	Pte.	Gallagher, J.	M.M.
32701	Pte.	Owen, F.	M.M.
25265	Pte.	Stott, J. R.	M.M.
23698	Pte.	Wilson, A.	M.M.
306890	Pte.	Bancroft, H.	M.M.
308112	Pte.	Armitage, W.	M.M.

2/4TH KING'S OWN YORKSHIRE LIGHT INFANTRY.

	Rank.	Name.	Award.
	Lt.-Col. ...	Chaytor, C. A.	D.S.O.
			Croix de Guerre
	Lt.-Col. ...	Power, R. E.	D.S.O.
	Major ...	Brook, —.	D.S.O.
	Major ...	Shearman, C.	D.S.O.
	Major ...	Beaumont, G.	M.C.
			Bar to M.C.
	Captain ...	Wellington, J. H.	M.C.
		(East Yorks. attached)	Bar to M.C.
	Captain ...	Bentley, P.	M.C.
			3 Bars to M.C.
	Captain ...	McNicol, M.	M.C.
	Capt. & Adjt. ...	Earle, A. E.	M.C.
			Bar to M.C.
	Captain ...	Clarke, J. T. E.	M.C.
	Lieut. ...	Lee, N.	M.C.
	Lieut. ...	Hale-White, R.	M.C.
	Lieut. ...	McCausland, C. J.	M.C.
	2/Lieut. ...	Hirst, C.	M.C.

2/4TH KING'S OWN YORKSHIRE LIGHT INFANTRY—*continued.*

Regtl. No.	Rank.	Name.	Award.
	2/Lieut. ...	Briggs, T. H.	M.C.
	2/Lieut. ...	Curtis. G. S. C.	M.C.
	2/Lieut. ...	Spencer, G. E.	D.S.O.
	2/Lieut. ...	Ireland, C. A.	M.C.
	2/Lieut. ...	Rodger, J. L.	M.C.
	2/Lieut. ...	Cocker, F.	M.C.
	2/Lieut. ...	Schools, P.	M.C.
240829	R.S.M.	Ledger, W. H.	M.C.
			D.C.M.
201304	R.Q.M.S. ...	Townend, E. W.	M.S.M.
	C.S.M.	Hudson, R.	D.C.M.
36812	C.Q.M.S. ...	Woods, E. S.	M.M.
200649	Sgt.	Naylor, B.	M.M.
8244	Sgt.	Fenton, J.	D.C.M.
240961	Sgt.	Robinson, A.	M.M.
242411	Sgt.	Howsley, J.	D.C.M.
200797	Sgt.	Walsh, J.	D.C.M.
241337	Sgt.	Andrew, R.	D.C.M.
			M.M.
			Bar to M.M.
34580	Sgt.	Stevens, W.	M.M.
201539	Sgt.	Hunt, F. A.	M.M.
	Sgt.	Cater, W. W.	M.S.M.
17262	Sgt.	Fox, W. R.	M.M.
235661	Sgt.	Davenport, C.	M.M.
8995	Sgt.	Hampson, E.	D.C.M.
11787	Sgt.	Parker, J. W.	M.M.
200866	Sgt.	Bryan, J.	D.C.M.
63249	Sgt.	Shaw, D. R.	D.C.M.
63250	Sgt.	Broughton, S.	D.C.M.
300670	Sgt.	Auty, J.	M.S.M.
202230	Sgt.	Hommingway, E.	M.S.M.
200958	Sgt.	Walker, H. V.	M.S.M.
240374	L.-Sgt.	Johnson. S.	D.C.M.
201303	L.-Sgt.	Turpin, A.	M.M.
201216	Cpl.	Maddox, E.	M.M.
			D.C.M.
16933	Cpl.	Game, J. G.	M.M.
			Bar to M.M.
201471	Cpl.	Baker, J.	M.M.
			Bar to M.M.
10400	Cpl.	Newbolt. A.	M.M.
201693	Cpl.	Thompson, H.	M.M.
39442	Cpl.	Carr, H.	M.M.
201154	Cpl.	Hampson, H.	M.M.
241765	Cpl.	Booth, H. E.	D.C.M.
201402	Cpl.	Dakin, S.	M.M.
35967	Cpl.	Barmby. F.	M.M.
63264	Cpl.	Beardsley, T. C.	M.M.
15780	Cpl.	Parr, G. H.	M.M.
			Bar to M.M.
200948	L.-Cpl.	Taylor, G.	M.M.
			Bar to M.M.
35540	L.-Cpl.	Cooke, A. H.	M.M.
201432	L.-Cpl.	Wimpenny, G. A.	M.M.
200778	L.-Cpl.	Lee, G.	M.M.
47618	L.-Cpl.	Chatterton, V.	M.M.
201213	L.-Cpl.	Shepherd. J. I....	M.M.
39343	L.-Cpl.	Kennedy, T.	M.M.
			Bar to M.M.
201517	L.-Cpl.	Scholey, J.	M.M.

2/4TH KING'S OWN YORKSHIRE LIGHT INFANTRY—*continued*.

Regtl. No.	Rank.	Name.	Award.
200267	L.-Cpl.	Benson, H.	D.C.M.
238009	L.-Cpl.	Geary, J.	M.M.
201388	L.-Cpl.	Simpson, E.	·M.M.
200807	L.-Cpl.	Elliott, R.	D.C.M.
235834	L.-Cpl.	Newton, J.	D.C.M.
201558	L.-Cpl.	Oakland, H.	M.M.
43549	L.-Cpl.	Mattingley, H.	M.M.
263112	L.-Cpl.	Sleightholme, A.	M.M.
241771	L.-Cpl.	Eayling, H. W.	M.M.
40620	L.-Cpl.	James, J. W.	M.M.
263113	L.-Cpl.	Mitchell, R.	M.M.
41329	L.-Cpl.	Kay, J. C.	M.M.
201319	L.-Cpl.	Armitage, G. T.	M.M.
202341	L.-Cpl.	Sheard, W.	M.M.
201816	L.-Cpl.	Rooker, E.	M.M.
41431	L.-Cpl.	Parker, L.	M.M.
203928	L.-Cpl.	Hayes, H.	M.M.
24729	Pte.	Sternburg, N.	M.M.
201216	Pte.	Maddox, E.	M.M.
238024	Pte.	Lockwood, M.	M.M.
202835	Pte.	Fairburn, F.	M.M.
201934	Pte.	Hazel, H. D.	M.M.
245289	Pte.	Simpson, S. J.	M.M.
200111	Pte.	Johnson, E.	M.M.
37455	Pte.	Jackson, G. W.	M.M.
263188	Pte.	Hum, W.	M.M.
63455	Pte.	Potts, W.	M.M.
52885	Pte.	Posser, J.	M.M.
201197	Pte.	Heaps, T.	M.M.
201817	Pte.	Ward, K.	M.M.
202215	Pte.	Wadsworth, F.	M.M.
202313	Pte.	Williamson, A.	M.M.
235832	Pte.	Haigh, W.	M.M.
601457	Pte.	Burton, C.	M.M.
63266	Pte.	Bosward, E. A.	M.M.
63899	Pte.	French, A.	M.M.
63940	Pte.	Strawbridge, W. P. ...	M.M.
63935	Pte.	O'Neill, S.	M.M.
32868	Pte.	Crookes, J.	M.M.
204328	Pte.	Gill, W. H.	M.M.
63899	Pte.	Cockman, V. C.	M.M.
242510	Pte.	Senior, H.	M.M.
253987	Pte.	Jones, J.	M.M.
63336	Pte.	Clewlow, H. E.	M.M.
200955	Pte.	Goodfellow, H.	M.M.
36194	Pte.	Lawler, T.	M.M.
38737	Pte.	Northin, G. J.	M.M.
51840	Pte.	Peacock, T. R.	M.M.
201288	Pte.	Whiteley, H.	M.M.
202468	Pte.	Machin, W.	M.M. Bar to M.M.
202451	Pte.	Greaves, E.	M.M.
5532	Bugler	Burkill, W.	M.M.

2/5TH KING'S OWN YORKSHIRE LIGHT INFANTRY.

	Lt.-Col. ...	Watson, O. C. S.	V.C. — 4
		¹⁸ Cou⁻ᵗ⁻ ᵒᶠ Lond⁻ ⁻⁻⁻⁻⁻⁻ ⁻⁻⁻⁻⁻	D.S.O. M.C.
	Lt.-Col. ...	Peter, F. H.	M.C. D.S.O.

2/5TH KING'S OWN YORKSHIRE LIGHT INFANTRY—*continued*.

Regtl. No.	Rank.	Name.	Award.
	Lt.-Col. ...	Barton, B. J.	D.S.O. Bar to D.S.O.
	Captain ...	Bentley, P.	M.C. Bar to M.C.
	Captain ...	Oliphant, T. A. H.	M.C. Bar to M.C.
	Captain ...	Crawford, W. L.	M.C.
	Captain ...	Crow, W.	M.C. Bar to M.C.
	Captain ...	Spencer, G. E.	M.C.
	Capt. & Adjt. ...	Robinson, A.	M.C.
	Capt. & Adjt. ...	Lynn, A. C.	M.C.
	Hon. Capt. & Qr. Mstr.	Barker, H.	M.C.
	Lieut. ...	Rose, A. R.	M.C.
	Lieut. ...	Houghton, R. A.	M.C.
	Lieut. ...:	Stansfield, J.	M.C. Bar to M.C.
	Lieut. ...	Townend, O. E.	M.C. Bar to M.C.
	Lieut. ...	Tomalin, H.	M.C. Bar to M.C.
	Lieut. ...	Champion, A. S.	M.C.
	Lieut. ...	Logan, R. B.	M.C.
	Lieut. ...	Trigg, G.	M.C.
	2/Lieut. ...	Prestall, W. G....	M.C.
	2/Lieut. ...	Doherty, F. J.	M.C.
	2/Lieut. ...	Moore, P.	M.C.
	2/Lieut. ...	Callear, E.	M.C.
	2/Lieut. ...	Gray, G. C.	M.C.
	2/Lieut. ...	Crofts, C. H.	M.C.
	2/Lieut. ...	Jenkins, W. J.	M.C.
	2/Lieut. ...	Atkins, J.	M.C.
	2/Lieut. ...	Mottram, T. W.	M.C.
	2/Lieut. ...	Platt, O. G.	M.C.
	2/Lieut. ...	Morris, E.	M.C.
	2/Lieut. ...	James, W. G.	D.S.O.
	2/Lieut. ...	Ibbott, W. C.	M.C.
	2/Lieut. ...	Haigh, E.	M.C.
	2/Lieut. ...	Douglass, A. F. S. ...	M.C.
240650	C.S.M.	Sampson, B.	D.C.M. M.M.
63076	C.S.M.	Younghusband, W.	D.C.M.
5541	C.S.M.	Watson, F. W.	D.C.M.
240829	C.S.M.	Ledger, W. H.	M.C.
242172	C.Q.M.S. ...	Wilson, G.	M.M.
240012	C.Q.M.S. ...	Firth, E.	M.M.
240020	C.Q.M.S. ...	Strudwick, E. E.	M.S.M.
241146	Sgt.	Fox, P.	M.M.
18805	Sgt.	Drage, H.	M.M.
241572	Sgt.	Ward, H. P.	D.C.M.
11777	Sgt.	Tordoff, H.	D.C.M.
8461	Sgt.	Boughby, E.	M.M. Bar to M.M.
205688	Sgt.	Hamilton, G.	M.M. Bar to M.M.
15368	Sgt.	Norbury, J.	M.M.
63132	Sgt.	Dawson, E.	M.M.
249099	Sgt.	Brooke, A. L.	M.M.
241315	Sgt.	Raywood, E.	M.M. Bar to M.M.

2/5TH KING'S OWN YORKSHIRE LIGHT INFANTRY—*continued*.

Regtl. No.	Rank.	Name.	Award.
240231	Sgt.	Robinson, W.	M.M.
240536	Sgt.	Chatterton, T. H.	M.M.
240683	Sgt.	Mulligan, J.	M.M.
240043	Sgt.	Westlake, F. A.	M.M.
240194	Sgt.	Calvert, L.	V.C. — M.M.
241658	Sgt.	Kirkham, B.	M.M.
241326	Sgt.	Hasky, J. W.	D.C.M.
241103	Sgt.	Thomas, O. C.	D.C.M.
242191	Sgt.	Roberts, F.	D.C.M.
240781	Sgt.	Foster, J. G.	D.C.M.
240537	Sgt.	Guy, W.	D.C.M.
240415	Sgt.	Leng, R. A.	M.S.M.
240349	C.S.M.	Fletcher, J. T.	D.C.M. M.M.
240075	C.S.M.	Cooper, C.	D.C.M.
240890	C.Q.M.S.	Schmidt, A. W.	M.M.
240675	C.Q.M.S.	Smith, H.	M.M. M.S.M.
242072	L.-Sgt.	Stocks, J. D.	M.M.
63846	Cpl.	Williamson, T. T.	M.M.
202150	Cpl.	Essery, J.	M.M.
42157	Cpl.	Close, S.	M.M.
242869	Cpl.	McNamara, J.	M.M.
242945	Cpl.	Machin, J.	M.M.
240592	Cpl.	Wright, J.	M.M.
235096	Cpl.	Womersley, H.	M.M.
202196	Cpl.	Harris, W.	M.M.
58137	Cpl.	Riddle, H. W.	M.M.
240658	Cpl.	Foulstone, W.	M.M.
242174	Cpl.	Wardle, S. G.	M.M.
240699	Cpl.	Marchington, B.	M.M.
58077	L.-Cpl.	Routledge, R.	M.M.
58112	L.-Cpl.	Yates, L.	M.M.
1336	L.-Cpl.	Martin, E.	M.M.
242887	L.-Cpl.	Reynolds, A.	M.M.
18329	L.-Cpl.	Jenkins, W.	M.M.
241690	L.-Cpl.	Hawes, H. J.	M.M.
65196	L.-Cpl.	Williamson, T.	M.M.
205687	L.-Cpl.	Clazey, J.	M.M.
263057	L.-Cpl.	Pallett, R.	M.M.
240668	L.-Cpl.	Stocks, H.	M.M.
241189	L.-Cpl.	Buck, G.	M.M.
55081	L.-Cpl.	Errington, J.	M.M.
35875	L.-Cpl.	Dungworth, W.	M.M.
39734	L.-Cpl.	Ayre, F.	M.M.
241455	L.-Cpl.	Porter, E. F.	M.M. Bar to M.M
19117	L.-Cpl.	Bennett, F.	M.M.
263053	L.-Cpl.	Crosland, J.	M.M.
19091	L.-Cpl.	Williams, A.	M.M.
241070	L.-Cpl.	Morris, B.	M.M.
63215	Pte.	Shaw, J. W.	M.M.
45520	Pte.	Turner, J.	M.M.
263042	Pte.	Ledger, W. H.	M.M.
241361	Pte.	Toplis, P.	M.M.
26080	Pte.	Norfolk, E.	M.M.
27233	Pte.	Smith, T.	M.M.
35055	Pte.	Hunter, L.	M.M.
240643	Pte.	Brompton, J.	M.M.
242650	Pte.	Bower, H.	M.M.

2/5TH KING'S OWN YORKSHIRE LIGHT INFANTRY—*continued.*

Regtl. No.	Rank.	Name.	Award.
241920	Pte.	Spiers, T.	M.M.
242640	Pte.	Bell, J.	M.M.
			Bar to M.M.
41157	Pte.	Broomhead, A....	D.C.M.
142701	Pte.	Smith, S. H.	M.M.
			Bar to M.M.
			2nd Bar to M.M.
62318	Pte.	Smith, E.	M.M.
24084	Pte.	Rendle, W. H.	M.M.
65193	Pte.	Bevans, G. H....	D.C.M.
			M.M.
205677	Pte.	Robinson, T.	M.M.
			Bar to M.M.
205708	Pte.	Shaw, A.	M.M.
60872	Pte.	Ayscough, T. L.	M.M.
240742	Pte.	Cragg, T.	M.M.
14701	Pte.	Flynn, F.	M.M.
60869	Pte.	Hooley, P.	M.M.
11245	Pte.	Hooley, C. D.	M.M.
63189	Pte.	Macfarlane, R. W.	M.M.
42996	Pte.	Hinchcliffe, H.	M.M.
27756	Pte.	Barnes, A.	M.M.
263004	Pte.	Lingley, J. W.	M.M.
202854	Pte.	Dickinson, W....	M.M.
243047	Pte.	Wilkinson, J.	M.M.
65183	Pte.	Duffy, L.	M.M.
62969	Pte.	Clark, N.	M.M.
36427	Pte.	Maiser, C.	M.M.
205202	Pte.	Humphries, F.	M.M.
203132	Pte.	Harrison, J. T....	M.M.
205677	Pte.	Robinson, T.	M.M.
203515	Pte.	Westoby, S.	M.M.
38208	Pte.	Peters, A.	D.C.M.
65177	Pte.	Allan, A. E.	D.C.M.
			Bar to D.C.M.
201923	Pte.	Malham, E.	M.M.
65192	Pte.	Shipley, M. C....	M.M.
23016	Pte.	Ferguson, H.	M.M.
64027	Pte.	White, J.	M.M.
203132	Pte.	Harrison, T. J....	M.M.
35035	Pte.	Graham, J.	M.M.
240328	Pte.	Crowcroft, T. R.	M.M.
240388	Pte.	Gladwin, C. H.	M.M.
241508	Pte.	Woodall, J.	M.M.
242605	Pte.	Greaves, G.	M.M.
4170	Pte.	Clarke, F.	M.M.
240990	Pte.	Beddoes, J.	M.M.
241025	Pte.	Boyer, W.	M.M.
242959	Pte.	Hird, H.	M.M.
46423	Pte.	Petty, F.	M.M.
40437	Pte.	Jessop, J.	M.M.
241829	Pte.	Benson, H.	M.M.
200765	Pte.	Hutchinson, A.	M.M.
26226	Pte.	Godfrey, W.	M.M.
241191	Pte.	Speight, B.	MS.M.
22262	Pte.	Budby, E.	D.C.M.
242753	Pte.	Boam, H. J.	M.M.
38454	Pte.	Muir, J.	M.M.
242439	Pte.	Fennel, G.	M.M.
242142	Pte.	Day, J. T.	M.M.
240455	Pte.	Abbott, A.	M.M.
42858	Pte.	Cooper, J. W.	M.M.

2/4TH YORK AND LANCASTER REGIMENT.

Regtl. No.	Rank.	Name.	Award.
	Lt.-Col. ...	Blacker, F. S. J.	D.S.O.
	Major ...	Ludgrab, C. W.	M.C.
	Major ...	Stickney, J. E. D.	D.S.O. M.C. Bar to M.C.
	Captain ...	Hill, C. M.	M.C.
	Captain ...	Smith, R.	M.C. Bar to M.C.
	Captain ...	Lucas, E.	M.C.
	Captain ...	Ormesher, A. H.	M.C.
	Captain ...	Wilson, A. F.	M.C. Bar to M.C.
	Captain ...	Ellse, J.	M.C.
	Captain ...	Maxwell, S. C....	M.C. Bar to M.C.
	Captain ...	Rodgers, J.	M.C.
	Captain ...	Pennington, B. C.	M.C.
	Lt.-Col. ...	Hart, L. H. P.	D.S.O. Bar to D.S.O. Croix de Guerre.
	Lieut. ...	Mitchell, A.	M.C.
	Lieut. ...	Hedges, N. H.	M.C.
	Lieut. ...	Dixon, C. V.	M.C.
	Lieut. ...	Skrine, D. V. D.	M.C. Bar to M.C.
	Lieut. ...	Perkins, S. M.	M.C.
	2/Lieut. ...	Munro, M.	M.C. 2 Bars to M.C.
	2/Lieut. ...	Halliday, A. H.	M.C.
	2/Lieut. ...	Carter, R. W.	M.C.
	2/Lieut. ...	Longmire. L. A.	M.C.
	2/Lieut. ...	Thackeray, E. A.	M.C.
	2/Lieut. ...	Revitt. C.	M.C. Bar to M.C.
	2/Lieut. ...	Penny, J. E.	M.C.
	2/Lieut. ...	Bradbury, J. C. L.	M.C.
	2/Lieut. ...	Summerbell, A. W.	M.C. Bar to M.C.
	2/Lieut. ...	Murrell-Talbot, E. R.... ...	M.C.
	2/Lieut. ...	Eckersley, J.	M.C. M.M.
	2/Lieut. ...	Simpkin, A. L.	M.C.
	2/Lieut. ...	May, W. B.	M.C.
	2/Lieut. ...	Dryden, G. A.	M.C.
	2/Lieut. ...	Fisher, T. D.	M.C.
	2/Lieut. ...	Proudfoot, F.	M.C.
	2/Lieut. ...	Bailey, R.	M.C. Bar to M.C.
200893	C.S.M.	Davis, J. C.	M.M. Bar to M.M.
201402	C.S.M.	Fish, P. V.	M.M.
200824	C.S.M.	Wyman, G.	D.C.M. M.M.
200850	Sgt.	Murfin, T.	M.M.
200797	Sgt.	Elsworth, A.	M.M.
201253	Sgt.	Turton, W.	M.M.
201312	Sgt.	Nelson, L.	M.M.
201861	Sgt.	Box, J. A.	M.M.
200955	Sgt.	Levesley, G.	M.M.
201006	Sgt.	Hunter, A. K.	M.M.
15496	Sgt.	Bissel, A.	M.M.

2/4TH YORK AND LANCASTER REGIMENT—*continued.*

Regtl. No.	Rank.	Name.	Award.
205353	Sgt.	Daykins, J.	V.C.
			M.M.
2984	Sgt.	Blakemore, G.	M.M.
200949	Sgt.	Askham, T. S.	M.M.
201550	Sgt.	Hodgson, A.	M.M.
263013	Sgt.	Murphy, G.	D.C.M.
19731	Sgt.	Bowman, T. W.	D.C.M.
202740	Sgt.	Slingsby, P.	M.M.
201042	Sgt.	Pashby, T.	M.M.
200971	Sgt.	Dickenson, A.	M.M.
200931	Sgt.	Pemberton, A.	M.M.
55779	Sgt.	Harrop, —.	M.M.
			Bar to M.M.
25989	Sgt.	Wellington, G.	M.M.
241246	Sgt.	Orwin, R.	M.M.
			Bar to M.M.
200202	Sgt.	Coldwell, B.	M.M.
32819	Sgt.	Munn, W.	M.M.
201350	Sgt.	Stephens, E.	M.S.M.
200810	Sgt.	Birtles, J.	D.C.M.
202582	L.-Sgt. ...	Robertson, A. H. ...	M.M.
201258	L.-Sgt. ...	Priest, W.	M.M.
202655	L.-Sgt. ...	Hulley, H.	M.M.
201568	Cpl.	Simpson, T.	M.M.
201432	Cpl.	Shelton, H. H.	M.M.
38319	Cpl.	Turner, R.	M.M.
24749	Cpl.	Park, J.	M.M.
201064	Cpl.	Pettit, F.	M.M.
19731	Cpl.	Bowman, T. W.	M.M.
57603	Cpl.	Thompson, S.	M.M.
205348	Cpl.	Coke, S. C.	M.M.
235930	Cpl.	Elridge, H. J.	M.M.
201906	Cpl.	Hudson, H.	M.M.
55597	Cpl.	Roddy, F.	M.M.
201884	Cpl.	Ibbotson, T. E.	M.M.
3–1479	Cpl.	Guy, J.	M.M.
7551	Cpl.	Flintham, J.	M.M.
58392	Cpl.	Leggett, G. T.	M.M.
			Bar to M.M.
			2nd Bar to M.M.
37698	L.-Cpl.	Shelly, L.	M.M.
201168	L.-Cpl.	Mann, A. E.	M.M.
241908	L.-Cpl.	Corbett, H.	M.M.
			Bar to M.M.
39445	L.-Cpl.	Winterbottom, W.	M.M.
235931	L.-Cpl.	Ferguson, J. E.	D.C.M.
205319	L.-Cpl.	Aherns, A. G.	D.C.M.
58246	L.-Cpl.	Lawson, M.	D.C.M.
24245	L.-Cpl.	Buck, W.	M.M.
57717	L.-Cpl.	Hill, L.	M.M.
18786	L.-Cpl.	Waldron, J. J.	M.M.
943	L.-Cpl.	Harrington C.	M.M.
236171	L.-Cpl.	Nash, E.	M.M.
235999	L.-Cpl.	McNeill, R.	M.M.
235937	L.-Cpl.	Wood, W.	M.M.
241934	L.-Cpl.	Riley, W.	M.M.
35560	L.-Cpl.	Gibbons, W.	M.M.
57269	L.-Cpl.	Jones, H.	D.C.M.
321926	L.-Cpl.	Lumley, F.	D.C.M.
27227	L.-Cpl.	Jackson, W. E.	M.M.
			Bar to M.M.

2/4TH YORK AND LANCASTER REGIMENT—*continued*.

Regtl. No.	Rank.	Name.	Award.
200095	L.-Cpl.	Hattersley, A.	M.S.M.
201406	Pte.	Rowe, H.	M.S.M.
201712	Pte.	Coggin, J. M.	M.M.
202468	Pte.	Machen, W.	M.M.
35616	Pte.	Hainring, J.	M.M.
204426	Pte.	Edwards, J. W.	M.M.
202486	Pte.	Danby, W. J.	M.M.
201180	Pte.	Bacon, W.	M.M.
205355	Pte.	Denton, A. B.	M.M.
202634	Pte.	Garside, A. B.	M.M.
732	Pte.	Milner, A.	M.M.
204405	Pte.	Willett, A.	M.M.
202405	Pte.	Farnham, R.	M.M.
37633	Pte.	Hewe, T. W.	M.M.
32914	Pte.	Stainthorpe, N. T.	M.M.
241683	Pte.	Greensmith, E.	M.M.
241168	Pte.	Dale, W.	D.C.M.
9578	Pte.	Turrell, J.	M.M.
901955	Pte.	Bagshaw, B.	M.M.
37618	Pte.	Vause, G. E.	M.M.
240732	Pte.	Slater, F.	M.M.
201540	Pte.	Bradley, O. H.	M.M.
201084	Pte.	Slater, G.	M.M.
202760	Pte.	Lewin, F. J.	M.M. Bar to M.M.
20491	Pte.	Adamson, F.	M.M.
265175	Pte.	Platt, B. T.	M.M.
200476	Pte.	Bradshaw, S.	M.M.
56751	Pte.	White, F.	M.M.
263185	Pte.	Kirton, T. W.	M.M.
265255	Pte.	Dickenson, H.	M.M.
202774	Pte.	Jubb, J.	M.M.
58081	Pte.	Dickins, G.	M.M.
57365	Pte.	Todd, E. J.	M.M.
9610	Pte.	Spreckley, G.	D.C.M.
241672	Pte.	Hinds, J.	D.C.M.
57911	Pte.	Powner, S.	D.C.M.
523874	Pte.	Horan, J.	D.C.M.
21198	Pte.	Rankin, F.	M.M.
57723	Pte.	Hill, J.	M.M.
200763	Pte.	Clark, H.	M.M.
204923	Pte.	Whyatt, J.	M.M.
201457	Pte.	Lockwood, B.	M.M.
58445	Pte.	Errington, W.	M.M.
241678	Pte.	Slater, H.	M.M.
58241	Pte.	Rogers, A.	M.M.
235994	Pte.	Arnold, E.	M.M.
203903	Pte.	Hammerton, P. W.	M.M.
32878	Pte.	Graham, T. W.	M.M.
35637	Pte.	Wigglesworth, T. H.	M.M.
57753	Pte.	Beever, W. H.	M.M.
58092	Pte.	Francis, J.	M.M.
32688	Pte.	Rawcliffe, S.	M.M.
57538	Pte.	Patterson, F. D.	M.M.
202430	Pte.	Cragg, J. W.	M.M.
222432	Pte.	Hunt, W. F.	M.M.
58383	Pte.	Cockerill, J. W.	M.M.
36446	Pte.	Spencer, A.	M.M.
57675	Pte.	Venus, R.	M.M.
240304	Pte.	Dye, J. C.	M.M.
202350	Pte.	Oxley, E.	M.M.

2/4TH YORK AND LANCASTER REGIMENT—*continued*.

Regtl. No.	Rank.	Name.	Award.
201164	Pte.	Mills, R.	M.M.
4132	Pte.	Brown, P.	D.C.M.
18786	Pte.	Waldren, J. J.	D.C.M.
57603	Pte.	Thompson, S.	D.C.M.

2/5TH YORK AND LANCASTER REGIMENT.

Regtl. No.	Rank.	Name.	Award.
	Lt.-Col. ...	Prince, P.	D.S.O.
	Cap.(R.A.M.C.)	Wilson, A. F.	M.C.
	Captain ...	Surridge, S. O. R.	M.C.
	Captain ...	Hall, R. C.	M.C.
	Captain ...	Lancaster, A. C.	Chevalier de l'Ordre de Leopold Belgian
	Captain ...	Bate, R. E. de B.	M.C.
	Lieut. ...	Stansee, J. R.	M.C.
	Lieut. ...	Hill, J. J.	M.C.
	Lieut. ...	Beetham, C. C.	M.C.
	Lieut. ...	Dunkerton, E. L. H.	M.C.
	2/Lieut. ...	Maxwell, S. C....	M.C.
	2/Lieut. ...	Wells, D.	M.C.
	2/Lieut. ...	Shooter, J. H.	M.C.
	2/Lieut. ...	Thompson, G.	M.C.
240370	C.S.M.	Rudd, F. W.	M.M. D.C.M.
240331	C.S.M.	Gray, G.	M.M.
1772	Sgt. ...	Williams, J. F.	M.M.
240791	Sgt. ...	Robinson, J.	M.M.
240279	Sgt. ...	Shenton, A.	M.S.M.
241974	Sgt. ...	Chadwick, A.	M.M.
241760	Sgt. ...	Rollett, E.	M.M.
240797	Sgt. ...	Gummer, T.	M.M.
240268	Sgt. ...	Pennington, J.	D.C.M.
242683	Sgt. ...	McGarrell, D.	M.M.
240318	L.-Sgt.	Whitaker, J. W.	M.M.
241248	Cpl. ...	Front, T.	M.M.
240580	Cpl. ...	Bareham, F.	M.M.
241363	Cpl. ...	Cutler, J. W.	M.M.
241135	L.-Cpl.	Evans, E.	M.M.
200637	L.-Cpl.	Jackson, A.	M.M.
2920	L.-Cpl.	Auty, S.	M.M.
241816	L.-Cpl.	Banks, H.	M.M.
3086	L.-Cpl.	Gledhill, J. W.	M.M.
3294	L.-Cpl.	Causer, J. H.	M.M.
3295	L.-Cpl.	Parkinson, M.	M.M.
3746	L.-Cpl.	Simpson, P.	M.M.
241327	L.-Cpl.	Hewitt, S.	M.M.
241714	L.-Cpl.	Guest, R. E.	M.M.
241922	L.-Cpl.	Blenkharn, A.	M.M.
242637	L.-Cpl.	Burn, M.	M.M.
241704	L.-Cpl.	Corbett, M.	M.M.
241047	L.-Cpl.	Cartledge, R.	M.M.
240956	L.-Cpl.	Statham, W.	M.M.
240042	L.-Cpl.	Longden, G.	M.M.
241882	L.-Cpl.	Hogg, R.	M.M.
240899	L.-Cpl.	Peat, W.	M.M.
241246	L.-Cpl.	Orwin, R.	M.M.
241949	L.-Cpl.	Smithson, J.	M.M.
241208	L.-Cpl.	Shepherd, B.	M.M.
241589	L.-Cpl.	Roberts, R.	M.M.
241636	L.-Cpl.	Lodge, J.	M.M.

2/5TH YORK AND LANCASTER REGIMENT—*continued.*

Regtl. No.	Rank.	Name.	Award.
240579	L.-Cpl. ...	Trout, G.	M.M.
473	L.-Cpl. ...	Pickersgill, F.	M.M.
203539	L.-Cpl. ...	Thompson, T. M.	M.M.
241687	L.-Cpl. ...	Wilson, W. V.	M.M.
241700	L.-Cpl. ...	Headley, T.	M.M.
241022	L.-Cpl. ...	Bamforth, W.	M.M.

1/5TH DEVONSHIRE REGIMENT.

Regtl. No.	Rank.	Name.	Award.
	Lt.-Col.	Bastow, H. V.	D.S.O.
	Captain	Windeatt, J.	M.C. Bar to M.C.
	Captain	Hamlyn, H.	M.M.
	Captain	Antony, G. H.	M.C.
	Captain	Pitts-Lewis G. F.	M.C.
	Lieut.	Treacher, H.	M.C. Bar to M.C.
	Captain	Bedford, R.	M.C. Bar to M.C.
	2/Lieut.	Edgar, J. H.	M.C.
	2/Lieut.	Steer, W.	M.C.
	2/Lieut.	Coleman, R. W.	M.C.
	2/Lieut.	Matthews, S. F.	M.C.
	2/Lieut.	Fisher, D. K.	M.C.
	2/Lieut.	Stanley, H.	M.C.
	Lieut.	Northey, T.	M.C.
240062	R.Q.M.S.	Bessell, S. J.	M.S.M.
240068	C.S.M. ...	Winsborrow, A. J.	M.M.
204679	Sgt. ...	Hepper, E. T.	D.C.M.
240601	Sgt. ...	Cowles, F. W.	M.M.
240113	Sgt. ...	Crispin, E. J.	M.M. Bar to M.M.
240917	Sgt. ...	Hodge, C.	M.M.
240586	Sgt. ...	Lethbridge, W. O.	M.M.
240070	Sgt. ...	Woolcott, L. W.	M.M.
240774	Sgt. ...	Sparkes, F. J.	M.M.
8733	Sgt. ...	Pascoe, W. G.	M.M.
240441	L.-Sgt. ...	Pook, F. E.	M.M.
240473	L.-Sgt. ...	Aggett, S.	M.M.
240034	Cpl. ...	Botterell, G.	M.M. Bar to M.M.
72002	Cpl. ...	Craigie, W.	M.M.
240075	Cpl. ...	Yolland, Y. H.	M.M. Bar to M.M.
37057	Cpl. ...	Sullivan, B. T.	M.M.
240682	Cpl. ...	Penwarden, W. T.	M.M.
240967	Cpl. ...	Hudson, W. H. D.	M.M.
67450	Cpl. ...	Matthews, W. H.	M.M.
241056	L.-Cpl. ...	**Tribble**, W.	M.M.
240124	L.-Cpl. ...	Radmore, W. G.	M.M.
240258	L.-Cpl. ...	Heath, C.	M.M.
240990	L.-Cpl. ...	Cooper, J. H. H.	M.M.
240468	L.-Cpl. ...	Ashton, A. C.	M.M.
23772	L.-Cpl. ...	Lang, J. J.	M.M.
45643	L.-Cpl. ...	Short, A. T.	M.M.
240452	L.-Cpl. ...	Phillips, P.	M.M.
240755	L.-Cpl. ...	Collman, E.	M.M.
240396	L.-Cpl. ...	Dollen, F. M.	M.M.
240640	L.-Cpl. ...	Cox, W. J.	M.M.
241182	L.-Cpl. ...	Walters, J. W.	M.M.

1/5TH DEVONSHIRE REGIMENT—*continued.*

Regtl. No.	Rank.	Name.	Award.
63831	L.-Cpl.	Leach, A. J.	M.M.
240176	L.-Cpl.	Willis, F. J.	M.M.
315348	Pte.	Skinner, W. F....	M.M.
240335	Pte.	Rice, S.	D.C.M.
241029	Pte.	Hale, G.	M.M.
67595	Pte.	Thomas, G.	M.M.
240338	Pte.	Sillitoe, W. T.	M.M.
241015	Pte.	Stone. G.	M.M.
241398	Pte.	Stephens, H.	M.M.
241072	Pte.	Martin, W. J.	M.M.
240244	Pte.	White, C. W.	M.M. Bar to M.M.
203600	Pte.	Ponsford, M.	M.M.
240159	Pte.	Mann, G. G.	M.M.
67466	Pte.	Crawshaw, R. L.	M.M.
241089	Pte.	Hooper, A. C.	M.M.
67275	Pte.	Bates, H.	M.M.
241046	Pte.	Foghill. J. L.	M.M.
241090	Pte.	Jarvis, T. H.	M.M.
240464	Pte.	Blight, A.	M.M.
32370	Pte.	Morris, T. B.	M.M.
240017	Pte.	Menhinnick, W.	M.M.
241160	Pte.	Roberts. W. J.	M.M.
65351	Pte.	Lawerence, W....	M.M.
240291	Pte.	Ball, J. T.	M.M.
240495	Pte.	Jolly, J. H.	M.M.
240882	Pte.	Taylor, J. R. B.	M.M.
67383	Pte.	Salter, H.	M.M.
240526	Pte.	Leach, J.	M.M.
32322	Pte.	Dunford, F. J. L.	M.M.
206144	Pte.	Baker, J.	M.M.
240233	Pte.	Warren, W.	M.M.
24155	Pte.	Furneaux, L. G.	M.M.
72039	Pte.	Brown, C. J.	M.M.
345266	Pte.	Eddy, R.	M.M·
241009	Pte.	Phillips, C. E.	M.M.
67150	Pte.	Wilcoxon, A. H.	M.M.
72015	Pte.	Arrowsmith, T.	M.M.
24594	Pte.	Williams, H. J.	M.M.
241253	Pte.	Metherell, W. G.	M.M.
240937	Pte.	Ridge, C. L.	M.M.
240324	Pte.	Potter, W. T.	M.M.
67397	Pte.	Trinder, R. J....	M.M.
206044	Pte.	Taylor, A. E.	M.M.
51273	Pte.	Taylor, F.	M.M.
30049	Pte.	Dean, A.	D.C.M.
67550	Pte.	Matthews, W. H.	M.M.
47479	Pte.	Duxbury, R.	M.M.
241180	Pte.	Pearce, R. J.	M.M.
240889	Pte.	Knight, S.	M.M.
240998	Pte.	Flood, W. R.	M.M.
240770	Pte.	Bearne, F.	M.M.
241145	Pte.	Grate, W.	M.M.
240713	Pte.	Southern, R. C.	M.M.
241115	Pte.	Hill, F....	M.M.
315728	Pte.	Johns, W. F.	M.M.
77313	Dmr.	Edwards, C. J.	M.M.

9TH DURHAM LIGHT INFANTRY.

Regtl. No.	Rank.	Name.	Award.
	L.t-Col....	Crouch, E.	D.S.O. D.C.M.
	Major	Wilson, P. P.	D.S.O.
	Captain	Jameson, T. B.	M.C.
	Captain	Thompson, W. D. B. ...	M.C. D.S.O. Croix de Guerre.
	Captain	Rickaby, J. D.	M.C.
	Captain	Marshall, C. A.	M.C. Bar to M.C.
	Captain	Gee, C. H. R.	M.C.
	Lieut.	Weightman, J. G.	M.C.
	Lieut.	Johnson, H.	M.C. Bar to M.C.
	Lieut.	Armstrong, J. R.	M.C. Bar to M.C.
	Lieut.	Plummer, H. C. V.	M.C. Bar to M.C.
	Lieut.	Meikle, W. E.	M.C.
	2/Lieut.	Cowling, F. W.	M.C.
	2/Lieut.	Blakey, J. F.	M.C.
	2/Lieut.	Dodds, L.	M.C.
203361	R.S.M. ...	Johnstone, W.	D.C.M.
S/1424	Sgt. ...	Simms, F.	M.S.M.
325082	Sgt. ...	Noble, F.	M.M.
327152	Sgt. ...	Carr, J. R.	M.M.
325025	Sgt. ...	Munro, J.	M.M.
325306	Sgt. ...	Wilson, G.	D.C.M.
325036	Sgt. ...	Hutton, J.	M.M. Bar to M.M.
248045	Sgt. ...	Graham, F.	M.M.
325066	Sgt. ...	Wilson, W. J. H.	M.M.
325314	Sgt. ...	Mason, T.	D.C.M.
327253	Sgt. ...	Paliant, E.	M.M.
325854	Cpl. ...	Jones, A.	M.M.
326790	Cpl. ...	Clay, H. S.	M.M.
27629	Cpl. ...	Williams, H.	M.M. Bar to M.M.
325063	Cpl. ...	Holburn, R.	M.M.
200536	Cpl. ...	Edmundson, F.	M.M.
325637	Cpl. ...	Gill, E.	D.C.M. M.M.
276275	Cpl. ...	Fenwick, M.	M.M.
327169	Cpl. ...	Outram, A.	M.M.
325981	Cpl. ...	Bickerton, C.	M.M.
348018	Cpl. ...	Scorer, W. H.	M.M.
325224	Cpl. ...	Garrity, M.	M.M.
325545	L.-Sgt. ...	Hammond, S.	M.M.
201310	L.-Cpl. ...	Moore, J. G.	M.M.
325617	L.-Cpl. ...	Waters, T.	M.M.
76439	L.-Cpl. ...	Jones, A. E.	M.M.
325586	L.-Cpl. ...	Farrow, R.	M.M.
325465	L.-Cpl. ...	Masters, J.	D.C.M.
325379	L.-Cpl. ...	Stirling, W.	M.M. Bar to M.M.
325479	L.-Cpl. ...	Landreth, G.	M.M. Bar to M.M. 2nd Bar to M.M.
325647	L.-Cpl. ...	Burnside, A.	M.M.
40519	L.-Cpl. ...	Henry, P.	M.M.

9TH DURHAM LIGHT INFANTRY—*continued*.

Regtl. No.	Rank.	Name.	Award.
325709	L.-Cpl. ...	Cobb, C. J.	M.M.
325498	L.-Cpl. ...	Hardy, J.	M.M.
325910	L.-Cpl. ...	Leadbitter, T.	M.M.
41052	L.-Cpl. ...	Smith, G. E.	M.M.
325054	L.-Cpl. ...	Taylor, J.	M.M.
325658	L.-Cpl. ...	Nobes, C.	M.M.
325833	L.-Cpl. ...	Robson, T. W....	M.M.
325832	L.-Cpl. ...	Hudson, T.	M.M.
25115	L.-Cpl. ...	Nichol, —.	M.M.
203391	L.-Cpl. ...	Wallace, G.	M.M.
325497	L.-Cpl. ...	Norris, J.	M.M.
39804	L.-Cpl. ...	Otley, R.	M.M.
325156	L.-Cpl. ...	Quinn, R.	M.M.
348014	L.-Cpl. ...	Nicholson, T.	M.M.
327247	L.-Cpl. ...	Wood, B.	D.C.M. M.M.
235673	L.-Cpl. ...	Hindmarsh, E.	M.M. Bar to M.M.
325178	L.-Cpl. ...	Henderson, T.	M.M.
204230	L.-Cpl. ...	Timothy, R.	M.M.
52854	L.-Cpl. ...	Baxendale, W.	M.M.
325054	L.-Cpl. ...	Carmichael, R.	M.M.
348022	L.-Cpl. ...	Fenwick, J.	M.M.
40531	Pte. ...	Gill, T.	M.M.
325326	Pte. ...	Caygill, C.	D.C.M. M.M.
325604	Pte. ...	Howe, J. W.	M.M.
203197	Pte. ...	Slack, J.	M.M.
325886	Pte. ...	Moore, J. W.	M.M.
325784	Pte. ...	Waterworth, J. W.	M.M.
43084	Pte. ...	Annable, M.	M.M.
325786	Pte. ...	Whittaker, S.	M.M.
325979	Pte. ...	Galley, E.	M.M.
325098	Pte. ...	Slater, D.	M.M.
325253	Pte. ...	Johnson, C.	M.M.
295094	Pte. ...	Todd, W.	M.M.
203582	Pte. ...	Cranny, P.	M.M.
325715	Pte. ...	Morgan, S.	M.M.
325493	Pte. ...	Watts, J.	M.M.
325111	Pte. ...	Timothy, F.	M.M.
327171	Pte. ...	Forbes, T.	M.M.
325513	Pte. ...	Parker, J.	M.M.
325394	Pte. ...	Dempsey, G.	M.M.
325474	Pte. ...	Morris, J.	M.M.
325697	Pte. ...	Hewitt, W. R.	M.M.
325055	Pte. ...	Cass, J.	M.M.
325165	Pte. ...	Smith, J.	M.M.
325952	Pte. ...	Fortune, A.	M.M.
325915	Pte. ...	Williamson, J. H.	M.M.
77892	Pte. ...	Skilbeck, G.	M.M.
350981	Pte. ...	Wood, C.	M.M.
325642	Pte. ...	Tebb, H.	Award.
61720	Pte. ...	Wright, F.	M.M.
325392	Pte. ...	Newton, F.	M.M.
200538	Pte. ...	Kitching, W.	M.M.
375495	Pte. ...	Wiseman, H.	M.M.
82592	Pte. ...	Munt, P.	M.M.
325705	Pte. ...	Radford, J.	M.M.
82159	Pte. ...	Jackson, —.	M.M.
277132	Pte. ...	Atkin, T. E.	M.M.
325492	Pte. ...	Byrne, F.	M.M.

9TH DURHAM LIGHT INFANTRY—*continued*.

Regtl. No.	Rank.	Name.	Award.
325212	Pte.	Edwards, R.	M.M.
25803	Pte.	Purvis, J. W.	M.M.
91404	Pte.	Holmes, C.	M.M.
273099	Pte.	Gundry, J.	D.C.M. M.M.
325975	Pte.	Thompson, T.	D.C.M.
8579	Pte.	O'Neill, P.	M.M.
12217	Pte.	Coombes, J. T.	M.M.
78047	Pte.	Jackson, W.	M.M.
12165	Pte.	Cooper, J.	M.M.
325410	Pte.	Prudham, T.	M.M.
44760	Pte.	Burton, T.	M.M.
203590	Pte.	Young, T.	V.C.
325256	Pte.	Brown, G. W.	M.M.
325977	Pte.	Laws, A. F.	M.M.
72989	Pte.	Lowes, J. W.	M.M.
325850	Pte.	Chambers, J.	M.M.
325863	Pte.	Fodden, A.	M.M.
302220	Pte.	McCoy, J.	M.M.
325291	Pte.	Gray, G.	M.M.
325091	Pte.	Wishart, W.	M.M.
40529	Pte.	Glanville, J.	M.M.
325623	Pte.	Taylor, F.	M.M.

2/4TH HAMPSHIRE REGIMENT.

Regtl. No.	Rank.	Name.	Award.
	Major ...	Parsons, B. E. T.	D.S.O.
	Captain ...	Cave, W. S.	D.S.O.
	Captain ...	Pulley, C. P.	M.C.
	Captain ...	Ledgard, W. H.	M.C.
	Captain ...	Cottam, H. C. B.	M.C.
	Lieut. ...	Cotelee, R. H.	M.C.
	2/Lieut. ...	Willsher, H. L.	M.C.
	2/Lieut. ...	Wheeler, H. F.	M.C.
	2/Lieut. ...	Wheeler, J. P.	M.C. Bar to M.C.
	2/Lieut. ...	Barker, A. H.	M.C.
	2/Lieut. ...	Neil, E. M.	M.C.
	2/Lieut. ...	Brierley, W.	M.C.
	2/Lieut. ...	Gadcey, C. A.	M.C.
	2/Lieut. ...	Turner, T.	M.C.
	2/Lieut. ...	Dear, R. R.	M.C.
	2/Lieut. ...	Young, W. G.	M.C.
	2/Lieut. ...	Shorland, J. W.	D.S.O.
	2/Lieut. ...	Lane, J. H.	M.C.
	2/Lieut. ...	Bryant, H.	M.C.
	2/Lieut. ...	Fenn, R. P.	M.C.
	2/Lieut. ...	Greenhalgh, S. D.	M.C. Bar to M.C.
	2/Lieut. ...	Holbrook, F. C.	M.C.
4893	R.S.M.	Hubert, A. R.	D.C.M.
200027	R.Q.M.S.	Porter, S.	M.S.M.
201105	C.S.M.	Dennett, H.	D.C.M.
200343	C.S.M.	Rilson, J. H.	M.M.
201335	C.S.M.	Corney, E. C.	M.M.
200069	C.S.M.	Walsh, W. P.	M.M.
201152	C.Q.M.S.	Barney, A. E.	M.M.
200031	Sgt.	Hamilton, T.	D.C.M. Bar to D.C.M.
39016	Sgt.	Morris, G.	D.C.M.

Regtl. No.	Rank.	Name.	Award.
12856	Sgt.	Jarvis, J.	M.M.
			Bar to M.M.
201328	Sgt.	Gundry, A.	M.M.
200100	Sgt.	Meaden, G.	M.M.
201109	Sgt.	Churcher, H. T.	M.M.
205050	Sgt.	Moscrop, T.	M.M.
306830	Sgt.	Redman, R.	M.M.
230378	Sgt.	Sandy, W.	M.M.
9657	Sgt.	Gardner, A. E....	M.M.
201136	Sgt.	Raymont, D.	M.M.
200183	Sgt.	Lansdowne, F.	M.M.
209966	Sgt.	Painting, C.	M.M.
201253	Sgt.	Samways, C.	D.C.M.
200305	Sgt.	Shadwell, W.	D.C.M.
202820	Sgt.	Tucker, M.	M.M.
19706	Sgt.	Harrison, H. G.	M.M.
205042	Sgt.	Charlton, T. C.	M.M.
			Bar to M.M.
202609	Cpl.	Williams, A.	M.M.
			Bar to M.M.
200534	Cpl.	Digweed, J. R.	M.M.
200613	Cpl.	Bone, W.	M.M.
202347	Cpl.	Hopkinson, J. J.	M.M.
37635	Cpl.	Holles, W.	M.M.
			Bar to M.M.
202440	Cpl.	Kent, R. A.	M.M.
40896	Cpl.	Brogden, E. G.	M.M.
356847	Cpl.	Broadley, W.	M.M.
200315	Cpl.	Hixon, H.	M.M.
202740	Cpl.	Baldwin, F.	D.C.M.
18801	Cpl.	Steere, W.	D.C.M.
			M.M.
21392	Cpl.	Hurford, E.	M.M.
205032	Cpl.	Horner, G. W.	M.M.
201193	Cpl. ...	Arnold, F. L.	M.M.
1238	L.-Cpl. ...	Pulham, F.	D.C.M.
12334	L.-Cpl. ...	Childs, F.	M.M.
201562	L.-Cpl. ...	Allen, F. J.	M.M.
11617	L.-Cpl. ...	Falder, C.	M.M.
356621	L.-Cpl. ...	Jameson, G.	M.M.
13714	L.-Cpl. ...	Langston, G.	M.M.
33627	L.-Cpl. ...	Tonge, S.	M.M.
			Bar to M.M.
42296	L.-Cpl. ...	Ford, V.	M.M.
200475	L.-Cpl. ...	Taylor, J. M.	M.M.
201206	L.-Cpl. ...	Higgins, E. C....	M.M.
357322	L.-Cpl. ...	Stevens, F.	M.M.
202496	L.-Cpl. ...	Kearley, J.	M.M.
201630	L.-Cpl. ...	Adams, T.	M.M.
11417	L.-Cpl. ...	Cavell, C.	M.M.
10161	L.-Cpl. ...	Ayling, P.	D.C.M.
45716	L.-Cpl. ...	Ward, W.	M.M.
201332	L.-Cpl. ...	Stewart, G.	M.M.
14031	L.-Cpl. ...	Fox, A.	M.M.
8630	L.-Cpl. ...	Purkiss, F.	M.M.
28438	L.-Cpl. ...	Tompkinson, J. L. ...	M.M.
204788	L.-Cpl. ...	Simms, E. T.	M.M.
20089	L.-Cpl. ...	Murrell, J.	M.M.
27031	L.-Cpl. ...	Starr, G.	M.M.
7728	L.-Cpl. ...	Marshall, W. C.	M.M.
200298	L.-Cpl. ...	May, H.	M.M.

2/4TH HAMPSHIRE REGIMENT—*continued.*

Regtl. No.	Rank.	Name.	Award.
205440	Pte.	Buckett, W.	M.M.
202427	Pte.	Kervill, A. E.	M.M.
202711	Pte.	Mitchell, J.	M.M.
201600	Pte.	Panker, A.	M.M.
202475	Pte.	Carter, G. H.	M.M.
202586	Pte.	Seevior, S.	M.M.
17079	Pte.	Raybould, T.	M.M.
31737	Pte.	Blunn, J.	M.M.
55034	Pte.	Holland, A.	M.M.
202848	Pte.	Hillier, J.	M.M.
202244	Pte.	Charlton, T.	M.M.
205041	Pte.	Austin, J.	M.M.
27630	Pte.	Hewitt, H.	M.M.
202423	Pte.	Earley, J. A.	M.M.
27928	Pte.	Box, J.	M.M.
202875	Pte.	Mannock, F.	M.M.
39033	Pte.	Hall, S.	M.M.
202475	Pte.	Cawte, G. H.	M.M.
236839	Pte.	Morson, F.	M.M.
201339	Pte.	Brandon, S.	M.M.
200757	Pte.	Ellis, J.	M.M.
202461	Pte.	Clarke, F. W.	M.M.
201652	Pte.	Banning, C. J.	M.M.
201825	Pte.	West, P.	M.M.
202815	Pte.	Tappenden, F.	M.M.
202428	Pte.	Street, A. G.	M.M.
8470	Pte.	Purdue, W.	M.M.
33560	Pte.	Tonkin, F.	M.M.
38473	Pte.	Stone, F. T.	D.C.M.
201824	Pte.	Moody, H. J.	M.M.
200464	Pte.	Bushby, S.	M.M.
202479	Pte.	Cooper, F. W.	M.M.
20570	Pte.	Ackerman, A. B.	M.M.
200897	Pte.	Piper, A. J.	M.M.
201459	Pte.	Stone, E.	M.M.
205099	Pte.	Spencer, J.	M.M.
200763	Pte.	Meager, W.	M.M.
40672	Pte.	Cuthbert, G. W. R.	M.M.
11227	Pte.	Bushell, S.	M.M.
43613	Pte.	Phillips, G. H.	M.M.
202769	Pte.	Hampton, W. J.	M.M.
30911	Pte.	Kenny, A.	M.M.
28714	Pte.	Vincent, A.	M.M.
201752	Pte.	Bennett, V.	M.M.
201452	Pte.	Richardson, A.	M.M.
203833	Pte.	Trasher, F.	M.M.
205037	Pte.	Anger, C.	M.M.
19186	Pte.	Nolan, P.	M.M.
55074	Pte.	Gleinster, F.	M.M.
202534	Pte.	Parfoot, S. A.	M.M.
202836	Pte.	Budden, B. C.	M.M.
45673	Pte.	Pickard, H.	M.M.
25199	Pte.	Kibby, A. E.	M.M.
26566	Pte.	Surridge, W.	M.M.
44119	Pte.	Dowie, J.	M.M.
202490	Pte.	Sheath, A.	M.M.
26452	Pte.	Fry, E.	M.M.
202527	Pte.	Trent, F.	M.M.
21480	Pte.	Squires, J.	M.M.
202746	Pte.	Chapman, D.	M.M.
31551	Pte.	Besant, T.	M.M.

2/4TH HAMPSHIRE REGIMENT—*continued*.

Regtl. No.	Rank.	Name.	Award.
45697	Pte.	Sellars, A.	M.M.
45692	Pte.	Robinson, W. H.	M.M.
201090	Pte.	Siggance, H.	M.M.
40399	Pte.	Ellis, R....	M.M.
28235	Pte.	Donsan, A.	M.M.
26456	Pte.	Collins, T.	M.M.
33126	Pte.	Lewington, E.	M.M.
54883	Pte.	Seymour, S.	M.M.
27705	Pte.	Frampton, E.	M.M.
44940	Pte.	Sullivan, P.	M.M.
17301	Pte.	Boyes, A. J.	M.M.
205069	Pte.	Hogg, J.	M.M.
38595	Pte.	Campbell, H.	M.M.
200212	Pte.	Gosse, J.	M.M.
28799	Pte.	Levey, E. F.	M.M.
201140	Pte.	Rivers, H.	M.M.
202792	Pte.	Newington, H. G.	M.M.

2/20TH LONDON REGIMENT.

Regtl. No.	Rank.	Name.	Award.
	Major	Craddock, W. M.	M.C. D.S.O.
	Capt. & Adjt. ...	Elliot, W. R.	M.C.
	Captain ...	Hunt, A. H.	M.C.
	Captain ...	Bacon, D. C.	M.C.
	Captain ...	Wilson, H. W.	M.C.
	Lieut. ...	Woolfe, B. T.	M.C.
	2/Lieut. ...	Pritchard, J. S.	M.C.
	2/Lieut. ...	Smout, P. L.	M.C.
	2/Lieut. ...	Rogers, W. J.	M.C.
6530	R.S.M.	Skeer, W. T.	D.C.M.
630283	R.Q.M.S. ...	Clyne, E. H.	M.S.M.
630905	C.S.M.	Salkeld, J. B.	M.M.
530828	Sgt.	Mahony, W.	M.S.M.
630662	Sgt.	Powell, F.	M.M.
630629	Sgt.	Cook, W.	M.M.
632883	Sgt.	Cannon, H. F.	M.M.
632750	Sgt.	Lewis, A.	M.M.
630570	Sgt.	Dickens, C.	M.M.
630957	Sgt.	Eames. J.	M.M.
630386	L.-Sgt.	Beckley, C. R.	M.M.
632492	L.-Sgt.	Graney, J.	M.M. Bar to M.M.
650720	Cpl.	Hadlow, H.	M.M.
630986	Cpl.	Crate, A. C.	M.M.
632016	Cpl.	Smith, G.	M.M.
634492	Cpl.	Feaver, W. G.	M.M.
630659	Cpl.	Challis, H. M.	M.M.
630022	Cpl.	Smith, T.	M.M.
630925	Cpl.	Robinson, C.	M.M.
631887	L.-Cpl.	Giddings, G.	M.M.
630313	L.-Cpl.	Crawley, C. F.	M.M.
632665	L.-Cpl.	McRobie, J.	M.M.
36678	L.-Cpl.	Gardner, J. H.	M.M.
632034	L.-Cpl.	White, W.	M.M.
632603	L.-Cpl.	Shaw, J.	M.M.
630149	Pte.	Smith, A.	M.M.
663040	Pte.	Westall, A.	M.M.
630463	Pte.	Woolfe, D.	M.M.
634306	Pte.	Hales, S. G.	M.M.

2/20TH LONDON REGIMENT—*continued*.

Regtl. No.	Rank.	Name.	Award.
38874	Pte.	Taylor, W. H.	M.M.
630071	Pte.	Tapsfield, W. J.	M.M.
633179	Pte.	Critchell, C.	M.M.
632788	Pte.	Roberts, H. G.	M.M.
630405	Pte.	Mardell, W.	M.M.
630350	Pte.	Barron, A.	M.M. Bar to M.M.
36604	Pte.	Earl, G.	M.M. Bar to M.M.
36659	Pte.	Clark, J. D.	M.M.
36617	Pte.	Bates, A.	M.M.
645067	Pte.	Timms, S.	M.M.
630780	Pte.	Owen, B. J.	M.M.
633010	Pte.	Meade, H. J.	M.M.
G/28610	Pte.	Allsopp, G.	M.M.
36750	Pte.	Ross, P.	M.M.
633837	Pte.	Barnett, J. T. P.	M.M.
633077	Pte.	Marrison, T. R.	M.M.
630061	Pte.	Haynes, J. L.	D.C.M.

BLACK WATCH.

241344	Cpl. ...	Graham, C.	M.M.
268658	Cpl. ...	Simonette, E.	M.M.
S/41332	L.-Cpl. ...	McMonagle, T.	M.M.
267467	L.-Cpl. ...	Hopkins, R.	M.M.
S/7978	Pte. ...	Prentice, A.	M.M.

62ND MACHINE GUN CORPS.

	Major ...	Pollak, L. A.	Croix de Guerre. M.C.
	Major ...	Lismore, F.	Bar to M.C. M.C.
	Major ...	Gordon, A. D.	Bar to M.C. M.C. Croix de Guerre.
	Captain ...	McSweeney, D. L.	M.C.
	Captain ...	Lang, J. E.	M.C.
	Captain ...	Williams, N. V.	M.C.
	Captain ...	King, C. B. R.	M.C.
	Lieut. ...	Horsley, W. F.	M.C. Bar to M.C.
	Lieut. ...	Margerison, J.	M.C.
	Lieut. ...	Gulston, A. S.	M.C.
	Lieut. ...	Lane, G. H.	M.C.
	Lieut. ...	Gordon, K.	M.C.
	Lieut. ...	Crossman, A. A.	M.C.
	2/Lieut. ...	Mann, F.	M.C.
	2/Lieut. ...	Waterhouse, H. A.	M.C.
	2/Lieut. ...	Blundell, T. H.	M.C.
	2/Lieut. ...	Madge, G. M. A.	M.C.
	2/Lieut. ...	Long, A. J.	M.C.
	2/Lieut. ...	Gadsby, T.	M.C.
	2/Lieut. ...	Boyd, F. J.	M.C.
	2/Lieut. ...	Baxendale, J.	M.C.
	2/Lieut. ...	Mason, P. N.	M.C.
	2/Lieut. ...	Madge, M. H. A.	M.C.
	2/Lieut. ...	Trimlett, E.	D.S.O.

62ND MACHINE GUN CORPS—*continued.*

Regtl. No.	Rank.	Name.	Award.
	2/Lieut. ...	Newman, W. A.	M.C.
	2/Lieut. ...	McFarlane, J.	M.C.
141703	R.S.M.	Keane, S.	M.S.M.
8238	R.Q.M.S.	Brown, J. K.	M.S.M.
5518	C.S.M. ...	Vernon, H. S.	M.S.M.
42523	Sgt.	Hazel, W.	D.C.M.
27800	Sgt.	Hogg, T.	M.M.
5828	Sgt.	Bennett, W.	M.M.
16908	Sgt.	Little, A.	M.M.
20100	Sgt.	Shepherd, J.	D.C.M.
66665	Sgt.	Littlefair, A. G.	D.C.M.
46188	Sgt.	Driver, H.	M.M.
35035	Sgt.	Wilkinson, F. W.	M.M.
65550	Sgt.	Carter, E.	M.M.
17312	Sgt.	Still, G....	D.C.M. Bar to D.C.M.
	Sgt.	Donnelly, R. J.	M.S.M.
23048	Sgt.	Macrea, M. ... ·	D.C.M.
9632	Cpl.	Read, G. P.	D.C.M.
67840	Cpl.	Turner, L. G.	M.M.
89602	Cpl.	Hitchcock, H. J.	M.M.
64401	Cpl.	Condon, T.	M.M.
26630	Cpl.	Hindle, A.	M.M.
34308	Cpl.	Todd, B. J.	M.M.
67866	Cpl.	Gardner, T.	M.M.
62735	Cpl.	Phillips, G.	D.C.M.
3663	Cpl.	Chapman, R. F.	M.M. Bar to M.M.
22714	Cpl.	Torkington, A. J.	M.M.
65650	Sgt.	Bate, F.	M.M.
148291	Cpl.	Knowles, A.	M.M.
81450	Cpl.	Newby, W.	M.M.
6776	L.-Cpl. ...	Gibson, G.	M.M.
63949	L.-Cpl. ...	Thorne, W. G.	M.M.
54666	L.-Cpl. ...	Thornleigh, A.	M.M.
63955	L.-Cpl. ...	Schofield, G. P.	M.M.
87182	L.-Cpl. ...	Wilson, J. W.	M.M.
7084	L.-Cpl. ...	Haigh, H.	M.M.
119135	L.-Cpl. ...	Kelly, G.	M.M.
66254	L.-Cpl. ...	Baseley, W.	M.M.
142545	L.-Cpl. ...	Dye, A. E.	M.M.
8546	L.-Cpl. ...	Tyles, F. W.	M.M.
63891	L.-Cpl. ...	Laws, F.	M.M.
126104	Pte.	Stiff, W.	M.M.
127375	Pte.	Wood, L. H.	M.M.
142589	Pte.	Spurr, A.	M.M.
67088	Pte.	Tracey, J.	M.M.
142099	Pte.	Howard, F.	M.M.
86963	Pte.	Pallington, A.	M.M.
146656	Pte.	McAlindin, J.	M.M.
123701	Pte.	Robins, E.	M.M.
117196	Pte.	Cawthan, C.	M.M.
142534	Pte.	Ratcliffe, G.	M.M.
136805	Pte.	Proctor, T.	M.M.
119562	Pte.	Carter, W.	M.M.
88251	Pte.	Compton, J.	M.M.
128062	Pte.	Smith, F.	M.M.
142612	Pte.	Beaumont, F.	M.M.
68560	Pte.	Constables, C.	D.C.M.
137277	Pte.	Whybrow, T. H. R.	M.M.
60242	Pte.	Johnson, J.	M.M.

62ND MACHINE GUN CORPS—*continued.*

Regtl. No.	Rank.	Name.	Award.
126041	Pte.	White, F.	M.M.
32796	Pte.	Russell, J. H.	M.M.
105266	Pte.	France, W.	M.M.
11266	Pte.	Wilson, J.	M.M.
87841	Pte.	Munleck, H.	M.M.
66254	Pte.	Webster, J.	M.M.
142500	Pte.	Leake, M. G.	M.M.
103908	Pte.	Pollard, J. W.	M.M.
146183	Pte.	May, J. H.	M.M.
132987	Pte.	Cawkwell, A.	M.M.
121759	Pte.	Renalls, C.	D.C.M.
66389	Pte.	Birkby, G. E.	M.M.
34041	Pte.	Lovett, F. M.	M.M.
67758	Pte.	Murray, G.	M.M.
44307	Pte.	Henderson, P. A.	M.M.
64420	Pte.	Bailey, A. D.	M.M.
64406	Pte.	Downes, W.	M.M.

62ND (W.R.) DIVISIONAL R.A.S.C.

Regtl. No.	Rank.	Name.	Award.
	Lt.-Col. ...	Wilberforce, H. H.	D.S.O.
	Major	Wright, P. W.	M.C.
	Lieut.	Wooliscroft, W.	M.C.
251981	S.-Sgt.	Park, J.	M.S.M.
T4/250911	Sgt.	Hanstock, J.	M.M.
T4/250951	Sgt.	Holdsworth, H.	M.M.
54/252530	Sgt.	Close, J. W.	M.M.
S/4251921	Sgt.	Martin, A. E.	M.M.
M2/053265	Sgt.	Dobbyn, W.	M.M.
M2/188488	Sgt.	Boyd, J.	M.M.
M2/052965	M. S. Sgt. ...	Grimshaw, J. H.	M.S.M.
M2/078332	Cpl.	Bailey, C. H.	M.M.
S/253855	Cpl.	Shuttlesworth, F.	M.S.M.
T4/253750	Cpl.	Carter, T.	M.M.
T4/250935	Cpl.	Simpson, H.	M.M.
T/249588	L.-Cpl.	Craven, W.	M.S.M.
T4/251497	Dr.	Stabler, F.	M.M.
T4/252514	Dr.	Nettleton, A.	M.M.
T/24988	Dr.	Tuffley, H.	M.M.
T4/260354	Dr.	Mackellor, A.	M.M.
T/364956	Dr.	Jordan, A. S.	M.M.
T4/253666	Dr.	Lockwood, W.	M.M.
T4/252331	Dr.	Parkin, E.	M.M.
T4/252477	Dr.	Faulkingham, H.	M.M.
T/21788	Dr.	Mannering, J.	M.M.
T4/253892	Dr.	Allet, J.	M.M.
M/206143	Dr.	Prothers, D.	M.M.

HEADQUARTERS, R.A.M.C.

Regtl. No.	Rank.	Name.	Award.
	Major ...	Steill, G.	M.C.
	Captain ...	Jack, G.	M.C.
	Cpatian ...	Scott, J. A.	M.C.
			Bar to M.C.
			2nd Bar to M.C.
	Captain ...	Hird, F. W.	M.C.
	Captain ...	Pringle, J. H.	M.C.
	Captain ...	Frew, J. W.	M.C.
	Captain ...	Hickey, W. J. L.	M.C.

HEADQUARTERS, R.A.M.C.—*continued.*

Regtl. No.	Rank.	Name.	Award.
405380	Sgt.	Gregson, W.	M.M.
401178	Sgt.	Hirst, E.	D.C.M. M.M.
403156	L.-Sgt.	Barber, J. H.	D.C.M.
403297	Cpl.	Langley, F. C.	M.M.
403389	Cpl.	Squire, G. H.	M.S.M.
405305	L.-Cpl.	Warner, T.	M.M.
403343	Pte.	Marsden, W. H.	M.M.
403640	Pte.	Green, A.	M.M.
401255	Pte.	Braddock, J. W.	M.M.
403533	Pte.	Edwards, N. E.	M.M.
403358	Pte.	Bourke, T. E.	M.M.
56962	Pte.	Thomas, L. J.	M.M.
403150	Pte.	Allen, W. H.	M.M.
79505	Pte.	Sayer, J.	M.M.
405470	Pte.	Evers, O.	M.M.
405300	Pte.	Charlesworth, C.	M.M.
47867	Pte.	Scholes, C.	M.M.
11445	Pte.	Smithson, W.	M.M.
457517	Pte.	Dayment, W. J.	M.M.
405223	Pte.	Smith, A.	M.M.

2/1ST WEST RIDING FIELD AMBULANCE.

Regtl. No.	Rank.	Name.	Award.
	Major ...	Pope, H. E.	M.C.
	Captain ...	Mackenzie, L. A.	M.C.
	Captain ...	Pickles, H. D.	M.C.
	Captain ...	Blackburn, J. H.	M.C.
401327	Sgt.	Knaggs, H.	D.C.M. M.M. Bar to M.M.
401178	Sgt.	Hirst, E.	M.M.
401144	Sgt.	Wood, F. D.	M.S.M.
401173	Sgt.	Micklethwaite, G. J.	M.M.
401152	Pte.	Odgers, A. D.	M.M.
401160	Pte.	Summerscales, D. G.	M.M.
22655	Pte.	Burdon, J.	M.M.
461489	Pte.	Williamson, A.	M.M.
M2/182142	Pte.	Titterton, W.	M.M.
53660	Pte.	McLean, R. W.	M.M.
401494	Pte.	Coates, R. W.	M.M.
403494	Pte.	Yates, O.	M.M. Bar to M.M.
401401	Pte.	Hunter, T. W.	M.M.
401225	Pte.	Braddick, J. W.	M.M. Bar to M.M.
51846	Pte.	Goodwin, J.	M.M.
	Pte.	Wood, G. H.	M.M.
M2/102446	Pte.	Coleahill, W.	M.M.

2/2ND WEST RIDING FIELD AMBULANCE.

Regtl. No.	Rank.	Name.	Award.
	Lt.-Col. ...	Eames, C. W.	D.S.O.
	Captain ...	Kenworthy, T. R.	M.C.
403183	Sgt.	Tamar, T. A.	M.S.M.
403173	Sgt.	Disbrey, W. T.	M.S.M.
403420	Sgt.	Fuguel, A.	M.S.M.
388039	Sgt.	Liddell, S.	M.S.M.
405068	Cpl.	Lake, H. H.	M.M.

2/2ND WEST RIDING FIELD AMBULANCE—*continued.*

Regtl. No.	Rank.	Name.	Award.
403117	Cpl.	Thomas, G. F....	M.M.
403567	L.-Cpl.	Hillaby, J.	M.M.
403528	Pte.	Watkinson, F.	M.M.
403249	Pte.	Peakman, G. J.	M.M.
405142	Pte.	Barker, S.	M.M.
403468	Pte.	Marshall, A.	M.M.
403330	Pte.	Wright, C. V.	M.S.M.
403642	Pte.	Cockerham, R.	M.S.M.
DM2/190928	Pte.	Horton, R.	M.S.M.
403410	Pte.	Boshell, A.	M.S.M.
403500	Pte.	Chadwick, S. S.	M.S.M.
402334	Pte.	Senior, J.	M.S.M.
403295	Pte.	Dawson, A. J.	M.S.M.

2/3RD WEST RIDING FIELD AMBULANCE.

Regtl. No.	Rank.	Name.	Award.
	Major	Wrigglesworth, F.	M.C.
	Captain ...	Young, J. C.	M.C.
T4/252459	S.S.M.	Roberts, F.	M.S.M.
405375	Q.M.S.	Fowler, G.	M.S.M.
405202	S.-Sgt.	Torr, J. W.	D.C.M.
405051	Sgt.	Pattison, A.	M.S.M. M.M.
46986	Sgt.	Wignall, W.	M.S.M.
405444	Pte.	Thornton, E.	M.M.
405309	Pte.	Harris, G. B.	M.M.
403103	Pte.	Robinson, H.	M.M.
36280	Pte.	Richardson, F. W.	M.M.
405052	Pte.	Shaw, N.	M.M.
M/321557	Pte.	Kinnear, H.	M.M.
65036	Pte.	Tipping, P. J.	M.M.

MISCELLANEOUS UNITS ATTACHED TO 62ND (W.R.) DIVISION.

QUEEN'S OWN OXFORD HUSSARS.

285372	Sgt.	Jones, N. F.	M.M.

KING EDWARD'S HORSE.

	Lt.-Col.... ...	Russell, C. G.	D.S.O.

2/1ST (W.R.) MOBILE VETERINARY SECTION.

TT/03262	Sgt.	Mollekin, ...	M.S.M.

ARMY ORDNANCE CORPS.

5788	Condtr. ...	Bush, A. G.	M.S.M.

MISCELLANEOUS UNITS ATTACHED TO 62ND (W.R.) DIVISION—*continued.*

Regtl. No.	Rank.	Name.	Award.
	MOUNTED MILITARY POLICE.		
P/2367	Sgt.	Hood, W.	M.S.M.
P/2899	L.-Cpl.	Jones, J.	M.M.
P/5963	L.-Cpl.	Dent, J. W.	M.M.
	62ND DIVISIONAL TRAFFIC CONTROL.		
241941	L.-Cpl.	Whitehead, A.	M.M.
623583	Pte.	Smale, A.	M.M.
	DIVISIONAL EMPLOYMENT COMPANY.		
224596	Sgt.	Town, P. A.	M.M.
	CHAPLAINS.		
	Revd.	Chavasse, C. M.	M.C.
	Revd.	Martin, O.	M.C.
	Revd.	Harland, C. H.	M.C.
	Revd.	Wood, D.	M.C.
	Revd.	Moran, M.	M.C.
	Revd.	Hindle, B. F.	M.C.
	Revd.	Price, H. G.	M.C.
	Revd.	Thornhill, R. W.	M.C.

HONOURS AND AWARDS OBTAINED BY WEST RIDING
TERRITORIAL TROOPS NOT SERVING WITH THE 49TH AND
62ND DIVISIONS.

Regtl. No.	Rank.	Name.	Award.
	YORKSHIRE HUSSARS.		
	Major ...	Watts, A. F.	D.S.O.
	Major ...	Pearson, R. S.	O.B.E.
	Captain ...	Collins, A. E. D.	Knight of the Crown (Belgian)
	Captain ...	Howard, A. H....	M.C.
	Captain ...	Preston, T.	M.C.
	Captain ...	Slingsby, H.	M.C.
	Lieut.	Mars, L. J.	M.B.E.
	Lieut.	Ferrier, C. G.	O.B.E.
	YORKSHIRE DRAGOONS.		
	Major	Thompson, R.	D.S.O.
	Major	Brooke, R. W.	D.S.O. M.C.
	Captain	Hirst, C. J.	M.C.
	Lieut.	Barrett, F. P.	M.C.
	Lieut.	Sheppard, M.	M.C.
	Lieut.	Unwin, H. T. H.	M.C.
	Lieut.	Thompson, R. C.	M.C.
	Lieut.	Watson, R. A.	M.C.
	Lieut.	Beilly, R. B.	M.C.
	Lieut.	Snowden, S.	M.C.
2484	Sgt.	Fanvel, L.	M.M.
2650	Sgt.	Storer, J.	M.M.
2361	Sgt.	Tinker, ...	M.M.
3172	Cpl.	Granswick, W.	M.M.
	WEST RIDING R.G.A.		
	2 Officers ...		M.C.
	1 Other Rank ...	Names not obtainable	Croix de Guerre
	18 Other Ranks ...		M.M.
	1 Other Rank ...		Bar to M.M.
	NORTHERN SIGNAL COMPANIES R.E.		
	Lieut.	Jackson, W. F....	M.C.
	YORKSHIRE MOUNTED BRIGADE FIELD AMBULANCE.		
	Captain ...	Downie, J.	D.S.O. Order of St. Anne, 4th Class (Russia)
1147	Cpl.	Carey, H.	D.C.M.

APPENDIX IV.

RETURN* OF CASUALTIES UP TO THE END OF DECEMBER, 1918.

UNIT.	OFFICERS.				OTHER RANKS.				REMARKS.
	Killed	Wounded	Missing	Sick	Killed	Wounded	Missing	Sick	
Yorkshire Hussars	3	4	—	7	11	42	—	120	
Yorkshire Dragoons	2	4	—	5	3	14	—	59	
West Riding R.H.A.	1	—	—	4	1	—	—	3	
Yorks. Mtd. Bde. R.A.S.C.	—	—	—	—	1	2	—	3	
Yorks. Mtd. Bde. Field Ambulance	—	4	—	2	—	4	—	8	
Signal Troops with Mtd. Bde.	—	—	—	1	—	1	—	2	
Headquarters W.R. Division	6	4	—	7	1	4	1	7	
245th Brigade R.F.A.	9	15	—	16	36	173	3	184	
246th Brigade R.F.A.	1	10	—	12	82	221	—	268	
247th Brigade R.F.A.	—	8	—	6	4	19	—	92	
248th Brigade R.F.A. (Howitzer)	1	3	—	3	4	20	1	61	
310th Brigade R.F.A.	3	26	—	6	20	204	1	375	
312th Brigade R.F.A.	—	24	—	2	47	177	—	291	
West Riding R.G.A. (Heavy Battery)	—	1	—	7	5	11	—	21	
Divisional Ammunition Column	2	5	2	2	80	103	2	306	
Trench Mortar Batteries	19	18	—	27	22	211	2	55	
W.R. Divisional Royal Engineers	—	26	11	54	110	635	20	983	
5th Bn. West Yorks. Regt.	33	105	5	48	497	1,902	323	1,339	
6th Bn. West Yorks. Regt.	38	96	4	51	374	1,488	196	1,044	
7th Bn. West Yorks. Regt.	28	70	11	60	433	1,642	145	1,535	
8th Bn. West Yorks. Regt.	46	116	4	57	528	2,917	237	1,689	
4th Bn. West Riding Regt.	38	107	9	64	720	2,651	251	1,731	
5th Bn. West Riding Regt.	28	121	3	43	535	2,404	437	1,517	
6th Bn. West Riding Regt.	24	66	2	66	252	1,396	131	868	
7th Bn. West Riding Regt.	22	70	2	83	375	1,514	100	1,101	
4th Bn. K.O.Y.L.I.	48	138	—	—	630	2,947	579	1,560	
Carried forward	352	1,041	53	633	4,771	20,702	2,429	15,222	

RETURN* OF CASUALTIES UP TO THE END OF DECEMBER, 1918—*continued.*

UNIT.	Officers. Killed.	Wounded.	Missing.	Sick.	Other Ranks. Killed.	Wounded.	Missing.	Sick.	REMARKS.
Brought forward	352	1,041	53	633	4,771	20,702	2,429	15,222	
5th Bn. K.O.Y.L.I.	48	103	7	58	676	2,878	493	1,867	
4th Bn. York and Lancaster Regt.	36	113	4	56	614	3,015	438	1,538	
5th Bn. York and Lancaster Regt.	35	83	5	40	481	1,861	216	851	
5th Devon Regt.	10	31	—	3	138	645	60	353	
4th Hants. Regt.	5	24	—	5	157	662	105	422	
19th Lancashire Fusiliers	—	6	—	3	18	433	—	194	
9th Durham Light Infantry	2	24	—	1	93	506	46	345	
2/20th London Regt.	4	11	—	7	91	421	40	210	
Machine-Gun Corps	2	47	—	7	109	702	16	627	
Divisional Cyclists Corps	—	1	—	4	4	45	—	58	
West Riding Divisional R.A.S.C.	—	—	—	8	4	25	—	300	
1st West Riding Field Ambulance	1	6	—	14	11	61	—	161	
2nd West Riding Field Ambulance	1	5	—	8	9	65	—	248	
3rd West Riding Field Ambulance	—	7	—	5	18	162	1	201	
Casualty Clearing Station	—	—	—	11	1	4	—	23	
Mobile Veterinary Section	—	—	—	1	—	1	—	20	
Sanitary Section	—	—	—	—	1	—	—	1	
Chaplains	—	2	—	—	1	—	—	—	
243rd Employment Company	—	—	—	—	1	4	—	10	
M.M.P.	—	—	—	—	—	—	—	2	
TOTAL	496	1,505	69	857	7,197	32,192	3,844	22,653	

Total   Officers ... 2,927
           Other Ranks 65,886
                      68,813

* This Return is provisional only, and, though so deplorably heavy, cannot be regarded as complete.